Simulation-Optimization in Logistics, Transportation, and SCM

Simulation-Optimization in Logistics, Transportation, and SCM

Editors

Angel A. Juan
Markus Rabe
David Goldsman
Javier Faulin

MDPI • Basel • Beijing • Wuhan • Barcelona • Belgrade • Manchester • Tokyo • Cluj • Tianjin

Editors

Angel A. Juan
Dept. of Applied Statistics and
Operations Research at the
Universitat Politècnica de
València
Spain

Markus Rabe
IT in Production and Logistics,
TU Dortmund University
Germany

David Goldsman
School of Industrial and Systems
Engineering, Georgia Institute of
Technology
USA

Javier Faulin
Institute of Smart Cities,
Department of Statistics,
Computer Science, and
Mathematics, Public University
of Navarre
Spain

Editorial Office
MDPI
St. Alban-Anlage 66
4052 Basel, Switzerland

This is a reprint of articles from the Special Issue published online in the open access journal *Algorithms* (ISSN 1999-4893) (available at: https://www.mdpi.com/journal/algorithms/special_issues/Simulation_Optimization).

For citation purposes, cite each article independently as indicated on the article page online and as indicated below:

LastName, A.A.; LastName, B.B.; LastName, C.C. Article Title. *Journal Name* **Year**, *Volume Number*, Page Range.

ISBN 978-3-0365-1260-0 (Hbk)
ISBN 978-3-0365-1261-7 (PDF)

Cover image courtesy of Angel A. Juan

Contents

About the Editors

Angel A. Juan

Angel A. Juan is a Full Professor in the Dept. of Applied Statistics and Operations Research at the Universitat Politècnica de València (Spain), as well as Invited Professor at University College Dublin (Ireland) and Universidade Aberta (Portugal). Dr. Juan holds a Ph.D. in Industrial Engineering and an M.Sc. in Mathematics. He completed a predoctoral internship at Harvard University and postdoctoral internships at the Massachusetts Institute of Technology and the Georgia Institute of Technology. His main research interests include applications of simheuristics and learnheuristics in computational logistics and finance. He has published over 140 articles in JCR-indexed journals and more than 300 papers indexed in Scopus. His website address is https://ajuanp.upv.es and his email address is ajuanp@upv.es.

Markus Rabe

Markus Rabe is Full Professor of IT in Production and Logistics (ITPL) at the Technical University Dortmund. Until 2010, he has been with Fraunhofer IPK in Berlin as head of the corporate logistics and processes department, head of the central IT department, and a member of the institute direction circle. His research focus is on information systems for supply chains, production planning, and simulation. Markus Rabe is vice chair of the "Simulation in Production and Logistics" group of the simulation society ASIM, member of the Editorial Board of the *Journal of Simulation*, member of several conference program committees, has chaired the ASIM SPL conference in 1998, 2000, 2004, 2008, and 2015, Local Chair of the WSC'2012 in Berlin and Proceedings Chair of the WSC'18. More than 200 publications and editions report from his work. His e-mail address is markus.rabe@tu-dortmund.de.

David Goldsman

David Goldsman is a Professor in the H. Milton Stewart School of Industrial and Systems Engineering at the Georgia Institute of Technology. His research interests include simulation output analysis, ranking and selection, and healthcare simulation. He was Program Chair of the Winter Simulation Conference in 1995 and a member of the WSC Board of Directors between 2001–2009. His e-mail address is sman@gatech.edu, and his webpage is www.isye.gatech.edu/~sman.

Javier Faulin

Javier Faulin is a Full Professor of Statistics and Operations Research at the Public University of Navarre (Spain). He holds a Ph.D. in Economics and Business and an M.S. in Applied Mathematics. His research interests include transportation and logistics, vehicle routing problems, and simulation modelling and analysis, along with the use of metaheuristics and simheuristics in real problems. His work is also related to the evaluation of the environmental impact of freight transportation. His email address is javier.faulin@unavarra.es.

Preface to "Simulation-Optimization in Logistics, Transportation, and SCM"

This book provides a selected collection of recent works in the growing area of simulation-optimization methods applied to transportation, logistics, and supply chain networks. Many of the authors that contribute to the book are internationally recognized experts in the field, as well as frequent speakers at the prestigious Winter Simulation Conference, where some of the Guest Editors organize an annual track on logistics, transportation and supply chains. Inside this track, it is usual to find several sessions on the concept of simheuristics, a special type of simulation optimization that combines metaheuristics with simulation to deal with complex and large-scale optimization problems under uncertainty conditions.

The chapters in the book cover a wide area of logistics and transportation applications, from bike-sharing systems to container terminals, parcel locker systems, or e-commerce applications. A short overview of each of these chapters is provided next:

In "Modeling and Optimization in Resource Sharing Systems: Application to Bike-Sharing with Unequal Demands", Xiaoting Mo et al. model a bike-sharing system as a Markovian queueing network, which is then optimized to maximize the total profit.

The chapter "Combining Heuristics with Simulation and Fuzzy Logic to Solve a Flexible-Size Location Routing Problem under Uncertainty", by Rafael Tordecilla et al., proposes an extension of the simheuristic concept that also makes use of fuzzy logic. This fuzzy simheuristic allows the authors to consider an integrated facility location and vehicle routing problem in which customers might show either stochastic or fuzzy demands.

In "Integrated Simulation-Based Optimization of Operational Decisions at Container Terminals", Marvin Kastner et al. take into account uncertainty sources in container terminals, and discuss how simulation-based optimization can be employed to efficiently optimize these systems, including both equipment configuration and operational policies.

The chapter "Simulation-Optimization Approach for Multi-Period Facility Location Problems with Forecasted and Random Demands in a Last-Mile Logistics Application", by Markus Rabe et al., discusses the optimal allocation of automated parcel locker systems (facilities) in the city of Dortmund, Germany. These authors propose a simulation optimization approach that utilizes system dynamics simulation to analyze a multi-period capacitated facility location problem.

In the context of e-commerce and considering different supermarkets in Pamplona, Spain, the chapter "Urban e-Grocery Distribution Design in Pamplona (Spain) Applying an Agent-Based Simulation Model with Horizontal Cooperation Scenarios" analyzes the impact of horizontal cooperation strategies on the cost reduction and on the improvement in service quality. With that purpose, Adrian Serrano-Hernandez et al. carry out a survey and, with the gathered data, generate an agent-based simulation model, in which multi-depot vehicle routing problems are solved using a biased, randomized algorithm.

The chapter "An Algorithm for Efficient Generation of Customized Priority Rules for Production Control in Project Manufacturing with Stochastic Job Processing Times" discusses a project planning and control problem with random job processing times. Mathias Kühn et al. present a simulation-based optimization approach that allows them to obtain combined priority rules for determining the next job in short-term production control. According to some computational experiments, their approach outperforms the standard priority rules that are currently employed by many industries.

In "Applying Neural Networks in Aerial Vehicle Guidance to Simplify Navigation Systems", Raúl de Celis et al. present an algorithm, based on neural networks, to estimate the gravity vector that is used in guidance, navigation, and control of air vehicles. A nonlinear simulation, based on real flight dynamics, is used to train the neural network, and a series of experiments allow the authors to test the performance and robustness of their approach.

The chapter "A Simulation-Based Optimization Method for Warehouse Worker Assignment", by Odkhishig Ganbold et al., a simulation-based optimization algorithm is proposed to cope with an assignment problem in a warehouse. Their approach combines a discrete event simulation framework with a random neighborhood search method. Results show that the proposed approach can be useful for warehouse managers when deciding on worker allocation under uncertainty scenarios.

In "Combining Optimization and Simulation for Designing a Robust Short-Sea Feeder Network", Carl Axel Benjamin Medbøen et al. analyze a sea feeder network design problem. In particular, they focus on how to synchronize vessels in order to perform the transshipment of cargo between them at appropriate sea locations. Using an optimization simulation framework, they are able to obtain robust solutions for the network design problem: while the optimization component generates efficient routes, the discrete event simulation component is able to determine their efficiency under uncertain weather conditions.

The chapter "Scheduling Algorithms for a Hybrid Flow Shop under Uncertainty", by Christin Schumacher and Peter Buchholz, studies a a hybrid flow shop with two stages, machine qualifications, skipping stages, and uncertainty in demands. For solving this rich optimization problem, they propose a hybrid methodology combining forecasting techniques, metaheuristics, and discrete event simulation. The authors validate their approach using a real production system, showing how more robust schedules tend to increase the expected makespan as well.

In "A Simheuristic Algorithm for Solving the Stochastic Omnichannel Vehicle Routing Problem with Pick-up and Delivery", Leandro do C. Martins et al. analyze the omnichannel vehicle routing problem with random travel times. This is a realistic but complex optimization problem that arises in the context of e-marketing. In order to solve it efficiently, the authors develop a biased-randomized algorithm, which is later extended into a simheuristic algorithm capable of providing reliable solutions with reasonably low transportation costs.

Finally, the chapter "Simheuristics Approaches for Efficient Decision-Making Support in Materials Trading Networks" studies the distribution process in business-to-business materials trading. Markus Rabe et al. investigate how reinforcement learning can reduce the response time of the system, as well as how domain-specific information can be employed in the development of a simheuristic algorithm that allows one to efficiently cope with real-life scenarios.

All in all, we sincerely hope that these selected contributions are useful for our readers and provide them with updated knowledge on simulation optimization applications in the fields of logistics, transportation, and supply chain management. Both the scale and complexity of these systems are growing at a fast speed, thus making it necessary to employ hybrid methodologies that combine the extraordinary scalability properties of metaheuristics with the advantages that simulation can provide when modeling uncertainty elements, which arise in most real-life applications.

Finally, we would like to thank all the authors, reviewers, and editors, who have made this book possible. In particular, we would like to thank Mr. Musea Wu, MDPI Assistance Editor, who has supported us during the entire process.

Angel A. Juan, Markus Rabe, David Goldsman, Javier Faulin
Editors

Article

Modeling and Optimization in Resource Sharing Systems: Application to Bike-Sharing with Unequal Demands

Xiaoting Mo, Xinglu Liu and Wai Kin (Victor) Chan *

Intelligent Transportation and Logistics Systems Laboratory, Tsinghua-Berkeley Shenzhen Institute, Shenzhen 518055, China; mxt17@tsinghua.org.cn (X.M.); liuxl18@mails.tsinghua.edu.cn (X.L.)
* Correspondence: chanw@sz.tsinghua.edu.cn

Abstract: The imbalanced distribution of shared bikes in the dockless bike-sharing system (a typical example of the resource-sharing system), which may lead to potential customer churn and lost profit, gradually becomes a vital problem for bike-sharing firms and their users. To resolve the problem, we first formulate the bike-sharing system as a Markovian queueing network with higher-demand nodes and lower-demand nodes, which can provide steady-state probabilities of having a certain number of bikes at one node. A model reduction method is then designed to reduce the complexity of the proposed model. Subsequently, we adopt an operator-based relocation strategy to optimize the reduced network. The objective of the optimization model is to maximize the total profit and act as a decision-making tool for operators to determine the optimal relocation frequency. The results reveal that it is possible for most of the shared bikes to gather at one low-demand node eventually in the long run under the influence of the various arrival rates at different nodes. However, the decrease of the number of bikes at the high-demand nodes is more sensitive to the unequal demands, especially when the size of the network and the number of bikes in the system are large. It may cause a significant loss for operators, to which they should pay attention. Meanwhile, different estimated values of parameters related with revenue and cost affect the optimization results differently.

Keywords: dockless bike-sharing system; Markovian queueing network; relocation; unequal demand

Academic Editor: Angel A. Juan

Received: 8 December 2020
Accepted: 27 January 2021
Published: 30 January 2021

Publisher's Note: MDPI stays neutral with regard to jurisdictional claims in published maps and institutional affiliations.

1. Introduction

The existence of idle resources and people's willingness to well use them to promote the sharing economy has brought several lifestyle changes, including various traffic modes. The sharing economy means people can share resources (e.g., services, skills, assets, etc.) through a network of private individuals and businesses, which may often but not always be at lower costs. Shared mobility, a typical resource sharing pattern, has become more popular and common, such as bike-sharing [1], ride-sharing [2], car-sharing [2] and electric vehicle sharing [3]. Apparently, the shared transport emergence contributes to protecting the environment, conserving energy, reducing traffic congestion and improving transportation resource utilization and availability [4].

However, there remain some limitations of current shared transport systems. For instance, users cannot find an available shared vehicle or bicycle nearby sometimes, or they have to spend too much time seeking idle ones when they are in a hurry. Sometimes, the idle cars or bikes are parked in low demand areas, causing potential profit loss for operators [3]. An essential reason is *tidal commuter flows* [1]; more specifically, citizens usually travel from residential areas (or home) to public transit locations (subway stations) or popular areas (e.g., commercial zones) during peak hours, thereby resulting in rare bikes in residential zones, whereas the overwhelming number of shared bikes near popular zones [5]. An optional solution for improving this is to rebalance or reposition shared resources, e.g., reposition shared-bikes by trucks in bike-sharing systems (see [6]) and reposition shared cars in vehicle sharing systems (see [3]).

This paper focuses on bike-sharing and aims at solving rebalance problems existing in bike-sharing systems. Generally, there are two typical types of bike-sharing systems: the traditional bike-sharing system with docking stations (e.g., Citi Bike, Divvy and Ford GoBike in America, see [1]) and the dockless bike-sharing system (e.g., Mobike in China, see [5]). The dockless bike-sharing system, the focus of this work and the latest type of bike-sharing system, also termed the free-floating bike-sharing system, implies users are allowed to park their bikes everywhere they want rather than fixed docking stations. As the dockless bike-sharing system emerges, the traditional bike-sharing system tends to lose competitiveness and gradually vanish in some countries, especially China.

Numerous previous studies concentrate on optimizing rebalance (or relocation) decisions, which includes two main streams: vehicle-based (also terms operator-based) approach and user-based approach [7]. For vehicle-based approach, the rebalance decision involves pick-up decisions (from which station to pick up how many idle bikes), drop off decisions (to which station to drop off bikes) and the routing decisions, and then the rebalance strategy is executed by a fleet of trucks (see, e.g., [6,8–10]). Such a rebalance approach requires accurate demand prediction and cannot handle dynamic settings in real-time well. The user-based approach attempts to guide customers to rebalance the shared-bikes by providing monetary incentives, e.g., recommend pick-up or drop-off areas for users (see [5]), design incentive programs (see, e.g., the Bike Angels program in [1]). Instead of determining the optimal practical level decisions (i.e., pick-up and delivery decisions) and incentive policies (for user-based rebalance), this work focuses on analyzing how the key factors affect system performance based on the Markovian queueing networks formulation and optimizing the rebalance frequency.

The rest of this paper is organized as follows. The relevant literature on resource-sharing system and rebalance in bike-sharing system is reviewed in Section 2. In Section 3, we first present a complete problem description and then introduce the Markovian queueing networks formulation in Section 3.1. Afterwards, the rebalance strategy optimization model is presented in Section 3.2. Section 4 provides the analysis and discussion of the steady-state probabilities derived from the theoretical models under the influence of unequal demands. Moreover, we address the profit analysis based on the optimization model in this section. Finally, some valuable conclusions and suggestions about the dockless bike-sharing system, especially from the operators' perspective, are presented in Section 6.

2. Literature Review

Initially, few articles focus on the feasibility and impacts of bike-sharing as a new public transportation mode in urban areas [11–13]. Recently, more papers begin to discuss the sustainable development of bike-sharing systems, especially the dockless bike-sharing systems [10,14–19]. Because the study of dockless bike-sharing is still in progress, and some mature studies on the station-based bike-sharing can guide the development of the study on dockless bike-sharing, we review the literature on both station-based bike-sharing and dockless bike-sharing. Some other typical transport sharing systems are mentioned due to their contributions to resource sharing. These related studies can be classified into three major categories: system design, system analysis and system optimization. Each category involves a review of some major topics and relevant progress.

2.1. System Design

To build or expand a bike-sharing system, bike-sharing firms need to select an area and investigate the potential demand for shared bikes. Based on the essential research, these firms decide the scale of the network system, select bike pick-up locations and allocate shared bikes to each node in the network to meet the potential demand. There are several ways to estimate demand by connecting with various factors. One traditional way is to do a population study and a sample survey to determine the locations of the pick-up/drop-off nodes in the system [20]. Frade and Ribeiro proposed a methodology considering the distance and slope of city paths between any two traffic zones [21]. In the age of big data, some researchers extract valuable information from a large amount of historical data collected from existing bike-sharing systems. Xu et al. used deep learning approach with trip data to estimate dynamic demand for a citywide dockless bike-sharing system [22]. Besides demand prediction, how to build a bike-sharing network and where to allocate a number of bikes to serve users in the network are considered. Çelebi et al. considered station locations and bike allocation using a set-covering model and a queueing model for a station-based bike-sharing system, given a number of stations [23]. Cheng et al. [18] found that the station-based bikes are used more frequently near subway stations and commercial zones, whereas the dockless shared bikes are preferred in residential areas and near major roads, which provides useful suggestions for system operators to enhance the system efficiency by allocating and deploying these two types of shared bikes well.

2.2. System Analysis

In the operation phase of bike-sharing systems, many data can be collected and analyzed to find patterns (e.g., system patterns, bike usage and trip characteristics) and make changes from operators' perspective. Mátrai and Tóth [16] aimed to identify the differences among various bike-sharing systems. According to their results, four main types of bike-sharing systems are involved after clustering: public systems, private systems, mixed systems and other systems. Bordagaray et al. used binary probit models to investigate travel behavior and impacts of different usage types (e.g., round trips, rental time reset and bike substitution) [24]. Gurumurthy et al. matched different single-person trips by identifying similar time and routes from cellphone-based real-time data using MATLAB [25]. Yang et al. used dockless bike data to analyze bike mobility patterns based on unique bike IDs, including spatial and temporal patterns [26]. Ji et al. compared regularity of bike usage between station-based bike-sharing and dockless bike-sharing [27]. Besides usage pattern analysis, Bakogiannis et al. paid attention to user perceptions and evaluated the information to get ideas about how to improve user experience [28]. For operators, gaining profits is important. Profits have a close relationship with costs and revenues. Yoon et al. investigated the impacts of different pricing plans in several cities on membership demand and ridership and presented a new pricing plan based on the estimated cost per trip and price sensitivity of customers to improve revenue [29]. Estrada et al. focused on how to determine operational cost based on defined performance, expected functionality of a system and cost driver analysis [30]. Chen et al. aimed at maximizing the profits by using the advantage of hassle costs, which are derived from the provided convenience of travel for customers [31].

Moreover, some literature analyze the impact of COVID-19 on the performance and the feasibility of the bike-sharing system [32–34]. According to the questionnaire survey and analysis results of reference [34], commuters who were previously commuting with taxis or ride-hailing/ride-sharing service now prefer shared bikes due to the safety concerns (reduce interpersonal contact). Teixeira et al. explored the relationship between bike sharing and subway systems by analyzing the trip data of New York City during the COVID-19 pandemic. The results reveal that travel demand in the bike-sharing system is more stable than subway system, and bike-sharing system enhances the robustness (the capability to resist disruptive events) of urban transport systems. Besides, they found a modal trend that some subway customers leave the systems and head to bike-sharing system. Hua et al. [32] examined that travel demand of bike sharing in Nanjing, China decreased significantly due to the pandemic control policies. These works implies that the COVID-19 leads to huge uncertainty and change in travel demand for bike-sharing systems, which bring new challenges on travel demand prediction and operation issues.

2.3. System Optimization

Several topics are involved in system optimization: fleet size management, rebalance of shared resources, etc. Sayarshad et al. proposed a multi-periodic optimization formulation to determine the minimum bike fleet size by maximizing the total profits [35]. Since that the main topic of system optimization related to this work is rebalance/relocation of shared resources, we mainly review rebalance related literature in this section. Optimizing resource-sharing systems by relocation, which means relocating shared resources (e.g., cars and bikes) to solve the problem of imbalanced distribution of resources and try to make supply meet demand, is mainly discussed. Taking shared bikes as an example, a main principle is to move extra bikes from locations which have a surplus supply of bikes to locations which have a shortage of bikes. Relocation strategies have two primary types: operator-based relocation strategy (see [6,8–10,14,15]) and user-based relocation strategy (see [1,5,7,36,37]). Some studies perform joint rebalance strategy by merging them together (see, e.g., [19]). An operator-based relocation strategy means relocation is driven by operators' behavior (e.g., reposition by trucks) and a user-based relocation strategy means relocation is directly driven by users (e.g., design appropriate incentives).

In the early stage, the user-based relocation strategy may be sufficient to handle imbalance for the system. When user-based relocation is insufficient, operator-based relocation is applied by using a fleet of trucks to relocate bikes through well-designed routes. Liu et al. solved a static relocation problem and minimized the weighted sum of three factors (inconvenience level of finding an available bike, lost demand and operational time) [38]. Brinkmann et al. proposed a stochastic-dynamic lookahead policy to cope with changing demand patterns [39]. Legros used a Markov decision process to determine the priority of stations where bikes need to be relocated and minimizes the ratio of arrival rate of unsatisfied users who cannot find any bikes to determine the number of relocated bikes at appointed stations [40]. Brendel et al. adopted a user-based relocation strategy to increase usage in an electric vehicle sharing system [41]. Reiss et al. combined operator-based relocation with user-based relocation, which is called as a hybrid relocation strategy, in a dockless bike-sharing system [42].

Several factors affect the performance of relocation strategy, e.g., region partitioning policy, demand prediction, faulty bikes, etc. Many studies optimize the relocation strategy based on region partitioning, but, usually, the region partitioning results seems to be inefficient due to no well-predefined geographical zones. For example, for irregular areas, inefficient zone partitioning decisions may lead to very large errors in relocation stage. Jin et al. [19] investigated the effects of geographical zone scale on the imbalance estimation of the dockless bike-sharing system and the relocation decisions. Besides, they developed a region decomposition approach to handle large scale instances based on appropriate scales. Cheng et al. [17] designed a recurrent neural networks-based real-time rental and return demand prediction approach, which can offer estimated demand information as input parameters for rebalance optimization model. Moreover, sometimes, faulty bikes will lead to infeasibility of relocation strategy [15]. More specificity, all the shared bikes in the system (including faulty ones) are assumed as available inventory if faulty bikes are not considered in the problem; this assumption makes operators fail to estimate the actual real-time supply information and is more likely to result in impractical rebalance decisions. Du et al. [15] formulated the bike rebalancing problem with faulty bikes and operator-based rebalance policy for dockless bike-sharing systems, where a fleet of heterogeneous trucks, multiple depots and multiple visiting are considered. Usama et al. [14] explicitly considered the shifting decisions of faulty bikes rather than relocating them to the nearest station, i.e., bring broken bikes to the depot for repair.

Most existing literature related to rebalancing optimization adopts integer programming, reinforcement learning and heuristic approaches, which aim to make operational level decisions (e.g., truck route and the number of bikes to pickup/drop off at each node). A few studies use queueing theory to model bike-sharing problems and provide tactical level decisions (e.g., rebalance frequency). Sayarshad et al. obtained the queueing delay by using the queueing-based approximation and related the delay to a cost constraint of a dynamic relocation optimization model [43]. Samet et al. presented a closed queuing network model for a station-based bike-sharing system [44]. For station-based bike-sharing systems, customers may wait at a station to pick up or return a bike, because the parking spaces are fixed and finite. For dockless bike-sharing systems, wait time is negligible. If customers can find an available bike to ride, they will not wait behind others. If customers cannot find one, they will leave quickly and feel dissatisfied.

3. Methodology

3.1. Markovian Queueing Networks

3.1.1. Assumptions and Notations

The dockless bike-sharing system is modeled by a closed Markovian queueing network with $N \in \mathbb{N}^*$ connected nodes and a total of $K \in \mathbb{N}^*$ bikes. The bikes are distributed among the nodes. $\mathcal{N} = \{1, 2, \cdots, N\}$ and $\mathcal{K} = \{1, 2, \cdots, K\}$ are the sets of N nodes and K bikes, separately. Customers arrive at node $i \in N$ to pick up bikes to ride and return bikes at node $j \in N$. Let p_{ij} be the transition probability from node $i \in N$ to node $j \in N$. All of the nodes are fully connected because of the customers' bike trips. The transition probabilities can reflect the information of customers' destinations as well as geographical environment. If the route between two nodes is long and steep, there will be a low probability of riding bikes between these two nodes. High demand leads to a large value of the arrival rate. The main assumptions are made as follows:

1. Customers arrive at a node one by one for picking up bikes rather than arriving in groups.
2. The inter-arrival times of customers are exponentially distributed (i.e., the number of customer arrivals within a unit time interval is Poisson distributed) with an arrival rate λ_i at node i, and the arrivals at each node are completely independent.
3. All of the probabilities are the same for each route from a start node to a destination node (which can also be the start node itself), which means $p_{ij} = \frac{1}{N}$ for every pair of i and j.
4. The time spent on picking up or dropping off bikes is negligible, which means customers do not have to wait in lines at any node in the network, and the trip time is not considered as an independent parameter in the theoretical models as our focus is the steady states in the long run, but it is included in the simulation model.
5. The number of bikes is evenly distributed at each node at the beginning of the operation, and the total number of bikes in the system is fixed.
6. The capacity of each node is large enough to accommodate K bikes.
7. If a node has no bike during a period of time, customers will still arrive randomly and leave immediately, and the service for these customers will be regarded as the lost demand.

The notations are summarized in Table 1.

Table 1. Overview of notations.

Notation	Units	Definitions
N	[nodes]	Total number of nodes in a system
K	[bikes]	Total number of bikes in a system ($K = \epsilon N$)
ϵ	[bikes]	The initial number of bikes at each node in the system
λ_i	[people/min]	Arrival rate at node $i \in N$
λ	[people/min]	A certain value of the arrival rate
$\alpha_{(m)}$	[people/min]	Transition rate of returning one bike to node i by a customer riding from one of the other nodes except node i ($m = 0, 1, \cdots, K-1$)
$\beta_{(m+1)}$	[people/min]	Transition rate of renting one bike from node i to one of the other nodes except node i ($m = 0, 1, \cdots, K-1$)
α	[people/min]	A certain value of the transition rate
β	[people/min]	A certain value of the transition rate
p_l	-	Probability of having l bikes at node i with no relocation ($l = 0, 1, \cdots, K$)

Table 1. *Cont.*

Notation	Units	Definitions
$\alpha_{i(m_1,m_2)}$	[people/min]	Transition rate of renting one bike at the virtual node and returning it at node i ($m_1, m_2 = 0, 1, \cdots, K-1$)
$\alpha_{j(m_1,m_2)}$	[people/min]	Transition rate of renting one bike at the virtual node and reurning it at node j ($m_1, m_2 = 0, 1, \cdots, K-1$)
$\beta_{i(m_1,m_2)}$	[people/min]	Transition rate of renting one bike at Node and returning it at the virtual node i ($m_1, m_2 = 0, 1, \cdots, K-1$)
$\beta_{j(m_1,m_2)}$	[people/min]	Transition rate of renting one bike at Node and returning it at the virtual node j ($m_1, m_2 = 0, 1, \cdots, K-1$)
$\alpha_i\beta_{j(m_1,m_2)}$	[people/min]	Transition rate of renting one bike at Node and returning it at node i ($m_1, m_2 = 0, 1, \cdots, K-1$)
$\alpha_j\beta_{i(m_1,m_2)}$	[people/min]	Transition rate of renting one bike at Node and returning it at node j ($m_1, m_2 = 0, 1, \cdots, K-1$)
p_{m_1}	-	Probability of having m_1 bikes at node i ($m_1 = 0, 1, \cdots, K$)
p_{m_2}	-	Probability of having m_2 bikes at node j ($m_2 = 0, 1, \cdots, K$)
p_{m_1,m_2}	-	Probability of having m_1 bikes at node i and having m_2 bikes at node j with no relocation ($m_1, m_2 = 0, 1, \cdots, K$)
p'_l	-	Adjusted probability of having l bikes at node i with relocation ($l = 0, 1, \cdots, K$)
r	[times]	Relocation frequency during operation time
c	-	Coefficient of variation in probability of having zero bikes at node i under the influence of relocation
μ	-	Index of measuring the influence of relocation on steady-state probabilities
B	-	Coefficient of variation in probability of having bikes at node i under the influence of relocation
c_{in}	[RMB ·min/(bike·person)]	Unit revenue per bike per person during operation time
c_{re}	[RMB /time]	Unit cost of one-time relocation
c_p	[RMB·min/person]	Penalty per person for unmet demands during operation time
$Y(r)$	[RMB]	Total profit with relocation
r_{max}	[times]	Optimal relocation frequency which corresponds to the maximum total profit with relocation
$Y(r_{max})$	[RMB]	Maximum total profit with relocation by adopting the optimal relocation frequency

3.1.2. A Markovian Queueing Network with Higher Demands

Samet et al. studied the possibility of applying a model reduction method to a closed queueing network [44]. The aim is to reduce the complexity of the network model. When the network model is used to model a dockless bike-sharing system, both the excessive nodes and their intricate relationship increase the burden of calculation rapidly and make the problem more difficult to solve. Considering the potential barrier, a model reduction method is adopted based on the basic idea proposed by Samet et al. [44]. The main idea of this method is to aggregate multiple nodes into a virtual single node. The additive property of independent Poisson random variables demonstrates its reliability from a demand-side perspective. If taking a three-node network as an example, we reduce a three-node system into a two-node system with a virtual node (i.e., a combination of two of the nodes). It is shown by the results that the aggregation of two nodes reduces the state space of the network significantly, from a three-tuple state space: $(K, 0, 0), \ldots, (0, K, 0), \ldots, (0, 0, K)$ to a two-tuple space: $(K, 0), (K-1, 1), \ldots, (1, K-1), (0, K)$. More generally, a simplified model with one single node (i.e., node i) and a combination of $N-1$ nodes as a virtual node is shown in Figure 1.

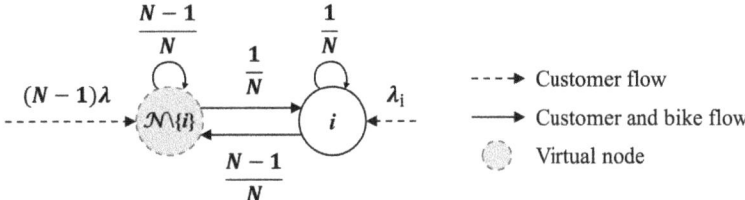

Figure 1. A reduced N-node network with the same probabilities and the same arrival rates at the nodes which are aggregated into a virtual node.

In this subsection, we build network models based on the model reduction method and differentiate a node with higher demands from the other nodes (i.e., $\lambda \le \lambda_i$). We assume that it is possible to have zero bikes at the nodes which are inside a virtual node during the state transition process of the dockless bike-sharing system (see Figure 2). The digits in circles represent the changing number of bikes at the high-demand node. The number of bikes at a virtual node is K minus the circled number. Therefore, each circled number can be described as a state of the system. $\alpha_{(0)}, \alpha_{(1)}, \cdots, \alpha_{(K-1)}$ and $\beta_{(1)}, \beta_{(2)}, \cdots, \beta_{(K)}$ are the state transition rates. $\{\alpha_{(m)}, m = 0, 1, \cdots, K-1\}$ means the rate of returning one bike, which is picked up at one of the nodes from the virtual node, at node i. $\{\beta_{(m+1)}, m = 0, 1, \cdots, K-1\}$ means renting one bike at node i and returning it at one of the other nodes except node i. Although the complexity increases with the increasing number of nodes in the system, general formulas are concluded.

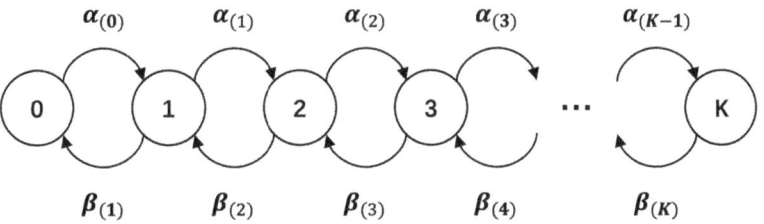

Figure 2. The state transition diagram with a high-demand node.

A three-node system:

$$\alpha_{(m)} = \frac{2}{3}\lambda\frac{K-m}{K-m+1}, \quad m = 0, 1, \cdots, K \tag{1}$$

A four-node system:

$$\alpha_{(m)} = \frac{3}{4}\lambda\frac{K-m}{K-m+2}, \quad m = 0, 1, \cdots, K \tag{2}$$

A N-node system:

$$\alpha_{(m)} = \frac{N-1}{N}\lambda\frac{K-m}{K-m+N-2}, \quad m = 0, 1, \cdots, K \tag{3}$$

$\beta_{(m+1)}$ is given by

$$\beta_{(m+1)} = \lambda_i \frac{N-1}{N}, m = 0, 1, \cdots, K-1 \tag{4}$$

The steady-state probabilities are given by

$$p_l = \frac{\alpha_{(m)}}{\beta_{(m+1)}} p_{l-1}, (l, m) = \{(1, 0), \cdots, (K, K-1)\} \tag{5}$$

Based on $\sum_{l=0}^{K} p_l = 1$, the formula of p_0 is yielded by

$$p_0 = \frac{1}{1 + \frac{\lambda}{\lambda_i} \frac{K}{K+N-2} + \frac{\lambda^2}{\lambda_i^2} \frac{K(K-1)}{(K+N-2)(K+N-3)} + \cdots + \frac{\lambda^K}{\lambda_i^K} \frac{K!}{(K+N-2)\cdots(N-1)}} \tag{6}$$

which leads to the formula of $p_l(l = 1, 2, \cdots, K)$:

$$p_l = \frac{\left(\frac{\lambda}{\lambda_i}\right)^l \frac{K(K-1)\cdots(K-l+1)}{(K+N-2)(K+N-3)\cdots(K+N-l-1)}}{1 + \frac{\lambda}{\lambda_i} \frac{K}{K+N-2} + \frac{\lambda^2}{\lambda_i^2} \frac{K(K-1)}{(K+N-2)(K+N-3)} + \cdots + \frac{\lambda^K}{\lambda_i^K} \frac{K!}{(K+N-2)\cdots(N-1)}} \tag{7}$$

The value of p_0 tends to be 1 when λ_i is far larger than λ.

3.1.3. A Markovian Queueing Network with Higher Demands and Lower Demands

In reality, a bike-sharing system may include multiple nodes with complex and diverse demands from customers. To make the models more related to a real-world network, the Markovian queueing network model is extended in the paper to analyze the system under the influence of unequal demands, which include the higher demands and the lower demands. The reduced N-node network of the extension model is shown in Figure 3. Node i refers to a node with higher demands, and node j refers to a node with lower demands than the nodes (whose arrival rates are the same and represented by λ) inside a virtual node (i.e., $\lambda_j \leq \lambda \leq \lambda_i$).

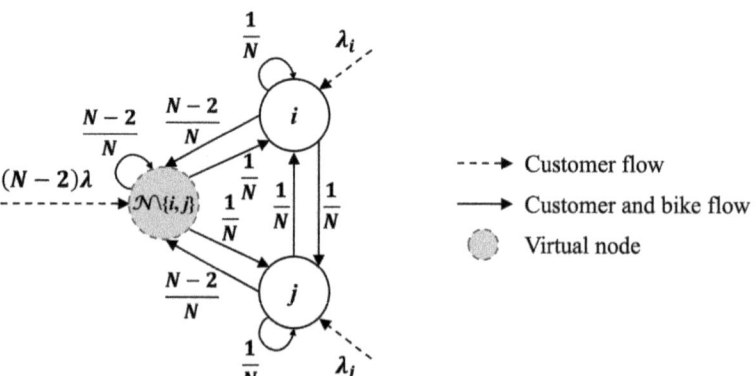

Figure 3. A reduced N-node network with the same probabilities and unequal demands.

With the existence of a virtual node and two single nodes, a three-tuple state space $\{(K, 0, 0), \cdots, (0, K, 0), \cdots, (0, 0, K)\}$ is used to represent the changing states of the whole system. Thanks to the fixed total number of bikes, a two-tuple state space $\{(K, 0), (K-1, 1), \ldots, (1, K-1), (0, K)\}$ performs a similar function, which represents the number of bikes at nodes i and j, separately (see Figure 4a,b). Each transition of the states means transferring one bike at a time. The six types of transition rates are defined as follows:

$$\beta_{i(m_1+1,m_2)} = \beta_i = \lambda_i \frac{N-2}{N}, \qquad \forall m_1, m_2 \tag{8}$$

$$\beta_{j(m_1,m_2+1)} = \beta_j = \lambda_j \frac{N-2}{N}, \qquad \forall m_1, m_2 \tag{9}$$

$$\alpha_j \beta_{i(m_1+1,m_2)} = \frac{\lambda_i}{N}, \qquad \forall m_1, m_2 \tag{10}$$

$$\alpha_i \beta_{j(m_1,m_2+1)} = \frac{\lambda_j}{N}, \qquad \forall m_1, m_2 \tag{11}$$

$$\alpha_{i(m_1,m_2)} = \frac{N-2}{N} \frac{\lambda(K-m_1-m_2)}{K-m_1-m_2+N-3} \tag{12}$$

$$\alpha_{j(m_1,m_2)} = \frac{N-2}{N} \frac{\lambda(K-m_1-m_2)}{K-m_1-m_2+N-3} \tag{13}$$

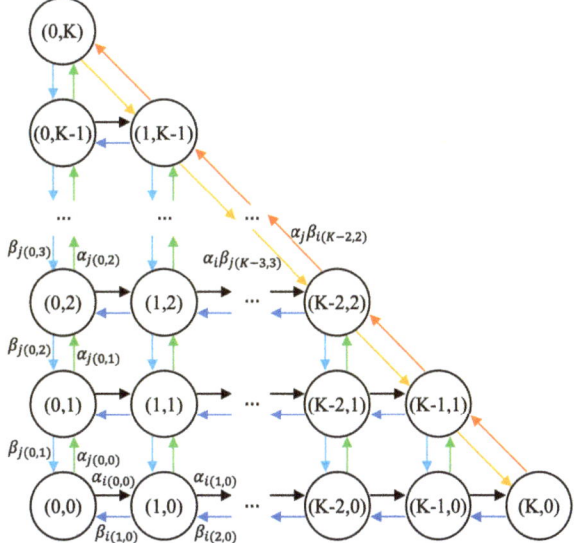

(**a**) The state transition diagram with unequal demands;

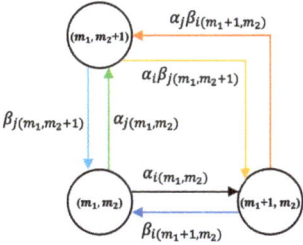

(**b**) The schematic symbols.

Figure 4. The detailed state transition diagram.

According to a main principle that the sum of the values of inflows equals to the sum of the values of outflows in a steady-state system, multiple equations (which are centered on each steady state and its directly-connected states) can be deducted. Equations are given as follows ($1 \leq m_1, m_2 \leq K - 1$):

$$\left(\alpha_{i(0,0)} + \alpha_{j(0,0)}\right)P_{(0,0)} = \beta_i p_{1,0} + \beta_j p_{0,1}, \tag{14}$$

$$\left(\beta_j + \frac{\lambda_j}{N}\right)p_{0,K} = \frac{\lambda_i}{N}p_{1,K-1} + \alpha_{j(0,K-1)}p_{0,K-1}, \tag{15}$$

$$\left(\beta_i + \frac{\lambda_i}{N}\right)p_{K,0} = \frac{\lambda_j}{N}p_{K-1,1} + \alpha_{i(K-1,0)}p_{K-1,0}, \tag{16}$$

$$\left(\beta_i + \beta_j + \alpha_{i(m_1,m_2)} + \alpha_{j(m_1,m_2)}\right)p_{m_1,m_2}$$
$$= \beta_i p_{m_1+1,m_2} + \beta_j p_{m_1,m_2+1} + \alpha_{i(m_1-1,m_2)}p_{m_1-1,m_2} + \alpha_{j(m_1,m_2-1)}p_{m_1,m_2-1}, \quad \forall m_1 + m_2 \leq K - 1 \tag{17}$$

$$\left(\beta_j + \alpha_{i(0,m_2)} + \alpha_{j(0,m_2)}\right)p_{0,m_2} = \beta_i p_{1,m_2} + \beta_j p_{0,m_2+1} + \alpha_{j(0,m_2-1)}p_{0,m_2-1} \tag{18}$$

$$\left(\beta_i + \alpha_{i(m_1,0)} + \alpha_{j(m_1,0)}\right)p_{m_1,0} = \beta_j p_{m_1,1} + \beta_i p_{m_1+1,0} + \alpha_{i(m_1-1,0)}p_{m_1-1,0} \tag{19}$$

$$\left(\beta_i + \frac{\lambda_i}{N} + \beta_j + \frac{\lambda_j}{N}\right)p_{m_1,K-m_1}$$
$$= \frac{\lambda_i}{N}p_{m_1+1,K-m_1-1} + \frac{\lambda_j}{N}p_{m_1-1,K-m_1+1} + \alpha_{i(m_1-1,K-m_1)}p_{m_1-1,K-m_1} + \alpha_{j(m_1,K-m_1-1)}p_{m_1,K-m_1-1} \tag{20}$$

In addition, there is a constraint toward the sum of the steady-state probabilities:

$$\sum_{\substack{m_1, m_2 \geq 0 \\ m_1 + m_2 \leq K}} p_{m_1,m_2} = 1 \tag{21}$$

A unique solution of the steady-state probabilities can be obtained by solving the set of equations. The probabilities of having m_1 bikes at node i and the probabilities of having m_2 bikes at node j are given by the following formulas:

$$p_{m_1} = \sum_{m_2=0}^{K-m_1} p_{m_1,m_2} \tag{22}$$

$$p_{m_2} = \sum_{m_1=0}^{K-m_2} p_{m_1,m_2} \tag{23}$$

Since it is a problem of solving non-homogeneous linear equations, we can use matrix inversion or other efficient algorithms to compute the solutions. In this paper, we use the open source R statistics software to obtain the values of steady-state probabilities. The limitation is that the burden of computation becomes huger with the increase of K.

3.2. Rebalance Strategy Optimization Model

According to the probabilistic results of the Markovian network model with one high-demand node, shared bikes are likely to leave the high-demand node and gather at the relatively low-demand nodes in the system in the long run. The basic relocation strategy we tend to adopt is to relocate the extra bikes from the relatively low-demand nodes (which have been aggregated into a virtual node in the network model with one high-demand node) to the high-demand node (which is represented as node i in the network model with one high-demand node) to reach the initial number of bikes at each node. The relocation strategy can be implemented as many times as needed during normal operation of the bike-sharing system, and the relocation frequency can reflect the number of times of relocation.

In this paper, we assume that a more effective relocation strategy is able to reduce the value of $p0$ more rapidly, which can be described as $p_0' \propto cr^{-\mu} p_0 (c > 0, \mu > 0)$. p_0' represents the steady-state probability of having zero bikes at node i under the influence of relocation. The formulas and descriptions are based on the Markovian queueing network model with higher demands. When operators implement the relocation strategy more frequently, p_0' decreases from a basic value of p_0. To determine the relationship between the probabilities without relocation and the probabilities with relocation, we have $p_0' = cr^{-\mu} p_0$. When p_0' equals p_0, $cr^{-\mu} = 1$, where the value of r represents no relocation is implemented in the system. $r > c^{\frac{1}{\mu}}$ means the operators start to relocate bikes. Considering that the sum of all the probabilities equals 1, the other probabilities are assumed to increase proportionately to satisfy the constraint, which are given by

$$p_l' = B p_l, \quad \forall l = 1, \cdots, K \tag{24}$$

For $\sum_{l=0}^{K} p_l' = 1$, we have

$$B = \frac{1 - cr^{-\mu} p_0}{1 - p_0} \tag{25}$$

$$p_l' = \begin{cases} cr^{-\mu} p_0, & l = 0 \\ \frac{1 - cr^{-\mu} p_0}{1 - p_0} p_l, & l = 1, \cdots, K \end{cases} \tag{26}$$

Our aim is to maximize the total profit obtained by the operators of the dockless bike-sharing system after implementing the relocation strategy. The operating revenue comes from the customers who rent the shared bikes and return them successfully without any trouble. In reality, the customers often have to pay for the time they spend using the bikes. We assume that the operating revenue is in proportion to the customer demand, the number of available bikes at each node and the unit price charged by the operators. If there is a high demand for shared bikes or there is a large number of available bikes in the area, it is likely to squeeze more revenue from the customers. Based on the adjusted probabilities of having a number of bikes at node i, the operating revenue is given by

$$\left[\sum_{l=0}^{K} p_l' l \lambda_i + \sum_{l=0}^{K} p_l' (K - l) \lambda \right] c_{in} = \left[K\lambda + \sum_{l=0}^{K} p_l' l (\lambda_i - \lambda) \right] c_{in} \tag{27}$$

The operating cost can be divided into the cost of relocations (which is assumed to be in proportion to the relocation frequency and the unit cost of implementing the relocation strategy) and the penalty derived from the unmet demands (which is assumed to be in proportion to the arrival rate, the possibility of having zero bikes at each node and the unit cost of penalties). Due to the given constraint for r, if no relocation is implemented in the system, the cost of relocations will not occur. According to the initial assumption that the nodes inside a virtual node are the same, it is assumed that, when the total number of bikes at these nodes (i.e., the nodes which are aggregated into one virtual node) is less than the number of the nodes inside the virtual node, there may be no bike available at some of these nodes. If the arrival rate at the node where there is no bike available for customers to use is large or the possibility of having zero bikes at the node is high, the cost of penalty from unmet demands will increase. The sum of the operating cost is given by

$$\left(r - c^{\frac{1}{\mu}}\right)c_{re} + \left(p_0'\lambda_i + \sum_{l=1}^{N-1} p_{K-N+1+l}' l\lambda\right)c_p \tag{28}$$

The total profit after implementing the relocation strategy can be calculated by the following formula:

$$\max Y(r_{\max}) = \left[K\lambda + \sum_{l=0}^{K} p_l'(r_{\max})l(\lambda_i - \lambda)\right]c_{in}$$
$$- \left(r_{\max} - c^{\frac{1}{\mu}}\right)c_{re} - \left[p_0'(r_{\max})\lambda_i + \sum_{l=1}^{N-1} p_{K-N+1+l}'(r_{\max})l\lambda\right]c_p \tag{29}$$

$Y(r)$ means the total profit with the corresponding relocation frequency r. $r_{\max}$ represents the optimal relocation frequency which corresponds to the maximum profit $Y(r_{\max})$ that the operators can obtain after relocating the bikes in the system. It is found that the relationship between $Y(r)$ and r takes the shape of a concave curve. Before the relocation frequency reaches the turning point, $Y(r)$ increases with the increase of r. After the turning point, $Y(r)$ decreases with the increase of r. The turning point turns out to be the best choice for the relocation frequency and the total profit. Therefore, we take a derivative of the total profit with respect to the relocation frequency in order to get the formula of $r_{\max}$. The first-order partial derivative of Equation (29) with respect to r is given by

$$\frac{\partial Y(r)}{\partial r} = \sum_{l=1}^{K} (\lambda_i - \lambda)c_{in}\frac{c\mu p_0 l p_l}{1 - p_0}r^{-\mu-1} + \lambda_i c_p c\mu p_0 r^{-\mu-1} - \sum_{l=1}^{N-1} \lambda c_p \frac{c\mu p_0 l p_{K-N+1+l}}{1 - p_0}r^{-\mu-1} - c_{re} \tag{30}$$

When the first-order partial derivative equals 0, $r_{\max}$ can be calculated by the following formula

$$r_{\max} = \left[\frac{\sum_{l=1}^{K}(\lambda_i - \lambda)c_{in}\frac{c\mu p_0 l p_l}{1-p_0} + \lambda_i c_p c\mu p_0 - \sum_{l=1}^{N-1}\lambda c_p \frac{c\mu p_0 l p_{K-N+1+l}}{1-p_0}}{c_{re}}\right]^{\frac{1}{\mu+1}} \tag{31}$$

4. Results

4.1. Probabilistic Results

The relationship between the steady-state probabilities and the arrival rates at different nodes in the network model with unequal demands is investigated in multiple cases by numerical experiments. The setting of the arrival rates and the corresponding figures of the cases are shown in Table 2.

Table 2. Setting of the arrival rates in the network model with unequal demands.

Case ID	λ	λ_i	λ_j	Figure
Case 1	1	1	0.8	Figure 5a
Case 2	1	1	0.6	Figure 5b
Case 3	1	1	0.4	Figure 5c
Case 4	1	1.2	0.8	Figure 5d
Case 5	1	1.2	0.6	Figure 5e
Case 6	1	1.2	0.4	Figure 5f
Case 7	1	1.2	0.2	Figure 5g
Case 8	1	1.2	0.1	Figure 5h
Case 9	1	1.2	0.05	Figure 5i

It can be concluded from the change of the arrival rates at different nodes that the long-term bike distribution in the dockless bike-sharing system is more sensitive to the higher demands than the lower demands. Due to the difference, the number of bikes at the

nodes with higher demands decreases more quickly and more likely than the increase of
the number of bikes at the nodes with lower demands. For the nodes with middle demands,
the number of bikes may decrease more mildly compared with the decreased number of
bikes at the nodes with higher demands. It is suggested that the operators should pay
more attention to the high-demand nodes, which may suffer the biggest loss in the system.
Unless one low-demand node has the smallest arrival rate which is terribly different from
the arrival rates at the other nodes, there is a relatively small possibility that all of the bikes
in the system are transferred to one low-demand node in a limited period of time, which
can be regarded as the biggest imbalance of bikes in the system.

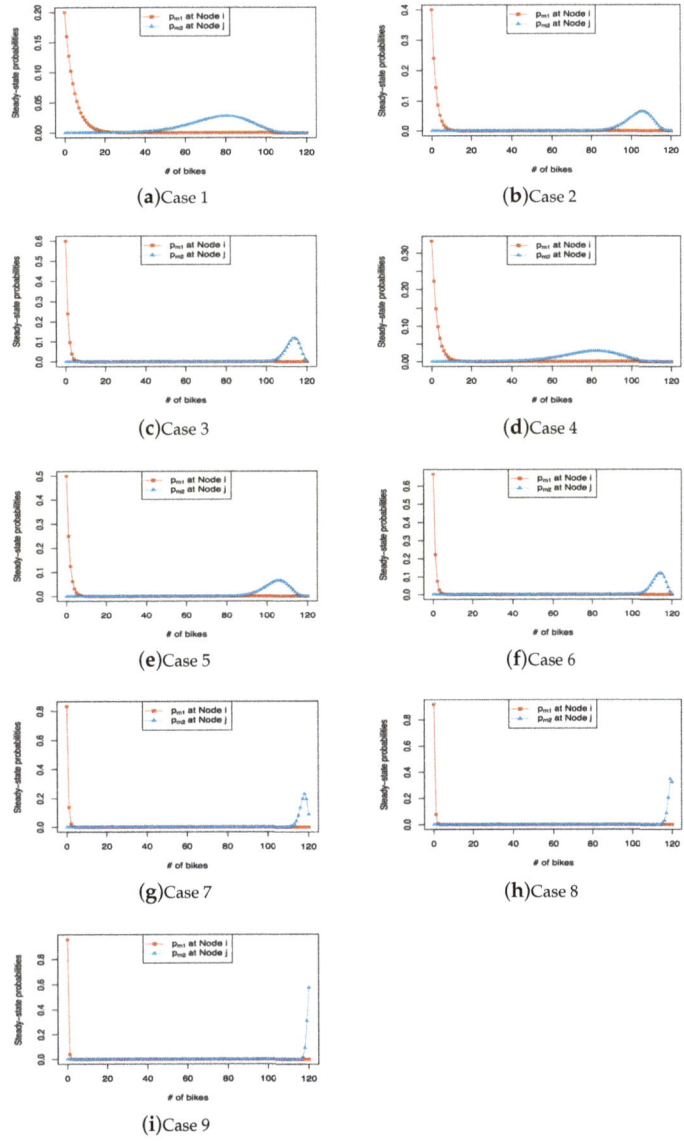

Figure 5. Probabilities with respect to the number of bikes at nodes *i* and *j*.

4.2. Profitability Results

4.2.1. The Effect of Relocation-Related Parameters

c and μ are two positive parameters which can be regarded as a measure of the effectiveness of an adopted relocation strategy. If the relocation strategy is more effective, c is supposed to decrease and μ is supposed to increase, which can contribute a low probability of having zero bikes at the high-demand node under the influence of relocations. In the numerical experiments, c and μ are changed separately to analyze their influence on the performance of the optimization model, as shown in Figure 6.

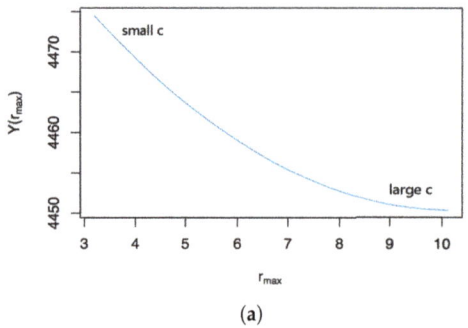
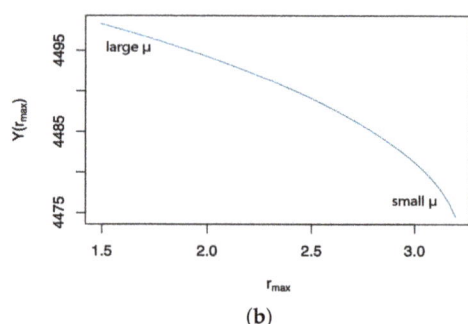

(a)   (b)

Figure 6. Effect of relocation-related parameters. (**a**) The maximum profit after implementing the relocation strategy with respect to the optimal relocation frequency under the influence of c; (**b**) The maximum profit after implementing the relocation strategy with respect to the optimal relocation frequency under the influence of m.

The value of $Y(r_{\max})$ decreases with the increase of $r_{\max}$ in Figure 6a,b. When c decreases or μ increases, the maximum profit tends to increase and the optimal relocation frequency tends to decrease. It is indicated that the relocation strategy works well. An effective relocation strategy can reduce the relocation frequency and save the expense of frequent relocations, which can increase the total profit indirectly. However, the concavity and convexity of the curves shown in these two figures is different between c and μ. In Figure 6a, $Y(r_{\max})$ is more sensitive when the value of c is small, and $r_{\max}$ is more sensitive when the value of c is large. In Figure 6b, $Y(r_{\max})$ is more sensitive when the value of μ is small, and $r_{\max}$ is more sensitive when the value of μ is large. Since it is preferable for operators to gain more profits, a combination of a small c and a large μ can properly decrease the sensitivity of $Y(r_{\max})$ and $r_{\max}$ to the effectiveness of relocation strategies, which allows the operators to make more flexible decisions about what kind of relocation strategies they want to adopt.

4.2.2. The Effect of Revenue-Related and Cost-Related Parameters

c_{in}, c_{re} and c_p are parameters related to the operating revenue and the operating cost. As shown in Figure 7a,b, $Y(r_{\max})$ increases with the increase of $r_{\max}$ under the influence of c_{in} and c_{re}. $Y(r_{\max})$ increases with the decrease of $r_{\max}$ under the influence of c_p (Figure 7c). It can be explained by the different meanings of these parameters. The relocation strategy can reset the number of bikes at each node to an initial state, which make the bike-sharing system able to supply the customers with enough bikes after each relocation. Due to the definition of c_{in}, the high price means operators can generate more revenue by satisfying the customer demand, which can be promised by frequent relocations. Therefore, with the increase of c_{in}, both the optimal relocation frequency and the maximum profit increase. According to the change of $r_{\max}$ and $Y(r_{\max})$, as shown in Figure 7a, $r_{\max}$ is insensitive to the increase of c_{in} and $Y(r_{\max})$ is sensitive to the increase of c_{in}. In reality, operators can make more profits by raising the unit price. However, they have to consider the unit price given by their competitors, who have the ability to pull regular customers from them.

Although acquiring a large revenue from customers can cover the expense on relocations to some extent, the increase of the optimal relocation frequency is slight. For operators, pricing decisions have a significant influence on the total profit but have a slight effect on the decision-making about relocating bikes. As shown in Figure 7b, with the increase of c_{re}, both r_{max} and $Y(r_{max})$ decrease. It is because that the high cost of relocating bikes is supposed to decrease the relocation frequency to save cost for operators. With the decrease of relocation frequency, the total profit decreases due to the huge expense on relocations and the decreased revenue caused by the occasional shortage of bikes at some nodes. The slope of the curve in Figure 7b indicates that r_{max} is more sensitive to the change of c_{re} than $Y(r_{max})$, especially when c_{re} has a small value.

It is suggested that operators should consider how to reduce the expense on relocating bikes in the system, which can be very beneficial to solve the imbalance problem of bike distribution. In Figure 7c, r_{max} increases and $Y(r_{max})$ decreases with the increase of c_p. The large value of c_p means a large penalty of losing customers, which happens when customers arrive at the node where there is no bike available. The increase of relocation frequency can minimize the losses by relocating bikes to the nodes with high demands. With the increase of the penalty and the increased cost derived from frequent relocations, the total profit decreases. In the real world, the unit cost of penalty from unmet demands is difficult to measure. In the numerical experiments, the value of c_p is set far larger than the values of c_{in} and c_{re}. It is because unmet demands may have a significant impact on the loyalty of the regular customers. If the customers often cannot find any bikes to ride, they are likely to feel dissatisfied with the dockless bike-sharing system and turn to alternatives, which may bring about great losses (e.g., an obvious decrease in the potential revenue) for the bike-sharing company. Therefore, setting a large value of c_p in the optimization model for a relocation problem can emphasize the need for a suitable relocation frequency.

4.2.3. The Effect of Arrival Rates

The arrival rate is the most important parameter which is concerned with the customer demand for bike service in the paper. The influence of the arrival rates at different nodes on the relocation problem is also investigated by a numerical experiment. In Figure 7d, r_{max} increases and $Y(r_{max})$ decreases with the decrease of $\frac{\lambda}{\lambda_i}$. It is because that the decrease of $\frac{\lambda}{\lambda_i}$ means the customer demand at different nodes becomes more unequal, which leads to an increased possibility of the imbalanced distribution of bikes in the system. Frequent relocations are needed to deal with this problem. Due to the high cost of frequent relocations, the total profit decreases. From the results, it is observed that, compared with the maximum profit, the optimal relocation frequency is more sensitive to the difference of the arrival rates at different nodes in the network, especially when $\frac{\lambda}{\lambda_i}$ is small. When $\frac{\lambda}{\lambda_i}$ gets close to 1, the optimal relocation frequency decreases rapidly and becomes very close to 0. Therefore, we suggest that the operators should pay attention to the difference of the customer demand among the nodes, especially when the demand is always changing as the time goes by. Not only does the unequal demand have a significant influence on the bike distribution in the long term, but also it requires multiple times of relocating bikes in the bike-sharing system. If the unit cost of relocations is high, the operators may have to spend a huge amount of money on relocating bikes under the influence of a small value of $\frac{\lambda}{\lambda_i}$.

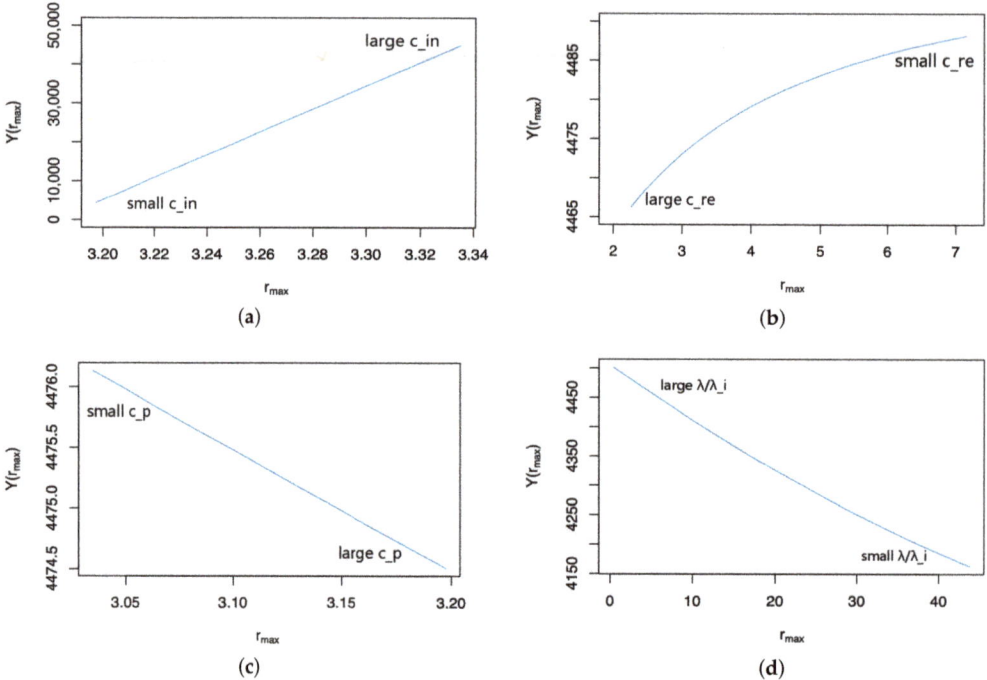

Figure 7. Effect of revenue- and cost-related parameters and arrival rates. (**a**) The maximum profit after implementing the relocation strategy with respect to the optimal relocation frequency under the influence of c_{in}; (**b**) The maximum profit after implementing the relocation strategy with respect to the optimal relocation frequency under the influence of c_{re}; (**c**) The maximum profit after implementing the relocation strategy with respect to the optimal relocation frequency under the influence of c_p. (**d**) The maximum profit after implementing the relocation strategy with respect to the optimal relocation frequency under the influence of $\frac{\lambda}{\lambda_i}$.

5. Discussion

By analyzing the results of Markovian queueing network, we can obtain the several interesting findings. Compared with the high-demand node, the number of bikes at the lower-demand node changes at a much slower rate. As a whole, we guess that the number of bikes at the higher-demand node is likely to be smaller than the number of bikes at each of the middle-demand nodes (if there are a relatively large number of middle-demand nodes) and is much smaller than the number of bikes at the lower-demand node. The bike distribution at the lower-demand node is not sensitive to the increase of the arrival rate at the higher-demand node, which means bikes at the higher-demand node are likely to be scattered at both the lower-demand node and some middle-demand nodes. It is suggested that the operators should pay more attention to the nodes with higher demands, where the number of bikes decreases rapidly, rather than the nodes with lower demands, where the number of bikes increases relatively slowly, although these all belong to two extremes of the nodes with different customer demand. When the total number of bikes in the system is fixed, the expected number of bikes at the low-demand node in the long run tends to decrease and its possible range becomes broader with the increase of the number of nodes and the decrease of the initial number of bikes at each node. It suggests that a large number of nodes in the network can reduce the influence of the unequal demands moderately and make the long-term bike distribution more balanced than a small number of nodes in the network. Meanwhile, a larger initial number of bikes at each node can lead to a more imbalanced distribution of shared bikes in the system without human intervention.

The rebalance problem is solved by an operator-based rebalance strategy based on the proper utilization of probabilistic results provided by the theoretical models. The main objective is to maximize the total profit and get the optimal relocation frequency. It is found that the relationship between the total profit and the relocation frequency takes the shape of a concave curve, which makes it quick to find the global optimal point by taking derivative of the expression.

There are various key parameters related to the optimization problem (i.e., the indexes which can measure the effectiveness of each relocation c and μ, the unit price c_{in}, the unit cost of relocation c_{re}, the unit cost of unmet demands c_p and the different ratios of arrival rates). It is common sense from a business perspective that operators prefer the solution which can bring more profits and requires a low frequency of relocating bikes.

The numerical experiments show that small values of c and c_p and large values of μ can fit the preference. A small value of c and a large value of μ can reduce the probability of having zero bikes at the high-demand node, which means an effective relocation strategy can result in a low frequency of relocation and increase the total profit mainly by saving the total cost. When the value of c is small, the maximum profit is more sensitive to the change of the optimal relocation frequency, while, when the value of μ is large, the maximum profit is less sensitive to the change of the optimal relocation frequency. Therefore, a small c and a large μ are complementary to each other, which can provide one of the criteria for operators to select useful relocation strategies.

When the ratio of arrival rates is changed in the optimization model, it is indicated that a large difference between the arrival rates is going to decrease the total profit and make the optimal relocation frequency increase rapidly, which totally deviates from the operators' purpose. The unequal demands not only have an adverse effect on bike distribution but also influence the relocation frequency and the profit operators can obtain. What the operators can do is to balance the customer demand among the nodes as much as possible, and their efforts spent on balancing can be directly reflected in the benefits. Differing from the influence of c_p, a large value of c_{in} and a small value of c_{re} can increase both the optimal relocation frequency and the maximum total profit, which means the operators can get a maximum profit and also have to carry out more frequent relocations. The change of c_{in} has a greater influence on the total profit and the change of c_{re} has a greater influence on the optimal relocation frequency. With the decrease of c_{re}, the maximum total profit becomes less sensitive to the change of the optimal relocation frequency, which means the benefit of relocating bikes gradually reduces.

Therefore, operators can consider increasing the unit price within a customer's acceptable range in order to make more profits. If the unit cost of each relocation can be reduced significantly, a high frequency of relocation can bring more profits and satisfy more demands. The unit cost of unmet demand is the most uncertain parameter for operators, so it is suggested that the operators should predict the value of c_p carefully by investigation and analysis and minimize the disappointment from customers who cannot find any available bikes to ride if possible.

6. Conclusions

In short, although our work takes a dockless bike-sharing system as an example, the developed methods and models can be extended to apply in some other resource-sharing systems when necessary. The theoretical models are general, flexible and extensible. In this work, we first formulate the bike-sharing system as a Markovian queueing network with higher-demand nodes and lower-demand nodes. Thereafter, we employ an operator-based rebalance strategy and optimize the rebalance frequency at the minimum cost. The results reveal that it is possible for most of the shared bikes to gather at one low-demand node eventually in the long run under the influence of the various arrival rates at different nodes. However, the decrease in the number of bikes at the high-demand nodes is more sensitive to the unequal demands, especially when the size of the network and the number of bikes in the system are large. It may cause a significant loss for operators, to which they should pay attention. Meanwhile, different estimated values of parameters related to revenue and cost affect the optimization results differently. By analysis of some factors with practical meanings, this paper can bring real-world insights.

There are also some limitations to the study, which can be regarded as directions for further research. The influence of different arrival rates on the distribution of bikes in the dockless bike-sharing system is the focus of our research. In the optimization model for solving the relocation problems, the relocation costs can be estimated based on how many bikes are relocated, but the distance of relocating bikes from one node to another is not considered, which is also a limitation of our proposed methods. The optimization models for solving relocation problems can be extended to apply to a more general Markovian network model with multiple high-demand nodes and low-demand nodes in the future study. Additionally, the impact of COVID-19 can also be involved in the future research, for instance, high/median/low risk areas can be regarded as various types of nodes in the Markovian network. These heterogeneous types of nodes are associated with various levels of demand decrease and uncertainty, which brings new challenges on system optimization in bike-sharing systems.

Author Contributions: Conceptualization, X.M. and W.K.C.; methodology, X.M.; software, X.L.; formal analysis, X.M.; investigation, X.M.; writing—original draft preparation, X.M. and X.L.; writing—review and editing, X.M. and X.L.; visualization, X.M. and X.L.; supervision, W.K.C.; and funding acquisition, W.K.C. All authors have read and agreed to the published version of the manuscript.

Funding: This paper was partially funded by Shenzhen Municipal Development and Reform Commission, Shenzhen Environmental Science and New Energy Technology Engineering Laboratory, Grant Number: SDRC [2016]172.

Data Availability Statement: Not Applicable.

Conflicts of Interest: The authors declare no conflict of interest.

References

1. Freund, D.; Henderson, S.G.; O'Mahony, E.; Shmoys, D.B. Analytics and bikes: Riding tandem with motivate to improve mobility. *INFORMS J. Appl. Anal.* **2019**, *49*, 310–323. [CrossRef]
2. Mourad, A.; Puchinger, J.; Chu, C. A survey of models and algorithms for optimizing shared mobility. *Transp. Res. Part B Methodol.* **2019**, *123*, 323–346. [CrossRef]
3. He, L.; Hu, Z.; Zhang, M. Robust repositioning for vehicle sharing. *Manuf. Serv. Oper. Manag.* **2020**, *22*, 241–256. [CrossRef]
4. Furuhata, M.; Dessouky, M.; Ordóñez, F.; Brunet, M.E.; Wang, X.; Koenig, S. Ridesharing: The state-of-the-art and future directions. *Transp. Res. Part B Methodol.* **2013**, *57*, 28–46. [CrossRef]
5. Pan, L.; Cai, Q.; Fang, Z.; Tang, P.; Huang, L. A deep reinforcement learning framework for rebalancing dockless bike sharing systems. *Proc. AAAI Conf. Artif. Intell.* **2019**, *33*, 1393–1400. [CrossRef]
6. Schuijbroek, J.; Hampshire, R.C.; Van Hoeve, W.J. Inventory rebalancing and vehicle routing in bike sharing systems. *Eur. J. Oper. Res.* **2017**, *257*, 992–1004. [CrossRef]
7. Pal, A.; Zhang, Y. Free-floating bike-sharing: Solving real-life large-scale static rebalancing problems. *Transp. Res. Part C Emerg. Technol.* **2020**, *80*, 92–116. [CrossRef]
8. O'Mahony, E.; Shmoys, D.B. Data analysis and optimization for (citi) bike sharing. *Proc. Aaai Conf. Artif. Intell.* **2015**, *29*, 687–694.
9. Liu, J.; Sun, L.; Chen, W.; Xiong, H. Rebalancing bike sharing systems: A multi-source data smart optimization. In Proceedings of the 22nd ACM SIGKDD International Conference on Knowledge Discovery and Data Mining, San Francisco, CA, USA, 13–17 August 2016; pp. 1005–1014.
10. Li, Y.; Zheng, Y.; Yang, Q. Dynamic bike reposition: A spatio-temporal reinforcement learning approach. In Proceedings of the 24th ACM SIGKDD International Conference on Knowledge Discovery & Data Mining, London, UK, 19–23 August 2018; pp. 1724–1733.
11. Parkes, S.D.; Marsden, G.; Shaheen, S.A.; Cohen, A.P. Understanding the Diffusion of Public Bikesharing Systems: Evidence from Europe and North America. *J. Transp. Geogr.* **2013**, *31*, 94–103. [CrossRef]
12. Wang, M.; Zhou, X. bike-sharing systems and congestion: Evidence from US cities. *J. Transp. Geogr.* **2017**, *65*, 147–154. [CrossRef]
13. Ma, Y.; Lan, J.; Thornton, T.; Mangalagiu, D.; Zhu, D. Challenges of collaborative governance in the sharing economy: The case of free-floating bike-sharing in Shanghai. *J. Clean. Prod.* **2018**, *197*, 356–365. [CrossRef]
14. Usama, M.; Zahoor, O.; Shen, Y.; Bao, Q. Dockless bike-sharing system: Solving the problem of faulty bikes with simultaneous rebalancing operation. *J. Transp. Land Use* **2020**, *13*, 491–515. [CrossRef]

15. Du, M.; Cheng, L.; Li, X.; Tang, F. Static rebalancing optimization with considering the collection of malfunctioning bikes in free-floating bike sharing system. *Transp. Res. Part E: Logist. Transp. Rev.* **2020**, *141*, 102012. [CrossRef]
16. Mátrai, T.; Tóth, J. Cluster Analysis of Public Bike Sharing Systems for Categorization? *IET Intell. Transp. Syst.* **2020**, *12*, 5501. [CrossRef]
17. Chen, P.C.; Hsieh, H.Y.; Su, K.W.; Sigalingging, X.K.; Chen, Y.R.; Leu, J.S. Predicting station level demand in a bike-sharing system using recurrent neural networks? *IET Intell. Transp. Syst.* **2020**, *14*, 554–561. [CrossRef]
18. Cheng, L.; Yang, J.; Chen, X.; Cao, M.; Zhou, H.; Sun, Y. How could the station-based bike sharing system and the free-floating bike sharing system be coordinated? *J. Transp. Geogr.* **2020**, *89*, 102896. [CrossRef]
19. Jin, X.; Tong, D. Station-Free Bike Rebalancing Analysis: Scale, Modeling, and Computational Challenges. *Isprs Int. J. Geo Inf.* **2020**, *9*, 691. [CrossRef]
20. Galatoulas, N.F.; Genikomsakis, K.N.; Ioakimidis, C.S. Analysis of potential demand and costs for the business development of an electric vehicle sharing service. *Sustain. Cities Soc.* **2018**, *42*, 148–161.
21. Frade, I.; Ribeiro, A. Bicycle Sharing Systems Demand. *Procedia Soc. Behav. Sci.* **2014**, *111*, 518–527. [CrossRef]
22. Xu, C.; Ji, J.; Liu, P. The station-free sharing bike demand forecasting with a deep learning approach and large-scale datasets. *Transp. Res. Part C Emerg. Technol.* **2018**, *95*, 47–60. [CrossRef]
23. Çelebi, D.; Yörüsün, A.; Işık, H. Bicycle sharing system design with capacity allocations. *Transp. Res. Part B Methodol.* **2018**, *114*, 86–98. [CrossRef]
24. Bordagaray, M.; Dell'Olio, L.; Fonzone, A.; Ibeas, Á; Capturing the conditions that introduce systematic variation in bike-sharing travel behavior using data mining techniques. *Transp. Res. Part C Emerg. Technol.* **2016**, *71*, 231–248. [CrossRef]
25. Gurumurthy, K.M.; Kockelman, K.M. Analyzing the dynamic ride-sharing potential for shared autonomous vehicle fleets using cellphone data from Orlando, Florida. *Comput. Environ. Urban Syst.* **2018**, *71*, 177–185. [CrossRef]
26. Yang, Y.; Heppenstall, A.; Turner, A.; Comber, A. A spatiotemporal and graph-based analysis of dockless bike-sharing patterns to understand urban flows over the last mile. *Comput. Environ. Urban Syst.* **2019**, *77*, 101361. [CrossRef]
27. Ji, Y.; Ma, X.; He, M.; Jin, Y.; Yuan, Y. Comparison of usage regularity and its determinants between docked and dockless bike-sharing systems: A case study in Nanjing, China. *J. Clean. Prod.* **2020**, *255*, 120110. [CrossRef]
28. Bakogiannis, E.; Siti, M.; Tsigdinos, S.; Vassi, A.; Nikitas, A. Monitoring the first dockless bike-sharing system in Greece: Understanding user perceptions, usage patterns and adoption barriers. *Res. Transp. Bus. Manag.* **2019**, *33*, 100432. [CrossRef]
29. Yoon, G.; Chow, J.Y. Unlimited-ride bike-share pass pricing revenue management for casual riders using only public data. *Int. J. Transp. Sci. Technol.* **2020**, *9*, 159–169. [CrossRef]
30. Estrada, A.; Romero, D.; Pinto, R.; Pezzotta, G.; Lagorio, A.; Rondini, A. A Cost-Engineering Method for Product-Service Systems Based on Stochastic Process Modelling: Bergamo's bike-sharing PSS. *Procedia CIRP* **2017**, *64*, 417–422. [CrossRef]
31. Chen, Y.; Zha, Y.; Wang, D.; Li, H.; Bi, G. Optimal pricing strategy of a bike-sharing firm in the presence of customers with convenience perceptions. *J. Clean. Prod.* **2020**, *253*, 119905. [CrossRef]
32. Hua, M.; Chen, X.; Cheng, L.; Chen, J. Should bike sharing continue operating during the COVID-19 pandemic? Empirical findings from Nanjing, China. *arXiv* **2020**, arXiv:2012.02946.
33. Teixeira, J.F.; Lopes, M. The link between bike sharing and subway use during the COVID-19 pandemic: The case-study of New York's Citi Bike. *Transp. Res. Interdiscip. Perspect.* **2020**, *6*, 100166.
34. Nikiforiadis, A.; Ayfantopoulou, G.; Stamelou, A. Assessing the Impact of COVID-19 on Bike-Sharing Usage: The Case of Thessaloniki, Greece. *Sustainability* **2020**, *12*, 8215. [CrossRef]
35. Sayarshad, H.; Tavassoli, S.; Zhao, F. A multi-periodic optimization formulation for bike planning and bike utilization. *Transp. Res. Part C Emerg. Technol.* **2012**, *36*, 4944–4951. [CrossRef]
36. Singla, A.; Santoni, M.; Bartók, G.; Mukerji, P.; Meenen, M.; Krause, A. Incentivizing users for balancing bike sharing systems. *Proc. Aaai Conf. Artif. Intell.* **2015**, *29*, 723–729.
37. Fricker, C.; Gast, N. Incentives and redistribution in homogeneous bike-sharing systems with stations of finite capacity. *Euro J. Transp. Logist.* **2016**, *5*, 261–291. [CrossRef]
38. Liu, Y.; Szeto, W.Y.; Ho, S.C. A static free-floating bike repositioning problem with multiple heterogeneous vehicles, multiple depots, and multiple visits. *Transp. Res. Part C Emerg. Technol.* **2018**, *92*, 208–242. [CrossRef]
39. Brinkmann, J.; Ulmer, M.W.; Mattfeld, D.C. Dynamic Lookahead Policies for Stochastic-Dynamic Inventory Routing in bike-sharing Systems. *Comput. Oper. Res.* **2019**, *106*, 260–279. [CrossRef]
40. Legros, B. Dynamic repositioning strategy in a bike-sharing system; how to prioritize and how to rebalance a bike station. *Eur. J. Oper. Res.* **2019**, *272*, 740–753. [CrossRef]
41. Brendel, A.B.; Lichtenberg, S.; Brauer, B.; Nastjuk, I.; Kolbe, L.M. Improving electric vehicle utilization in carsharing: A framework and simulation of an e-carsharing vehicle utilization management system. *Eur. J. Oper. Res.* **2018**, *64*, 230–245. [CrossRef]
42. Reiss, S.; Bogenberger, K. A Relocation Strategy for Munich's bike-sharing System: Combining an operator-based and a user-based Scheme. *Transp. Res. Procedia* **2017**, *22*, 104–114. [CrossRef]

43. Sayarshad, H.R.; Chow, J.Y. Non-myopic relocation of idle mobility-on-demand vehicles as a dynamic location-allocation-queueing problem. *Transp. Res. Part E Logist. Transp. Rev.* **2017**, *106*, 60–77. [CrossRef]
44. Samet, B.; Couffin, F.; Zolghadri, M.; Barkallah, M.; Haddar, M. Model reduction for studying a bike-sharing System as a closed queuing network. *Procedia Manuf.* **2018**, *25*, 39–46. [CrossRef]

 **algorithms**

Article

Combining Heuristics with Simulation and Fuzzy Logic to Solve a Flexible-Size Location Routing Problem under Uncertainty

Rafael D. Tordecilla [1,2,*], Pedro J. Copado-Méndez [1,3], Javier Panadero [1,3], Carlos L. Quintero-Araujo [4], Jairo R. Montoya-Torres [2] and Angel A. Juan [1,3]

1   IN3–Computer Science Department, Universitat Oberta de Catalunya, 08018 Barcelona, Spain; pcopadom@uoc.edu (P.J.C.-M.); jpanaderom@uoc.edu (J.P.); ajuanp@uoc.edu (A.A.J.)
2   School of Engineering, Universidad de La Sabana, Chia 250001, Colombia; jairo.montoya@unisabana.edu.co
3   Department of Data Analytics & Business Intelligence, Euncet Business School, 08221 Terrassa, Spain
4   International School of Economics and Administrative Sciences, Universidad de La Sabana, Chia 250001, Colombia; carlosqa@unisabana.edu.co
*   Correspondence: rtordecilla@uoc.edu or rafael.tordecilla@unisabana.edu.co

Abstract: The location routing problem integrates both a facility location and a vehicle routing problem. Each of these problems are *NP-hard* in nature, which justifies the use of heuristic-based algorithms when dealing with large-scale instances that need to be solved in reasonable computing times. This paper discusses a realistic variant of the problem that considers facilities of different sizes and two types of uncertainty conditions. In particular, we assume that some customers' demands are stochastic, while others follow a fuzzy pattern. An iterated local search metaheuristic is integrated with simulation and fuzzy logic to solve the aforementioned problem, and a series of computational experiments are run to illustrate the potential of the proposed algorithm.

Keywords: location routing problem; uncertainty; heuristics; simulation; fuzzy logic

 check for updates

Citation: Tordecilla, R.D.; Copado-Méndez, P.J.; Panadero, J.; Quintero-Araujo, C.L.; Montoya-Torres, J.R.; Juan, A.A. Combining Heuristics with Simulation and Fuzzy Logic to Solve a Flexible-Size Location Routing Problem under Uncertainty. *Algorithms* **2021**, *14*, 45. https://doi.org/10.3390/a14020045

Academic Editor: Javier Del Ser Lorente

Received: 15 December 2020
Accepted: 26 January 2021
Published: 30 January 2021

Publisher's Note: MDPI stays neutral with regard to jurisdictional claims in published maps and institutional affiliations.

1. Introduction

When designing and managing supply chains, one of the most relevant problems is the simultaneous location of distribution facilities and the routing of vehicles to deliver products to a set of geographically dispersed customers. The former is considered a strategic decision, while the latter is operational. This problem is known in the scientific literature as the location routing problem (LRP). The LRP addresses these two types of decisions in an integrated manner. From the formal view of the operational research community, the LRP is known to be *NP-hard*, since it can be reduced to either the facility location problem (FLP), the vehicle routing problem (VRP) or the multidepot VRP, which are all known to be *NP-hard*. This computational complexity means that optimal solutions are really difficult to obtain in a reasonable computational time. Thus, heuristic approaches are required to solve medium- and large-sized instances. Due to its complexity, some of the first studies tackled the problem by splitting it into the corresponding subproblems [1,2]. Nevertheless, this approach might lead to suboptimal solutions.

Due to the increase in computational power and the development of fast heuristic approaches, the LRP has been studied in an integrated way, which clearly has improved the obtained results [3]. One of the most studied versions of the LRP is the capacitated LRP, in which both depot and vehicle capacity constraints must be satisfied (the acronym LRP will henceforth refer to this version). However, all previous works consider the depot capacity as a fixed value for each location. This could not be a suitable approach when dealing with realistic problems, since it is usual that decision-makers can select the size of a facility from a discrete set of known available sizes, or even freely. For real-world problems, this set is usually associated with investment activities, such as building facilities [4], purchasing equipment [5] or qualifying workforce [6]. From an academic point of view, despite the increasing number of published works on the LRP, the consideration of flexible sizes for facilities has been rarely addressed in the literature. Nevertheless, real-life examples from both LRP [4,7,8] and non-LRP [5,6] contexts show the relevance of considering a variety of facility sizes to select from.

Traditional LRP approaches consider that parameters are deterministic or crisp, i.e., they assume that inputs are known in advance. This assumption is far from reality in many applications, such as waste collection, humanitarian logistics and urban freight distribution, where uncertainty is a key factor to consider. Despite this, the literature on the LRP addressing uncertain parameters is still scarce. In order to overcome this problem, articles employing stochastic approaches can be found in the literature. Customers' demand is one of the most addressed stochastic parameters [9–13]. Other parameters might also be considered as stochastic, such as transportation costs and travel speeds [14] or logistic costs and travel distance [15]. In general, many articles addressing stochasticity in routing problems hybridize simulation models with heuristic or metaheuristic algorithms to tackle efficiently both uncertainty and *NP-hardness*. In many real-life situations, however, it might not be possible to accurately model all uncertainty sources as stochastic variables following a probability distribution. This might be the case, for instance, when the volume of observations is low or the available data does not have enough quality [16]. Hence, uncertainty in the LRP has also been tackled through the use of fuzzy sets. Parameters such as customers' demands [17–20], travel times [21,22] or time windows [23] have been modeled as fuzzy in several studies. Notice that, whenever possible, modeling uncertainty as stochastic variables might allow a deeper statistical analysis of the results.

To the best of our knowledge, there are no works in the literature simultaneously addressing stochastic and fuzzy approaches to model demand uncertainty in a flexible-size LRP. This is a realistic scenario, since many companies might have historical data on trustworthy customers and not enough data on new or unreliable ones. Hence, the main contributions of this paper are two-fold: on the one hand, a new variant of the location routing problem is studied, where facility sizing decisions and hybrid fuzzy-stochastic demands are simultaneously considered. On the other hand, this paper proposes a competitive solution approach based on the hybridization of a metaheuristic algorithm with both simulation and fuzzy logic, i.e., a so-called fuzzy simheuristic, to solve the aforementioned problem. Indeed, simheuristics have been traditionally proposed to deal with stochastic issues in hard combinatorial optimization problems [24]. However, their hybridization with fuzzy logic has been rarely studied.

The remainder of this paper is organized as follows: Section 2 describes previous works on the topic. Section 3 presents a description of our addressed problem. Section 4 explains the fuzzy simheuristic approach used to solve the problem. Section 5 describes a series of computational experiments. Section 6 analyzes our obtained results. Finally, Section 7 draws some conclusions and future research perspectives.

2. Literature Review

This section presents a summary of the published manuscripts on the main topics addressed by this work. Thus, Section 2.1 outlines works related to the location routing problem in both its deterministic version and the variant including uncertain parameters. Additionally, Section 2.2 summarizes the main contributions on the field of simheuristics and fuzzy logic as methodologies to handle uncertain parameters in routing problems.

2.1. The Location Routing Problem

Perhaps the first work related to the location routing problem is the one by Maranzana [25], who analyze the influence of transportation costs on location decisions. Moreover, Salhi and Rand [1] quantify for the first time the benefits of considering routing decisions when locating facilities. They also state that solving each subproblem (location and routing) independently does not provide optimal solutions. Multiple variants of the LRP have been proposed over time. These variants depend on the characteristics of depots (capacitated or not), vehicles (capacitated or not, homogeneous or heterogeneous fleet), costs (symmetric or asymmetric) or the consideration of uncertain parameters. All capacitated variants addressed by these authors assume that depot sizes are fixed and cannot be changed.

Considering the limited computational power available at that time, the initial works on the LRP firstly solved the underlying location problem and used the obtained solution as a starting point to handle the corresponding routing problem. However, as the computational power has notably increased in recent years, the newest approaches deal with the LRP in an integrated manner [26,27]. Among the recently published works on the deterministic LRP, Escobar et al. [28] propose a granular tabu search within a VNS framework to speed up computational times without decreasing the solutions quality. A biased-randomization-based metaheuristic of two phases is developed by Quintero-Araujo et al. [27] to solve the capacitated version of the problem. Ferdi and Layeb [29] propose a GRASP with a novel technique used to create clusters around the open depots. Traditional applications of the LRP include horizontal cooperation [30], electric vehicle routing problems [31–33], city logistics [34], humanitarian logistics [35] or supply chain network design [36]. Moreover, most recent applications are related to environmental issues [37], cold supply chains [38] or waste management [39].

When dealing with uncertainty, most works have focused on the use of stochastic modeling. One of the utilized approaches has been the hybridization of simulation techniques with metaheuristics. For instance, Quintero-Araujo et al. [9] propose a simheuristic to solve an LRP with stochastic demands, by hybridizing Monte Carlo simulation with an iterated local search metaheuristic. A similar approach is employed by Tordecilla et al. [13], who address an LRP where the sizes of facilities to locate are also a variable to consider. Rabbani et al. [10] also propose a simheuristic approach that combines a nondominated sorting genetic algorithm-II (NSGA-II) and Monte Carlo simulation. They tackle a multiobjective multiperiod LRP in the context of the hazardous waste management industry. Both generated waste and number of people at risk are stochastic. Inventory decisions are also taken into account. Sun et al. [11] address a real-world case from an express delivery company in Shanghai. These authors tackle an LRP in which demand is stochastic and can be split for self-pickup. Then a simulation-based optimization model is proposed and two heuristics results are compared.

Other parameters are also considered to be uncertain. For instance, Herazo-Padilla et al. [14] hybridize an ant colony optimization metaheuristic with discrete-event simulation to solve an LRP in which transportation costs and vehicle travel speeds are considered stochastic. Authors demonstrate that their proposed approach is not only efficient but is able to find statistical interactions among the different parameters. Zhang et al. [15] present an approach that hybridizes a genetic algorithm with simulation to solve a sustainable multiobjective LRP in the context of emergency logistics. The authors consider the travel distance, the demand and the cost of opening a depot as uncertain variables. Additionally, the emergence of new technologies introduces new challenges. This is the case of Zhang et al. [12], who address the problem of locating battery swap stations and routing electric vehicles with stochastic demands. This problem is solved using a hybrid approach that combines a variable neighborhood search with a binary particle swarm optimization algorithm. The problem's complexity increases when considering the low autonomy of this type of vehicles, since route failures can frequently be present when demands are not known in an accurate manner.

Uncertainty in the LRP has been studied using either stochastic or fuzzy parameters. Table 1 shows an overview of works addressing this topic, which includes: (i) whether the uncertainty is addressed stochastically or in a fuzzy fashion; (ii) the considered uncertain parameter; (iii) the mathematical modeling approach; (iv) the approach used to solve the problem; and (v) the objective function. Analyzed works show a clear preference for considering an uncertain demand, as well as for using fuzzy chance constrained models.

Given both the considered uncertainty and the combinatorial nature of the LRP, most works employ a hybrid approach combining simulation with a metaheuristic algorithm. Finally, cost minimization is the prevalent objective, although a few works also consider the minimization of risk or the minimization of the additional travel distance due to route failures. Regarding works on fuzzy parameters, Zhang et al. [17] propose a hybrid particle swarm optimization (PSO) algorithm to solve a capacitated LRP with fuzzy triangular demands (CLRP-FD). The hybrid PSO algorithm is composed of three phases including a local search method and stochastic simulation. In addition, the authors propose a chance-constrained programming model for the CLRP-FD. Zarandi et al. [21] consider a multidepot LRP with fixed depot capacity and fuzzy travel times. Mehrjerdi and Nadizadeh [18] present a fuzzy chance constrained programming model where demands are modeled as fuzzy numbers. A four-phase method called "greedy clustering" is proposed, in which both an ant colony system metaheuristic and stochastic simulation are included. Fazayeli et al. [19] propose an LRP with time windows and fuzzy demands as the delivery part of a multimodal transport network. The mixed integer mathematical fuzzy model is coded and solved using GAMS and compared to the results provided by a genetic algorithm. Nadizadeh and Kafash [20] analyze a LRP with simultaneous pick-up and delivery in the context of reverse logistics. Both types of demands (pick-up and deliveries) are fuzzy variables. A fuzzy chance constrained programming model is proposed to represent the problem, and a greedy clustering method is used to solve it.

Table 1. Recent works related to the location routing problem with uncertain parameters.

Reference	Type of Uncertainty	Uncertain Parameter	Mathematical Approach	Solving Approach	Objective Criterion
Quintero-Araujo et al. [9]	Stochastic	Demand	Mixed-integer linear programming	Simheuristic Iterated local search Monte Carlo simulation	Minimize cost
Rabbani et al. [10]	Stochastic	Demand Number of people at risk	Mixed-integer non-linear programming	Simheuristic NSGA-II Monte Carlo Simulation	Minimize cost Minimize environmental risk
Sun et al. [11]	Stochastic	Demand	Mixed-integer linear programming	Biogeography-based optimization Adaptive large neighborhood search	Minimize cost
Zhang et al. [12]	Stochastic	Demand	—	Variable neighborhood search Particle swarm optimization	Minimize cost
Tordecilla et al. [13]	Stochastic	Demand	—	Simheuristic Iterated local search Monte Carlo simulation	Minimize cost
Herazo-Padilla et al. [14]	Stochastic	Transportation cost Travel speed	Mixed-integer linear programming	Ant colony optimization Discrete-event simulation	Minimize cost
Zhang et al. [15]	Stochastic	Demand Travel distance Depot opening cost	Mixed-integer non-linear programming	Genetic algorithm Uncertain simulation	Minimize travel time Minimize emergency relief cost Minimize CO_2 emissions
Zhang et al. [17]	Fuzzy	Demand	A fuzzy chance constrained model	Particle swarm optimization Variable neighborhood search Stochastic simulation	Minimize cost Minimize additional travel distance due to route failures
Mehrjerdi and Nadizadeh [18]	Fuzzy	Demand	A fuzzy chance constrained model	A greedy clustering method Ant colony system Stochastic simulation	Minimize cost
Fazayeli et al. [19]	Fuzzy	Demand	Mixed-integer non-linear programming	Exact approach Genetic algorithm	Minimize cost
Nadizadeh and Kafash [20]	Fuzzy	Demand	A fuzzy chance constrained model	A greedy clustering method Ant colony system Stochastic simulation	Minimize cost
Zarandi et al. [21]	Fuzzy	Travel time	A fuzzy chance constrained model	Simulated annealing Fuzzy simulation	Minimize cost
Zarandi et al. [22]	Fuzzy	Demand Travel time	A fuzzy chance constrained model	Simulated annealing Fuzzy simulation	Minimize cost Minimize additional travel distance due to route failures

Table 1. *Cont.*

Reference	Type of Uncertainty	Uncertain Parameter	Mathematical Approach	Solving Approach	Objective Criterion
Ghezavati and Morakabatchian [23]	Fuzzy	Time windows	Mixed-integer linear programming	Exact approach	Minimize cost Minimize risks
Ghaffari-Nasab et al. [40]	Fuzzy	Demand	A fuzzy chance constrained model	Simulated annealing Stochastic simulation	Minimize cost Minimize additional travel distance due to route failures
Nadizadeh and Nasab [41]	Fuzzy	Demand	A fuzzy chance constrained model	A hybrid heuristic algorithm Ant colony system Stochastic simulation	Minimize cost Minimize additional travel distance due to route failures
Wei et al. [42]	Fuzzy	Transportation cost Number of people that may be at risk	A fuzzy chance constrained model	Genetic algorithm Fuzzy simulation	Minimize cost Minimize risks

The analyzed works show that uncertainty in the LRP has been addressed either by using stochastic or fuzzy demands but never considering both types of uncertainty at the same time—e.g., that some customers' demands are modeled as stochastic variables while others are modeled as fuzzy values. In addition, to the best of our knowledge, there are no previous studies on the LRP with facility sizing decisions and hybrid fuzzy-stochastic demands. Only Tordecilla et al. [13] have studied a similar LRP variant, although considering all customers' demands as stochastic. Thus, our work aims to fulfill the existing gap by considering a flexible-size LRP and two different types of uncertain parameters: stochastic and fuzzy demands.

2.2. Simheuristics and Fuzzy Logic for Vehicle Routing Problems under Uncertainty

When dealing with combinatorial optimization problems subject to uncertain parameters, one of the most recommended approaches is the combination of simulation (to handle stochasticity) with heuristic-based methods (to deal with the optimization part of the problem) [43,44]. In that sense, a simheuristic approach is a relatively new and efficient technique to tackle combinatorial optimization problems under uncertainty [24,45]. In general, a simheuristic algorithm works as follows: (i) given a stochastic problem, the random variables are transformed into their deterministic counterpart by using expected values; (ii) an approximated framework (heuristic or metaheuristic) is used to generate high-quality solutions for the transformed deterministic instance that can also be "promising" solutions for the stochastic version of the problem; (iii) these promising solutions are sent to a simulation engine in order to estimate its quality in a stochastic environment. The simulation engine, in addition, provides feedback to better guide the search used by the approximated procedure; and (iv) an improved estimation of the quality of the solutions is obtained for a subset of "elite" solutions using a longer simulation process. Different simheuristic algorithms have been presented in the literature to solve routing problems.

Stochastic demands in vehicle routing problems are addressed by Quintero-Araujo et al. [46] and Gruler et al. [47]. Moreover, stochastic demands are also studied in arc routing problems [48]. Stochastic versions of the inventory routing problem can be found in Gruler et al. [49]. Real applications like the waste collection problem with stochastic demands are analyzed in Gruler et al. [50]. Intermodal routing problems have also considered other stochastic parameters, such as capacity [51] or travel times [52,53]. Additionally, the need of using fuzzy logic in vehicle routing problems arises when there are some vague or uncertain parameters. The literature presents various works in which fuzzy logic is added, for instance, to model uncertain demands [54–57], travel times [58,59], capacity [57,59], and service times [60]. Additional aspects are also considered by these works, such as time windows [57,61,62], environmental aspects [59], multiple objectives [59], intermodal transportation [57,59] and an open VRP [63]. Additional applications of metaheuristics combined either with Monte Carlo simulation or fuzzy logic can be found in several fields, such as scheduling [64,65], controller optimization [66,67] parameter estimation [68], finance [69], facility location [70], etc.

3. Problem Description

The location routing problem is a well-known problem in which three main decisions must be made: (i) locating one or more facilities; (ii) allocating customers to open facilities without exceeding their capacity; and (iii) designing a number of routes whose aggregated customers' demand does not exceed a vehicle capacity. Each route must start and finish at the same facility. Furthermore, we consider a location routing problem with facility sizing decisions, where the size of each open facility is also a variable to decide on. Furthermore, we also consider both stochastic and fuzzy demands. Hence, a percentage of the vehicles' capacity is reserved as a safety stock (*SS*), in case the demand is higher than expected. Therefore, the main decision variables in this problem are related to the number of facilities to open, the facilities' size and location, which customers must be allocated to each open facility, how many vehicles must be used and how to design the associated routes. This problem is *NP-hard* since it contains, as special cases, the capacitated vehicle routing problem, the multidepot VRP and the facility location problem, all of them known to be computationally hard. Figure 1 provides an example of a complete LRP solution. Facilities are represented by diamonds and customers by circles. Black (solid) diamonds are the open facilities, while noncolored diamonds correspond to nonopen facilities. For each open depot, a set of routes starting and finishing at the corresponding depot location is designed to serve all customers' demands. Each route is assigned a single vehicle.

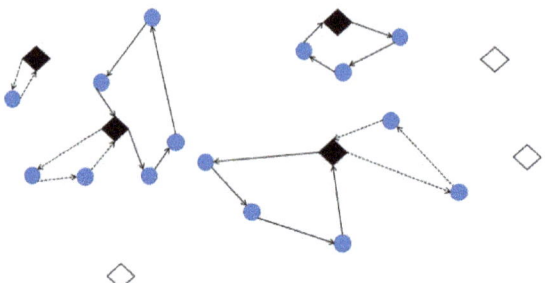

Figure 1. Graphical representation of a location routing problem (LRP) solution.

Formally speaking, the LRP can be defined on a complete, weighted, and undirected graph $G(V, E, C)$, in which $V = J \cup I$ is the set of nodes (comprising the subset J of potential facility locations and subset I of customers), E is the set of edges, and C is the cost matrix of traversing each edge. Delivery routes are performed by a set K of unlimited homogeneous vehicles with limited capacity. This problem also assumes that all vehicles are shared by all facilities (i.e., no depot has a specific fleet) and each edge $e \in E$ satisfies the triangle inequality. The customers' demands are uncertain and are modeled using stochastic values for a subset of customers I_1, and fuzzy values for a subset of customers I_2, such that $I_1 \cup I_2 = I$. The variant of the LRP considered in this paper is the one in which a decision must be made about the size of the facilities to open. Hence, a set L of alternative sizes for each facility and associated fixed and variable opening costs are provided as inputs. Depots might have equal or different capacities. Each customer node must be served by exactly one vehicle that starts and finishes its route in the facility to which it has been allocated (i.e., split deliveries are not allowed). The following notation is used to describe our problem:

Parameters

s_l = Available size of type $l \in L$
D_i = Uncertain demand of customer $i \in I$
f_j = Fixed opening cost of depot $j \in J$
o_{jl} = Variable opening cost of depot $j \in J$ with size of type $l \in L$
c_e = Cost of traversing arc $e \in E$

q = Capacity of each vehicle

%SS = Safety stock percentage

Decision variables

y_{jl} = Binary variable that indicates whether the depot $j \in J$ is open with size $l \in L$ or not.

x_{ij} = Binary variable that indicates whether customer $i \in I$ is assigned to the depot $j \in J$ or not

w_{ek} = Binary variable that indicates whether arc $e \in E$ is used in the route performed by vehicle $k \in K$ or not

The objective is to minimize the total cost (TC), which includes opening facilities costs (OC), routing costs (RC), and failure costs (FC), i.e., $TC = OC + RC + FC$. These parts are defined in Equations (1)–(3).

$$OC = \sum_{j \in J} \sum_{l \in L} (f_j + o_{jl}) y_{jl} \tag{1}$$

$$RC = \sum_{e \in E} \sum_{k \in K} c_e w_{ek} \tag{2}$$

$$FC = \min\{c_{reac}, c_{prev}\} \tag{3}$$

FC represents the cost incurred whenever the actual demand of a route is greater than the vehicle capacity, where c_{reac} and c_{prev} depend on the corrective action considered, namely:

1. A reactive strategy with a cost c_{reac}, in which a vehicle must perform a round-trip to its assigned facility for a replenishment if the actual current-customer demand is higher than the vehicle's current load.
2. A preventive strategy with a cost c_{prev}, in which a vehicle must perform a detour to the facility before visiting the next customer. The decision about performing this detour depends on the type of demand of the next customer. If the demand is stochastic, the detour is carried out whenever the expected demand of the next customer is higher than the current capacity of the vehicle. Alternatively, if the demand is fuzzy, this decision depends on the comparison between the fuzzy values of both the demand of the next customer and the current capacity.

Let $\varnothing \neq S \subset V$ be a subset of nodes, $\delta^+(S)$ the set of edges leaving S, $\delta^-(S)$ the set of edges entering S, and $A(S)$ the set of edges with both ends in S. Hence, the location routing problem with facility sizing decisions and uncertain demands can be modeled as the following integer program:

$$Minimize \ \ TC \tag{4}$$

subject to:

$$\sum_{k \in K} \sum_{e \in \delta^-(i)} w_{ek} = 1 \quad \forall i \in I \tag{5}$$

$$\sum_{i \in I} \sum_{e \in \delta^-(i)} D_i w_{ek} \leq (1 - \%SS) q \quad \forall k \in K \tag{6}$$

$$\sum_{e \in \delta^+(n)} w_{ek} = \sum_{e \in \delta^-(n)} w_{ek}, \quad \forall k \in K, \forall n \in V \tag{7}$$

$$\sum_{e \in \delta^+(J)} w_{ek} \leq 1 \quad \forall k \in K \tag{8}$$

$$\sum_{e \in A(S)} w_{ek} \leq |S| - 1 \quad \forall S \subseteq I, \forall k \in K \tag{9}$$

$$\sum_{e\in\delta^+(j)} w_{ek} + \sum_{e\in\delta^-(i)} w_{ek} \leq 1 + x_{ij} \quad \forall i \in I, \forall j \in J, \forall k \in K \tag{10}$$

$$\sum_{j\in J} x_{ij} = 1 \quad \forall i \in I \tag{11}$$

$$\sum_{i\in I} D_i x_{ij} \leq \sum_{l\in L} s_l y_{jl} \quad \forall j \in J \tag{12}$$

$$\sum_{l\in L} y_{jl} \leq 1 \quad \forall j \in J \tag{13}$$

$$\forall y_{jl}, x_{ij}, w_{ek} \in \{0,1\} \tag{14}$$

The objective function (4) minimizes the total cost. Constraint (5) ensures that each customer is served by a single route and a single vehicle. Constraint (6) guarantees that the total demand served by a vehicle in a route does not exceed its capacity. This limit is reduced by a safety stock, which is a percentage of the vehicle capacity reserved to respond more effectively to the uncertain demand. Constraint (7) guarantees the continuity of each route. Constraint (8) ensures the return of each vehicle to its starting depot. Constraint (9) guarantees the subtour elimination. Constraint (10) ensures that a customer is served by a route departing from an open depot only if this customer is allocated to this depot. Constraint (11) guarantees that a customer is assigned to only one depot. Constraint (12) ensures that the total demand served from a depot does not exceed its assigned size. Constraint (13) guarantees that only one size is assigned to an open depot. Finally, Constraint (14) determines that all decision variables are binary.

4. Solution Approach

Since the problem described in Section 3 is known for being *NP-hard*, the formulated mathematical model is not employed to find an optimal solution but just to provide a better understanding of the problem details Hence, we propose a fuzzy simheuristic approach [24] for minimizing the expected total cost. Traditionally, simheuristics have been used to solve optimization problems with stochastic components, such as arc routing problems with stochastic demands [48], stochastic waste collection problems [50] or team orienteering problems with stochastic travel times [71]. We have extended the simheuristic framework by including fuzzy components in order to deal with combinatorial optimization problems with uncertainty components of both stochastic and nonstochastic nature. In particular, our methodology combines an iterated local search (ILS) metaheuristic with Monte Carlo simulation and fuzzy inference systems (FIS) to deal with stochastic and fuzzy variables, respectively. As discussed in Ferone et al. [72], several metaheuristic frameworks offer a well-balanced combination of efficiency and relative simplicity and can be easily extended to a fuzzy simheuristic. In general, our approach is composed of three stages. During the first stage, a set of promising LRP solutions are generated using a constructive heuristic, which employs biased-randomization techniques [73]. In the second stage, the ILS metaheuristic tries to improve each of these promising solutions by iteratively exploring the search space and conducting a short number of simulations. Finally, in the third stage, a refinement procedure using a larger number of simulation runs is applied to these elite solutions, which allows one to obtain a more accurate estimation of the expected total cost.

Algorithm 1 outlines the main components of Stage 1. It generates quickly a ranked list of "promising" LRP solutions. The main input parameters of this heuristic are: the list of customers with both their demand and location in Cartesian coordinates, the list of facilities including their opening costs and the vehicle capacity. The algorithm procedure is as follows: initially, the minimum and maximum ($nbDepots_0$ and $maxNbDepots$, respectively) numbers of facilities required to serve the total demand are computed. Both bounds are calculated by dividing the total demand by the maximum available facility size, and the minimum available facility size, respectively, and they are rounded up to the next integer number. Then we run our algorithm for each number of facilities between $nbDepots_0$ and $maxNbDepots$ (line 3). Later, for each iteration of the line 4 loop, a new set of random locations are generated (line 5). This is stored in $usedOpenDepots$ to avoid repeating. Next, if the available capacity of facilities in $openDepots$ is enough to satisfy customers demand, customers' allocation and routing procedures are carried out; otherwise, $openDepots$ is rejected. The customers' allocation procedure is performed by producing a new map (line 9) where each facility has a list of all customers sorted by savings. These savings represent the benefit of allocating each customer to the current depot instead to the best alternative facility. Then a facility in $openDepots$ is selected randomly, and a biased-randomized procedure is used to allocate a customer of the list to the current depot. This procedure ends when all customers have been allocated. In the step in line 10 a VRP is solved for each subset facility-customers in the map. Finally, a feasible LRP solution is yielded and stored in the pool of solutions $poolSol$. The algorithm ends returning a top list of complete LRP solutions, assessed in terms of opening and routing costs.

Algorithm 1 Constructive heuristic ($cust, depots, vehCap, \beta, iter_{max}$)

1: $usedOpenDepots \leftarrow \varnothing$

2: $\langle nbDepots_0, maxNbDepots \rangle \leftarrow computeDepotsBound(depots)$

3: **for** $nbDepots \leftarrow nbDepots_0$ to $maxNbDepots$ **do**

4:     **for** $iter \leftarrow 1$ to $iter_{max}$ **do**

5:         $openDepots \leftarrow depotsToOpen(nbDepots)$

6:         **if** $openDepots \notin usedOpenDepots$ **then**

7:             **if** $capacity(openDepots) \geq demand(cust)$ **then**

8:                 $usedOpenDepots \leftarrow add(usedOpenDepots, openDepots)$

9:                 $map \leftarrow allocateCustomers(openDepots, cust)$

10:                 $lrpSol \leftarrow CWS(map, \beta, vehCap)$

11:                 $poolSol \leftarrow add(poolSol, lrpSol)$

12:             **end if**

13:         **end if**

14:     **end for**

15: **end for**

16: **return** $sortingByCost(poolSol)$

Algorithm 2 outlines Stages 2 and 3. During the second stage, each "promising" map generated by the constructive heuristic is processed by the simulation and the fuzzy components to estimate its safety stock (line 4). This procedure is carried out by performing a low number of runs, where a new value is assigned to each random or fuzzy element based on its probability distribution or fuzzy function, respectively. We use Monte Carlo simulation in order to estimate the stochastic variables, whilst a fuzzy inference system is used to estimate the fuzzy variables. Then, the objective function and the constraints are evaluated under the random/fuzzy generated values to compute the expected cost of each promising map. Next, the ILS metaheuristic tries to improve the set of "promising" maps by iteratively exploring the search space and conducting a second process of fuzzy/simulation runs. We start the process by perturbing the current base solution $baseSol$ (line 8). In this phase we use two different strategies. In the first one, the algorithm randomly selects a set of customers and tries to reassign them in a random way to another facility without violating its capacity. Regarding the second strategy, the algorithm randomly exchanges the allocation of a percentage of customers among facilities. This process is dependent on the value of k, which represents the degree of exchange to be applied. This value is updated in each iteration between K_{min} and K_{max}, i.e., it is reset to K_{min} whenever a new solution *newSol* outperforms the *baseSol*, and it is increased whenever the algorithm fails to improve the current solution until a maximum value K_{max}. The strategy to be used in each iteration of the algorithm is randomly selected.

Algorithm 2 ILS-based Fuzzy Simheuristic $(inputs, \alpha, \beta, \lambda, Inc, T_0, K_{min}, K_{max}, I_0, t_{max})$

1: $initSol \leftarrow$ genInitSol(inputs,α, β)

2: $baseSol \leftarrow initSol$

3: $bestSol \leftarrow baseSol$

4: **fastSimulation**(baseSol) *% Fuzzy and Monte Carlo Simulation*

5: $T \leftarrow T_0$

6: **while** (time $\leq t_{max}$) **do** *% ILS stage*

7:     $k \leftarrow K_{min}$

8:     perturbationSol $\leftarrow$ perturbation(baseSol, k, α, β)

9:     newSol $\leftarrow$ localSearch(perturbationSol)

10:     **if** (detCost(newSol) < detCost(baseSol)) **then**

11:         **fastSimulation**(newSol) *% Fuzzy and Monte Carlo simulation*

12:         **if** (expCost(newSol) < expCost(baseSol)) **then**

13:             baseSol $\leftarrow$ newSol

14:             **if** (expCost(newSol) < expCost(bestSol)) **then**

15:                 bestSol $\leftarrow$ newSol

16:                 insert(poolBestSol,bestSol)

17:             **end if**

18:             $k \leftarrow K_{min}$

19:         **end if**

20:     **else** *% SA-based acceptance criterion*

21:         temperature $\leftarrow$ updateTemperature(detCost(newSol), detCost(baseSol), T)

22:         **if** ($\mathcal{U}(0,1) \leq$ temperature) **then**

23:             baseSol $\leftarrow$ newSol

24:             $k \leftarrow K_{min}$

25:         **else**

26:             $k \leftarrow$ min(k * Inc,K_{max})

27:         **end if**

28:     **end if**

29:     $T \leftarrow \lambda T$

30: **end while**

31: **for** (sol $\in$ poolBestSol) **do** *% Refinement stage - Fuzzy and Monte Carlo simulation*

32:     **longSimulation**(sol)

33:     **if** (expCost(sol) < expCost(bestSol)) **then**

34:         bestSol $\leftarrow$ sol

35:     **end if**

36: **end for**

37: **return** bestSol

Afterwards, the algorithm starts a local search around the perturbed solution in order to improve it (line 9). This stage consists in a *two-opt inter-route* operator, which interchanges two chains of randomly selected customers between different facilities. A *newSol* is returned whenever no more improvements are achieved. Later, whenever the deterministic cost of the *baseSol* is improved (line 10), the *newSol* is processed by the simulation and the fuzzy components to deal with the uncertainty of the proposed problem, using a low number of runs to compute the expected cost of the solution (line 11). Notice that this procedure does not only provide estimated values to the expected cost associated with the solutions generated by our approach, but it also reports feedback to the metaheuristic search process. If the *newSol* is also able to improve the expected cost of the *baseSol* (line 12), the latter is updated. In the same way, if the expected cost of the *newSol* improves the cost of the best solution (*bestSol*) found so far (line 14), the latter is updated and added to the pool of elite solutions (line 16). This pool contains the best stochastic/fuzzy solutions found so far. The number of solutions in this pool is a known parameter that depends on the available computational time. Moreover, by limiting the size of this pool we ensure that we only keep track of the top solutions as the algorithm evolves. In order to further diversify the search, the algorithm might occasionally accept nonimproving solutions following an acceptance criterion (lines 20–28). Specifically, we have used a simulated-annealing acceptance criterion, which contains a decaying probability that is regulated by a dynamic temperature parameter (T).

Finally, a refinement procedure using a larger number of simulation runs is executed in the third stage for each elite solution (lines 31–36). Hence, a more accurate summary of output variables can be obtained. As before, both probability distributions and fuzzy functions are employed in this simulation, depending on whether the element has a stochastic or fuzzy nature. Finally, the "best" solution (or pull of best alternative solutions) is returned, considering that the decision maker might be not only interested in the average value associated with a solution but also in its variability level. Particularly, the main output variables in our experiments are: the opening and routing costs, the cost incurred whenever a route fails and the safety stock.

5. Computational Experiments

Multiple sets of instances are found in the literature to test the algorithms designed to solve the LRP [74–76]. Nevertheless, these sets do not consider characteristics such as parameters uncertainty and flexible facility sizes, i.e., instances must be adapted to our problem's features. Therefore, we use Akca's [74] instances and introduce the following modifications:

1. Traditional LRP instances consider that a single fixed size is available to assign to open depots. We extend this unit set to five alternative sizes, so that our algorithm selects one of them for each open depot. If s_j is the size proposed by the original instance for each potential depot $j \in J$, and L is the set of available sizes, our approach' alternative sizes are $s_{jl} \in \{(1-2r)s_j, (1-r)s_j, s_j, (1+r)s_j, (1+2r)s_j\}$, where $l \in L$, $0.0 < r < 0.5$, and r is the range of difference between available sizes. When $r = 0$, the case is the same as the traditional LRP. We consider that $r = 0.25$.

2. Traditional LRP instances consider a fixed cost (f_j) incurred whenever a depot $j \in J$ is open. We keep this parameter unaltered. Additionally, we introduce a variable cost (o_{jl}) depending on f_j and s_{jl}, namely: $o_{jl} = \dfrac{(s_{jl} - s_j)}{2s_j} \dfrac{\sum_j f_j}{|J|}$. This formula preserves o_{jl} in the same order as f_j for each depot $j \in J$. Besides, it yields negative costs whenever $s_{jl} < s_j$, positive costs whenever $s_{jl} > s_j$, and a null cost when $s_{jl} = s_j$. Thus our results can be compared with those found in the LRP literature.

3. An uncertain demand D_i for each customer $i \in I$ is considered. The demand of half of the customers is assumed to follow a log-normal probability distribution. If ϕ_i is the deterministic demand in the Akca's set, then $E[D_i] = \phi_i$. In addition, three different values of variance are considered: low, medium and high, i.e., for $\lambda \in \{0.05, 0.10, 0.20\}$,

$Var[D_i] = \lambda \phi_i$. These variability values are preserved identical to the ones used by Tordecilla et al. [13], in order to perform a suitable results comparison. The demand of the other half of the customers is considered to be fuzzy. In this case, D_i can be estimated as low (DL), medium (DM) or high (DH). The demand in each of these fuzzy sets is represented by a triangular fuzzy number $D_i = (d_{1i}, d_{2i}, d_{3i})$. If q is the vehicle total load capacity, all fuzzy demand values are expressed as a proportion of q in order to perform an appropriate comparison between the demand and the vehicle available capacity, i.e., $0 \leq D_i \leq 1$. The membership function of these fuzzy sets are displayed in Figure 2.

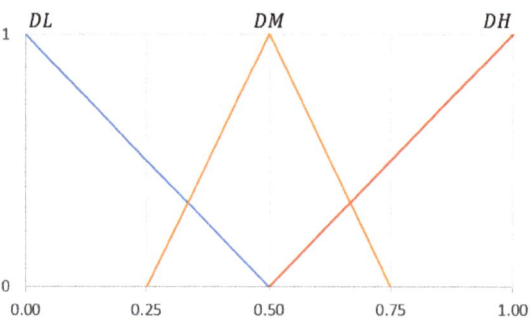

Figure 2. Fuzzy sets for the demand of the customer i.

A Fuzzy Approach for the Demand and the Vehicle Available Capacity

When considering customers with stochastic demands, the decision about visiting the next customer in a route is made simply by comparing its expected demand with the vehicle's current capacity. If this demand is greater, the vehicle will perform a detour to the depot for a replenishment. Nevertheless, when the next customer demand is fuzzy, the decision about serving it is made employing a preference index p_i [77]. It indicates the strength of our inclination to visit the next node in a route. This index depends on both the estimated demand of the next node D_{i+1} and the vehicle capacity C_i that remains available after serving the customer $i \in I$. C_i is expressed as a proportion of q, i.e., $0 \leq C_i \leq 1$. It also can be treated as low (CL), medium (CM) or high (CH), and it is represented by a triangular fuzzy number $C_i = (c_{1i}, c_{2i}, c_{3i})$. The membership function of the capacity fuzzy sets are displayed in Figure 3.

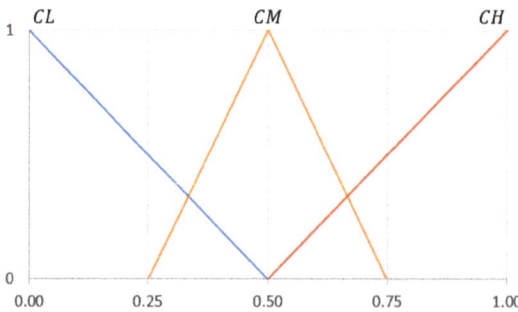

Figure 3. Fuzzy sets for the vehicle available capacity after visiting the customer i.

The preference index is defined between 0 and 1, i.e., $0 \leq p_i \leq 1$. When $p_i = 1$, we will definitely visit the next node in a route since the vehicle available capacity can for sure meet its demand. When $p_i = 0$, we are sure that D_{i+1} exceeds C_i and the vehicle must return to the depot for a replenishment. We consider that the preference can be very low (PVL), low (PL), medium (PM), high (PH) or very high (PVH). Each of these categories is represented by a fuzzy set, whose membership function is depicted in Figure 4. Additionally, we define a set of reasoning rules (Table 2) to determine the preference to visit the next node depending on the levels of both the demand and the vehicle available capacity.

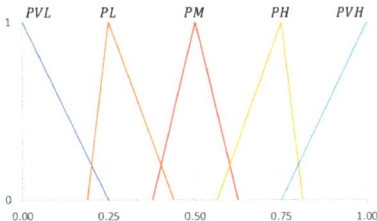

Figure 4. Fuzzy sets for the preference strength to visit the customer i.

Table 2. Reasoning rules determining the visit preference strength.

Demand	Available Capacity		
	CL	**CM**	**CH**
DL	PM	PH	PVH
DM	PL	PM	PH
DH	PVL	PL	PM

Figure 5 displays the procedure used to compute the preference index p_i after serving the customer $i \in I$. This procedure is described as follows:

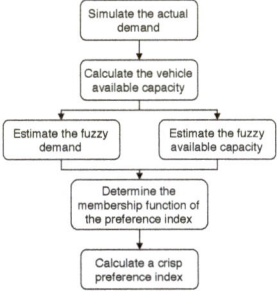

Figure 5. Procedure used to compute the preference index p_i.

1. Simulate the actual demand of each customer employing a fuzzy simulation approach. Based on the works by Teodorović and Pavković [77], Sun et al. [59] and Sun [78], we follow the steps described below:

    (a) Generate a random demand d_i between a lower bound and an upper bound. Since the objective is preserving the variability conditions similar to the stochastic demands, the lower and upper bounds are given by the expressions $\frac{\phi_i - \sqrt{3\lambda\phi_i}}{q}$ and $\frac{\phi_i + \sqrt{3\lambda\phi_i}}{q}$, respectively.

    (b) Calculate the membership degree $\mu(d_i)$ of this demand. Notice that $\mu(d_i) \in [0,1]$.
    (c) Generate a random number $\rho \in [0,1]$.
    (d) Compare ρ and $\mu(d_i)$. If $\rho \leq \mu(d_i)$, then assume the actual demand of the customer i as d_i; otherwise, repeat steps (a)–(d) until this condition is fulfilled.

2. Calculate the vehicle available capacity subtracting from q the sum of the simulated demand of the first m customers visited in the current route, including the customer i. Whenever the route fails and the vehicle must perform a trip to the depot for a replenishment, the counting of m starts again from 1.

3. Estimate the fuzzy demand and the fuzzy available capacity according to the categories previously defined: low, medium or high.

4. Determine the membership function of the preference index using the reasoning rules defined in Table 2.

5. Calculate a crisp preference index using the center of gravity as defuzzification method. Additional methods can be found in Klir and Yuan [79], and Opricovic and Tzeng [80].

We define a known threshold p^*, such that $0 \leq p^* \leq 1$. The computed preference index p_i must be compared with p^* in order to make a decision about the vehicle next destination. If $p_i \geq p^*$, the vehicle should visit the next customer directly; otherwise, we estimate that the vehicle available capacity cannot meet the next customer demand. In this case, both preventive (c_{prev}) and reactive (c_{reac}) costs are calculated (see Section 3). If $c_{prev} < c_{reac}$, the vehicle should perform a detour to the depot for a preventive replenishment; otherwise, it should visit the next customer directly and react to its real demand. The lower the threshold level, the greater the inclination to unload the vehicle as much as possible before making a replenishment trip to the depot. In this case, less preventive detours are performed. Hence, the number of times that a reactive round-trip must be carried out increases. Previous tests using modified Akca's instances yielded lower costs when $p^* = 0.45$.

The following parameters are used by our algorithm to run the experiments: (i) 350 iterations for map perturbations; (ii) 150 iterations for the biased-randomized savings heuristic; (iii) 150 iterations for splitting; (iv) a random value between 0.05 and 0.80 for β_1, the parameter of the geometric distribution associated with the biased-randomized selection during the allocation map process; (v) a random value between 0.07 and 0.23 for β_2, the parameter of the geometric distribution associated with the biased-randomized heuristic for routing; (vi) $n = 100$ runs for the initial simulation stage; (vii) $N = 5000$ runs for the intensive simulation stage; and (viii) 100 iterations to estimate the safety stock (SS), testing only discrete values between 0% and 10%. Our proposed algorithm was coded as a Java application. All experiments were executed on a standard Windows PC with a Core $i5$ processor and 6 GB RAM. A total of ten different random seeds were used for each instance.

6. Results and Discussion

Table 3 shows our obtained results for 12 Akca's instances. Five main indicators are computed: depots opening costs (OC), which is formed by both fixed and variable costs; routing costs (RC); failure costs (FC), which is incurred whenever the vehicle must perform either a detour or a round-trip to the depot; total costs (TC); and the estimated safety stock (SS) level. Four types of solutions are compared. All of them are flexible, i.e., they consider facility sizing decisions. Firstly, our best deterministic solutions are shown, i.e, there is no uncertainty in the customers' demand and its realization is exactly as expected. In this case, a safety stock is not necessary and there are no failure costs. Secondly, we show the best stochastic solutions reported by Tordecilla et al. [13], in which the exact customers' demand is not known. Instead, all of them follow a log-normal distribution with known mean and standard deviation. Thirdly, our best hybrid fuzzy-stochastic solutions are displayed, in which half of the customers' demand follows a log-normal distribution, and half of the customers' demand is considered to be fuzzy. Finally, our best fuzzy solutions are shown, in which all customers' demand is considered to be fuzzy, due to a high level of uncertainty. Additionally, results for three levels of variability (λ) are shown. Clearly, our best deterministic solutions are the same regardless of the variability level, given the total absence of uncertainty.

Table 3. Comparative results between our flexible solutions under different uncertainty levels.

Instance	Best Deterministic Solution			Best Stochastic Solution [13]					Best Hybrid Solution					Best Fuzzy Solution				
	OC	RC	TC	OC	RC	FC	TC	SS	OC	RC	FC	TC	SS	OC	RC	FC	TC	SS
Low variability																		
Cr30x5a-1	200.00	575.14	775.14	200.00	575.14	2.37	777.51	0%	200.00	575.14	3.31	778.45	2%	200.00	575.14	5.86	781.00	2%
Cr30x5a-2	200.00	607.28	807.28	200.00	607.28	0.04	807.32	3%	200.00	607.28	0.12	807.40	3%	200.00	607.28	0.12	807.40	3%
Cr30x5a-3	187.50	507.92	695.42	187.50	509.25	10.99	707.74	3%	187.50	509.25	17.48	714.22	3%	187.50	509.25	25.50	722.25	3%
Cr30x5b-1	225.00	623.22	848.22	225.00	623.22	9.37	857.59	0%	225.00	623.22	14.59	862.81	0%	225.00	623.22	22.85	871.07	1%
Cr30x5b-2	187.50	625.32	812.82	187.50	625.32	0.00	812.82	2%	187.50	625.32	0.00	812.82	2%	187.50	625.32	0.00	812.82	2%
Cr30x5b-3	187.50	684.58	872.08	187.50	684.58	2.25	874.33	1%	187.50	684.58	6.35	878.43	1%	187.50	684.58	9.50	881.58	1%
Cr40x5a-1	162.50	731.84	894.34	162.50	731.84	0.03	894.37	1%	162.50	731.84	0.07	894.41	1%	162.50	731.84	0.59	894.93	1%
Cr40x5a-2	225.00	637.26	862.26	225.00	639.02	0.10	864.12	0%	225.00	639.02	0.81	864.83	1%	225.00	642.02	0.03	867.05	3%
Cr40x5a-3	162.50	752.88	915.38	162.50	752.88	0.97	916.35	0%	162.50	752.88	3.26	918.64	0%	162.50	752.88	6.82	922.21	1%
Cr40x5b-1	162.50	852.04	1014.54	162.50	852.04	6.90	1021.45	1%	162.50	852.04	12.24	1026.78	1%	162.50	852.04	20.79	1035.33	1%
Cr40x5b-2	225.00	690.57	915.57	225.00	690.57	0.08	915.65	1%	225.00	690.57	0.62	916.18	1%	225.00	690.57	1.23	916.79	1%
Cr40x5b-3	175.00	764.33	939.33	175.00	772.87	0.07	947.93	2%	175.00	772.87	0.29	948.16	2%	175.00	772.87	0.35	948.22	2%
Average	191.67	671.03	862.70	191.67	672.00	2.76	866.43	1.17%	191.67	672.00	4.93	868.59	1.42%	191.67	672.25	7.80	871.72	1.75%
Medium variability																		
Cr30x5a-1	200.00	575.14	775.14	200.00	575.14	7.63	782.77	2%	200.00	575.14	9.67	784.81	2%	200.00	575.14	12.91	788.05	2%
Cr30x5a-2	200.00	607.28	807.28	200.00	607.28	0.46	807.74	3%	200.00	607.28	1.94	809.22	3%	200.00	607.28	1.43	808.71	3%
Cr30x5a-3	187.50	507.92	695.42	187.50	509.25	18.50	715.25	3%	187.50	509.25	24.10	720.85	3%	187.50	509.25	29.73	726.48	3%
Cr30x5b-1	225.00	623.22	848.22	225.00	623.22	14.63	862.85	0%	225.00	623.22	18.32	866.53	3%	225.00	623.22	24.23	872.45	3%
Cr30x5b-2	187.50	625.32	812.82	187.50	625.32	0.00	812.82	2%	187.50	625.32	0.00	812.82	2%	187.50	625.32	0.00	812.82	2%
Cr30x5b-3	187.50	684.58	872.08	187.50	684.58	10.21	882.28	0%	187.50	684.58	12.79	884.87	1%	187.50	684.58	12.88	884.96	1%
Cr40x5a-1	162.50	731.84	894.34	162.50	739.24	0.01	901.75	3%	162.50	739.24	0.01	901.75	3%	162.50	739.24	0.00	901.74	3%
Cr40x5a-2	225.00	637.26	862.26	225.00	643.52	3.07	871.59	1%	225.00	642.02	0.24	867.26	3%	225.00	642.02	0.57	867.59	3%
Cr40x5a-3	162.50	752.88	915.38	162.50	752.88	4.46	919.85	1%	162.50	752.88	8.57	923.95	1%	162.50	752.88	11.83	927.22	1%
Cr40x5b-1	162.50	852.04	1014.54	162.50	858.58	4.54	1025.62	2%	162.50	858.58	8.01	1029.09	2%	237.50	795.18	0.00	1032.68	4%
Cr40x5b-2	225.00	690.57	915.57	225.00	690.57	2.06	917.63	1%	225.00	690.57	3.77	919.33	0%	225.00	690.57	5.80	921.37	1%
Cr40x5b-3	175.00	764.33	939.33	175.00	772.87	1.42	949.29	2%	175.00	772.87	2.53	950.40	2%	175.00	772.87	2.96	950.82	2%
Average	191.67	671.03	862.70	191.67	673.54	5.58	870.79	1.67%	191.67	673.41	7.50	872.57	2.08%	197.92	668.13	8.53	874.57	2.33%

Table 3. *Cont.*

Instance	Best Deterministic Solution			Best Stochastic Solution [13]					Best Hybrid Solution					Best Fuzzy Solution				
	OC	RC	TC	OC	RC	FC	TC	SS	OC	RC	FC	TC	SS	OC	RC	FC	TC	SS
High variability																		
Cr30x5a-1	200.00	575.14	775.14	200.00	575.14	19.66	794.80	2%	200.00	575.14	19.82	794.96	0%	200.00	575.14	24.25	799.38	1%
Cr30x5a-2	200.00	607.28	807.28	200.00	607.74	0.02	807.76	5%	200.00	611.41	0.02	811.43	7%	200.00	607.74	0.04	807.78	5%
Cr30x5a-3	187.50	507.92	695.42	187.50	509.25	27.86	724.61	2%	187.50	509.25	29.95	726.70	4%	187.50	509.25	33.41	730.16	3%
Cr30x5b-1	225.00	623.22	848.22	225.00	623.22	19.99	868.21	10%	225.00	623.22	20.73	868.95	10%	225.00	623.22	24.86	873.08	10%
Cr30x5b-2	187.50	625.32	812.82	187.50	625.32	0.10	812.92	3%	187.50	625.32	0.20	813.02	5%	187.50	625.32	0.15	812.97	3%
Cr30x5b-3	187.50	684.58	872.08	187.50	684.58	24.93	897.00	1%	187.50	684.58	29.03	901.11	5%	187.50	684.58	34.01	906.09	5%
Cr40x5a-1	162.50	731.84	894.34	162.50	737.20	2.85	902.55	2%	162.50	735.84	7.83	906.17	1%	162.50	735.84	9.38	907.71	1%
Cr40x5a-2	225.00	637.26	862.26	225.00	642.02	1.79	868.82	3%	225.00	642.02	1.48	868.50	3%	225.00	642.02	2.25	869.27	3%
Cr40x5a-3	162.50	752.88	915.38	162.50	763.69	5.78	931.97	2%	162.50	763.69	7.76	933.96	2%	162.50	752.88	18.65	934.04	1%
Cr40x5b-1	162.50	852.04	1014.54	237.50	786.00	4.65	1028.14	3%	237.50	792.36	2.84	1032.70	4%	237.50	786.00	8.47	1031.97	3%
Cr40x5b-2	225.00	690.57	915.57	225.00	690.57	9.35	924.91	2%	225.00	690.57	12.59	928.15	2%	225.00	690.57	14.96	930.53	2%
Cr40x5b-3	175.00	764.33	939.33	175.00	780.62	4.14	959.76	3%	175.00	780.62	4.90	960.52	3%	175.00	780.62	5.86	961.48	2%
Average	191.67	671.03	862.70	197.92	668.78	10.09	876.79	3.17%	197.92	669.50	11.43	878.85	3.83%	197.92	667.77	14.69	880.37	3.33%

Results in Table 3 show a slight average increase in total costs when increasing the variability level for all types of solutions, except the best deterministic solution. This growth is caused mainly by the rise in failure costs, since a greater number of detours and round-trips is expected when the demand variability level is higher. Additionally, total costs also increase when the uncertainty level is higher regardless of the variability level, i.e., the deterministic solution is the cheapest one, and the fuzzy solution is the most costly. If we compare only the average deterministic cost of each set of solutions, formed by the sum of OC and RC, we obtain values with negligible differences. Hence, the contrasts in total costs are caused mainly by failure costs. For example, for the instance *Cr30x5a-3* in the low variability scenario, 1.6% of total costs are failure costs in the best stochastic solution. However, in the best fuzzy solution this percentage rises to 3.5%. Most instances show this steady growth when increasing the uncertainty level, which confirms that fuzzy scenarios have a higher uncertainty level when compared with deterministic and stochastic scenarios. Finally, the average safety stock increases when both variability and uncertainty levels rise, since more protection against uncertainty is necessary in both cases.

Results corresponding to our best deterministic solution in Table 3 were yielded assuming that the realized demand is deterministic. Hence, an additional experiment has been performed, in which this solution (called henceforth OBD) is tested in a hybrid fuzzy-stochastic environment, using 0% of safety stock protection against uncertainty. Figure 6 compares this solution's results with our best-found hybrid fuzzy-stochastic solution (OBF) in terms of failure costs. Results for 12 Akca's instances are depicted for each demand variability scenario. Extreme points in dashed lines indicate the average cost for each set of data. As expected, average failure costs show an increasing trend when the variability grows, regardless of the type of solution. Conversely, Figure 6 shows that OBF outperforms OBD when tested under uncertainty conditions. This fact demonstrates the quality of our fuzzy simheuristic approach, especially in scenarios where the demand variability is high.

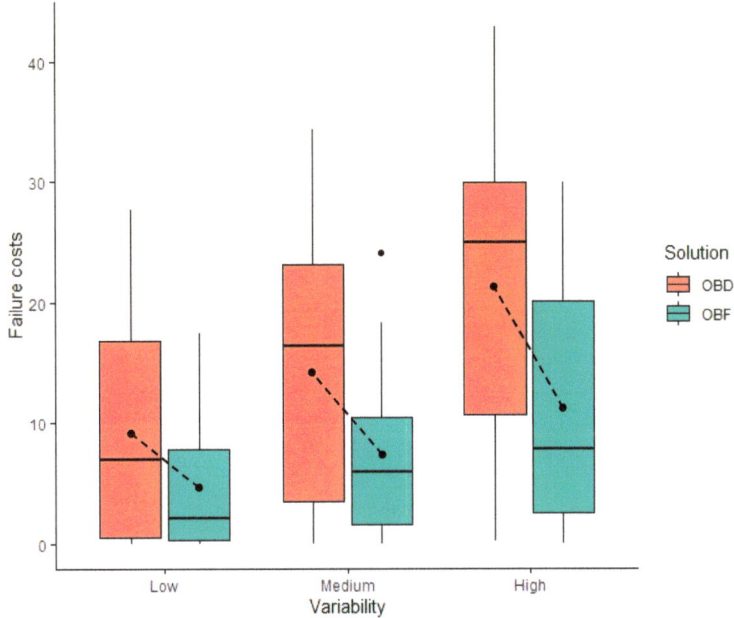

Figure 6. Failure costs of our best deterministic and our best hybrid solutions.

Table 4 compares two types of hybrid fuzzy-stochastic solutions. Firstly, we show our best solution with a single facility size alternative given by the original Akca's instances—

i.e., the solution is not flexible since only one size is available to select. Secondly, we show our best flexible solution, which corresponds to our best hybrid solution in Table 3. When comparing the total costs of both types of solutions, the negative gap obtained for all instances and under all variability levels shows the advantages of considering facility sizing decisions. For example, we reach a maximum absolute gap of 7.71% in total cost savings for a single instance. In average, both opening and routing costs decrease whenever alternative depot sizes are available. Nevertheless, each instance shows different results regarding OC and RC. The most evident case is that in which opening costs decrease. Clearly, this is a direct result of having smaller facility size alternatives. Without loss of generality, all examples below take as reference the high variability scenario. For example, the instance *Cr30x5b-3* has a total demand of 1620. Both flexible and nonflexible approaches design the same routes and yield equal routing costs. Nevertheless, the nonflexible approach locates two depots of size 1000 each. Conversely, our flexible approach locates one depot of size 1000 and one depot of size 750. Hence, the nonflexible solution assigns an extra capacity that is not necessary under the problem's current conditions.

Table 4. Comparative results between our hybrid solutions when considering facility sizing decisions.

| Instance | Best Nonflexible Hybrid Solution | | | | | Best Flexible Hybrid Solution | | | | | Gap |
	OC	RC	FC	TC	SS	OC	RC	FC	TC	SS	TC
				Low variability							
Cr30x5a-1	200.00	619.51	3.45	822.96	1%	200.00	575.14	3.31	778.45	2%	−5.41%
Cr30x5a-2	200.00	626.01	0.04	826.05	1%	200.00	607.28	0.12	807.40	3%	−2.26%
Cr30x5a-3	200.00	507.99	17.56	725.55	2%	187.50	509.25	17.48	714.22	3%	−1.56%
Cr30x5b-1	200.00	682.97	0.32	883.29	2%	225.00	623.22	14.59	862.81	0%	−2.32%
Cr30x5b-2	200.00	625.32	0.00	825.32	2%	187.50	625.32	0.00	812.82	2%	−1.51%
Cr30x5b-3	200.00	684.58	5.95	890.53	1%	187.50	684.58	6.35	878.43	1%	−1.36%
Cr40x5a-1	200.00	733.47	3.22	936.70	0%	162.50	731.84	0.07	894.41	1%	−4.51%
Cr40x5a-2	200.00	691.47	11.15	902.63	1%	225.00	639.02	0.81	864.83	1%	−4.19%
Cr40x5a-3	200.00	748.64	9.88	958.52	1%	162.50	752.88	3.26	918.64	0%	−4.16%
Cr40x5b-1	200.00	858.58	1.94	1060.53	2%	162.50	852.04	12.24	1026.78	1%	−3.18%
Cr40x5b-2	300.00	690.57	0.65	991.22	2%	225.00	690.57	0.62	916.18	1%	−7.57%
Cr40x5b-3	200.00	780.62	0.07	980.69	2%	175.00	772.87	0.29	948.16	2%	−3.32%
Average	208.33	687.48	4.52	900.33	1.42%	191.67	672.00	4.93	868.59	1.42%	−3.45%
				Medium variability							
Cr30x5a-1	200.00	619.51	9.17	828.68	0%	200.00	575.14	9.67	784.81	2%	−5.29%
Cr30x5a-2	200.00	626.01	0.60	826.61	2%	200.00	607.28	1.94	809.22	3%	−2.10%
Cr30x5a-3	200.00	507.99	24.30	732.29	2%	187.50	509.25	24.10	720.85	3%	−1.56%
Cr30x5b-1	200.00	681.50	14.31	895.80	1%	225.00	623.22	18.32	866.53	3%	−3.27%
Cr30x5b-2	200.00	625.32	0.01	825.33	2%	187.50	625.32	0.00	812.82	2%	−1.52%
Cr30x5b-3	200.00	684.58	15.60	900.18	1%	187.50	684.58	12.79	884.87	1%	−1.70%
Cr40x5a-1	200.00	733.47	7.69	941.17	1%	162.50	739.24	0.01	901.75	3%	−4.19%
Cr40x5a-2	200.00	700.80	12.59	913.39	3%	225.00	642.02	0.24	867.26	3%	−5.05%
Cr40x5a-3	200.00	748.64	20.15	968.79	0%	162.50	752.88	8.57	923.95	1%	−4.63%
Cr40x5b-1	200.00	863.91	2.32	1066.23	3%	162.50	858.58	8.01	1029.09	2%	−3.48%
Cr40x5b-2	300.00	690.57	4.18	994.75	1%	225.00	690.57	3.77	919.33	0%	−7.58%
Cr40x5b-3	200.00	780.62	0.94	981.56	3%	175.00	772.87	2.53	950.40	2%	−3.17%
Average	208.33	688.58	9.32	906.23	1.58%	191.67	673.41	7.50	872.57	2.08%	−3.63%
				High variability							
Cr30x5a-1	200.00	619.51	20.69	840.20	0%	200.00	575.14	19.82	794.96	0%	−5.38%
Cr30x5a-2	200.00	621.45	5.66	827.12	3%	200.00	611.41	0.02	811.43	7%	−1.90%
Cr30x5a-3	200.00	507.99	30.16	738.15	4%	187.50	509.25	29.95	726.70	4%	−1.55%
Cr30x5b-1	200.00	681.50	18.85	900.35	0%	225.00	623.22	20.73	868.95	10%	−3.49%
Cr30x5b-2	200.00	625.32	0.14	825.46	5%	187.50	625.32	0.20	813.02	5%	−1.51%
Cr30x5b-3	200.00	684.58	30.23	914.81	1%	187.50	684.58	29.03	901.11	5%	−1.50%
Cr40x5a-1	200.00	737.94	5.78	943.73	2%	162.50	735.84	7.83	906.17	1%	−3.98%
Cr40x5a-2	200.00	700.80	15.98	916.78	3%	225.00	642.02	1.48	868.50	3%	−5.27%
Cr40x5a-3	200.00	748.64	32.89	981.54	0%	162.50	763.69	7.76	933.96	2%	−4.85%
Cr40x5b-1	200.00	858.58	22.53	1081.11	2%	237.50	792.36	2.84	1032.70	4%	−4.48%
Cr40x5b-2	300.00	693.03	12.66	1005.69	0%	225.00	690.57	12.59	928.15	2%	−7.71%
Cr40x5b-3	200.00	772.87	13.22	986.09	2%	175.00	780.62	4.90	960.52	3%	−2.59%
Average	208.33	687.68	17.40	913.42	1.83%	197.92	669.50	11.43	878.85	3.83%	−3.68%

Some instances show an opposite behavior, i.e., opening costs either increase or remain the same while routing costs decrease. For example, the nonflexible solution of the instance *Cr30x5a-1* opens two depots of size 1000 each. Alternatively, the flexible solution opens one depot of size 1500 and one depot of size 500, i.e., the total capacity is equal and, given our defined costs structure, also the opening costs. However, this slight change drives a redesign of routes that decreases RC. An additional example is given by the instance *Cr40x5a-2*. Figure 7 depicts the best solution found by the nonflexible approach (a) and our flexible approach (b). The solution in Figure 7a locates two depots of size 1750 each, and the solution in Figure 7b locates three depots of size 875 each. The latter case has a total capacity that is smaller than the former's; however, opening costs are higher since the fixed cost is clearly greater when 3 facilities are open instead of 2. This new configuration decreases considerably routing costs (Table 4), which shows that considering facility sizing decisions not only reduces total costs by decreasing depots capacity but also by increasing it, since shorter routes can be designed.

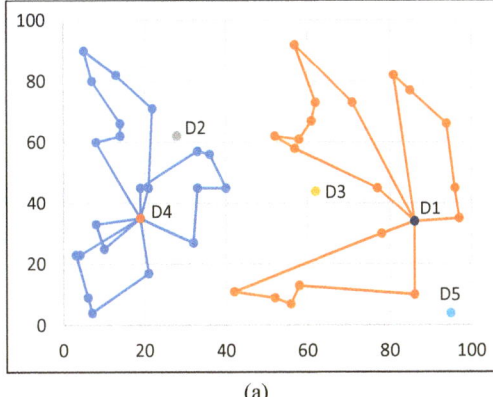
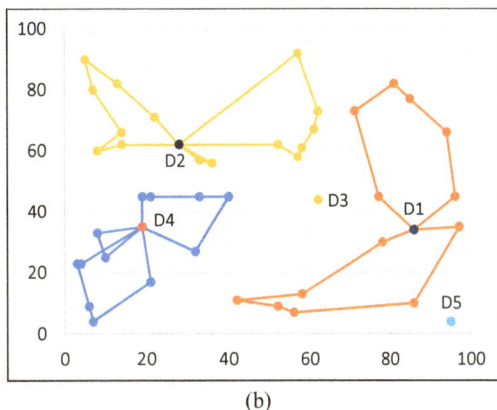

(a)   (b)

Figure 7. Best-found solution by a nonflexible (**a**) and a flexible (**b**) fuzzy LRP for the instance *Cr40x5a-2*.

Managerial Insights

From a managerial perspective, we have shown a general algorithm useful to solve a flexible-size LRP where a subset of customers provides enough information to model stochastically their demand, while the complementary subset provides scarce data. In this case, decision makers may estimate a fuzzy demand. Our algorithm is general because scenarios where the demand of all customers is deterministic, stochastic or fuzzy represent particular cases of our described problem. Hence, decision makers can employ our approach more extensively than other algorithms. We analyze these scenarios through some numerical results and assess how the level of uncertainty influences opening, routing and route-failure costs. Clearly, more precise data decrease total costs. Furthermore, we have calculated the cost of assuming a deterministic demand when the real scenario is fuzzy or stochastic. It has been shown that our hybrid approach yields less average costs, which leads to a more competitive supply chain. Additionally, we have also shown that important cost savings are generated whenever a set of facility size alternatives are analyzed by decision makers, instead of considering a single alternative—as in most LRP studies. Finally, our algorithm is able to generate detailed information about the location-allocation-routing decisions that should be made.

7. Conclusions

This work presented a location routing problem where the facility size is an additional variable, instead of a known parameter as the traditional LRP assumes. Moreover, we consider a hybrid fuzzy-stochastic setting in which some customers' demands are fuzzy and others are stochastic. Hence, a fuzzy simheuristic approach is proposed to solve this problem cost- and time- efficiently. Initially, our algorithm selects the best size for each open facility from a set of provided alternatives. We perform an iterative procedure in which a set of location-allocation-routing configurations are assessed in terms of opening and routing costs. Then a top list of complete LRP solutions is iteratively perturbed and simulated. The perturbation stage is performed by employing an iterated local search metaheuristic. The simulation stage is carried out by running a classic Monte Carlo simulation for the stochastic demands and a fuzzy simulation for the fuzzy demands. Failure costs are introduced as an additional performance indicator. Finally, a set of elite solutions is assessed through a refinement procedure where a larger number of simulation runs is executed.

Our fuzzy simheuristic approach has been proved to be flexible enough not only to combine efficiently stochastic and fuzzy demands in a single execution but also to address less general scenarios in which demands of all customers are either deterministic or fuzzy. Our approach has also been proved to be a cost-efficient algorithm when considering uncertainty scenarios. It decreases route failure costs when compared with the best deterministic solution tested in a hybrid fuzzy-stochastic environment. The use of a safety stock policy as a protection against uncertainty has also contributed to this decrease. In order to design a time-efficient algorithm, our current approach employs stochastic and fuzzy simulation only to assess the designed routes. Hence, our algorithm results can be enhanced by introducing fuzzy-stochastic aspects from the construction stage. However, this approach might also increase computational times.

To the best of our knowledge, this is the first time that a hybrid fuzzy-stochastic LRP with facility sizing decisions is addressed. Medium-sized benchmark instances considering three demand variability levels were used. Obtained results show that introducing such flexibility decreases total costs in two mutually nonexclusive ways: firstly, yielding savings in opening costs by locating facilities of smaller size; and secondly, yielding savings in routing costs by locating facilities of higher size, which drives a routes redesign that reduces the total traveled distance. We also have demonstrated that these savings are always incurred regardless of the demand variability level.

Multiple challenges remain open for future research. Since we are considering that only routes fail when demands are higher than expected, future work can include the simulation of facility failures, which would prompt a revision of location-allocation decisions. In addition, failure costs are currently measured only by considering the distances traveled to perform round-trips and detours. Still, real-life customers might not allow a delivery delay, e.g., because a time windows constraint must be met. This delay may drive lost sales or a goodwill reduction. Hence, this type of costs can be included in the computation of failure costs. Finally, large-sized instances can be used to assess the influence of the number of nodes in our approach performance.

Author Contributions: Conceptualization, R.D.T. and A.A.J.; methodology, R.D.T., P.J.C.-M. and J.P.; software, P.J.C.-M. and J.P.; formal analysis, R.D.T.; investigation, R.D.T., P.J.C.-M., C.L.Q.-A. and J.R.M.-T.; writing—original draft preparation, all authors; writing—review and editing, R.D.T. and A.A.J. All authors have read and agreed to the published version of the manuscript.

Funding: This work has been partially supported by the Spanish Ministry of Science (PID2019-111100RB-C21/AEI/10.13039/501100011033). In addition, it has received the support of the Doctoral School at the Universitat Oberta de Catalunya (Spain) and the Universidad de La Sabana (INGPhD-12-2020).

Data Availability Statement: Data are available upon reasonable request to the corresponding author.

Conflicts of Interest: The authors declare no conflict of interest.

References

1.   Salhi, S.; Rand, G.K. The effect of ignoring routes when locating depots. *Eur. J. Oper. Res.* **1989**, *39*, 150–156. [CrossRef]
2.   Nagy, G.; Salhi, S. Location-routing: Issues, models and methods. *Eur. J. Oper. Res.* **2007**, *177*, 649–672. [CrossRef]
3.   Prodhon, C.; Prins, C. A survey of recent research on location-routing problems. *Eur. J. Oper. Res.* **2014**, *238*, 1–17. [CrossRef]

4. Zhou, L.; Lin, Y.; Wang, X.; Zhou, F. Model and algorithm for bilevel multisized terminal location-routing problem for the last mile delivery. *Int. Trans.Oper. Res.* **2019**, *26*, 131–156. [CrossRef]

5. Tordecilla-Madera, R.; Polo, A.; Muñoz, D.; González-Rodríguez, L. A robust design for a Colombian dairy cooperative's milk storage and refrigeration logistics system using binary programming. *Int. J. Prod. Econ.* **2017**, *183*, 710–720. [CrossRef]

6. Correia, I.; Melo, T. Multi-period capacitated facility location under delayed demand satisfaction. *Eur. J. Oper. Res.* **2016**, *255*, 729–746. [CrossRef]

7. Hemmelmayr, V.; Smilowitz, K.; de la Torre, L. A periodic location routing problem for collaborative recycling. *IISE Trans.* **2017**, *49*, 414–428. [CrossRef]

8. Tunalıoğlu, R.; Koç, Ç.; Bektaş, T. A multiperiod location-routing problem arising in the collection of Olive Oil Mill Wastewater. *J. Oper. Res. Soc.* **2016**, *67*, 1012–1024. [CrossRef]

9. Quintero-Araujo, C.L.; Guimarans, D.; Juan, A.A. A simheuristic algorithm for the capacitated location routing problem with stochastic demands. *J. Simul.* **2019**, 1–18. [CrossRef]

10. Rabbani, M.; Heidari, R.; Yazdanparast, R. A stochastic multi-period industrial hazardous waste location-routing problem: Integrating NSGA-II and Monte Carlo simulation. *Eur. J. Oper. Res.* **2019**, *272*, 945–961. [CrossRef]

11. Sun, Z.; Yan, N.; Sun, Y.; Li, H. Location-routing optimization with split demand for customer self-pickup via data analysis and heuristics search. *Asia-Pac. J. Oper. Res.* **2019**, *36*, 1940013. [CrossRef]

12. Zhang, S.; Chen, M.; Zhang, W. A novel location-routing problem in electric vehicle transportation with stochastic demands. *J. Clean. Prod.* **2019**, *221*, 567–581. [CrossRef]

13. Tordecilla, R.D.; Panadero, J.; Quintero-Araujo, C.L.; Montoya-Torres, J.R.; Juan, A.A. A simheuristic algorithm for the location routing problem with facility sizing decisions and stochastic demands. In Proceedings of the 2020 Winter Simulation Conference, IEEE, Marriott, Orlando, FL, USA, 14–18 December 2020; pp. 1265–1275.

14. Herazo-Padilla, N.; Montoya-Torres, J.R.; Nieto Isaza, S.; Alvarado-Valencia, J. Simulation-optimization approach for the stochastic location-routing problem. *J. Simul.* **2015**, *9*, 296–311. [CrossRef]

15. Zhang, B.; Li, H.; Li, S.; Peng, J. Sustainable multi-depot emergency facilities location-routing problem with uncertain information. *Appl. Math. Comput.* **2018**, *333*, 506–520. [CrossRef]

16. Corlu, C.G.; Panadero, J.; Onggo, S.; Juan, A.A. On the scarcity of observations when modelling random inputs and the quality of solutions to stochastic optimisation problems. In Proceedings of the 2020 Winter Simulation Conference, IEEE, Marriott, Orlando, FL, USA, 14–18 December 2020; pp. 2105–2113.

17. Zhang, H.; Liu, F.; Ma, L.; Zhang, Z. A hybrid heuristic based on a particle swarm algorithm to solve the capacitated location-routing problem with fuzzy demands. *IEEE Access* **2020**, *8*, 153671–153691. [CrossRef]

18. Mehrjerdi, Y.Z.; Nadizadeh, A. Using greedy clustering method to solve capacitated location-routing problem with fuzzy demands. *Eur. J. Oper. Res.* **2013**, *229*, 75–84. [CrossRef]

19. Fazayeli, S.; Eydi, A.; Kamalabadi, I.N. Location-routing problem in multimodal transportation network with time windows and fuzzy demands: Presenting a two-part genetic algorithm. *Comput. Ind. Eng.* **2018**, *119*, 233–246. [CrossRef]

20. Nadizadeh, A.; Kafash, B. Fuzzy capacitated location-routing problem with simultaneous pickup and delivery demands. *Transp. Lett.* **2019**, *11*, 1–19. [CrossRef]

21. Zarandi, M.H.F.; Hemmati, A.; Davari, S. The multi-depot capacitated location-routing problem with fuzzy travel times. *Expert Syst. Appl.* **2011**, *38*, 10075–10084. [CrossRef]

22. Zarandi, M.H.F.; Hemmati, A.; Davari, S.; Turksen, I.B. Capacitated location-routing problem with time windows under uncertainty. *Knowl. Based Syst.* **2013**, *37*, 480–489. [CrossRef]

23. Ghezavati, V.; Morakabatchian, S. Application of a fuzzy service level constraint for solving a multi-objective location-routing problem for the industrial hazardous wastes. *J. Intell. Fuzzy Syst.* **2015**, *28*, 2003–2013. [CrossRef]

24. Juan, A.A.; Kelton, W.D.; Currie, C.S.; Faulin, J. Simheuristics applications: dealing with uncertainty in logistics, transportation, and other supply chain areas. In Proceedings of the 2018 Winter Simulation Conference, IEEE, Marriott, Orlando, FL, USA, 14–18 December 2018; pp. 3048–3059.

25. Maranzana, F. On the location of supply points to minimize transport costs. *J. Oper. Res. Soc.* **1964**, *15*, 261–270. [CrossRef]

26. Dai, Z.; Aqlan, F.; Gao, K.; Zhou, Y. A two-phase method for multi-echelon location-routing problems in supply chains. *Expert Syst. Appl.* **2019**, *115*, 618–634. [CrossRef]

27. Quintero-Araujo, C.L.; Caballero-Villalobos, J.P.; Juan, A.A.; Montoya-Torres, J.R. A biased-randomized metaheuristic for the capacitated location routing problem. *Int. Trans. Oper. Res.* **2017**, *24*, 1079–1098. [CrossRef]

28. Escobar, J.W.; Linfati, R.; Baldoquin, M.G.; Toth, P. A granular variable tabu neighborhood search for the capacitated location-routing problem. *Transp. Res. Part B Methodol.* **2014**, *67*, 344–356. [CrossRef]

29. Ferdi, I.; Layeb, A. A GRASP algorithm based new heuristic for the capacitated location routing problem. *J. Exp. Theor. Artif. Intell.* **2018**, *30*, 369–387. [CrossRef]

30. Quintero-Araujo, C.L.; Gruler, A.; Juan, A.A.; Faulin, J. Using horizontal cooperation concepts in integrated routing and facility-location decisions. *Int. Trans. Oper. Res.* **2019**, *26*, 551–576. [CrossRef]

31. Hof, J.; Schneider, M.; Goeke, D. Solving the battery swap station location-routing problem with capacitated electric vehicles using an AVNS algorithm for vehicle-routing problems with intermediate stops. *Transp. Res. Part B Methodol.* **2017**, *97*, 102–112. [CrossRef]

32. Almouhanna, A.; Quintero-Araujo, C.L.; Panadero, J.; Juan, A.A.; Khosravi, B.; Ouelhadj, D. The location routing problem using electric vehicles with constrained distance. *Comput. Oper. Res.* **2020**, *115*, 104864. [CrossRef]
33. Theeraviriya, C.; Sirirak, W.; Praseeratasang, N. Location and routing planning considering electric vehicles with restricted distance in agriculture. *World Electr. Veh. J.* **2020**, *11*, 61. [CrossRef]
34. Nataraj, S.; Ferone, D.; Quintero-Araujo, C.; Juan, A.; Festa, P. Consolidation centers in city logistics: A cooperative approach based on the location routing problem. *Int. J. Ind. Eng. Comput.* **2019**, *10*, 393–404. [CrossRef]
35. Ukkusuri, S.V.; Yushimito, W.F. Location routing approach for the humanitarian prepositioning problem. *Transp. Res. Record* **2008**, *2089*, 18–25. [CrossRef]
36. Lashine, S.H.; Fattouh, M.; Issa, A. Location/allocation and routing decisions in supply chain network design. *J. Model. Manag.* **2006**, *1*, 173–183. [CrossRef]
37. Leng, L.; Zhao, Y.; Zhang, J.; Zhang, C. An effective approach for the multiobjective regional low-carbon location-routing problem. *Int. J. Environ. Res. Public Health* **2019**, *16*, 2064. [CrossRef]
38. Wang, Z.; Leng, L.; Wang, S.; Li, G.; Zhao, Y. A hyperheuristic approach for location-routing problem of cold chain logistics considering fuel consumption. *Comput. Intell. Neurosci.* **2020**, *2020*, 8395754 . [CrossRef]
39. Rabbani, M.; Sadati, S.A.; Farrokhi-Asl, H. Incorporating location routing model and decision making techniques in industrial waste management: Application in the automotive industry. *Comput. Ind. Eng.* **2020**, *148*, 106692. [CrossRef]
40. Ghaffari-Nasab, N.; Ahari, S.G.; Ghazanfari, M. A hybrid simulated annealing based heuristic for solving the location-routing problem with fuzzy demands. *Sci. Iran.* **2013**, *20*, 919–930.
41. Nadizadeh, A.; Nasab, H.H. Solving the dynamic capacitated location-routing problem with fuzzy demands by hybrid heuristic algorithm. *Eur. J. Oper. Res.* **2014**, *238*, 458–470. [CrossRef]
42. Wei, M.; Yu, L.; Li, X. Credibilistic Location-Routing Model for Hazardous Materials Transportation. *Int. J. Intell. Syst.* **2015**, *30*, 23–39. [CrossRef]
43. Faulin, J.; Gilibert, M.; Juan, A.A.; Vilajosana, X.; Ruiz, R. SR-1: A simulation-based algorithm for the capacitated vehicle routing problem. In Proceedings of the 2008 Winter Simulation Conference, IEEE, Miami, FL, USA, 7–10 December 2008; pp. 2708–2716.
44. Juan, A.A.; Faulin, J.; Ruiz, R.; Barrios, B.; Gilibert, M.; Vilajosana, X. Using oriented random search to provide a set of alternative solutions to the capacitated vehicle routing problem. In *Operations Research and Cyber-Infrastructure*; Springer: Berlin, Germany, 2009; pp. 331–345.
45. Oliva, D.; Copado, P.; Hinojosa, S.; Panadero, J.; Riera, D.; Juan, A.A. Fuzzy simheuristics: Solving optimization problems under stochastic and uncertainty scenarios. *Mathematics* **2021**, *1*, 00005.
46. Quintero-Araujo, C.L.; Gruler, A.; Juan, A.A.; de Armas, J.; Ramalhinho, H. Using simheuristics to promote horizontal collaboration in stochastic city logistics. *Prog. Artif. Intell.* **2017**, *6*, 275–284. [CrossRef]
47. Gruler, A.; Panadero, J.; de Armas, J.; Moreno, J.A.; Juan, A.A. A variable neighborhood search simheuristic for the multiperiod inventory routing problem with stochastic demands. *Int. Trans. Oper. Res.* **2020**, *27*, 314–335. [CrossRef]
48. Gonzalez-Martin, S.; Juan, A.A.; Riera, D.; Elizondo, M.G.; Ramos, J.J. A simheuristic algorithm for solving the arc routing problem with stochastic demands. *J. Simul.* **2018**, *12*, 53–66. [CrossRef]
49. Gruler, A.; Panadero, J.; de Armas, J.; Moreno, J.A.; Juan, A.A. Combining variable neighborhood search with simulation for the inventory routing problem with stochastic demands and stock-outs. *Comput. Ind. Eng.* **2018**, *123*, 278–288. [CrossRef]
50. Gruler, A.; Fikar, C.; Juan, A.A.; Hirsch, P.; Contreras-Bolton, C. Supporting multi-depot and stochastic waste collection management in clustered urban areas via simulation–optimization. *J. Simul.* **2017**, *11*, 11–19. [CrossRef]
51. Uddin, M.; Huynh, N. Reliable routing of road-rail intermodal freight under uncertainty. *Netw. Spat. Econ.* **2019**, *19*, 929–952. [CrossRef]
52. Hrušovský, M.; Demir, E.; Jammernegg, W.; Van Woensel, T. Hybrid simulation and optimization approach for green intermodal transportation problem with travel time uncertainty. *Flex. Serv. Manuf. J.* **2018**, *30*, 486–516. [CrossRef]
53. Zhao, Y.; Liu, R.; Zhang, X.; Whiteing, A. A chance-constrained stochastic approach to intermodal container routing problems. *PLoS ONE* **2018**, *13*, e0192275. [CrossRef]
54. Werners, B.; Drawe, M. Capacitated vehicle routing problem with fuzzy demand. In *Fuzzy Sets Based Heuristics for Optimization*; Springer: Berlin, Germany, 2003; pp. 317–335.
55. Erbao, C.; Mingyong, L. A hybrid differential evolution algorithm to vehicle routing problem with fuzzy demands. *J. Comput. Appl. Math.* **2009**, *231*, 302–310. [CrossRef]
56. Xue, L.; Dai, X.X. Research on the vehicle routing problem with fuzzy demands. In *Advanced Materials Research*; Trans Tech Publications Ltd.: Stafa-Zurich, Switzerland, 2011; Volume 186, pp. 570–575.
57. Sun, Y. Fuzzy approaches and simulation-based reliability modeling to solve a Road–Rail intermodal routing problem with soft delivery time windows when demand and capacity are uncertain. *Int. J. Fuzzy Syst.* **2020**, *22*, 2119–2148. [CrossRef]
58. Zheng, Y.; Liu, B. Fuzzy vehicle routing model with credibility measure and its hybrid intelligent algorithm. *Appl. Math. Comput.* **2006**, *176*, 673–683. [CrossRef]
59. Sun, Y.; Hrušovský, M.; Zhang, C.; Lang, M. A time-dependent fuzzy programming approach for the green multimodal routing problem with rail service capacity uncertainty and road traffic congestion. *Complexity* **2018**, *2018*, 8645793. [CrossRef]
60. Gupta, R.; Singh, B.; Pandey, D. Fuzzy vehicle routing problem with uncertainty in service time. *Int. J. Contemp. Math. Sci.* **2010**, *5*, 497–507.

61. Tang, J.; Pan, Z.; Fung, R.Y.; Lau, H. Vehicle routing problem with fuzzy time windows. *Fuzzy Sets Syst.* **2009**, *160*, 683–695. [CrossRef]
62. López-Castro, L.F.; Montoya-Torres, J.R. Vehicle routing with fuzzy time windows using a genetic algorithm. In Proceedings of the 2011 Workshop On Computational Intelligence In Production And Logistics Systems, IEEE, Paris, France, 11–15 April 2011; pp. 1–8.
63. Cao, E.; Lai, M. The open vehicle routing problem with fuzzy demands. *Expert Syst. Appl.* **2010**, *37*, 2405–2411. [CrossRef]
64. Gonzalez-Neira, E.M.; Ferone, D.; Hatami, S.; Juan, A.A. A biased-randomized simheuristic for the distributed assembly permutation flowshop problem with stochastic processing times. *Simul. Model. Pract. Theory* **2017**, *79*, 23–36. [CrossRef]
65. Zarandi, M.H.F.; Asl, A.A.S.; Sotudian, S.; Castillo, O. A state of the art review of intelligent scheduling. *Artif. Intell. Rev.* **2020**, *53*, 501–593. [CrossRef]
66. Ochoa, P.; Castillo, O.; Soria, J. High-Speed Interval Type-2 Fuzzy System for Dynamic Crossover Parameter Adaptation in Differential Evolution and Its Application to Controller Optimization. *Int. J. Fuzzy Syst.* **2019**, *22*, 414–427. [CrossRef]
67. Bernal, E.; Castillo, O.; Soria, J.; Valdez, F. Generalized type-2 fuzzy logic in galactic swarm optimization: Design of an optimal ball and beam fuzzy controller. *J. Intell. Fuzzy Syst.* **2020**, *39*, 3545–3559. [CrossRef]
68. Anter, A.M.; Gupta, D.; Castillo, O. A novel parameter estimation in dynamic model via fuzzy swarm intelligence and chaos theory for faults in wastewater treatment plant. *Soft Comput.* **2020**, *24*, 111–129. [CrossRef]
69. Panadero, J.; Doering, J.; Kizys, R.; Juan, A.A.; Fito, A. A variable neighborhood search simheuristic for project portfolio selection under uncertainty. *J. Heuristics* **2020**, *26*, 353–375. [CrossRef]
70. de Armas, J.; Juan, A.A.; Marquès, J.M.; Pedroso, J.P. Solving the deterministic and stochastic uncapacitated facility location problem: From a heuristic to a simheuristic. *J. Oper. Res. Soc.* **2017**, *68*, 1161–1176. [CrossRef]
71. Panadero, J.; Juan, A.A.; Bayliss, C.; Currie, C. Maximising reward from a team of surveillance drones: A simheuristic approach to the stochastic team orienteering problem. *Eur. J. Ind. Eng.* **2020**, *14*, 485–516. [CrossRef]
72. Ferone, D.; Gruler, A.; Festa, P.; Juan, A.A. Enhancing and extending the classical GRASP framework with biased randomisation and simulation. *J. Oper. Res. Soc.* **2019**, *70*, 1362–1375. [CrossRef]
73. Ferrer, A.; Guimarans, D.; Ramalhinho, H.; Juan, A.A. A BRILS metaheuristic for non-smooth flow-shop problems with failure-risk costs. *Expert Syst. Appl.* **2016**, *44*, 177–186. [CrossRef]
74. Akca, Z.; Berger, R.; Ralphs, T. A branch-and-price algorithm for combined location and routing problems under capacity restrictions. In *Operations Research and Cyber-Infrastructure*; Springer: Boston, MA, USA, 2009; pp. 309–330.
75. Barreto, S.; Ferreira, C.; Paixao, J.; Santos, B.S. Using clustering analysis in a capacitated location-routing problem. *Eur. J. Oper. Res.* **2007**, *179*, 968–977. [CrossRef]
76. Belenguer, J.M.; Benavent, E.; Prins, C.; Prodhon, C.; Calvo, R.W. A branch-and-cut method for the capacitated location-routing problem. *Comput. Oper. Res.* **2011**, *38*, 931–941. [CrossRef]
77. Teodorović, D.; Pavković, G. The fuzzy set theory approach to the vehicle routing problem when demand at nodes is uncertain. *Fuzzy Sets Syst.* **1996**, *82*, 307–317. [CrossRef]
78. Sun, Y. A Fuzzy Multi-Objective Routing Model for Managing Hazardous Materials Door-to-Door Transportation in the Road-Rail Multimodal Network With Uncertain Demand and Improved Service Level. *IEEE Access* **2020**, *8*, 172808–172828. [CrossRef]
79. Klir, G.; Yuan, B. Fuzzy Sets and Fuzzy Logic: Theory and Applications. *Possibility Theory Versus Probab. Theory* **1996**, *32*, 207–208.
80. Opricovic, S.; Tzeng, G.H. Defuzzification within a multicriteria decision model. *Int. J. Uncertain. Fuzziness Knowl. Based Syst.* **2003**, *11*, 635–652. [CrossRef]

Article

Integrated Simulation-Based Optimization of Operational Decisions at Container Terminals

Marvin Kastner *,†, **Nicole Nellen** †, **Anne Schwientek** † and **Carlos Jahn**

Institute of Maritime Logistics, Hamburg University of Technology, 21073 Hamburg, Germany;
nicole.nellen@tuhh.de (N.N.); a.schwientek@tuhh.de (A.S.); carlos.jahn@tuhh.de (C.J.)
* Correspondence: marvin.kastner@tuhh.de; Tel.: +49-40-42878-4793
† These authors contributed equally to this work.

Abstract: At container terminals, many cargo handling processes are interconnected and occur in parallel. Within short time windows, many operational decisions need to be made and should consider both time efficiency and equipment utilization. During operation, many sources of disturbance and, thus, uncertainty exist. For these reasons, perfectly coordinated processes can potentially unravel. This study analyzes simulation-based optimization, an approach that considers uncertainty by means of simulation while optimizing a given objective. The developed procedure simultaneously scales the amount of utilized equipment and adjusts the selection and tuning of operational policies. Thus, the benefits of a simulation study and an integrated optimization framework are combined in a new way. Four meta-heuristics—Tree-structured Parzen Estimator, Bayesian Optimization, Simulated Annealing, and Random Search—guide the simulation-based optimization process. Thus, this study aims to determine a favorable configuration of equipment quantity and operational policies for container terminals using a small number of experiments and, simultaneously, to empirically compare the chosen meta-heuristics including the reproducibility of the optimization runs. The results show that simulation-based optimization is suitable for identifying the amount of required equipment and well-performing policies. Among the presented scenarios, no clear ranking between meta-heuristics regarding the solution quality exists. The approximated optima suggest that pooling yard trucks and a yard block assignment that is close to the quay crane are preferable.

Keywords: container terminal; simulation; simulation-based optimization; meta-heuristic; horizontal transportation; hyper-parameter optimization

Citation: Kastner, M.; Nellen, N.; Schwientek, A.; Jahn, C. Integrated Simulation-Based Optimization of Operational Decisions at Container Terminals. *Algorithms* **2021**, *14*, 42. https://doi.org/10.3390/a14020042

Academic Editor: Angel A. Juan
Received: 6 December 2020
Accepted: 25 January 2021
Published: 28 January 2021

Publisher's Note: MDPI stays neutral with regard to jurisdictional claims in published maps and institutional affiliations.

1. Introduction

Seaports are the interface between various transport modes in the maritime supply chain. In 2019, the volume of global maritime containerized trade had tripled to 152 million TEU (Twenty-foot Equivalent Unit, the size of a standard container) from its value in 1997 [1]. Moreover, ship sizes have also tripled in the past 20 years, from an 8000 TEU capacity to around 24,000 TEU. This implies that, in addition to adjustments to the port's infrastructure and superstructure, container terminals have to substantially increase their efficiency in ship handling in order to keep unproductive berthing times as short as possible while container volumes that are handled during one ship call increase. Thus, the challenge for terminals is to handle a large number of containers within a very short period of time. Terminals can address this challenge by creating technical prerequisites (i.e., using more and higher-performance equipment) and by optimizing operational processes. While the use of more equipment entails correspondingly more investment and higher running costs, intelligent control of operational processes leads to more efficient cargo handling without additional costs. Therefore, it is reasonable to minimize the amount of necessary equipment and to coordinate operational processes.

Container handling requires a large number of process steps in the terminal. When a ship is berthed, Quay Cranes (QCs) unload the containers and set them onto waiting

Yard Trucks (YTs), which then transport them to the storage area. There, Rubber-Tired Gantry (RTGs) cranes lift the containers into the respective Yard Block (YB) for short-term storage until the container is picked up. The steps in the process of loading a ship run in the opposite direction. The processes are coupled because YTs are passive equipment and are not able to lift the containers themselves. As a result, waiting times and utilization of the respective equipment must be weighed against each other. In order to perform ship handling as quickly as possible and to reduce the waiting times of the QCs, it is preferable to use more YTs however, this leads to longer waiting times and lower utilization of YTs. Furthermore, using too many YTs leads to congestion and, therefore, to delays in ship handling [2]. The better the balance between these conflicting objectives, the more efficiently the terminal works.

There are several decision problems in the design and operation of container terminals, which strongly influence the efficiency of container handling. Figure 1 shows an overview of typical decision problems at container terminals.

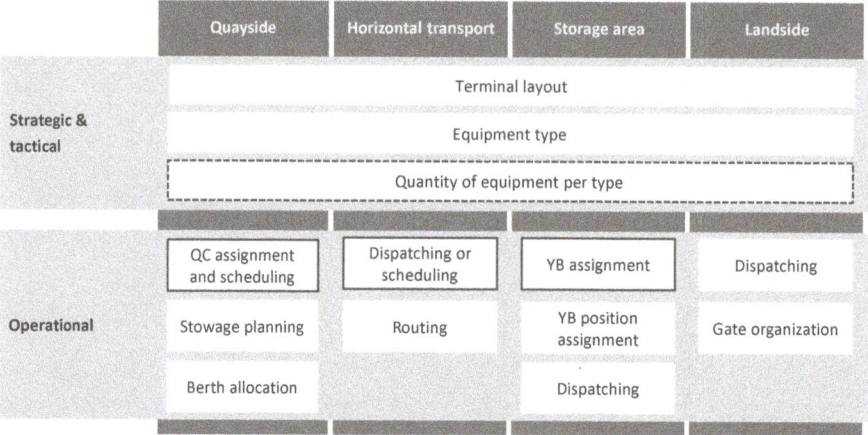

Figure 1. Decision problems at container terminals.

Decisions regarding the design of the terminal layout (e.g., location and size of the YBs) or the equipment that must be used and how much of it to procure have a rather long-term influence (refer to [3] for a recent overview). From a short-term perspective, on the quayside, decisions include berth allocation, stowage planning, and QC assignment and scheduling (refer to [4] for an overview). In horizontal transport, the decision problems are dispatching or scheduling (assigning vehicles and transport orders) and routing. Dispatching (assigning RTGs and storage orders), YB assignment, and YB position assignment are the primary decision problems in the storage area. On the land side, there are also questions of order assignment and gate control. Kizilay and Eliiyi [5] provide a recent overview of container terminal decision problems.

These decision problems influence each other [6]. For example, berth allocation directly influences the YB assignment and vice versa. The distances between the ship at the berth and the assigned YBs should be as short as possible, and at the same time, sufficient YBs should be assigned to a berth or QC. RTGs in the yard can typically move 15 containers within one hour, while QCs have a productivity of around 30 moves/h. Thus, at least two YBs (each being served by at least one RTG) have to be connected to one QC. Another example is the relationship between gate organization and dispatching in the yard: If the number of truck arrivals is regulated by a truck appointment system, then this also influences the number of handling orders for RTGs and thus affects dispatching [7]. These are just two examples of the numerous interactions between decision problems. Therefore, there is a risk that the overall solution will deteriorate if only one decision problem is optimized. Hence, it is necessary to combine the different related decision problems into a single integrated decision problem. Usually, the operations on the waterside are focused on due to the high costs related to the berth time of a ship. This means that the number of QCs, YTs, and RTGs as well as the integration of the handling processes need to be jointly considered to ensure efficient operations. Thus, this study analyzes a combination of QC assignment and dispatching, as well as YB assignment as shown with a dark frame around the respective boxes in Figure 1. Additionally, the dashed frame around the quantity of equipment per type indicates that the number of YTs used is modified.

Integrated decision problems covering QCs, YTs, and RTGs have been traditionally solved by formulating and solving a mathematical model. At first glance, this seems like a reasonable approach. However, this results in a very complex problem for which a solution is difficult to find and, especially under the real-time requirements of a container terminal, is almost impossible to solve in terms of computing power. Therefore, it is worthwhile stepping back and considering different methods, including the use of policies.

1.1. Literature Review on Integrated Decision Problems

There are two main approaches to addressing the operational decision problems of container terminals [8]. The first approach takes into account the complex dynamic environment of a container terminal. It typically uses priority rules, which are analyzed with the help of simulation models that can represent stochastic processes. Simulation models involving container terminals are reviewed in [9,10]. In the second approach, a simplified deterministic mathematical model is formulated. Either the model can be solved optimally for small instances, or an approximation can be found with the help of heuristics.

While the first approach is better suited to volatile processes at container terminals, simulation studies that aim to investigate several decision problems quickly become very complex [11]. The second approach also quickly reaches its limits. In this context, Zhen et al. [12] showed that the integrated QC and YT scheduling problem is non-deterministic polynomial-time hard, which means that the computing time required to optimally solve the problem is too long to be used in practice. To take advantage of both approaches, especially in order to investigate integrated decision problems that influence each other, the approach of combining simulation and optimization has been developed in recent years. He et al. [13] addressed integrated QC, YT, and RTG scheduling. They developed a mixed-integer programming model and proposed a simulation-based optimization method. Their optimization algorithm integrates genetic and particle swarm optimization algorithms. Cao et al. [14] aimed to schedule RTGs and YTs simultaneously in order to decrease the ship turnaround time. They introduced a multi-layer genetic algorithm to solve the scheduling problem and designed an algorithm-accelerating strategy. Castilla-Rodríguez et al. [15] focused on the QC scheduling problem: They integrated artificial intelligence techniques and simulation, combining an evolutionary algorithm with a simulation model to embed uncertainty. Kizilay et al. [16] studied the integrated problem of QC assignment and scheduling, YB assignment, and YT dispatching. They proposed a mixed-integer programming and constraint programming model and showed that the constraint programming model performed much better in terms of calculating time. Integrated quayside problems can also be investigated with other aims, such as saving costs and energy simultaneously [17] or exploring different modes of integration [18]. Sislioglu et al. [19] combined discrete event simulation, data envelopment analysis, and cost-efficiency analysis to investigate different investment alternatives based on the number of QCs, total length of a quay, YTs, and RTGs. They applied their model to 16 different scenarios but did not modify the operating policies. Furthermore, other research has combined different simulation paradigms to solve optimization problems at different decision levels. For example, in [20], a system-dynamic model was used to optimize the main parameters of a dry port, and in [21], a combination of system-dynamic and discrete-event simulation models was used. Kastner et al. [22] provide a literature overview of simulation-based optimization at container terminals. They focused on the covered problems, chosen meta-heuristics, and the shapes of the parameter configuration space in the respective publications. Similarly, Zhou et al. [23] present a summary of publications on the integration of simulation and optimization for maritime logistics. They classified five modes of integration according to the interaction of the two techniques.

Kastner et al. [24] proposed applying the Tree-structured Parzen Estimation (TPE) approach to scale the amount of utilized equipment in a simulation model. With the help of simulation-based optimization, only a subset of the experiments was executed. At the same time, a fine search grid (all equipment was scaled in step sizes of 1) enabled a very good approximation of the unknown optimum.

The presented study is an extension of [24]. The reviewed literature is expanded and updated. Previously, the three meta-heuristics TPE, Simulated Annealing (SA), and Random Search (RS) were used to scale the number of QCs and YTs. In this study, in addition, the number of YBs is alternated, and the coordination of equipment is varied by using different policies. This enrichment required several extensions of the simulation model and the parameter configuration space. In the new study, the number of QCs is considered to be fixed during an optimization run and a caching mechanism is implemented to speed up optimization. As a new meta-heuristic, Bayesian Optimization (BO) is introduced. The application of dispatching and other policies differentiates this publication from most of the previously mentioned publications. Previous works often directly search for near-optimal sequences of container handling tasks. For larger container terminals, terminal operating systems integrate the computed schedules of different equipment [25]. Smaller container terminals tend to use less complex IT solutions that lack automated scheduling methods, relying more on operational rules of thumb, such as dispatching policies [26]. This study presents a solution method that is applicable for these smaller container terminals. The simulation results describe the near-optimal combination of multiple decisions, such as the quantity of equipment, the dispatching policy, and other policies for a given situation. In this study, optimization plays a role that is very different from that in the above-mentioned scheduling methods. Several parameters, some of them categorical, some discrete, and some continuous, are adjusted in parallel. It is known from similar prior studies (e.g., [11]) that different parameters also affect each other. In this study, therefore, a multivariate optimization problem is solved.

1.2. Optimizing Objective Functions without Mathematical Optimization

The integration of several operational problems leads to many decisions that are made in parallel. In the presented study, the number of utilized resources is scaled, while, concurrently, different storage and equipment control policies are taken into account, potentially allowing for policy tuning. All of these parameters are optimized without a mathematical model. This section elaborates on the options that a simulator can choose from if no mathematical model is present but an optimum, or at least its approximation, is sought.

For simulation studies, a full factorial design is often used, where each parameter combination is tested by running a corresponding simulation experiment [27]. The parameter combination that performs best according to an objective function is then reported as the best known solution. In other words, it is the best available approximation of the unknown optimum. Such simulation studies do not include a mathematical model, and hence, the distance between the best approximation of the optimum and the optimum of the mathematical model cannot be reported.

A study that covers a full factorial design is only feasible for finite sets, such as categorical values or selected numerical values. Continuous parameters (e.g., real numbers) need to be restricted to a finite set of selected values. The search grid for such a study needs to be sufficiently fine (i.e., for natural numbers, few omissions within a given range; for real numbers, small step sizes are used) so that the optimum can be approximated well. For high-dimensional parameter configuration spaces, the combination of all concurrently varied parameters, at some point, becomes too large for exhaustive examination. This holds true for large simulation studies as well as for hyper-parameter optimization in machine learning. Furthermore, if all permissible values of a parameter are exhaustively examined, for real numbers, only an approximation for the optimal input parameter might be identified.

As soon as the combination of all varied parameters results in an amount of expensive simulation runs that could not be executed within a reasonable time frame, some of the simulation runs need to be skipped or simplified. If the goal of the study is to approximate an optimum, expensive simulation runs which are expected to result in a lower objective function value need to be avoided. Several approaches presented in the following paragraphs exist. However, if the simulation model is sufficiently complex, any approach might fail to identify the best approximated optimum in the set of feasible solutions.

One option to reduce computational time is to use a multi-fidelity approach [28]. With a low-fidelity simulation model, each parameter combination is evaluated. These results are used to identify promising parameter configurations, which are further examined with a high-fidelity simulation model. From that subset, the best solution can be determined. This approach requires the simulator to create two simulation models of a different fidelity. The low-fidelity simulation model requires special skills during creation as all important aspects need to be covered in the model because, otherwise, a promising parameter configuration for the high-fidelity simulation experiment may be omitted. At the same time, the processes must be sufficiently simplified to improve the required time for running the experiments.

An alternative option to reduce computational time is to maintain a computing budget, i.e., the total amount of computing resources that are available to approximate the optimal solution [29]. The initial experiments are randomly chosen from the parameter configuration space [30]. If, during the evaluation, a given parameter configuration is identified as having superior performance, more computing resources are invested to obtain a better picture of the corresponding objective function value. The longer the total observed time range for a given simulation model, the more that typically noisier sample statistics approximate the population parameters. AlSalem et al. [29] stated that this approach does not necessarily create optimal solutions, but solutions that are close to the optimum with a very high probability. Furthermore, in industry, such approximations often satisfy requirements [29]. Even if optimal input parameters are calculated for a given simulation model, the difference in performance might be of little practical relevance.

Another option to reduce computational time is to embed the simulation into an outer loop of optimization. The simulation model itself is regarded as a black-box function. If the optimization problem (i.e., the objective values derived from the simulation model) has some known structural properties, one might prefer to derive a simpler representation that enables optimization with other tools than simulation [31]. The optimization algorithm in the outer loop tests a subset of the feasible parameter configurations to approximate the optimum of the black-box function. This concept goes by many different names, such as "simulation optimization" [32], "simulation evaluation" [33], "simulation integrated into optimization" [34], and "simulation-based optimization" [23]. For cases in which a combinatorial optimization problem is solved, the term "simheuristic" has been coined [35]. This concept is the only combination of simulation and optimization that does not rely on maintaining an additional mathematical model [34]. If the simulation model is sufficiently complex, then the optimization algorithm can only consist of general guidelines for searching good (but not necessarily optimal) solutions. These general guidelines, which are applicable across research domains, are also referred to as meta-heuristics [36]. Meta-heuristics often start with several randomly drawn parameter configurations, and the first objective values that are obtained direct further search. A good meta-heuristic balances exploration and exploitation. During exploration, parameter configurations that are quite different from the previous samples are tested. During exploitation, well-performing parameter configurations are slightly altered to obtain an improved parameter configuration. After several iterations, a stopping criterion is reached, and the best solution found so far is returned as an approximation of the global optimum. For a guided search, a meta-heuristic needs to keep track of past evaluations. The large number of meta-heuristics reported in the literature stems from the fact that it is a non-trivial decision as to how to continue a search given a set of observations.

To the best of the authors' knowledge [37], and the authors' previous study [24] are the only ones that have used the simulation-based optimization approach at a container terminal for scaling the amount of several utilized resources. Kotachi et al. [37] simultaneously optimized the berth length, the number of QCs, the number of gates, the fleet size of YTs, the number of export and import rows, and the number of RTGs per row. The objective function balanced the throughput and the utilization, weighted by investment costs. While a high throughput was achieved with more resources, the weighted utilization ensured that no superfluous resources were added to the container terminal. Even though not all permissible realistic values were taken into account, the authors calculated 72,576 possible parameter combinations. They decided that these were too many to fully cover in a simulation study. They built an optimization framework that consisted of two stages: First, the interactions between resources were examined to determine the most promising sequence of resource optimization tasks. As seven different types of resources were checked, $7! = 5040$ possible permutations existed. Second, the gained sequence was utilized to optimize each resource one by one. The resources that were not yet optimized were selected according to stochastic sampling. Following the proposed optimization framework, the number of executed experiments could be reduced by 34% and it is stated that further enhancements are possible. In the following, some applicable ideas for such an optimization framework are explored.

1.3. Relationship between Hyper-Parameter Optimization and Simulation-Based Optimization

Identifying high-performing solutions for a given model is a typical research question in many fields of science. The speed of the necessary search process has increased since the advent of computers and the new possibility of automating tedious and complex computations. Complex computations often become quite resource-intensive and tend to contain a large number of parameters that can be varied. Each parameter configuration describes an alternative shape of the executed computation. For categorical parameters (i.e., an element of a finite set), the size of the parameter configuration space grows exponentially with every additional parameter. For continuous parameters (e.g., a range of real numbers), even for a single parameter, the search space is infinite. Therefore, for many applications, the parameter configuration reaches a size that is impossible or impractical to cover. Hence, scientists are forced to evaluate only a subset of all feasible parameter configurations. This search process is further complicated if the model contains stochastic components. Therefore, a single parameter configuration often needs to be tested several times before the resulting statistics reliably inform the scientist of the quality of a parameter configuration.

One field of science that faces similar difficulties is machine learning. Here, often learning algorithms that consist of many exchangeable components are optimized according to some metric. For neural networks, e.g., for the activation function, different mathematical functions can be inserted, the weights inside a neural network can be adjusted by different algorithms, the number of neurons for each layer can vary, etc. [38]. These decisions are referred to as hyper-parameters. They are usually considered to be constant during one experiment. It is a non-trivial problem to identify the best hyper-parameters for a given machine learning problem. Since machine learning pipelines often contain stochastic components, a repeated evaluation is often necessary.

The task of constructing and adjusting machine learning is so complex that, in some cases, randomly picking parameter configurations outperforms manual model calibration by scientists [39]. The authors explain these results by the higher resolution of the search grid and less wasting of the computational budget on the variation of parameters that have little or no impact on the final result. To support the expert in automating the search through a parameter configuration space, Hutter et al. [40] were the first to present an optimization procedure that can deal with numerical and categorical parameters in a problem-independent manner. Bergstra et al. [41] quickly followed with an alternative approach that they called TPE. A comparison between several data sets showed that the performance of such a hyper-parameter optimization technique varies with each setup [42–44]. This research topic is often referred to as hyper-parameter optimization and is the subject of active research and development [44–46].

In the past several years, many newly developed hyper-parameter optimization approaches have advanced the field. Studies such as [42–44] have empirically compared different meta-heuristics. This approach is the key to identifying characteristics of each meta-heuristic, which, in turn, can result in the recommendation of one meta-heuristic. Such an empirical approach is necessary because of the No Free Lunch Theorem (NFLT) in the optimization of black-box functions: One cannot determine the most successful optimization algorithm for an unseen problem [47]. This means that, for simulation-based optimization, a meta-heuristic that has worked well in one study might fail to lead to good approximations of the optimum for a different "problem", i.e., the black-box function that consists of a simulation model and an objective function. In machine learning, the black-box function can be understood as a combination of the learning algorithm and the data set on which it operates. Once one of the components is changed, it constitutes "an unseen problem" according to the NFLT.

As McDermott [48] elaborated, this claim might not be in harmony with observations from scientific literature as often, certain meta-heuristics tend to provide better results than others. Therefore, no published ranking of different optimization algorithms is guaranteed to be reproducible for other problem instances. However, when several optimization studies are considered together, the observed characteristics of each optimization algorithm (e.g., a meta-heuristic) should fit into the broader picture. Hence, a comparison study such as [42–44] or this publication contributes to these deeper insights.

This study uses simulation-based optimization on a multivariate optimization problem at a container terminal. As parameters, only categorical, discrete, and continuous value ranges are permissible. This makes it suitable for choosing policies, determining the amount of employed equipment, and defining policies that accept tuning parameters. The simulation model and the objective function together are treated as a black-box function that is repeatedly evaluated because of its stochasticity. The novelty of this optimization study is that meta-heuristics that have also been used in the context of hyper-parameter optimization are applied to a discrete event simulation model that models several integrated problems of a container terminal. As only meta-heuristics are deployed, the parameter configuration space and the simulation model can both be extended to represent additional complex integrated decisions with little effort. Alternative approaches that couple simulation and optimization require that both the simulation model and mathematical model remain aligned [34].

2. Materials and Methods

First, the simulation model is presented in Section 2.1. Then, the subsequently used meta-heuristics are presented in Section 2.2. Section 2.3 describes the method of identifying good parameter configurations for the simulation model. In this context, the objective function is presented.

2.1. Simulation Model

In the following, the created simulation model of the container terminal and its restrictions are presented. The discrete-event simulation model is implemented in Tecnomatix Plant Simulation and is based on the data of a real terminal. The layout of the terminal is shown in Figure 2.

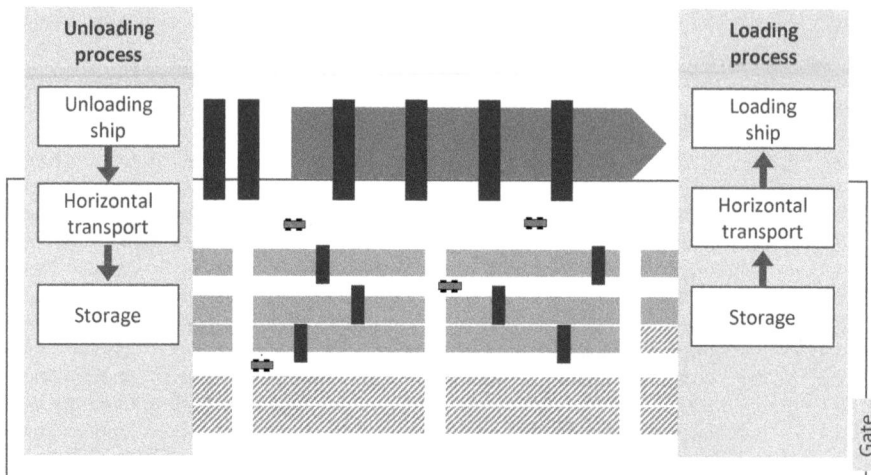

Figure 2. Layout and process illustration of the simulation model.

The terminal has a quay length of 800 m and a total of 20 YBs. The simulation model represents container handling between the quayside and container yard. As displayed in Figure 2, the specifics of the design of the land-side transport interface as well as the berths are not considered in detail. In this study, parallel handling of several ships is not modeled. Consequently, the simulation model of the container terminal is stressed by the arrival of a single ship. For this, 12 bays of the ship with a total of 4000 containers have to be handled. About half of them are import containers to be unloaded and the other half are export containers to be loaded. The container transport orders are pre-defined and contain details such as the origin and destination of the containers at the terminal and the availability time for handling in the yard or quayside by gantry cranes. To reduce the execution time of a simulation run, three variations for each parameter combination are generated before all experiments. Depending on the experiment, at least 3 and at most 6 QCs are available for loading and unloading the ship. The ship is unloaded and loaded bay by bay, whereby the QC always handles the entire bay that is assigned to it. Thus, the QC moves after the unloading of a bay and before the loading of the next bay. These bay changes are represented by a delay between the handling of two containers of the same QC. When fewer QCs are used for one ship, more bays are served by each QC.

In the simulation model, an average quayside handling rate of 30 containers per hour is assumed, which is represented by an expected handling frequency of 120 s by each QC. To model stochastic influences, a triangular distribution of the QC handling times is assumed with a minimum handling time of 80 s and a maximum value of 180 s. YTs carry out horizontal transport between the quay and yard. Since YTs are unable to lift containers themselves, the transfer between the QC and YT must be synchronized. The travel times of the YTs are determined by the distances between QCs and YBs, as specified by the terminal layout. For calculating the travel times, an average speed of 8.4 m/s is assumed for the YTs. By inserting a triangular distribution, stochastic influences are taken into account when calculating the travel times. The total number of YTs used per experiment is generated in the yard at the beginning of the simulation.

The inbound and outbound yard operations are performed by RTGs. For the simulation model, it is assumed that RTGs can handle an average of 15 containers per hour, which corresponds to an expected value of 240 s per handling. Deviations and irregularities in the process are modeled by a triangular distribution with a minimum handling time of 180 s and a maximum value of 420 s. For all experiments, at least two YBs are required for each active QC. Thus, it can be ensured that sufficient stowage space is available for the containers to be handled. Depending on the experiment, one of the two storage policies *random YB assignment* and *close YB assignment* is investigated with the simulation model. For the storage policy *random YB assignment*, containers from all active YBs can be transported to and from each of the QCs. In addition, import containers are randomly assigned to YBs, regardless of which QC is used for the unloading. All active YBs are ensured to be equally burdened as much as possible. The second storage policy is *close YB assignment*, which seeks to minimize the distance between QCs and YBs. YBs with the shortest possible distance for horizontal transport are assigned to every QC. The handling of containers only takes place between the defined QCs and YBs.

Furthermore, the two different dispatching policies *fixed QC-YT assignment* and *free QC-YT assignment* are implemented in the simulation model. In the first policy, *fixed QC-YT assignment*, a fixed number of YTs are assigned to each QC. This policy is typically used in practical terminal operations, as it is the simplest to apply. Every YT receives an attribute that assigns it to a specific QC. In the second dispatching policy, *free QC-YT assignment*, each YT can approach every QC. This policy is a modified version of the hybrid method from Schwientek et al. [11]. The next suitable job is chosen on the basis of the necessary driving time at the terminal and the waiting time of orders. The driving time and waiting time can be weighted differently for each experiment, controlled by the policy tuning parameter *Dispatching Weight*. For the selection of the next suitable order, each free YT inspects the next 20 orders. The order with the earliest availability time is determined. For the other 19 orders, the difference between the order's availability time and the earliest availability time is determined. Additionally, the required travel time to the start position of the respective order is calculated. Both values are multiplied by the intended weighting factor *Dispatching Weight* of the experiment. Finally, the results are added, and the order with the smallest sum is chosen by the YT. If no YT is available at the quay, the QCs have to wait. Otherwise, the containers can be loaded directly onto the YTs. Loaded YTs drive the containers to the defined YB. There, the YTs and containers are separated from each other. The same process steps for handling export containers occur in the reverse sequence of that described above.

2.2. Employed Meta-Heuristics

Meta-heuristics are used to approximate the best parameter configuration for the given simulation model described in the previous subsection. The corresponding process is depicted in Figure 3. First, the history H and the counter i are initialized as an empty set and 0, respectively. Since no prior observations are recorded in H, the meta-heuristic must select the experiment randomly. In the next step, the meta-heuristic suggests a parameter configuration $x^{(i)}$. If this is a previously unseen parameter configuration, a simulation experiment is executed and the fitness is calculated. Otherwise, from the previous experiment runs stored in H, the fitness value corresponding to $x^{(i)}$ is retrieved. In both cases, H is extended with the new value, and the meta-heuristic is set up with this H. After 50 evaluations, the results are reported, and the optimization study is completed. The history H is implemented with a global database that shares the history over several optimization runs independently from the employed meta-heuristic during the retrieval phase, which helps to reduce the wall time. The meta-heuristic is only set up with experiments that are previously suggested within the same optimization run to ensure the independence of each optimization run for the subsequent evaluation.

Without having executed any simulation experiments, the simulation model must be considered a black-box. It is, therefore, impossible to know which of a set of given meta-heuristics would lead to the best approximation. Since many meta-heuristics themselves have a stochastic component, even two different optimization runs of the same meta-heuristic can result in different approximations of the optimum. Hence, for a yet unknown simulation model, it is unpredictable whether the optimum will be approximated sufficiently well and, if so, which meta-heuristic will achieve this. Each meta-heuristic needs to empirically prove its applicability to a problem [48]. In this study, TPE was applied to a discrete event simulation model and compared with SA, BO, and RS. These meta-heuristics are introduced next.

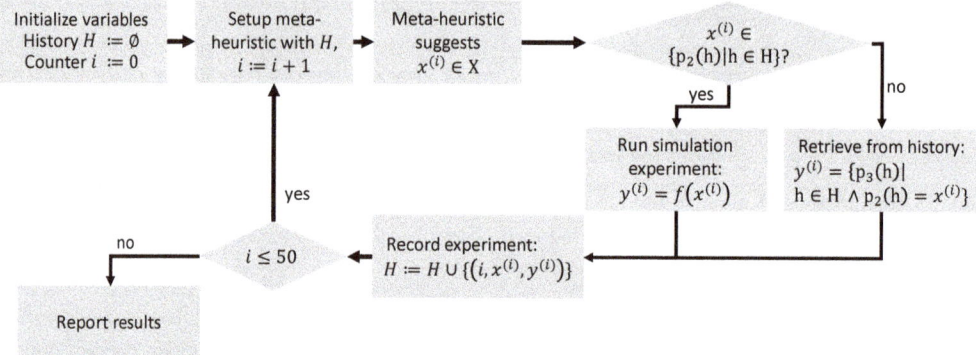

Figure 3. The optimization process.

2.2.1. Tree-Structured Parzen Estimator

TPE was developed to automate the search for a sufficiently well-performing configuration of a Deep Belief Network [41]. For a Deep Belief Network, parameters are either categorical variables (e.g., the decision whether to use pre-processed or raw data) or continuous variables (e.g., the learning rate). Integer values can be modeled as either categorical variables (the numbers are mere labels) or continuous variables that are rounded before further use. In addition, dependencies between variables exist: One variable determines the number of network layers and then each layer is configured on its own. Having the configuration of the third layer as part of a parameter configuration is only reasonable if the variable encoding the number of layers is set to at least three. Such a parameter is called a conditional parameter. To reflect the dependencies, this type of parameter configuration space is adequately represented as a tree. This requires specific meta-heuristics that support such a tree structure. The TPE approach has produced good benchmark results [42,49], and the initial paper is among the most cited publications on hyper-parameter optimization; at the time of writing, Scopus indicates that there are 939 citations.

The TPE models $p(y < y*)$, $p(x|y < y*)$, and $p(x|y \geq y*)$, where p denotes a probability density function (short: density), y is a point evaluation of the model, and x is a parameter configuration. The first density $p(y < y*) = \gamma$ is a fixed value (e.g., 0.15 was used in the first publication) set by the experimenter, and $y*$ is altered to fit the set value of γ for each iteration. The other two densities can be summarized as $p(x|y)$: The probability that a certain parameter configuration has been used, given a desired point evaluation value. Typically, TPE is formulated to find a minimum and, therefore, $p(x|y < y*)$ describes the density of parameters that have shown better results, whereas $p(x|y \geq y*)$ describes the density of the parameters that have led to poorer performance. As the true densities are unknown, they need to be estimated based on the obtained evaluations in each iteration. For each categorical parameter, two probability vectors are maintained and updated: Given the prior vector of probabilities $p = (p_1, ..., p_N)$, with each probability p_i for $i \in 1, ..., N$ representing one category, the posterior vector elements are proportional to $N \cdot p_i + C_i$, where C_i counts the occurrences of choice i in the recorded evaluations so far. An example is depicted in Figure 4a. The estimator for the better-performing parameters (the top 15%) and that for the worse-performing parameters (the bottom 85%) are calculated based on the observations already recorded. For each continuous parameter, two adaptive Parzen estimators are used. Given a prior probability density distribution determined by the experimenter, with each point evaluation of the parameter configuration space with the help of the simulation model and the objective function, the densities are further approximated. An example is depicted in Figure 4b. The parameter choices of the better- and worse-performing models are used to create the respective densities. In each iteration, the model consisting of the two densities is used to select the next parameter configuration x to evaluate. To achieve this, several parameters x are sampled from the promising distribution $p(x|y < y*)$. The parameter configuration x with the greatest expected improvement is chosen. This criterion is positively correlated with the ratio $p(x|y < y*)/p(x|y \geq y*)$ [41]. In Figure 4, this is referred to as ratio. The criterion favors the parameter configuration that has a high probability of leading to small evaluation values and a low probability of obtaining large evaluation values for the minimization problem at hand. After the parameter configuration has been evaluated by running the experiment and calculating the objective function value, the probability estimators are updated. For this publication, the reference implementation [49] in version 0.2.5 (the newest at the time of conducting the study), provided by the original authors, was chosen. As the prior distribution, a uniform distribution was chosen.

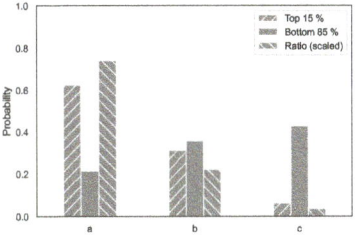
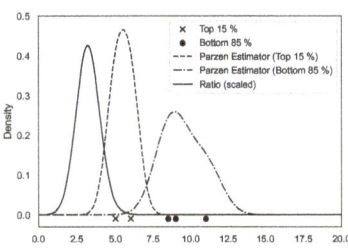

(**a**) Categorical variable. (**b**) Continuous variable.

Figure 4. The Tree-structured Parzen Estimation (TPE) uses the ratio of better- and worse-performing parameters to guide the search. In the example on the left, the categorical variable takes one of the three values "a", "b", and "c". For the continuous variable, in the example on the right the values range from 0 to 20.

2.2.2. Simulated Annealing

SA is a meta-heuristic that is applicable to both combinatorial and multivariate problems [50], the latter of which is relevant for this optimization study. For this publication, the implementation of [49] in version 0.2.5 (the newest at the time of conducting the study) was used. This version of SA works on the tree structure presented in Figure 5. The tree structure requires some specific adjustments of the algorithm documented in [51]. The default initialization values of the implementation were used.

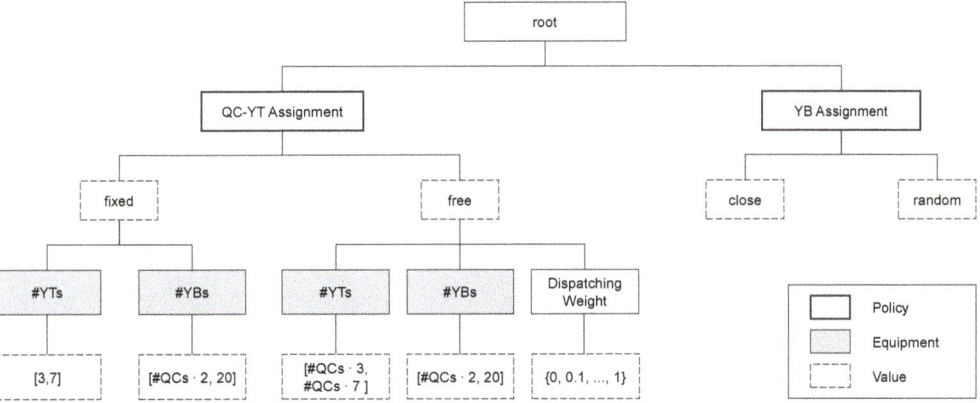

Figure 5. The parameter configuration space in tree form.

2.2.3. Bayesian Optimization

BO, also referred to as Gaussian process optimization, aims to minimize the expected deviation [52]. The response surface (i.e., the objective function values for given parameter configurations), including the uncertainty about the result, is estimated. For this publication, the implementation from [53] in version 1.2.6 (the newest at the time of conducting the study) was used. Since this procedure does not support tree-structured parameter configuration spaces, two simplifications are made. First, the numbers of YTs for the *QC-YT Assignment fixed* and *free* are grouped together. The parameter value ranges as in the right branch. If the fixed assignment is chosen, the number of YTs is divided by the number of QCs, and the result is rounded to the closest integer. Second, the dispatching weight is always set, even if it is not interpreted by the simulation model. During the initialization of an optimization run, five random experiments are conducted before BO takes over and guides the search.

2.2.4. Random Search

RS serves as a baseline. According to the NFLT, for some optimization problems, meta-heuristics perform worse than RS. It is crucial to identify meta-heuristics that misguide the search (e.g., by becoming stuck in local optima). For this publication, the implementation of [49] in version 0.2.5 (the newest at the time of conducting the study) was used, which is capable of sampling from a tree-structured parameter configuration space.

2.3. Optimization Procedure

The optimization procedure is written as an external program that encapsulates the simulation. First, the simulation model is initialized with the parameter configuration to examine. After the simulation runs for one experiment are finished, the output of the simulation model is read. The communication between the two programs is realized through the COM-Interface. The output values of the simulation model are inserted into the objective function, which determines the fitness of a given solution. This optimization procedure is described in more detail in the following.

2.3.1. Parameter Configuration Space

During initialization, each parameter of the parameter configuration is set as a global variable in the simulation model. The interpretation of one global variable in the simulation model can depend on another global variable. For example, the parameter *#YTs* is interpreted as the number of YTs for each QC for a fixed QC-YT assignment, but it is interpreted as the number of YTs for all QCs for a free QC-YT assignment. The parameter *Dispatching Weight* is the weight for the travel time and ranges from 0 to 1 in steps of 0.1. The weight for the availability time for handling is deduced by calculating $1 - dispatching\ weight\ for\ travel\ time$. This parameter is only used for a free QC-YT assignment. Although setting this uninterpreted parameter does not harm the simulation experiment, the recorded observations for the meta-heuristic are flawed. This is because the meta-heuristic might use a record that includes the uninterpreted parameter to guide further search, despite the lack of any effect, which might guide the search process in the wrong direction.

In Figure 5, the parameter configuration space is depicted in its tree form. It is dependent on the number of QCs, which can be either 3, 4, 5, or 6. Each case is considered to be independent and requires optimization.

The presented tree is used for TPE, SA, and RS. For BO, a vector representation is derived whereby each of the parameters *QC-YT Assignment, YB Assignment, #YTs, #YBs,* and *Dispatching Weight* are represented by one dimension of this vector. The different interpretation of *#YTs* is alleviated by varying the value over the range from $\#QCs \cdot 3$ to $\#QCs \cdot 7$ and, in the case of a fixed assignment, dividing by *#QCs* and then rounding that value to the closest integer value before using it to parameterize the simulation model. The parameter *Dispatching Weight* can theoretically take any value between 0 and 1. To make use of the caching mechanism, only steps of 0.1 were permitted in this study.

2.3.2. Objective Function

After a simulation run is executed, the objective function is invoked to calculate the fitness for the given parameter configuration. The objective function needs to reflect the fact that the unloading and loading process needs to be fast, while at the same time, resources are only added if they are needed. Therefore, the following objective function was developed (based on [37]):

$$fitness = \frac{\widetilde{t_{ship}}}{t_{ship}} \cdot \frac{50 \cdot \#QCs \cdot util_{QCs} + 5 \cdot \#RTGs \cdot util_{RTGs} + \#YTs \cdot util_{YTs}}{50 \cdot \#QCs + 5 \cdot \#RTGs + \#YTs} \tag{1}$$

The left factor of the multiplication reflects the inverted relative makespan of the ship. t_{ship} is the time used to unload and load the ship. As an approximation of $\widetilde{t_{ship}}$, prior to the optimization runs, 100 random samples are drawn from the parameter configuration space, and the makespan for the ship is measured. This normalization process centers the left factor to around 1 and ensures that it remains in proportion to the right factor. The shorter the makespan, the larger the left factor becomes.

The right factor of the multiplication is the weighted utilization. $\#QCs$ refers to the number of QCs, $\#RTGs$ is the number of RTGs and, therefore, also the number of YBs, and $\#YTs$ is the number of trucks. $util_{<equipment>}$ refers to the ratio of the time for which the equipment has been working to the overall makespan. When summarizing these utilization values to one factor, weights are assigned according to the investment costs. It is assumed that a QC is 50 times more expensive than a truck, and the cost of an RTG is 10% of a QC [37]. The higher the equipment utilization (with a special focus on expensive equipment), the larger the right factor becomes.

2.3.3. Structure of Optimization Study

For each scenario (3, 4, 5, and 6 QCs) and meta-heuristic (TPE, BO, SA, and RS), 50 optimization runs are executed. This allows for gaining insights on the reproducibility of the optimization results using meta-heuristics. Each optimization run consists of 50 experiments. For each experiment, 30 simulation runs are executed. The results of each simulation run vary slightly due to stochastic factors. These are implemented by drawing handling times from random distributions, as described in Section 2.1.

3. Results and Discussion

In the following, the experimental results of the optimization study are analyzed. Then, the solutions found for the different meta-heuristics are compared and discussed.

3.1. Preparatory Study

The objective function (see Equation (1)) requires $\widetilde{t_{ship}}$, the median of t_{ship}. The population parameter is only known after exhaustive coverage of the parameter configuration space, which must be avoided for an optimization study. As a replacement, a sample estimate must suffice. For this purpose, for each scenario, 100 parameter configurations were sampled randomly, and the corresponding simulation experiments were run. For each of these simulation experiments, the makespan of the ship was recorded. The median, minimum, and maximum of the makespan are noted in Table 1. The values in the median column are used as $\widetilde{t_{ship}}$ for the respective scenario.

Table 1. Makespan of the ship for 100 randomly drawn experiments.

Number of QCs	Makespan (in Hours, Rounded)		
	Median	Minimum	Maximum
3	61	51	158
4	49	39	161
5	47	38	160
6	35	29	161

Table 1 shows that the median and minimum both decrease as the number of QCs increases. The median shows that using 4 QCs instead of 3 results in a reduction of ca. 20% in the makespan. By doubling the number of QCs from 3 to 6, the performance can be increased by ca. 57%. This is not true for the maximum, which remains nearly constant at around 160 h. Furthermore, the difference between 4 and 5 QCs is rather small. This can be explained by the fact that in the simulation model, 12 bays of the ship are handled. With 4 QCs, each QC handles exactly 3 bays. With 5 QCs, 3 QCs are responsible for 2 bays each, and 2 QCs are responsible for 3 bays each. Thus, 3 QCs complete the container handling task earlier, but the makespan is based on the QC that finishes last.

3.2. Observations from All Experiments

In the scope of the optimization study, 40,000 experiments in total were evaluated. For each scenario (3, 4, 5, and 6 QCs) and each meta-heuristic (TPE, BO, SA, and RS), 50 optimization runs were executed, each consisting of 50 experiments. This set of experiments covers many randomly chosen experiments (e.g., RS or initialization phase of any of the meta-heuristics) in addition to experiments that are biased by the manner in which each meta-heuristic works during its search process. This overview, which omits the search process, provides some insights into the characteristics of the simulation model.

For each experiment, among others, the makespan, as well as the utilization of the equipment, is measured. The utilization is the arithmetic mean of the working time of all equipment of its respective type. In Figure 6, the utilization of YTs, YBs, and QCs is shown. Due to the larger investment costs, the weighted utilization is closest to the QCs. The median of the utilization of the YTs is the lowest. Since a YT cannot lift a container itself, it must wait for a gantry crane (either QC or RTG) to load or unload the YT. High utilization of QCs and YBs is only possible if enough YTs are available, which inevitably results in lower utilization on the YT side. As the utilization of YTs is assigned a rather small weight in the fitness function, the lower utilization rate carries no relevant weight.

In Figure 7, the difference between the maximum and minimum working times of the YTs for each experiment that used the global assignment policy is depicted. This is an indicator of how effectively the work is shared among YTs. As a general tendency, it can be seen that more QCs lead to less statistical scattering.

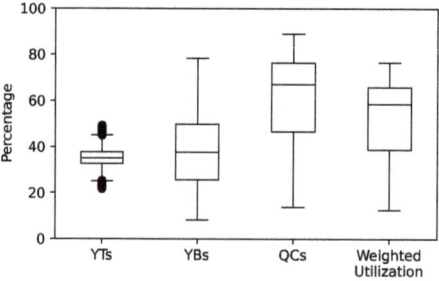

Figure 6. The utilization of the equipment over all experiments.

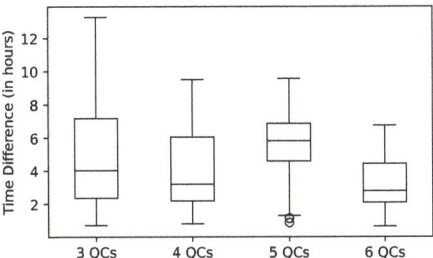

Figure 7. Time difference between maximum and minimum working times of YTs.

3.3. Approximated Optima

Both the preparatory study and the first screening of all executed experiments created first impressions of the underlying processes. Within the parameter configuration tree, there are exceptionally low-performing solutions. This raises the following question: Which of the meta-heuristics identified the best parameter configuration? To determine this, for each optimization run, the experiment with the highest fitness is extracted. During optimization, both TPE and BO select the next experiment with the greatest expected improvement. Hence, in contrast to SA, after a phase of exploitation (i.e., minor adjustments), a phase of exploration (i.e., larger changes) can follow. RS is the most extreme example since exploitation is never sought. This, in turn, means that the best result of an optimization run can appear at any position of the sequence of recorded experiments.

In Figure 8, the four meta-heuristics TPE, BO, SA, and RS are compared for each scenario with 3, 4, 5, and 6 QCs. Consistent with the preparatory study, the results for 5 QCs are far worse than those of all other scenarios. Each of the meta-heuristics shows outliers in at least three of the boxplots, which indicates the importance of stochastic influences during the search process. There is no clear ranking among the meta-heuristics. For 3 QCs, BO performs considerably worse than the other three meta-heuristics. These results are similar for 4 and 5 QCs, although with less severity. This is especially interesting since, for 6 QCs, BO produces the highest median. Over the first three scenarios, RS and SA have very similar performances, and for 6 QCs, SA has the worst median, with outliers in both directions. TPE performs very well in the first three scenarios, providing many of the best solutions with few outliers that are substantially worse. For 6 QCs, the median of TPE is much lower than that of BO. However, in two instances, BO arrived at substantially lower-performing solutions.

The differences between meta-heuristics were examined statistically. A significance level of $\alpha = 0.01$ was chosen for the whole study and corrected for each test using Bonferroni correction. To make general statements regarding the meta-heuristics, all scenarios (different numbers of QCs) are agglomerated. The large number of outliers for some of the meta-heuristics precludes the assumption of a normal distribution and requires a nonparametric approach. Hence, a Kruskal–Wallis H test was employed. The test statistic of $H = 31.303$ leads to $p \ll 0.005$. Hence, the null hypothesis that the four groups stem from a single population is rejected. In a posthoc Nemenyi's test for pairwise comparison, only TPE was significantly different from the other meta-heuristics. In other words, BO and SA are not significantly different from RS. The comparison of descriptive statistics (as the reader can approximate from Figure 8) shows the superiority of TPE in this study.

The wide range of approximated optima and the large difference between meta-heuristics are indicators of the complexity of the simulation model. The parameter configurations of all optima are more closely examined in the following. The meta-heuristics always determine that the fixed assignment of YTs to QCs leads to an inferior performance compared with pooling. Furthermore, in all instances, the pairing of each QC with its closest YBs performs better than delivering each container to a randomly chosen YB. In contrast to these parameters, the parameter *Dispatching Weight* shows no clear interpretable results.

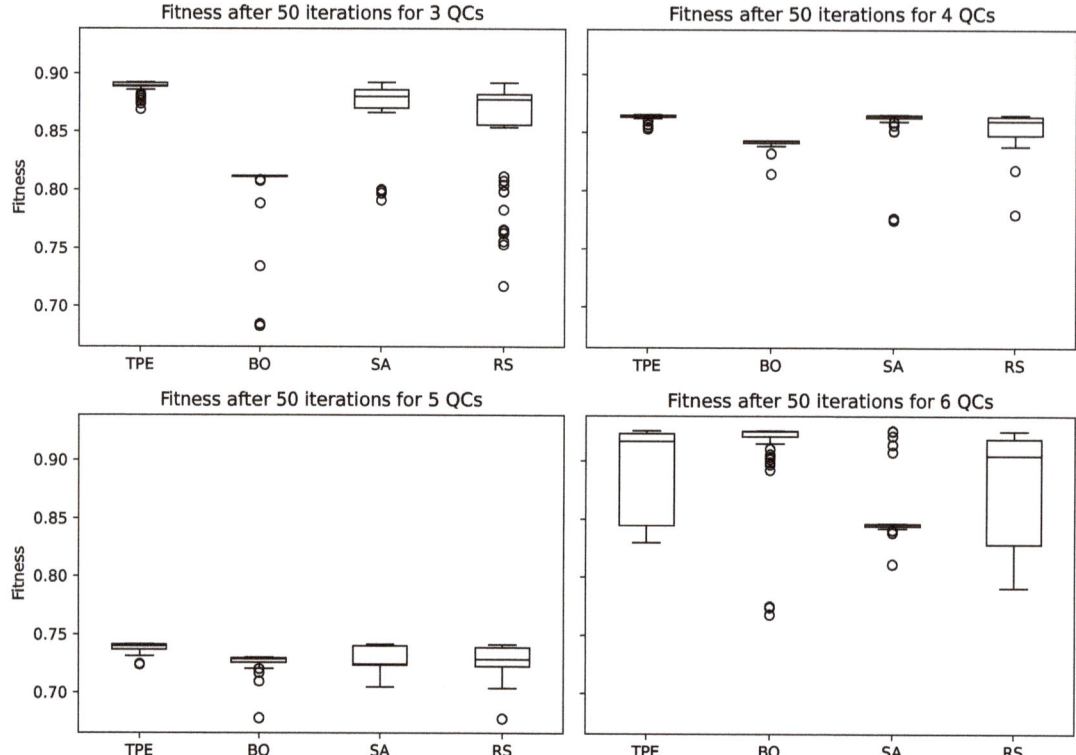

Figure 8. The approximated optima for each scenario and each meta-heuristic.

In Figure 9, the frequencies of specific numbers of YBs for 3, 4, 5, and 6 QCs are depicted. A small number of YBs creates a bottleneck in the yard, while having too many YBs leads to a low utilization of each YB as well as longer travel paths of the YTs. The fewer YBs are used, the shorter the traveled paths, the higher the probability that an unloading job and a loading job can be combined. The number of used YBs is often a multiple of the number of QCs. This can be explained by the rather conservative transportation job assignment policy in place, which is designed to avoid traffic jams but rather postpones a job.

In Figure 10, the number of YTs per QC for each scenario is presented. The large number of outliers to the right can be explained by the rather small impact of the number of trucks on the weighted utilization and, therefore, on the objective function.

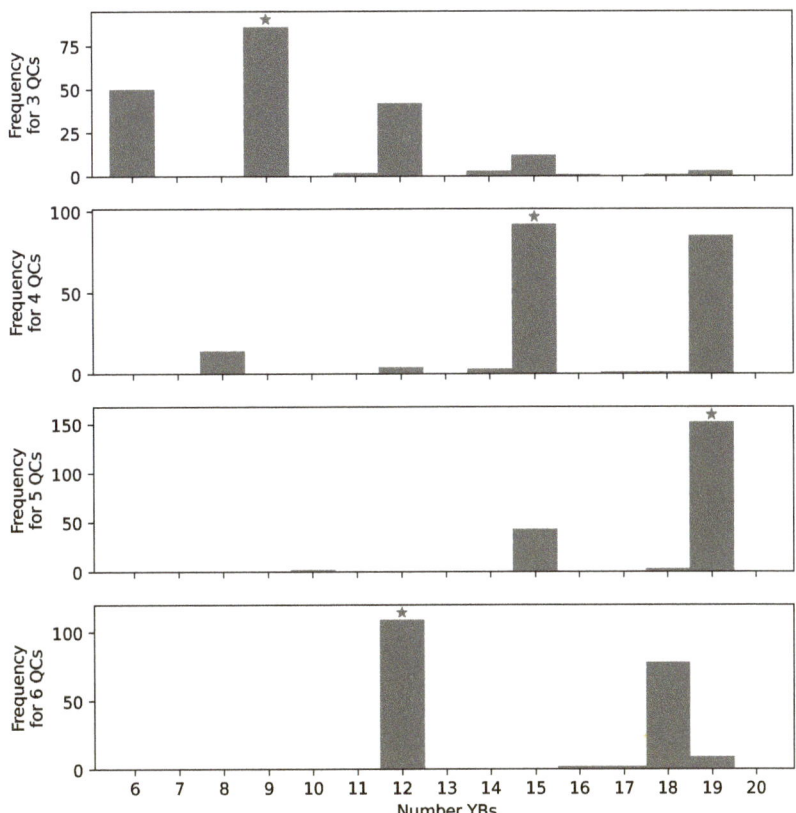

Figure 9. The number of YBs in the set of approximated optima. The parameter value that leads to the best objective function value over all optimization runs is marked with an asterisk.

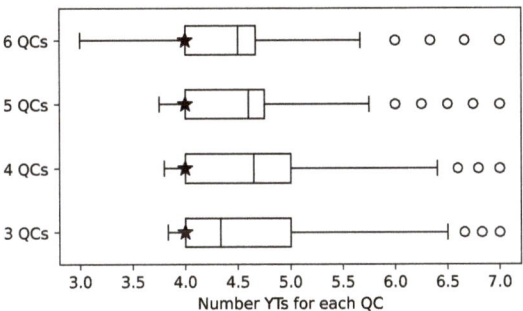

Figure 10. The number of YTs in the set of approximated optima. The parameter value that leads to the best objective function value over all optimization runs is marked with an asterisk.

In this study, as in [24], TPE exhibits the most robust behavior. Of the 200 optimization runs, TPE never returns the worst approximation of the optimum. For some scenarios, other meta-heuristics provide better medians of approximations. At the same time, only TPE is significantly different from RS when the data are agglomerated over all scenarios.

These observations provide evidence that TPE is an appropriate approach. For an explicit recommendation, meta-analyses of several publications using the same meta-heuristics are required in future to accumulate such evidence.

In comparison with [37], this study shows an alternative approach to calibrating the quantity of equipment used in different functional areas of a container terminal. In addition, policies are selected and tuned (if the policy accepts a parameter). The approach of Kotachi et al. [37] requires all parameters to be at least on an ordinal scale since the mutation is defined as changing a parameter one level up or down. For categorical parameters that can take more than two values, there is no order. For continuous parameters, this mutation makes it necessary to define a step size. The approach presented in this study also discretizes the parameter *Dispatching Weight* to the the set $\{0, 0.1, ..., 1\}$. However, this is performed to enable caching to speed up the optimization study. All of the meta-heuristics used support continuous parameters, which might be of interest for future optimization studies.

4. Conclusions

This study provides an approach to solving integrated decision problems at container terminals. Earlier studies have often approached such problems by using a mathematical model that aims to optimize the schedule of jobs. Depending on the concept, sometimes the schedule is determined hours before the actual execution of a job, which is an appropriate approach in rather deterministic environments. Another common approach in the literature is to define a policy that is evaluated using a simulation study. The design of experiments—e.g., a full-factorial design with a coarse grid—leads to either very large simulation studies or a selection of experiments biased by the researcher's beliefs. These shortcomings of optimization alone and manually designed large simulation studies are partly overcome by the presented simulation-based optimization approach. This approach uses simulation to evaluate the quality of a given solution, and only in this way can the dynamics of real systems be properly represented. Simulation-based optimization allows for the possibility of illustrating these dynamics, providing an approximated solution to the problem without maintaining a separate mathematical model. Therefore, further decision problems can be integrated into the simulation model and the parameter configuration space with little effort.

The authors showed the transferability of meta-heuristics, which originate from the domain of machine learning or have been successfully applied in that area. These methods could be used to optimize discrete event simulation models. A special focus was placed on discrete and continuous parameters that were potentially interdependent. Several optimization runs guided by different meta-heuristics were executed and with a restricted computational budget, promising parameter configuration ranges were identified. This publication focused on examining the results of different optimization runs. For this purpose, the numbers of QCs, YTs, and YBs were modified during different experiments. At the same time, different dispatching policies, as well as QC-YB assignment policies, were investigated. Furthermore, different allocation policies of YBs were applied. In this study, the approximated optima suggest that the pooling of YTs was preferable to free allocation. Furthermore, a YB assignment close to the QCs was considered better than a random one. By choosing more QCs, the number of bays to be served per QC decreased. Thus, a reduction of the makespan could be achieved. A doubling of the number of QCs from 3 to 6 led to a reduction of the makespan by 57%.

Due to the NFLT, it is not clear whether these empirical results can be generalized to future studies that use simulation-based optimization. The applicability of meta-heuristics such as TPE or BO needs to be demonstrated by further optimization studies, potentially with various simulation models, different objective functions, and additional meta-heuristics or different fine-tuning of the same meta-heuristic for comparison.

Author Contributions: Conceptualization, M.K., A.S., C.J., and N.N.; methodology, M.K., A.S., and N.N.; software, M.K., A.S., and N.N.; validation, M.K.; formal analysis, M.K.; investigation, N.N.,

M.K.; resources, N.N.; data curation, M.K.; writing—original draft preparation, M.K., A.S., and N.N.; writing—review and editing, A.S., C.J.; visualization, N.N., M.K.; supervision, C.J.; project administration, M.K. All authors have read and agreed to the published version of the manuscript.

Funding: This research received no external funding.

Data Availability Statement: The data presented in this study are openly available in zenodo at 10.5281/zenodo.4473251.

Conflicts of Interest: The authors declare no conflict of interest.

Abbreviations

The following abbreviations are used in this manuscript:

BO	Bayesian Optimization
NFLT	No Free Lunch Theorem
QC	Quay Crane
RS	Random Search
RTG	Rubber-tired Gantry Crane
SA	Simulated Annealing
TPE	Tree-structured Parzen Estimator
TEU	Twenty-foot Equivalent Unit
YB	Yard Block
YT	Yard Truck

References

1. UNCTAD. *Review of Maritime Transport*; United Nations: New York, NY, USA, 2020.
2. Karam, A.; Eltawil, A.; Harraz, N. Simultaneous assignment of quay cranes and internal trucks in container terminals. *Int. J. Ind. Syst. Eng.* **2016**, *24*, 107–125. [CrossRef]
3. Gharehgozli, A.; Zaerpour, N.; de Koster, R. Container terminal layout design: transition and future. *Marit. Econ. Logist.* **2020**, *22*, 610–639. [CrossRef]
4. Bierwirth, C.; Meisel, F. A follow-up survey of berth allocation and quay crane scheduling problems in container terminals. *Eur. J. Oper. Res.* **2015**, *244*, 675–689. [CrossRef]
5. Kizilay, D.; Eliiyi, D.T. A comprehensive review of quay crane scheduling, yard operations and integrations thereof in container terminals. *Flex. Serv. Manuf. J.* **2020**, *1*, 1–42. [CrossRef]
6. Chen, L.; Langevin, A.; Lu, Z. Integrated scheduling of crane handling and truck transportation in a maritime container terminal. *Eur. J. Oper. Res.* **2013**, *225*, 142–152. [CrossRef]
7. Lange, A.K.; Schwientek, A.K.; Jahn, C. Reducing truck congestion at ports—Classification and trends. Digitalization in Maritime and Sustainable Logistics. In *Proceedings of the Hamburg International Conference of Logistics (HICL)*; Jahn, C., Kersten, W., Ringle, C.M., Eds.; Epubli: Berlin, Germany, 2017; pp. 37–58.
8. Cordeau, J.F.; Legato, P.; Mazza, R.M.; Trunfio, R. Simulation-based optimization for housekeeping in a container transshipment terminal. *Comput. Oper. Res.* **2015**, *53*, 81–95. [CrossRef]
9. Dragovic, B.; Tzannatos, E.; Park, N.K. Simulation modelling in ports and container terminals: Literature overview and analysis by research field, application area and tool. *Flex. Serv. Manuf. J.* **2017**, *29*, 4–34. [CrossRef]
10. Angeloudis, P.; Bell, M.G. A review of container terminal simulation models. *Marit. Policy Manag.* **2011**, *38*, 523–540. [CrossRef]
11. Schwientek, A.K.; Lange, A.K.; Jahn, C. Effects of terminal size, yard block assignment, and dispatching methods on container terminal performance. In *Winter Simulation Conference 2020*; Bae, K.H., Feng, B., Kim, S., Zheng, Z., Roeder, T., Thiesing, R., Eds.; IEEE Press: New York, NY, USA, 2020.
12. Zhen, L.; Yu, S.; Wang, S.; Sun, Z. Scheduling quay cranes and yard trucks for unloading operations in container ports. *Ann. Oper. Res.* **2016**, *122*, 21. [CrossRef]
13. He, J.; Huang, Y.; Yan, W.; Wang, S. Integrated internal truck, yard crane and quay crane scheduling in a container terminal considering energy consumption. *Expert Syst. Appl.* **2015**, *42*, 2464–2487. [CrossRef]
14. Cao, P.; Jiang, G.; Huang, S.; Ma, L. Integrated simulation and optimisation of scheduling yard crane and yard truck in loading operation. *Int. J. Shipp. Transp. Logist.* **2020**, *12*, 230–250. [CrossRef]
15. Castilla-Rodríguez, I.; Expósito-Izquierdo, C.; Melián-Batista, B.; Aguilar, R.M.; Moreno-Vega, J.M. Simulation-optimization for the management of the transshipment operations at maritime container terminals. *Expert Syst. Appl.* **2020**, *139*, 112852. [CrossRef]
16. Kizilay, D.; Eliiyi, D.T.; van Hentenryck, P. Constraint and mathematical programming models for integrated port container terminal operations. Integration of Constraint Programming, Artificial Intelligence, and Operations Research. *Lect. Notes Comput. Sci.* **2018**, *10848*, 344–360. [CrossRef]

17. Karam, A.; Eltawil, A.; Hegner Reinau, K. Energy-Efficient and Integrated Allocation of Berths, Quay Cranes, and Internal Trucks in Container Terminals. *Sustainability* **2020**, *12*, 3202. [CrossRef]
18. Karam, A.; Eltawil, A. Functional integration approach for the berth allocation, quay crane assignment and specific quay crane assignment problems. *Comput. Ind. Eng.* **2016**, *102*, 458–466. [CrossRef]
19. Sislioglu, M.; Celik, M.; Ozkaynak, S. A simulation model proposal to improve the productivity of container terminal operations through investment alternatives. *Marit. Policy Manag.* **2019**, *46*, 156–177. [CrossRef]
20. Muravev, D.; Rakhmangulov, A.; Hu, H.; Zhou, H. The introduction to system dynamics approach to operational efficiency and sustainability of dry port's main parameters. *Sustainability* **2019**, *11*, 2413. [CrossRef]
21. Muravev, D.; Hu, H.; Rakhmangulov, A.; Mishkurov, P. Multi-agent optimization of the intermodal terminal main parameters by using AnyLogic simulation platform: Case study on the Ningbo-Zhoushan Port. *Int. J. Inf. Manag.* **2020**, *1*, 102133. [CrossRef]
22. Kastner, M.; Pache, H.; Jahn, C. Simulation-based optimization at container terminals: A literature review. In *Digital Transformation in Maritime and City Logistics, Proceedings of the Hamburg International Conference of Logistics (HICL)*; Jahn, C., Kersten, W., Ringle, C.M., Eds.; Epubli GmbH: Berlin, Germany, 2019; pp. 111–135. [CrossRef]
23. Zhou, C.; Li, H.; Liu, W.; Stephen, A.; Lee, L.H.; Peng Chew, E. Challenges and opportunities in integration of simulation and optimization in maritime logistics. In Proceedings of the 2018 Winter Simulation Conference, Gothenburg, Sweden, 9–12 December 2018, pp. 2897–2908. [CrossRef]
24. Kastner, M.; Nellen, N.; Jahn, C. Model-based optimisation with tree-structured parzen estimation for container terminals. In *ASIM 2019 Simulation in Produktion und Logistik 2019*; Putz, M., Schlegel, A., Eds.; Wissenschaftliche Scripten: Auerbach, Germany, 2019; pp. 489–498.
25. Singgih, I.K.; Jin, X.; Hong, S.; Kim, K.H. Architectural design of terminal operating system for a container terminal based on a new concept. *Ind. Eng. Manag. Syst.* **2016**, *15*, 278–288. [CrossRef]
26. Schwientek, A. Abilities of the Used Terminal Operating Systems: Personal Conversation, 2012–2013.
27. Barton, R.R. Simulation experiment design. iN Proceedings of the 2010 Winter Simulation Conference, Piscataway, NJ, USA, 5–8 December 2010; pp. 75–86. [CrossRef]
28. Li, H.; Zhou, C.; Lee, B.K.; Lee, L.H.; Chew, E.P.; Goh, R.S.M. Capacity planning for mega container terminals with multi-objective and multi-fidelity simulation optimization. *IISE Trans.* **2017**, *49*, 849–862. [CrossRef]
29. Al-Salem, M.; Almomani, M.; Alrefaei, M.; Diabat, A. On the optimal computing budget allocation problem for large scale simulation optimization. *Simul. Model. Pract. Theory* **2017**, *71*, 149–159. [CrossRef]
30. Ho, Y.C.; Zhao, Q.C.; Jia, Q.S., Eds. *Ordinal Optimization: Soft Optimization for hard Problems*; Springer: New York, NY, USA, 2007.
31. Xu, J.; Huang, E.; Chen, C.H.; Lee, L.H. Simulation optimization: A review and exploration in the new era of cloud computing and big data. *Asia-Pac. J. Oper. Res.* **2015**, *32*, 1–34. [CrossRef]
32. Fu, M.C.; Glover, F.W.; April, J. Simulation optimization: A review, new developments, and applications. In Proceedings of the 2005 Winter Simulation Conference, Orlando, FL, USA, 4–7 December 2005; pp. 351–380.
33. Figueira, G.; Almada-Lobo, B. Hybrid simulation–optimization methods: A taxonomy and discussion. *Simul. Model. Pract. Theory* **2014**, *46*, 118–134. [CrossRef]
34. Hanschke, T.; Krug, W.; Nickel, S.; Zisgen, H. VDI 3633 Blatt 12 - Simulation und Optimierung. In *VDI-Handbuch Fabrikplanung und -Betrieb-Band 2: Modellierung und SIMULATION*; Beuth: Berlin, Germany, 2016.
35. Juan, A.A.; Faulin, J.; Grasman, S.E.; Rabe, M.; Figueira, G. A review of simheuristics: Extending metaheuristics to deal with stochastic combinatorial optimization problems. *Oper. Res. Perspect.* **2015**, *2*, 62–72. [CrossRef]
36. Chopard, B.; Tomassini, M. *An Introduction to Metaheuristics for Optimization*, 1st ed.; Natural Computing Series; Springer International Publishing: Cham, Switzerland, 2018.
37. Kotachi, M.; Rabadi, G.; Seck, M.; Msakni, M.K.; Al-Salem, M.; Diabat, A. Sequence-based simulation optimization: An application to container terminals. In Proceedings of the 2018 IEEE Technology & Engineering Management Conference, Piscataway, NJ, USA, 27 June–1 July 2018; pp. 1–7. [CrossRef]
38. Géron, A. *Hands-on Machine Learning with Scikit-Learn, Keras, and TensorFlow: Concepts, Tools, and Techniques to Build Intelligent Systems*, 2nd ed.; O'Reilly UK Ltd.: Newton, MA, USA, 2019.
39. Bergstra, J.; Bengio, Y. Random search for hyper-parameter optimization. *J. Mach. Learn. Res.* **2012**, *13*, 281–305.
40. Hutter, F.; Hoos, H.H.; Leyton-Brown, K. Sequential model-based optimization for general algorithm configuration. In *Learning and Intelligent Optimization*; Coello, C.A.C., Ed.; Springer: Berlin/Heidelberg, Germany, 2011; pp. 507–523.
41. Bergstra, J.; Bardenet, R.; Bengio, Y.; Kégl, B. Algorithms for hyper-parameter optimization. In Proceedings of the 25th Annual Conference on Neural Information Processing Systems, Granada, Spain, 12–14 December 2011; Volume 24, pp. 2546–2554.
42. Eggensperger, K.; Feurer, M.; Hutter, F.; Bergstra, J.; Snoek, J.; Hoos, H.; Leyton-Brown, K. Towards an empirical foundation for assessing Bayesian optimization of hyperparameters. In Proceedings of the NIPS Workshop on Bayesian Optimization in Theory and Practice, Lake Tahoe, NV, USA, 10 December 2013; pp. 1–5.
43. Madrigal, F.; Maurice, C.; Lerasle, F. Hyper-parameter optimization tools comparison for multiple object tracking applications. *Mach. Vis. Appl.* **2019**, *30*, 269–289. [CrossRef]
44. Yang, L.; Shami, A. On hyperparameter optimization of machine learning algorithms: Theory and practice. *Neurocomputing* **2020**, *415*, 295–316. [CrossRef]

45. Gijsbers, P.; LeDell, E.; Poirier, S.; Thomas, J.; Bischl, B.; Vanschoren, J. An open source AutoML benchmark. In Proceedings of the 6th ICML Workshop on Automated Machine Learning, Long Beach, CA, USA, 14–15 June 2019.
46. Akiba, T.; Sano, S.; Yanase, T.; Ohta, T.; Koyama, M. Optuna: A next-generation hyperparameter optimization framework. In Proceedings of the 25th ACM SIGKDD International Conference on Knowledge Discovery & Data Mining, Anchorage, AK, USA, 4–8 August 2019; pp. 2623–2631. [CrossRef]
47. Wolpert, D.H.; Macready, W.G. No free lunch theorems for optimization. *IEEE Trans. Evol. Comput.* **1997**, *1*, 67–82. [CrossRef]
48. McDermott, J. When and why metaheuristics researchers can ignore "No Free Lunch" theorems. *Metaheuristics* **2019**, *1*, 67. [CrossRef]
49. Bergstra, J.; Yamins, D.; Cox, D.D. Making a science of model search: hyperparameter optimization in hundreds of dimensions for vision architectures. In Proceedings of the 30th International Conference on Machine Learning, Atlanta, GA, USA, 16–21 June 2013; pp. 115–123.
50. Kirkpatrick, S.; Gelatt, C.D.; Vecchi, M.P. Optimization by simulated annealing. *Science* **1983**, *220*, 671–680. [CrossRef]
51. Bergstra, J. Simulated Annealing. Available online: https://github.com/hyperopt/hyperopt/blob/master/hyperopt/anneal.py (accessed on 29 December 2020).
52. Močkus, J. On Bayesian methods for seeking the extremum. In *Optimization Techniques IFIP Technical Conference*; Spring: Berlin/Heidelberg, Germany, 1975; pp. 400–404.
53. The GPyOpt authors. GPyOpt: A Bayesian Optimization Framework in Python. Available online: http://github.com/SheffieldML/GPyOpt (accessed on 29 December 2020).

algorithms

MDPI

Article

Simulation-Optimization Approach for Multi-Period Facility Location Problems with Forecasted and Random Demands in a Last-Mile Logistics Application

Markus Rabe [1], Jesus Gonzalez-Feliu [2], Jorge Chicaiza-Vaca [1,*] and Rafael D. Tordecilla [3,4]

[1]   IT in Production and Logistics, Faculty of Mechanical Engineering, TU Dortmund, 44227 Dortmund, Germany; markus.rabe@tu-dortmund.de
[2]   Centre de Recherche en Intelligence et Innovation Managériales, Excelia Business School, 17000 La Rochelle, France; gonzalezfeliuj@excelia-group.com
[3]   IN3—Computer Science Department, Universitat Oberta de Catalunya, 08018 Barcelona, Spain; rtordecilla@uoc.edu
[4]   School of Engineering, Universidad de La Sabana, 53753 Chia, Colombia; rafael.tordecilla@unisabana.edu.co
*   Correspondence: jorge.chicaiza@tu-dortmund.de

check for
updates

Citation: Rabe, M.; Gonzalez-Feliu, J.; Chicaiza-Vaca, J.; Tordecilla, R.D. Simulation-Optimization Approach for Multi-Period Facility Location Problems with Forecasted and Random Demands in a Last-Mile Logistics Application. *Algorithms* 2021, 14, 41. https://doi.org/10.3390/a14020041

Academic Editor: Alberto Policriti

Received: 14 December 2020
Accepted: 24 January 2021
Published: 28 January 2021

Publisher's Note: MDPI stays neutral with regard to jurisdictional claims in published maps and institutional affiliations.

Abstract: The introduction of automated parcel locker (APL) systems is one possible approach to improve urban logistics (UL) activities. Based on the city of Dortmund as case study, we propose a simulation-optimization approach integrating a system dynamics simulation model (SDSM) with a multi-period capacitated facility location problem (CFLP). We propose this integrated model as a decision support tool for future APL implementations as a last-mile distribution scheme. First, we built a causal-loop and stock-flow diagram to show main components and interdependencies of the APL systems. Then, we formulated a multi-period CFLP model to determine the optimal number of APLs for each period. Finally, we used a Monte Carlo simulation to estimate the costs and reliability level with random demands. We evaluate three e-shopper rate scenarios with the SDSM, and then analyze ten detailed demand configurations based on the results for the middle-size scenario with our CFLP model. After 36 months, the number of APLs increases from 99 to 165 with the growing demand, and stabilizes in all configurations from month 24. A middle-demand configuration, which has total costs of about 750,000€, already locates a suitable number of APLs. If the budget is lower, our approach offers alternatives for decision-makers.

Keywords: hybrid modeling; system dynamics; facility location problems; Monte Carlo simulation; automated parcel lockers; last-mile delivery

1. Introduction

Last-mile logistics (LML) is known as the least efficient and most complex part of the supply chain. LML activities have negative impacts on pollution and traffic congestion in urban areas [1]. The growth of e-commerce activities has increased the number of individual home deliveries, thus driving up LML flows. Improving the efficiency of LML in urban areas through research is an important driver for the success of e-commerce and helps to reduce the negative externalities associated with urban logistics (UL).

An automated parcel locker (APL) is a potential solution to LML challenges. In our current work, we analyze the use of APLs such as packstations or locker boxes as a promising alternative to improve UL activities [2]. An APL is a group of electronic lockers with variable opening codes. APLs can be used by different consumers whenever it is convenient for them. APLs are located near consumers' homes, workplaces, and train stations, where online shoppers deliver or ship packages. The costs of home delivery and the related risk of missed delivery are likely to be higher compared APL systems. Online shoppers are likely to use APLs more often in the future [3]. Third-party logistics providers such as DHL, InPost, Norway Post, UPS, or Amazon continue to invest in APLs to gain a competitive advantage [3].

The general overview of experiences with APLs is presented in [1,4]. APLs have several advantages, such as less traffic in city centers, out-of-hours deliveries, fewer kilometers and stops, and cost reductions for e-retailers and delivery companies [5]. Unattended delivery could reduce the number of failed deliveries [4,6,7]. In addition, the use of APLs also offers environmental benefits, such less pollutant emissions [8]. Furthermore, online shoppers are free to choose any pickup time for their parcels, and they can use it as both a delivery and a collection point to return unsatisfactory items. However, APLs have some disadvantages, such as limited payment flexibility in situ, limited storage space, and susceptibility to crime or vandalism [6].

Despite the advantages of the APL concept, from a scientific point of view this strategy has not been discussed sufficiently in the field of LML [9]. Urban parcel deliveries need to be studied in more detail. Most current research shows that the simulation of system dynamics (SD) applied in the LML field [10] is almost completely missing. In the available publications, local visions are adopted without a systemic or holistic perspective. Most of these did not take into account the different viewpoints of stakeholders, processes, interactions, and others [7,11]. Furthermore, for online buyers, the location of APLs is important to decide on their use [6,7]. Many studies have focused on analyzing the savings potential of using APLs, but have not addressed network design issues such as their number and review the associated installation costs. In this paper, we focus on a challenging and appropriate approach to analyze a number of APL configurations in an uncertain demand environment.

Different methods can be used for decision support in UL [1,12], such as empirical approaches, statistical analyses, or integrated computer science models and algorithms, to name a few. As for the last category of methods, researchers use simulation and optimization (SO) techniques as separate approaches in the field of operational research to solve complex problems [13]. On the one hand, exploring the behavior of systems and estimating their response to various environmental changes is a main purpose of using simulation [14]. On the other hand, optimization seeks to solve logistic problems, minimize total costs of ownership, or maximize profit. However, in real complex systems there are very specific properties that make it almost impossible to address the complexity of the problem with only one specific approach. Therefore, it is better to develop models that reflect the complexity of real systems and combine different modeling approaches. This type of combination is called a hybrid modeling approach [15]. By combining different modeling approaches, a hybrid model could provide a more comprehensive and holistic view of the system and a useful approach to understanding complexity. Moreover, according to the authors of [16] a good model is the one that is not only solved with a relevant method (and has an internal coherence and robustness proven), but also the one that represents the reality it aims to relate to in a satisfactory way with respect to the stakeholders that will use it and the decisions it involves. Given that, hybrid methods allow firstly for involving different capabilities, as they result of mixing different methods (so taking the advantages of each involved method). Second, hybrid methods can highlight synergies between the involved methods, as well as complements, aiming at a better representation of a reality [17].

This paper deals with the case of the city of Dortmund, which is located in the federal state North Rhine-Westphalia, Germany. With a population of about 600,000 people, it is the seventh largest city in Germany and the 34th largest city in the European Union. Based on the case study, we propose an SO approach as a hybrid model that integrates a system dynamics simulation model (SDSM) with a multi-period capacitated facility location problem (CFLP). We propose this integrated model as a decision support tool for future APL implementations as a last-mile distribution scheme. The paper is structured as follows. First, we use an SDSM to understand the behavior of the components of APL systems with respect to the specific customers and characteristics of the city of Dortmund. A planning horizon of three years (divided into months) is considered. Second, the problem is modeled as a multi-period CFLP. Taking into account the needs to be satisfied by the users, the goal is to find the minimum number of APLs to be installed per month within the time horizon. Several scenarios from the SDSM are considered and solved, taking into account different estimates for the requirements. Third, the performance of the associated solutions in a stochastic environment is evaluated using a Monte Carlo simulation. Finally, the conclusions present possible future work and applications.

2. Related Work

2.1. System Dynamics Modeling

The System Dynamics (SD) methodology was developed by Jay W. Forrester [18]. SD was originally introduced to facilitate the understanding of industrial processes. SD is used as a methodological approach to explain the effects of decisions in complex dynamic systems. The SD approach emphasizes time functions [19,20]. SD Models undergo constant interaction, continuous questioning, testing, and refinement. Based on the feedback concepts of control theory, the SD methodology generates the dynamic behavior of the associated model. The feedback loop structure of systems is represented by causal loop diagrams (CLD) [19,21]. A feedback loop contains two or more causality-related variables that are self-contained. The variable relationships in the loop can be either positive or negative. A positive relationship means that when one variable increases, the other one increases, too. In a balanced relationship, the change in the variables is inverse. The stock and flow diagram (SFD) is the underlying physical structure of the system. The SFD is normally structured according to the CLD. The stock (level) represents the state of the system and the flow (rate) is changed by decisions based on the state of the system. The stock and flow structure (including feedback) of a system determines the quantitative modes of behavior that the system can adopt. For the development of an SD model, the work in [19] presents a modeling process with the following steps: (i) problem analysis, (ii) system conceptualization, (iii) model formulation, (iv) simulation and verification, and (v) policy analysis and improvement. Figure 1 illustrates the SDSM process.

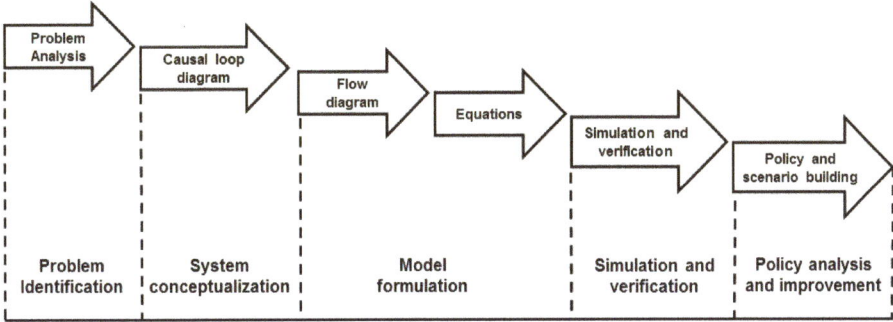

Figure 1. Steps to build an system dynamics simulation model (SDSM) based on the work in [19].

In the context of logistics, some studies show the application of SD to LML activities. In [22], the authors analyzed the decisions and interdependencies between customers, retailers, and suppliers using an SD model from an economic perspective. In [23], the authors applied an SD approach to model interdependencies of decisions by various stakeholders and their impact on city logistics. In [24], the authors presented a specific SD application in UL operations. They also used an SD model in [25] to understand customer behavior from an LML perspective. Although modeling efforts are important in urban logistics [12,26], the simulation seems to be still in the development phase [10] . The most popular simulation approaches remain multi-agent approaches [10,27] . While SD is still preliminary in its applications for urban freight distribution, it has great potential because it can take into account the complexity of the dynamics and heterogeneity of the systems [23].

2.2. Facility Location Problems

Facility location determination is a critical strategic business decision. There are several factors that determine facility location, including competition, costs, and associated impacts. The facility location decision has a profound impact on tactical and operational operations. For dealing with this strategic decision, the Facility Location Problem (FLP) was introduced to the field of operations research in the 1960s [28] and was initially called the Plant Location Problem.

FLPs consist of determining the optimal location for one or more facilities to serve a range of demand points. The importance of the optimal location depends on the nature of the problem in terms of the constraints and optimality criteria considered for the site [29]. FLPs are useful for determining the location of facilities such as hospitals, fire stations, bus stops, train stations, truck terminals, gas stations, blood bank centers, retail stores, neighborhoods, libraries, parks, post offices, airports, and landfills. The FLP can be seen as a generalization of the vehicle routing problem with fixed costs for the installation of facilities. An exhaustive review and discussion of the FLPs is provided in [30].

In a basic formulation, the FLP consists of a number of potential plant locations at which a plant can be opened and a number of demand points that must be served. The aim is to determine what subset of facilities needs to be opened in order to minimize the total costs of delivering goods to customers plus the sum of the facility opening costs. A simple example of a classic FLP instance is shown in Figure 2, where each customer (blue circle) is assigned to the nearest open facility (red square) via an active connection.

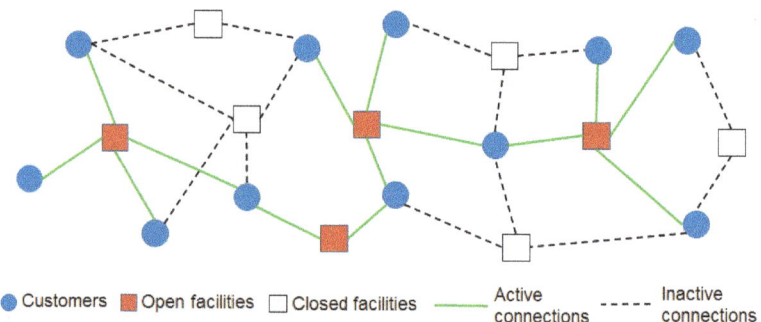

Figure 2. Illustrative example of the classical FLP based on the work in [31].

One of the most frequently investigated discrete location problems is the uncapacitated facility location problem (UFLP). The UFLP is the problem of determining the best location for a given facility—or the best locations for a given group of facilities—given some limitations on the environment in which it can be placed. This contrasts with the capacitated FLP, where facilities limit the number of customers they can serve. In the uncapacitated version, there is no such limitation. Some applications of FLP in UL context are presented in [31–38].

2.3. Monte Carlo Simulation

Monte Carlo simulation (MCS) generates distributions of possible result values. By using probability distributions, variables can have different probabilities of different outcomes occurring. Probability distributions are a suitable way to describe the uncertainty in variables of a risk analysis. During an MCS process, values are randomly selected from input probability distributions. Each set of samples is called an iteration, and the result of that sample is recorded. MCS conducts this hundreds or thousands of times, and the result is a probability distribution of possible outcomes. In this way, MCS provides a much more complete prediction of what may happen because it also delivers the probability that it will happen [39].

Many quantitative problems in science, engineering, and finance are solved today with MCS techniques. We list some important application areas, such as industrial engineering and operations research, physical processes, economics and finance, computer-based statistics and parallel computing, adaptive Monte Carlo Algorithms, spatial processes, and quasi Monte Carlo [40]. The MCS has been applied to last mile logistics in the real-world, which depends on many external random factors. This is especially true for last-mile deliveries. Challenging factors include—but are not limited to—traffic, weather, and the size of individual orders. To this end, MCS has found great use in assessing the risk and reliability of supply chains.

3. Integrated Simulation-Optimization Approach

Hybrid models play an important role in most real-world systems. Multiple perspectives can be obtained, each of which can answer a different important question. For answering the range of questions that can be asked with respect to a system, a combined set of model types can be the answer. Hybrid methods can bring more comprehensive and efficient estimations of a reality by enhancing the synergies among different methods and giving the suitable output for decision-makers [41]. One of the main goals of the SO method as a hybrid model is to efficiently address both the optimization and the uncertainty. An overview of the application of SO methods in designing resilient supply chain networks is presented in [42]. There are many ways to combine simulation and optimization, and the appropriate design depends strongly on the properties of the problem. The guideline 3633.12 [43] by the German Association of Engineers (Verein Deutscher Ingenieure (VDI)) provides a classification for different combinations of simulation and optimization in terms of sequential and hierarchical combination, which has been in detail elaborated by the Arbeitsgemeinschaft Simulation (ASIM) in Germany [44]. A sequential combination assumes that either simulation or optimization is completed before the other one can be executed. Within a hierarchical combined approach that can be called several times during the overall execution. Moreover, the details of the main classifications of various SO combinations are described in [13]. According to their classifications, we consider an analytical model improvement approach, where simulation is used to improve the model results, either by refining its parameters or by extending them, e.g., by considering different scenarios. In this context, the SDSM, based on an SO concept for APLs presented in [45], provides a suitable methodology to determine the behavior of the parameters in our multi-period capacitated FLP model. A well-proven SO approach to solve this kind of problems is provided by simheuristic algorithms [46,47].

In particular, our approach consists of the following steps, which are shown in Figure 3: (i) for each district, we use the SDSM to generate an estimate of expected demand; (ii) for different scenarios, each scenario being defined by a different level of demand (e.g., lower than expected, as expected, or higher than expected), solve the associated CFLP model; and (iii) use a Monte Carlo simulation to evaluate the solutions obtained in the previous step when used in a stochastic environment. Here, we assumed that the demand per district is uncertain and follows a known probability distribution, with the aim of comparing total costs with the reliability.

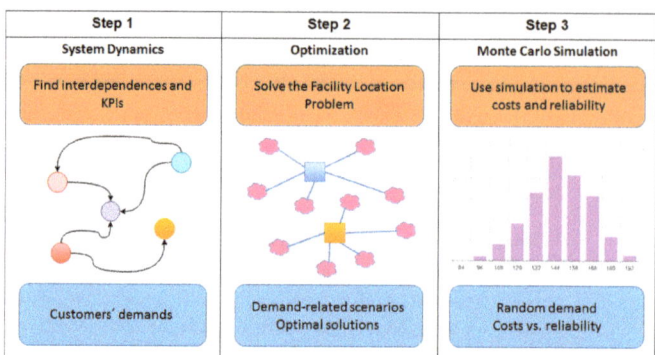

Figure 3. Schema of the integrated simulation-optimization approach.

4. Application in the City of Dortmund

This paper deals with the case of the city of Dortmund, which is divided into 62 districts, codified from 000 to 960. Figure 4 shows the map of the city of Dortmund with its respective districts.

Figure 4. The map of city of Dortmund with its codified districts.

4.1. System Dynamics Simulation Model

We propose an SDSM for APL as a UL delivery scheme. The SDSM is designed to understand the behavior of components of APL systems, and it will be used as a decision support for future implementations. To develop an SD model, we followed the steps shown in Figure 1.

4.1.1. Problem Identification

E-commerce does not necessarily mean the absence of physical shops, but rather an evolution in the way retailers carry out orders. For this reason, e-commerce has led to an increase in innovative combinations of physical and digital solutions, resulting in different ways of preparing, distributing, and collecting orders from customers [48].

Examples include home delivery, collection points, and APLs. We focus on understanding APL systems as a UL delivery scheme in the context of e-commerce and evaluating its components over time.

4.1.2. System Conceptualization

From a qualitative point of view, we use an SDSM to understand the behavior and interdependencies of the components of APL systems. From the existing literature on APLs (mainly based on case studies and field data), we define the main components that have an impact on the system. Following SD standard procedures [19], we use the software tool Vensim to create the causal-loop and stock-flow diagrams. Figure 5 describes the main APL system components that third-party logistics service providers will need to consider for future APL applications.

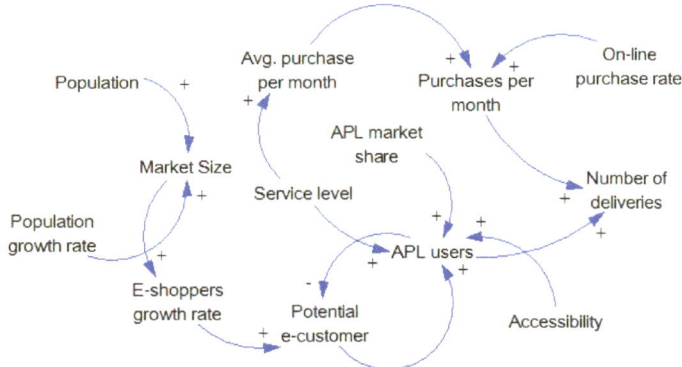

Figure 5. The automated parcel locker (APL) system causal-loop diagram.

The CLD describes that the market size is positively influenced by the population and the population growth rate. The potential number of e-customers is positively influenced by the e-shoppers growth rate and balanced by the number of APL users. In turn, the number of deliveries is positively reinforced by purchases per month and number of APL users. In turn, the purchases per month are positively reinforced by the average purchases per month and the online purchase rate.

4.1.3. Model Formulation

From a quantitative perspective, we present the evaluation of the APL components. Based on the CLD, we built the SFD, as shown in Figure 6. First, the variables of market size, potential e-customers, purchases per month, and APL users are defined as stocks (squared). Then, population growth rate, e-shoppers growth rate, online purchase rate, and APL market growth rate are defined as flows. Finally, population, accessibility, service level, average purchase per month, APL market share, and number of deliveries are auxiliary variables. The main output in this model is the number of deliveries, which are used as input values in the FLP model.

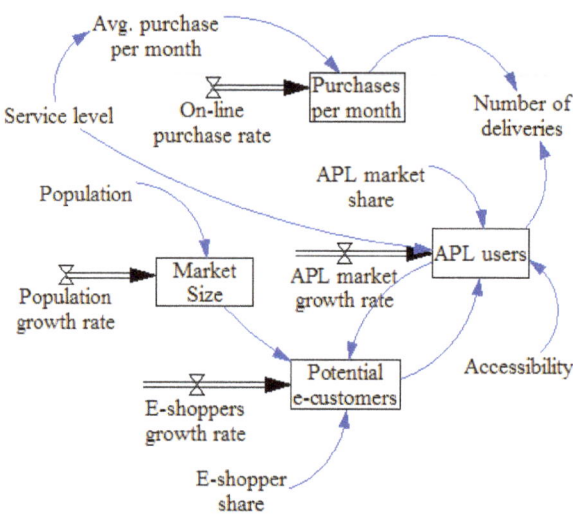

Figure 6. The APL systems stock-flow diagram.

4.1.4. Simulation and Verification

We apply the SDSM based on public data of the city of Dortmund and using the e-commerce trends in the German context. Taking into account the volatility of the e-commerce sector, the SDSM evaluates the system components of APL for a planning horizon of three years (divided into 36 months). Table 1 shows the components used in the SDSM application and their values.

Table 1. List and characteristics of variables used on the SDSM of the APL systems

Parameter	Definition	Initial Values
Population	Number of inhabitants in city of Dortmund	602,566 inhabitants
Population growth rate	Factor	0.02/12 (%) per month
Market Size	Population×Population growth rate	Population
Service level	Factor	90 (%)
Accessibility	Factor	70 (%)
Potential e-customers	(Market Size×E-shopper share-APL users) × E-shoppers growth rate	Market Size× E-shopper share
E-shoppers growth rate	Factor	0.2/12 (%)
E-shoppers share	Factor	50 (%)
APL market share	Factor	15 (%)
Avg. purchase per month	Constant×Service level	3 units per month
On-line purchase rate	Factor	10 (%)
Purchases per month	Avg. purchase per e-customer× On-line purchase rate	Avg. purchase per month
APL users	(Potential e-customers×APL market share× APL market growth rate)× (Service level×Accessibility)	Potential e-customers ×APL market share
Number of deliveries	APL users×Purchases per month	0 Units

4.1.5. Policy Analysis and Scenario Building

Table 2 shows the significant changes in the e-shoppers rate to build the scenarios. We consider Scenario 1 (S1), Scenario 2 (S2), and Scenario 3 (S3) with increasing rates of e-shoppers.

Table 2. Value changes to develop the scenarios.

Variable	S1	S2	S3
E-shoppers rate	50%	60%	70%

4.2. Multi-Period Facility Location Problem

The FLP is a well-known optimization challenge where the typical goal is to find the minimum costs and location of facilities that must be open to meet customer requirements, either deterministically [30] or stochastically [31,49]. If routing decisions are also included, the FLP turns into the so-called location routing problem [50,51]. In general, FLPs are classified either as capacitated or uncapacitated. The former refers to the case where the facilities have a known limit to the demand they can meet. The latter is the case where the service capacity of each facility exceeds the total demand of customers. Figure 7 illustrates the capacitated FLP (CFLP) for the APL network in the city of Dortmund. Here, each district is a potential APL location (yellow square) and each APL is connected to each other in the APLs configuration (dashed lines). These connections are used to calculate the distance matrix between districts.

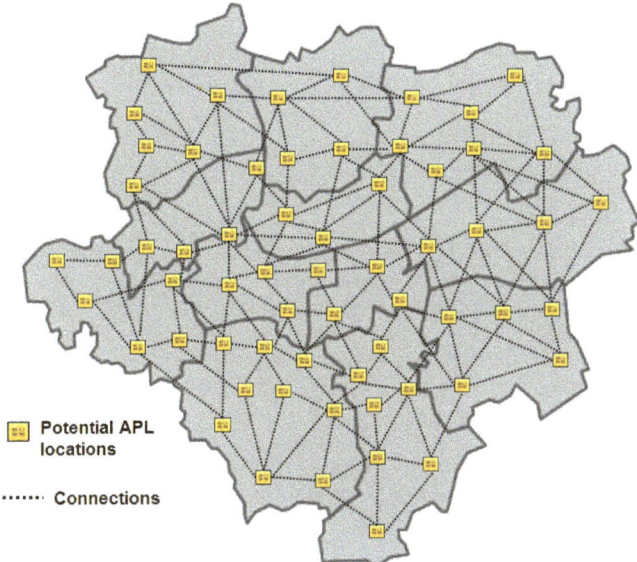

Figure 7. Illustrative CFLP for APLs in the city of Dortmund.

A multi-period CFLP is taken into account in our work. Decisions made in a given period affect future periods over a time horizon of T. In particular, as demand is expected to increase in future periods, we assume that whenever an APL is opened within a period $t \in T$, it must remain open until the end of the time horizon, i.e., for all $t' \in T : t' > t$. Similarly, third-party logistics providers indicate that a minimum percentage of $m \in (0,1)$ of total installed capacity must be used. Therefore, with the set I of nodes representing all districts in the city, each district $i \in I$ could contain no, one, or more APLs, each with a known capacity $a_i > 0$. Similarly, each district $j \in I$ has an aggregated demand in the period $t \in T$, $d_{jt} > 0$. For two districts $i,j \in I$, the unit costs of assigning an APL located in the district i to a customer located in the district j is $c_{ij} > 0$. Similarly, the costs of opening an APL in district $i \in I$ during the period $t \in T$ is indicated as $f_{it} > 0$. In this context, the binary variable x_{ijt} takes the value 1 if customers in the district $j \in I$ are assigned to an APL in the district $i \in I$ during the period $t \in T$; otherwise, the value is 0. Similarly, the integer variable y_{it} represents the number of APLs that are open in district $i \in I$ and in period $t \in T$. Then, our multi-period CFLP can be formulated as follows.

$$\textit{Minimize} \quad \sum_{i \in I} \sum_{j \in I} \sum_{t \in T} c_{ij} d_{jt} x_{ijt} + \sum_{i \in I} \sum_{t \in T} f_{it}(y_{it} - y_{it-1}) \tag{1}$$

subject to:

$$\sum_{i \in I} x_{ijt} = 1 \quad \forall j \in I, \forall t \in T \tag{2}$$

$$y_{it} \geq y_{it-1} \quad \forall i \in I, \forall t \in T \setminus \{1\} \tag{3}$$

$$\sum_{j \in I} d_{jt} x_{ijt} \leq a_i y_{it} \quad \forall i \in I, \forall t \in T \tag{4}$$

$$\sum_{j \in I} d_{jt} \geq m \sum_{i \in I} a_i y_{it} \quad \forall t \in T \tag{5}$$

$$x_{ijt} \in \{0,1\} \quad \forall i \in I, \forall j \in I, \forall t \in T \tag{6}$$

$$y_{it} \in \mathbb{Z}^+ \quad \forall i \in I, \forall t \in T \tag{7}$$

The expression (1) indicates the objective function that minimizes the total costs: The first term indicates the service costs of APLs, while the second represents the fixed costs of opening new APLs in the time horizon. Constraints (2) ensure that for each period $t \in T$ and each district $j \in I$ exactly one APL is assigned. Restrictions (3) ensure that once an APL is opened, it remains open until the end of the time horizon. Constraints (4) ensure that for each APL in district $i \in I$ and time period $t \in T$, the demand served by that APL does not exceed its capacity. Constraints (5) guarantee a minimum utilization percentage of the total installed capacity of APLs for each $t \in T$ period. Finally, constraints (6) and (7) specify the ranges of the decision variables.

5. Computational Results and Discussion

Based on the city of Dortmund as a real-world case, a set of experiments considering a 36-month planning horizon has been tested. Table 1 shows the parameters provided by the SDSM. It yields multiple outputs, from which the yearly demand per district is the most relevant one to feed the multi-period CFLP model. Then, the integrated SO approach described in Section 3 is applied to obtain a set of solutions assessed in terms of stochastic cost and reliability level.

5.1. System Dynamics Simulation Model Results

The market size increases in line with the population growth rate from from 602,666 in month 1 to 606,182 inhabitants in month 36. The purchases per month, the number of deliveries and the number of APLs show an increasing trend over time. The number of deliveries increases from $125,353$ to $277,910$ packages per month. We applied the SDSM and changed the average purchases per month as shown in Table 2. The results for APL users in the first month are 45,666 for S1, 54,799 for S2, and 63,933 for S3, and at the 36th month 64,331 for S1, 77,202 for S2, and 90,071 for S3. The results of the number of deliveries (units) in the first month are 125,353 for S1, 150,423 for S2, and 175,496 for S3, and in the 36th month 277,910 for S1, 333,512 for S2, and 389,106 for S3. Figure 8 illustrates the scenario comparison of the users of APL and the number of deliveries. The complete results generated by the SDSM of the default scenarios are shown in Tables A1–A3 in Appendix A.

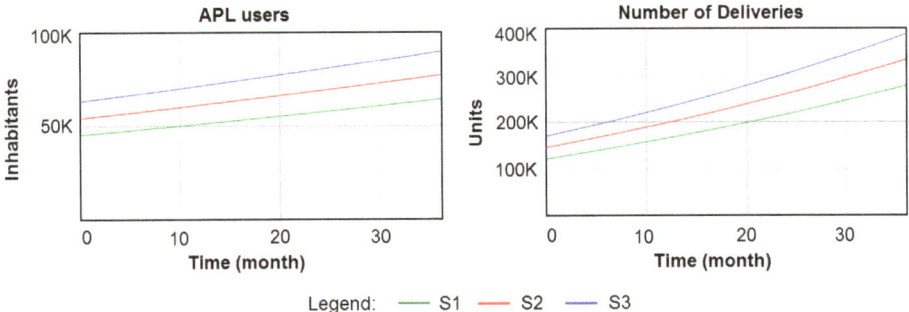

Figure 8. Scenario comparison: APL users (**left**) and number of deliveries (**right**).

5.2. Generating and Simulating Optimal Configurations

As soon as our SDSM provides the number of deliveries (expected demand) for the three scenarios ($s \in S$, where $S = \{S1, S2, S3\}$) under consideration of Table 2, are used to feed our CFLP model. We evaluate ten APL network configurations ($k \in K$, where $K = \{1, 2, ..., 10\}$) with the demand increasing proportional to k, based on the scenario S2. Each configuration is obtained by optimally solving the CFLP model using the procedure described below.

1. Consider a uniformly distributed random demand D_{jtk} per district $j \in J$ during the period $t \in T$ for generating the configurations.
2. Define $\mu_{jt} = E[D_{jtk}]$ and assume that μ_{jt} is the medium demand corresponding to the scenario S2.
3. Define a factor $\delta = 0.01$ to increase the size of the uniform interval as we move forward into future periods.
4. Generate the random demand using Equation (8). The expression $1 + \frac{k-1}{|K|-1}$ is useful to increase μ_{jt} proportionally to the value of k. In this way, we guarantee that generated configurations differ in size.

$$D_{jtk} \sim U\left(\left[1 + \frac{k-1}{|K|-1}\right](1 - \delta t)\mu_{jt}, \left[1 + \frac{k-1}{|K|-1}\right](1 + \delta t)\mu_{jt}\right) \quad \forall j \in I, \forall t \in T, \forall k \in K \tag{8}$$

The variable costs c_{ij} are proportional to the distance between each pair of districts. They were estimated using a web mapping service. The fixed costs are $f_{it} = 5500€$ for the first year and each district, and increase according to an average inflation rate of 2% per year. The capacity of each APL in a district $i \in I$ is $a_i = 6000$ units per month, and the minimum utilization percentage is $m = 40\%$. Then, our CFLP model is solved with Cplex for all ten configurations. The number of resulting open APLs per month is shown in Figure 9 for three out of these configurations. The lowest and highest lines represent solutions for the lowest and highest demand, respectively. The rest of the solutions are in between. As the demand μ_{jt} increases over time, the number of open APLs will behave the same regardless of the configuration. However, this consistent behavior does not extend beyond the year 1 for $k = 10$ and beyond the year 2 for $k = 1$ and $k = 5$, when the total installed APLs are sufficient to cover the total demand by the end of the planning horizon. Furthermore, there is a sharp increase in open APLs from months 11 to 12. This behavior is caused by two parameters: The annual growth of the fixed costs f_{it} drives the APLs that are opened when they are less expensive, but always limited by the minimum utilization percentage m. Finally, the total number of APLs installed varies significantly from one scenario to another, for example, while 165 APLs are required for $k = 10$, only 99 APLs are installed in the configuration $k = 1$ at the end of the planning horizon. All configuration results are stored in Tables A4–A6 in Appendix B.

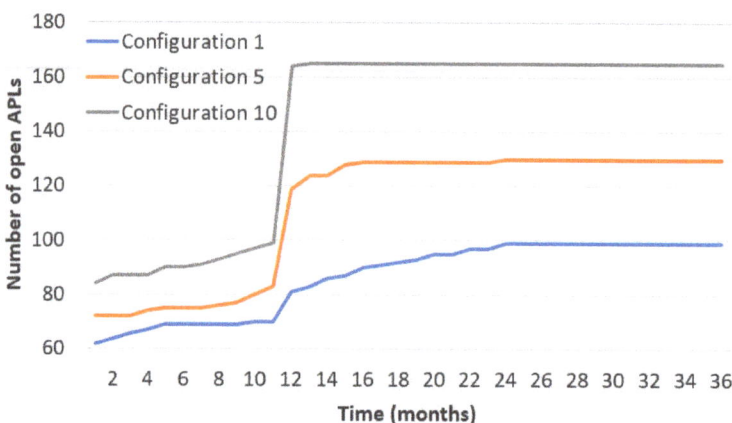

Figure 9. Number of total open APLs along the planning horizon for three configurations ($k = 1, 5, 10$).

Once all configurations have been generated, they are tested in a stochastic environment, assuming that the demand per district is uncertain and follows a known probability distribution. Consider a random demand D_{jts} whose mean and standard deviation are μ_{jts} and σ_{jts}, respectively, per district $j \in J$ during the period $t \in T$ for the scenario $s \in S$. We assume that μ_{jts} is the demand generated by our SDSM. Now, as the goal is to evaluate the performance of each configuration, they must be tested under the same demand conditions; therefore, the demand does not depend further on the configuration. Then, D_{jts} is simulated and each configuration is evaluated in terms of total costs (Equation (1)) and reliability. Studies on reliability in supply chains are found in [52,53]. We define the reliability R_{ks} of the configuration $k \in K$ for the scenario $s \in S$ as the probability that the stochastic demand of all districts in the city can be successfully satisfied, i.e.,

$$R_{ks} = \left(1 - \frac{b_{ks}}{n}\right) \cdot 100\% \quad \forall k \in K, \forall s \in S \tag{9}$$

where b_{ks} is the total number of simulation runs where the configuration does not cover all district demands, and n is the total number of runs. In other words, if at least one APL in a configuration is not able to cover all assigned needs, that configuration will fail. In our experiments, a total of $n = 5000$ runs are performed for each combination of scenario s and configuration k. Without losing generality, we assume that demand is independent of the customers' district, but our methodology can easily be adapted to take into account correlated demand. For the realization of the demand, three probability distributions have been tested:

1. A uniform distribution, according to Equation (10). In this case, $\sigma_{jts} = \frac{\sqrt{3}}{3}\delta t \mu_{jts}$.

$$D_{jts} \sim U\big([1 - \delta t]\mu_{jts}, [1 + \delta t]\mu_{jts}\big) \tag{10}$$

2. A symmetric triangular distribution, according to Equation (11), i.e., the mode equals μ_{jts}. To obtain conditions similar to 1, the lower and upper limits of this distribution are calculated assuming that the standard deviation is equal.

$$D_{jts} \sim T\left(\left[1 - \sqrt{2}\delta t\right]\mu_{jts}, \mu_{jts}, \left[1 + \sqrt{2}\delta t\right]\mu_{jts}\right) \tag{11}$$

3. A lognormal distribution, according to Equation (12). Again, the standard deviation is the same as in the point 1 to preserve similar conditions.

$$D_{jts} \sim Lognormal\big(\mu_{jts}, \sigma_{jts}\big) \tag{12}$$

Figure 10 shows the main results of the simulation process for each configuration. Blue, orange, and green lines represent the results from the demand for uniform, triangular, or log-normal distribution. In addition, dotted, solid, and dashed lines represent the results for the scenarios $S1$ (low demand), $S2$ (medium demand), and $S3$ (high demand), respectively. Each dot on each line represents a single configuration. In general, more expensive configurations result in higher reliability, because they include a larger number of installed APLs. When the demand follows either a uniform or a triangular distribution, the most expensive half of the configurations always achieve a 100.0% reliability level, regardless of the scenario. In other words, the configuration $k = 6$, with total costs of 748,660€, already locates a suitable number of APLs and eliminates the need to consider more expensive configurations. However, if the budget is lower, our approach offers other good alternatives for the decision makers.

In general, configurations are less reliable when demand scenarios are increased. For example, configuration $k = 4$, with total costs of 661,100€, only achieves a reliability level of 14.0% under the high demand scenario and a log-normal distribution. Conversely, this configuration achieves a reliability level of 98.8% under the low demand scenario. Furthermore, the reliability is very sensitive to the probability distribution. Broadly speaking, a configuration fails if the demand is too high (Equation (9)). Therefore, configurations simulating a log-normal demand, which has no upper limit, are less reliable than those where the probability distribution is either uniform or triangular (Equations (10) and (11)). This fact underlines the relevance of integrating the study to determine the behavior of demand in the real case.

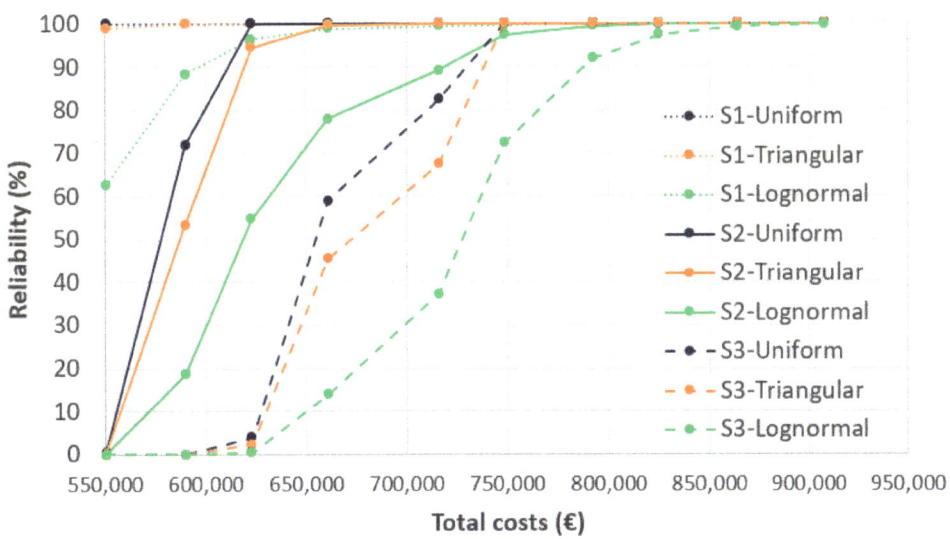

Figure 10. Optimal solutions evaluated in terms of costs and reliability.

6. Conclusions

With the goal of determining the optimal number and location of automated parcel locker (APL) systems in a multi-period time horizon, this paper has proposed the use of an integrated simulation-optimization approach combining system dynamics with exact optimization and Monte Carlo simulation. We propose this integrated model as a decision support tool for future APL implementations as a last-mile distribution scheme. The analysis is based on a real-world case study where service requirements are considered as random variables that evolve over time. First, a system dynamics simulation model is designed to determine the 36-month performance of parameters such as APL users and number of deliveries. Then, these results feed a multi-period facility location model that provides the optimal number of APLs. To deal with the demand uncertainty, different scenarios are considered and solved with precise methods. The solutions associated with each scenario are then sent to a Monte Carlo simulation to estimate both their costs and reliability level.

The model provides an optimal number of APLs, taking into account the expectations of user demands. We have considered three scenarios $S1$, $S2$, and $S3$ for 50%, 60%, and 70% of the e-shopper rate. The results for the number of deliveries (units) after 36 months show a wide range of shipments from about 277,000 in $S1$ to nearly 400,000 in $S3$. We used our CFLP to evaluate ten APL network configurations ($k = 1, ..., 10$) with increasing demand in relation to each scenario. Obviously, there is a strong impact on the number of APLs that the city needs. After 36 months, the number of APLs increases from 99 in the case of the lowest demand to 165 at maximum demand. Interestingly, the number of APLs stabilizes from month 24 in all configurations. Thus, we can conclude that the effect on APLs appears linear in relation to the potential users of APL with no obvious scale effects. From a stochastic environment, we assumed that the demand per district is uncertain and follows a known probability distribution. Whenever the demand follows either a uniform or a triangular distribution, the most expensive configurations always reach a reliability level of 100.0% regardless of the scenario. The configuration $k = 6$, with total costs of 748,660€, already locates a suitable number of APLs. However, if the budget is lower, our approach offers other alternatives for decision makers.

All in all, the work illustrates the potential of combining different simulation and optimization techniques to correctly address complex optimization problems in real urban logistics, where uncertainties must also be taken into account. The following research lines are still open for the future: (i) increasing the level of detail on the demand side, taking into account correlated and individual customers' demands instead of aggregated ones—which will significantly increase the size of the problem; (ii) develop a metaheuristic-based approach for the optimization phase, as this will be a necessary step when larger instances are to be analyzed; and (iii) extend the approach to a fully simheuristic algorithm, so that the feedback provided by the Monte Carlo simulation can be reused to guide the metaheuristic search.

Author Contributions: Conceptualization, M.R., J.G.-F., and J.C.-V.; methodology, J.C.-V. and R.D.T.; software, J.C.-V. and R.D.T.; validation, J.C.-V. and R.D.T.; formal analysis, M.R. and J.G.-F.; writing—original draft preparation, J.C.-V. and R.D.T.; writing—review and editing, M.R. and J.G.-F. All authors have read and agreed to the published version of the manuscript.

Funding: This work has been partially supported by the German Academic Exchange Service (DAAD) Research Grants—Doctoral Programmes in Germany, 2017/18.

Institutional Review Board Statement: Not applicable.

Informed Consent Statement: Not applicable.

Data Availability Statement: Data are available upon reasonable request to the corresponding author.

Conflicts of Interest: The authors declare no conflict of interest.

Appendix A. Results Generated by the SDSM for the Horizon Planning in the Proposal Scenarios

Appendix A shows the results by the SDSM for the first three years.

Table A1. Results generated by the SDSM in the first year.

Output Parameter	Month											
	1	2	3	4	5	6	7	8	9	10	11	12
Market size (thousands)												
S1	602.6	602.7	602.8	602.9	603	603.1	603.2	603.3	603.4	603.5	603.6	603.7
S2	602.6	602.7	602.8	602.9	603	603.1	603.2	603.3	603.4	603.5	603.6	603.7
S3	602.6	602.7	602.8	602.9	603	603.1	603.2	603.3	603.4	603.5	603.6	603.7
Potential e-customers (thousands)												
S1	303.4	305.5	307.6	309.7	311.9	314	316.1	318.5	320	322.4	324.5	326.6
S2	364.1	366.6	369.2	371.7	374.3	376.8	379.3	381.9	384.4	386.9	389.4	391.9
S3	424.7	427.7	430.7	433.7	436.6	439.6	442.6	445.5	448.5	451.4	454.3	457.3
APL users (thousands)												
S1	45.6	46.1	46.6	47.1	47.5	48	48.5	49	49.5	50	50.5	51.1
S2	54.7	55.3	55.9	56.6	57.1	57.7	58.2	58.8	59.4	60.1	60.7	61.3
S3	63.9	64.6	65.2	65.9	66.6	67.3	68	68.7	69.4	70.1	70.8	71.5
Number of deliveries (thousands)												
S1	125.3	128.7	132.1	135.6	139.2	142.8	146.4	150.1	153.9	157.7	161.6	165.5
S2	150.4	154.4	158.6	162.8	167	171.3	175.7	180.2	184.7	189.3	193.9	198.6
S3	175.4	180.2	185	189.9	194.9	199.9	205	210.2	215.5	220.8	226.3	231.8

Table A2. Results generated by the SDSM in the second year.

Output Parameter	Month											
	13	14	15	16	17	18	19	20	21	22	23	24
Market size (thousands)												
S1	603.8	603.9	604	604.1	604.2	604.3	604.4	604.5	604.6	604.7	604.8	604.9
S2	603.8	603.9	604	604.1	604.2	604.3	604.4	604.5	604.6	604.7	604.8	604.9
S3	603.8	603.9	604	604.1	604.2	604.3	604.4	604.5	604.6	604.7	604.8	604.9
Potential e-customers (thousands)												
S1	328.7	330.8	332.9	334.9	337	339.1	341.2	343.2	345.3	347.3	349.425	351.4
S2	394.4	396.9	399.4	401.9	404.4	406.9	409.4	411.9	414.3	416.8	419.3	421.7
S3	457.3	460.2	463.1	466	468.9	471.8	474.7	477.6	480.5	483.4	486.3	489.1
APL users (thousands)												
S1	51.6	52.1	52.6	53.1	53.7	54.2	54.7	55.3	55.8	56.3	56.9	57.4
S2	61.9	62.5	63.1	63.8	64.4	65	65.7	66.3	67	67.6	68.3	68.9
S3	72.2	72.9	73.7	74.4	75.1	75.9	76.6	77.4	78.1	78.9	79.7	80.4
Number of deliveries (thousands)												
S1	169.5	173.5	177.7	181.8	186	190.3	194.6	199	203.5	208	212.6	217.2
S2	203.4	208.3	213.2	218.2	223.3	228.4	233.6	238.9	244.2	249.6	255.1	260.7
S3	237.3	243	248.7	254.6	260.5	266.5	272.5	278.7	284.9	291.3	297.7	304.2

Table A3. Results generated by the SDSM in the third year.

Output Parameter	Month											
	25	26	27	28	29	30	31	32	33	34	35	36
Market size (thousands)												
S1	605	605.1	605.2	605.3	605.4	605.5	605.6	605.7	605.8	605.9	606	606.1
S2	605	605.1	605.2	605.3	605.4	605.5	605.6	605.7	605.8	605.9	606	606.1
S3	605	605.1	605.2	605.3	605.4	605.5	605.6	605.7	605.8	605.9	606	606.1
Potential e-customers (thousands)												
S1	353.5	355.5	357.5	359.6	361.6	363.6	365.6	367.6	369.6	371.6	373.6	375.6
S2	424.2	426.6	429	431.5	433.9	436.3	438.8	441.2	443.6	446	448.4	450.8
S3	494.9	497.7	500	503.4	506.2	509.1	511.9	514.7	517.5	520.3	523.1	525.9
APL users (thousands)												
S1	58	58.5	59.1	59.7	60.2	60.8	61.4	61.9	62.5	63.1	63.7	64.3
S2	69.6	70.3	70.9	71.6	72.3	73	73.7	74.4	75	75.7	76.4	77.2
S3	81.2	82	82.8	83.6	84.4	85.1	85.9	86.8	87.6	88.4	89.2	90
Number of deliveries (thousands)												
S1	221.9	226.7	231.5	236.4	241.4	246.4	251.5	256.6	261.8	267.1	272.5	277.9
S2	266.4	272.1	277.9	283.7	289.7	295.7	301.8	308	314.2	320.6	327	333.5
S3	310.8	317.4	324.2	331	338	345	352.1	359.3	366.6	374	381.5	389.1

Appendix B. Number of APLs by Period and Configuration

Appendix B shows the results for the required number of APLs for the first three years.

Table A4. Number of APLs in the first year.

Output Parameter	Month											
	1	2	3	4	5	6	7	8	9	10	11	12
Number of APLs												
$k1$	62	64	66	67	69	69	69	69	69	70	70	81
$k2$	69	69	69	69	69	69	70	71	71	71	73	92
$k2$	69	69	70	70	70	71	72	73	73	73	74	101
$k4$	71	71	72	72	72	73	74	75	76	76	76	110
$k5$	72	72	72	74	75	75	75	76	77	80	83	119
$k6$	73	75	75	76	76	76	78	80	82	84	86	130
$k7$	75	76	76	77	77	81	83	83	85	87	90	139
$k8$	76	76	78	80	83	85	88	89	89	90	91	148
$k9$	80	81	83	86	87	89	89	89	90	92	92	153
$k10$	84	87	87	87	90	90	91	93	95	97	99	164

Table A5. Number of APLs in the second year.

Output Parameter	Month											
	13	14	15	16	17	18	19	20	21	22	23	24
Number of APLs												
$k1$	83	86	87	90	91	92	93	95	95	97	97	99
$k2$	94	97	100	100	100	102	104	105	105	106	106	107
$k3$	102	106	108	110	112	112	113	113	113	113	113	113
$k4$	113	113	118	119	119	119	120	120	120	120	120	120
$k5$	124	124	128	129	129	129	129	129	129	129	129	130
$k6$	132	135	135	135	135	135	135	135	135	135	136	136
$k7$	143	144	144	144	144	144	144	144	144	144	144	144
$k8$	149	149	149	149	149	149	149	149	149	149	149	150
$k9$	157	157	157	157	157	157	157	157	157	157	157	157
$k10$	165	165	165	165	165	165	165	165	165	165	165	165

Table A6. Number of APLs in the third year.

Output Parameter	Month											
	25	26	27	28	29	30	31	32	33	34	35	36
Number of APLs												
$k1$	99	99	99	99	99	99	99	99	99	99	99	99
$k2$	107	107	107	107	107	107	107	107	107	107	107	107
$k3$	113	113	113	113	113	113	113	113	113	113	113	113
$k4$	120	120	120	120	120	120	120	120	120	120	120	120
$k5$	130	130	130	130	130	130	130	130	130	130	130	130
$k6$	135	135	135	135	135	135	135	135	135	135	136	136
$k7$	144	144	144	144	144	144	144	144	144	144	144	144
$k8$	150	150	150	150	150	150	150	150	150	150	150	150
$k9$	157	157	157	157	157	157	157	157	157	157	157	157
$k10$	165	165	165	165	165	165	165	165	165	165	165	165

References

1. Gonzalez-Feliu, J. *Sustainable Urban Logistics: Planning and Evaluation*; ISTE Ltd./John Wiley and Sons Inc.: Hoboken, NJ, USA, 2017.
2. Boudoin, D.; Morel, C.; Gardat, M. Supply Chains and Urban Logistics Platforms. In *Sustainable Urban Logistics: Concepts, Methods and Information Systems*; Gonzalez-Feliu, J., Semet, F., Routhier, J., Eds.; Springer: New York, NY, USA, 2013; pp. 1–20.
3. Moroz, M.; Polkowski, Z. The Last Mile Issue and Urban Logistics: Choosing Parcel Machines in the Context of the Ecological Attitudes of the Y Generation Consumers Purchasing Online. *Transp. Res. Procedia* **2016**, *16*, 378–393. [CrossRef]

4. Zurel, Ö.; van Hoyweghen, L.; Braes, S.; Seghers, A. Parcel Lockers, an Answer to the Pressure on the Last Mile Delivery? In *New Business and Regulatory Strategies in the Postal Sector*; Parcu, P., Brennan, T., Glass, V., Eds.; Springer International Publishing: Cham, Switzerland, 2018; pp. 299–312.
5. Verlinde, S.; Rojas, C.; Buldeo Rai, H.; Kin, B.; Macharis, C. E-Consumers and Their Perception of Automated Parcel Stations. In *City Logistics 3: Towards Sustainable and Liveable Cities*; Taniguchi, E., Thompson, R., Eds.; ISTE Ltd./John Wiley and Sons Inc.: Hoboken, NJ, USA, 2018; pp. 147–160.
6. Vakulenko, Y.; Hellstrom, D.; Hjort, K. What's in the Parcel Locker? Exploring Customer Value in E-commerce Last Mile Delivery. *J. Bus. Res.* **2018**, *88*, 421–427. [CrossRef]
7. Iwan, S.; Kijewska, K.; Lemke, J. Analysis of Parcel Lockers' Efficiency as the Last Mile Delivery Solution—The Results of the Research in Poland. *Transp. Res. Procedia* **2016**, *12*, 644–655. [CrossRef]
8. Faulin, J.; Grasman, S.; Juan, A.; Hirsch, P. *Sustainable Transportation and Smart Logistics: Decision-Making Models and Solutions*; Elsevier: Oxford, UK, 2018.
9. Guerrero, J.; Dıaz-Ramırez, J. A Review on Transportation Last-mile Network Design and Urban Freight Vehicles. In Proceedings of the 2017 International Conference on Industrial Engineering and Operations Management, Bristol, UK, 24–25 July 2017; pp. 533–552.
10. Jlassi, S.; Tamayo, S.; Gaudron, A. Simulation Applied to Urban Logistics: A State of the Art. In *City Logistics 3: Towards Sustainable and Liveable Cities*; Taniguchi, E., Thompson, R., Eds.; ISTE Ltd./John Wiley and Sons Inc.: Hoboken, NJ, USA, 2018; pp. 32–58.
11. Morganti, E.; Dablanc, L.; Fortin, F. Final Deliveries for Online Shopping: The Deployment of Pickup Point Networks in Urban and Suburban Areas. *Res. Transp. Bus. Manag.* **2014**, *11*, 23–31. [CrossRef]
12. Gonzalez-Feliu, J. (Ed.) *Logistics and Transport Modeling in Urban Goods Movement*; IGI Global: Hershey, PA, USA, 2019.
13. Figueira, G.; Almada-Lobo, B. Hybrid Simulation-Optimization Methods: A Taxonomy and Discussion. *Simul. Model. Pract. Theory* **2014**, *46*, 118–134. [CrossRef]
14. Crainic, T.G.; Perboli, G.; Rosano, M. Simulation of Intermodal Freight Transportation Systems: A Taxonomy. *Eur. J. Oper. Res.* **2018**, *270*, 401–418. [CrossRef]
15. Martinez-Moyano, I.; Macal, C. A Primer for Hybrid Modeling and Simulation. In Proceedings of the 2016 Winter Simulation Conference (WSC), Washington, DC, USA, 11–14 December 2016; Roeder, T.M., Frazier, P.I., Szechtman, R., Zhou, E., Huschka, T., Chick, S.E., Eds.; Institute of Electrical and Electronics Engineers, Inc.: Piscataway, NJ, USA, 2016; pp. 133–147.
16. Ackoff, R.L. Optimization + Objectivity = Optout. *Eur. J. Oper. Res.* **1977**, *1*, 1–7. [CrossRef]
17. Le Bouthillier, A.; Crainic, T.G. A Cooperative Parallel Metaheuristic for the Vehicle Routing Problem with Time Windows. *Comput. Oper. Res.* **2005**, *32*, 1685–1708. [CrossRef]
18. Forrester, J.W. Industrial Dynamics after the First Decade. *Manag. Sci.* **1968**, *14*, 398–415. [CrossRef]
19. Sterman, J. *Business Dynamics*; Irwin/McGraw-Hill: Boston, MA, USA, 2000.
20. Taniguchi, E.; Thompson, R.; Yamada, T. Emerging Techniques for Enhancing the Practical Application of City Logistics Models. *Procedia Soc. Behav. Sci.* **2012**, *39*, 3–18. [CrossRef]
21. Bala, B.K.; Arshad, F.M.; Noh, K.M. *System Dynamics: Modelling and Simulation*; Springer: Singapore, 2017.
22. Villa, S.; Gonçalves, P.; Arango, S. Exploring Retailers' Ordering Decisions Under Delays. *Syst. Dyn. Rev.* **2012**, *31*, 1–27. [CrossRef]
23. Kunze, O.; Wulfhorst, G.; Minner, S. Applying Systems Thinking to City Logistics: A Qualitative (and Quantitative) Approach to Model Interdependencies of Decisions by Various Stakeholders and their Impact on City Logistics. *Transp. Res. Procedia* **2016**, *12*, 692–706. [CrossRef]
24. Villa, S.; Gonçalves, P.; Arango, S. Describing and Explaining Urban Freight Transport by System Dynamics. *Transp. Res. Procedia* **2017**, *25*, 1075–1094. [CrossRef]
25. De La Torre, G.; Gruchmann, T.; Kamath, V.; Melkonyan, A.; Krumme, K. A System Dynamics-Based Simulation Model to Analyze Consumers' Behavior Based on Participatory Systems Mapping—A "Last Mile" Perspective. In *Innovative Logistics Services and Sustainable Lifestyles*; Melkonyan, A., Krumme, K., Eds.; Springer Science and Business Media: New York, NY, USA, 2013; pp. 165–194.
26. Anand, N.; van Duin, J.R.; Quak, H.; Tavasszy, L. Relevance of City Logistics Modeling Efforts: A Review. *Transp. Rev.* **2015**, *35*, 701–719.
27. Anand, N.; van Duin, J.R.; Tavasszy, L. Framework for Modeling Multi-Stakeholder City Logistics Domain Using the Agent Based Modeling Approach. *Transp. Res. Procedia* **2016**, *16*, 4–15. [CrossRef]
28. Balinski, M.L. Integer Programming: Methods, Uses, Computations. *Manag. Sci.* **1965**, *12*, 253–313. [CrossRef]
29. Laporte, G.; Nickel, S.; Saldanha da Gama, F. *Location Science*; Springer International Publishing: Cham, Switzerland, 2015. [CrossRef]
30. Melo, M.T.; Nickel, S.; Saldanha-da-Gama, F. Facility Location and Supply Chain Management—A Review. *Eur. J. Oper. Res.* **2009**, *196*, 401–412.
31. De Armas, J.; Juan, A.; Marquès, J.M.; Pedroso, J.P. Solving the Deterministic and Stochastic Uncapacitated Facility Location Problem: From a Heuristic to a Simheuristic. *J. Oper. Res. Soc.* **2017**, *68*, 1161–1176. [CrossRef]
32. Absi, N.; Feillet, D.; Garaix, T.; Guyon, O. The City Logistics Facility Location Problem. In Proceedings of the ODYSSEUS 2012, Fifth International Workshop on Freight Transportation and Logistics, Mykonos Island, GR, USA, 21–25 May 2012. [CrossRef]
33. Pamučar, D.; Vasin, L.; Atanasković, P.; Miličić, M. Planning the City Logistics Terminal Location by Applying the Green-Median Model and Type-2 Neurofuzzy Network. *Comput. Intell. Neurosci.* **2016**, *2016*. [CrossRef]

34. Sopha, B.M.; Asih, A.M.S.; Pradana, F.D.; Gunawan, H.E.; Karuniawati, Y. Urban Distribution Center Location: Combination of Spatial Analysis and Multi-Objective Mixed-Integer Linear Programming. *Int. J. Eng. Bus. Manag.* **2016**, *8*.
35. Dell'Amico, M.; Novellani, S. A Two-Echelon Facility Location Problem with Stochastic Demands for Urban Construction Logistics: An Application within the SUCCESS Project. In Proceedings of the 2017 IEEE International Conference on Service Operations and Logistics, and Informatics (SOLI), Bari, Italy, 18–20 September 2017; pp. 90–95. [CrossRef]
36. Gan, M.; Li, D.; Wang, M.; Zhang, G.; Yang, S.; Liu, J. Optimal Urban Logistics Facility Location with Consideration of Truck-Related Greenhouse Gas Emissions: A Case Study of Shenzhen City. *Math. Probl. Eng.* **2018**, *2018*. [CrossRef]
37. Nataraj, S.; Ferone, D.; Quintero-Araujo, C.; Juan, A.; Festa, P. Consolidation Centers in City logistics: A Cooperative Approach Based on the Location Routing Problem. *Int. J. Ind. Eng. Comput.* **2018**, *10*, 393–404.
38. Herrmann, E.; Kunze, O. Facility Location Problems in City Crowd Logistics. *Transp. Res. Procedia* **2019**, *41*, 117–134. [CrossRef]
39. Brandimarte, P. *Handbook in Monte Carlo Simulation: Applications in Financial Engineering, Risk Management, and Economics*; John Wiley and Sons.: Hoboken, NJ, USA, 2014. [CrossRef]
40. Kroese, D.P.; Brereton, T.; Taimre, T.; Botev, Z.I. Why the Monte Carlo Method is so Important Today. *Wiley Interdiscip. Rev. Comput. Stat.* **2014**, *6*, 386–392. [CrossRef]
41. Palacios-Argüello, L.; Gonzalez-Feliu, J.; Gondran, N.; Badeig, F. Assessing the Economic and Environmental Impacts of Urban Food Systems for Public School Canteens: Case Study of Great Lyon Region. *Eur. Transp. Res. Rev.* **2018**, *10*, 37.
42. Tordecilla, R.D.; Juan, A.A.; Montoya-Torres, J.R.; Quintero-Araujo, C.L.; Panadero, J. Simulation-Optimization Methods for Designing and Assessing Resilient Supply Chain Networks under Uncertainty Scenarios: A Review. *Simul. Model. Pract. Theory* **2021**, *106*, 102166. [CrossRef]
43. VDI 3633 Part 12. *Simulation of Systems in Materials Handling, Logistics, and Production—Simulation and Optimisation*; Beuth: Berlin, Germany, 2020. [CrossRef]
44. Maerz, L.; Krug, W.; Rose, O.; Weigert, G. (Eds.) *Simulation und Optimierung in Produktion und Logistik*; Springer: Berlin/Heidelberg, Germany, 2010. [CrossRef]
45. Rabe, M.; Chicaiza-Vaca, J. A Simulation-Optimization Conceptual Model of Automated Parcel Lockers on Macro and Micro Planning Levels. In Proceedings of the 2019 Winter Simulation Conference (WSC), National Harbor, MD, USA, 8–11 December 2019; Mustafee, N., Bae, K.-H., Lazarova-Molnar, S., Rabe, M.C., Szabo, C., Haas, P., Son, Y.-J., Eds.; Institute of Electrical and Electronics Engineers, Inc.: Piscataway, NJ, USA, 2019; pp. 2904–2905.
46. Juan, A.; Faulin, J.; Grasman, S.; Rabe, M.; Figueira, G. A Review of Simheuristics: Extending Metaheuristics to Deal with Stochastic Combinatorial Optimization Problems. *Oper. Res. Perspect.* **2015**, *2*, 62–72.
47. Juan, A.A.; Kelton, W.D.; Currie, C.S.; Faulin, J. Simheuristics Applications: Dealing with Uncertainty in Logistics, Transportation, and other Supply Chain Areas. In Proceedings of the 2019 Winter Simulation Conference (WSC), National Harbor, MD, USA, 8–11 December 2019; Rabe, M., Juan, A.A., Mustafee, N., Skoogh, A., Jain, S., Johansson, B., Eds.; Institute of Electrical and Electronics Engineers, Inc.: Piscataway, NJ, USA, 2019; pp. 3048–3059.
48. Durand, B.; Gonzalez-Feliu, J. Urban Logistics and E-grocery: Have Proximity Delivery Services a Positive Impact on Shopping Trips? *Procedia Soc. Behav. Sci.* **2012**, *39*, 510–520. [CrossRef]
49. Pages-Bernaus, A.; Ramalhinho, H.; Juan, A.A.; Calvet, L. Designing E-commerce Supply Chains: A Stochastic Facility-location Approach. *Int. Trans. Oper. Res.* **2019**, *26*, 507–528.
50. Quintero-Araujo, C.L.; Caballero-Villalobos, J.P.; Juan, A.A.; Montoya-Torres, J.R. A Biased-randomized Metaheuristic for the Capacitated Location Routing Problem. *Int. Trans. Oper. Res.* **2017**, *24*, 1079–1098. [CrossRef]
51. Quintero-Araujo, C.L.; Gruler, A.; Juan, A.A.; Faulin, J. Using Horizontal Cooperation Concepts in Integrated Routing and Facility-location Decision. *Int. Trans. Oper. Res.* **2019**, *26*, 551–579. [CrossRef]
52. Adenso-Diaz, B.; Mena, C.; Garcia-Carbajal, S.; Liechty, M. The Impact of Supply Network Characteristics on Reliability. *Supply Chain. Manag. Int. J.* **2012**, *17*, 263–276. [CrossRef]
53. Peng, P.; Snyder, L.V.; Lim, A.; Liu, Z. Reliable Logistics Networks Design with Facility Disruptions. *Transp. Res. Part B Methodol.* **2011**, *45*, 1190–1211. [CrossRef]

Article

Urban e-Grocery Distribution Design in Pamplona (Spain) Applying an Agent-Based Simulation Model with Horizontal Cooperation Scenarios

Adrian Serrano-Hernandez [1,2,*], Rocio de la Torre [3], Luis Cadarso [2] and Javier Faulin [1]

1   Institute of Smart Cities, Public University of Navarre, 31006 Pamplona, Spain; javier.faulin@unavarra.es
2   Aerospace Systems and Transport Research Group, EIATA Institute, Rey Juan Carlos University, 28942 Fuenlabrada, Spain; luis.cadarso@urjc.es
3   INARBE Institute, Public University of Navarre, 31006 Pamplona, Spain; rocio.delatorre@unavarra.es
*   Correspondence: adrian.serrano@unavarra.es; Tel.: +34-948169213

Abstract: E-commerce has boosted in the last decades because of the achievements of the information and telecommunications technology along with the changes in the society life-style. More recently, the groceries online purchase (or e-grocery), has also prevailed as a way of making the weekly shopping, particularly, the one including fresh vegetables and fruit. Furthermore, this type of virtual shopping in supermarkets is gaining importance as the most efficient delivery system in cost and time. Thus, we have evaluated in this study the influence of the cooperation-based policies on costs and service quality among different supermarkets in Pamplona, Spain. Concerning methodology, first of all, we carried out a survey in Pamplona having the purpose of modelling the demand patterns about e-grocery. Second, we have developed an agent-based simulation model for generating scenarios in non-cooperative, limited cooperation, and full cooperation settings, considering the real data obtained from the survey analysis. At this manner, Vehicle Routing Problems (VRP) and Multi Depot VRPs (MDVRP) are dynamically generated and solved within the simulation framework using a biased-randomization algorithm. Finally, the results show significant reductions in distance driven and lead times when employing horizontal cooperation in e-grocery distribution.

Keywords: agent-based simulation; horizontal cooperation; e-groceries; optimization

Citation: Serrano-Hernandez, A.; de la Torre, R.; Cadarso, L.; Faulin, J. Urban e-Grocery Distribution Design in Pamplona (Spain) Applying an Agent-Based Simulation Model with Horizontal Cooperation Scenarios. *Algorithms* **2021**, *14*, 20. https://doi.org/10.3390/a14010020

Received: 14 December 2020
Accepted: 6 January 2021
Published: 12 January 2021

Publisher's Note: MDPI stays neutral with regard to jurisdictional claims in published maps and institutional affiliations.

1. Introduction

During the last decade, consumers' shopping habits have drastically changed, not only because of the massive incorporation of new technologies into our lives but also because of a greater awareness of environmental and social sustainability, growing urbanization, and time pressures. The outcome is a challenging scenario mainly driven by the increment on demand for e-groceries (i.e., the online purchase of groceries, including fresh products) because of an exceptional development of e-commerce. As a consequence of this paradigm shift in consumption, companies have also adapted to this new order by adopting proactive sustainable strategies and developing sustainable supply chain management practices. However, and despite the complexity that features the growing demand, the existing literature does not demonstrate the challenges of the field, especially those related to the logistic process. Further, despite the promising development of the e-grocery business, the lack of interest in developing cost-effective operations is also evident in companies, since there are only a few e-grocers which have made progress on leading to profitable operations [1,2]. Thus, the challenges in e-grocery logistics include from a wide-range of food safety-related issues to differences in storage temperatures, including perishability over time [3]. In addition, environmentally responsible customer profiles must also be considered, who demand consumption of local products [4]. Note that, considering these consumer requirements, it is more than likely that consumers' wishes differ from the seller's desires. While consumers usually prefer products from a close origin with long date of expiry [5], sellers would benefit from shipping first items with shorter shelf lives in order to reduce food waste [6].

In fact, many researchers recognize the strategic importance of sustainability as an essential aspect in the supply chain management [7,8] . It is widely accepted that sustainability cannot be achieved by companies in isolation, and that requires the involvement of supply chain members [9]. Reinforcing the same idea, Soosay and Hyland [10] plead that supply chain members operate in more dynamic environments, characterized by globalization, rapidly evolving technologies, and increased customer responsiveness. Therefore, more integrative and cooperative efforts are required to reach the aforementioned supply chain characteristics. Likewise, horizontal cooperation may be paramount when meeting the requirements of demand and sellers in an efficient and sustainable way, for example, improving efficiency in logistics. Therefore, the partnering sellers aim at increasing productivity through close cooperation, for example, by optimizing vehicle capacity utilization, reducing empty mileage and cutting costs of non-core/supporting activities to increase the competitiveness of their logistics networks [11,12]. At this manner, Cruijssen et al. [13] have enumerated the potential benefits of cooperation as follows: *(i)* reduction of cost of transportation; *(ii)* improvement of service quality by reducing operation times and lost goods; *(iii)* diminution of environmental and social impacts; *(iv)* mitigation of risks; *(v)* and enhancement of market share. Consequently, extrapolating the previous benefits, horizontal cooperation might be particularly interesting for e-grocery, where a wide range of customers are widespread in big cities or in rural areas, which generates long empty backhauls after deliveries. In this regard, load factors can be improved by means of cooperation (i.e., supermarkets sharing their logistics operations) to reduce empty backhauls.

Accordingly, the main contributions of the this paper can be summarized as follows: *(i)* modeling the demand patterns about e-grocery (including ordering frequency, preference of supermarket, and delivery windows); *(ii)* an agent-based simulation model for generating scenarios in cooperative and non-cooperative settings, considering the real data obtained from the survey analysis, and *(iii)* the integration of Vehicle Routing Problems (VRP) and Multi Depot VRP within the simulation framework.

The remainder of the paper is organized as follows—Section 2 reviews concepts related to e-groceries, Horizontal Cooperation, and Agent-Based Simulation. Section 3 contains information about the geographical scope of our experiments, including the details of the survey and the main insights. Section 4 describes the simulation model, the cooperative protocols, and the routing algorithms. Section 5 presents the results of our simulation model. Finally, Section 6 summarizes the main findings of this paper and points out some future research lines.

2. Literature Review

This section presents an analysis of the literature regarding topics that are addressed in this work: e-groceries, Horizontal Cooperation, and Agent-Based Simulation.

2.1. e-Grocery

Nowadays, online shopping has become a key element for reaching the development and proper operation of our society. According to Fraser et al. [14], the electronic commerce (e-commerce) is the process of trading goods, information, or services via computer networks including the Internet. This concept is included within a wider concept (e-business), that refers to any business operation developed by means of information networks (i.e., customer services and knowledge sharing). Hence, this change in consumer habits has impulsed many traditional sellers to adapt their operations and business strategy to be adapted to more competitive scenarios. This situation has generated new challenges related to the e-commerce integration—the customization in order to be competitive enough, a sustainable logistic process (i.e., guarantee the optimum provisioning and delivery of goods), and a company internationalization [15]. Similarly, this change in the supply chain value needs to be accompanied by procedures and methodologies that help to: *(i)* reduce the transaction costs, *(ii)* facilitate just-in-time production strategies, *(iii)* boost short delivery-times, *(iv)* and improve information gathering and processing. Focusing on e-groceries, it refers to the purchase or acquisition of products by internet that provides relative convenience to the consumers, since they can obtain the required groceries from the comfort of their homes or offices and at a convenient time [16]. Regarding sellers, two types of retailers can be distinguished: the ones that have their own vehicle fleets for regional delivery, and the ones that ship nationwide via parcel delivery services. Furthermore, the first group of retailers presents the competitive advantage of having specialized vehicle fleets for different requirements and offering small time windows, although featuring local narrowness [17]. As a consequence, some sellers within this first group are not delivering any refrigerated food, making additional grocery shopping necessary (with the associated risk of losing clients). Therefore, it is in this context where horizontal cooperation plays an important role for survival of small retailers within the marketplace.

All this complex new system have led some authors, such as Wilson-Jeanselme and Reynolds [18], to study the preferences of consumers who demand these services. In particular, they find out that ordering, product quality, time, and reliability in the delivery process are the most important characteristics to know the client preferences to decide the purchase timing and the bought product. But, the design of a sustainable e-grocery service, in both economic and environmental terms, involves not only the consideration of those multiple attributes, but also a market segmentation based on the consumers' preferences knowledge. Similarly, the development of a precise service offer, enhancing the quality service (i.e., punctual delivery) is another key aspect of the sustainable e-grocery distribution.Thus, Ellinger et al. [19] have highlighted the importance of collaboration between logistics and marketing. Reinforcing the same idea, Seidel et al. [20] and Boyer et al. [21] show that being able to balance the desires for short delivery time-windows, that are more attractive to consumers (marketing desire), with longer delivery windows, which produce more efficient routes (sellers desire), can improve the outcome performance of the e-grocery service and foster the positioning of the seller within the marketplace.

As a result, some authors, such as Fikar et al. [22], have designed and implemented a simulation and optimization-based Decision Support System (DSS) that can help decision-makers in developing e-grocery sustainable operations and proper service offers (e.g., perishability management or safety related issues). For addressing this topic, the most common methodology is the Vehicle Routing Problem (VRP) and its variations (e.g., the Capacity Vehicle Routing Problem (CVRP) or the Vehicle Routing Problem with Backhauls (VRPB)). For example, Emeç et al. [16] designed a mathematical program for efficient delivery services of online groceries to fulfill a diverse consumer demand without incurring in additional inventory costs. That model is based on a distribution network in which the goods are acquired from an external set of vendors, sited at multiple locations within the supply network, and delivered to consumers in a single visit in an e-grocery environment. Furthermore, Hornstra et al. [23] introduced the VRP with simultaneous pickup and delivery, and managerial costs. In this work, the fleet of vehicles operates from a single depot for serving all the orders, which considers a delivery and a pickup demand such that all delivery items originate from and all pickup items go to the depot. Finally, it is important to mention that the increment in the popularity of this new type of good consumption has helped to reduce the carbon footprint in urban areas [24]. Note that, this is one of the reasons of its success along with its excellent results when it is managed by means of horizontal cooperation [25].

2.2. Horizontal Cooperation

Recently, new characteristics related to the current economic status quo, such as strong competition in global markets, introduction of products with shorter life cycles, or heightened customers expectations, have forced companies to invest in developing stronger and mutually beneficial relationships between them. This collaborative-sharing process usually involves multiple companies or autonomous business entities engaging in strategic relationships. Consequently, they can share improved outcomes and benefits [10] in supply chain in inter-organizational and inter-functional stages [26]. In this context, Bahinipati et al. [27] refers to horizontal cooperation as a set of actions developed by the partnership of several companies within the same supply chain level and oriented to improve their outcome in economic and sustainable terms. Lambert et al. [28] defined horizontal cooperation as a business-oriented relationship that is based on mutual trust, commitment, and openness, in which the main goal is to foster competitive advantage in the marketplace (i.e., assuming that the cooperative outcome would be greater than the one achieved in solitary, promoting the positioning within the market).

The partnering aims at increasing productivity through close cooperation, that is, small and medium enterprises could act as large enterprise, and consequently, would increase their benefits from economies of scale. For example, optimizing vehicle capacity utilization, reducing empty mileage, and cutting costs of non-core/supporting activities to increase the competitiveness of logistic networks [11]. According to Cao and Zhang [29], the main cooperative advantages and the most desired synergic outcomes are the strategic benefits gained over competitors through partnership, that enables inventory centralization and ordering. In the same line, Nooteboom [30] depicted that some of the expected results of the cooperative process are: *(i)* efficiency in the exploitation of resources; *(ii)* development of new competencies along with strengthening of the production capacity; and *(iii)* better positioning in markets.

However, some problems are expected to may arise in the process [31]—inequality in power distribution, where less powerful partners are likely to feel discriminated against; or the appearance of opportunism and dysfunctional disputes, because partnering firms are competing for the same customers. Nevertheless, as Rindfleisch [32] pointed out, these problems emerged within the same supply chain level are supposed to be lower in intensity, since companies usually do not rely on the output of partners for developing their core activity.

2.3. Agent-Based Simulation

Agent-based models (ABMs) are computational simulations in which artificial entities interact over time within customized environments [33]. That means, ABMs try to reproduce individual processes of movement, behavior, birth, growth, and death according to a set of information, such as genotype, history, and location of agents (i.e., crucial components of the analysis). Furthermore, ABMs permit an unequaled control and some statistical power by allowing to specify the behavior of any number of agents and observe their interactions over time. In this scenario, an agent is considered an actor who plays a role within a given environment and who functions independently (i.e., according to the nature and behavior of other agents, responses can vary too) from other agents (i.e., settlements, people, political entities or companies, among others). In order to be able to respond to this dynamic system, agents have protocols or mechanisms that describe how they interact with other agents, having themselves their own characteristic idiosyncrasies [34]. Moreover, an agent is an identifiable, discrete individual with a set of characteristics or attributes, behaviors, and decision-making capability which can be considered as a particular individual [35]. Also, agents are adaptive in that they respond to their environment through learning and evolution and are autonomous in that they control their own goals, states, and conducts [36].

In addition, ABMs present an ideal framework for social simulation that helps to specify causal mechanisms, that is, models that simulate not only individual behavior but also social interaction that characterizes society development and criterion [37]). Considering the aforementioned approach, ABMs are present in the literature in a wide variety of fields, such as economics [38], sociology [39], political science [40], or artificial intelligence [41]. Their use is widespread in modeling human social and organizational behavior and individual decision-making [42,43], where individual and group behavior, social interaction, and collaboration, among others, are main actors. This trend seems likely to continue in the same line, so their implementation will become frequent in geography and in urban and regional planning [44].

According to Macal and North [45], the main reasons for popularity in the use of agent-based modeling are: *(i)* the current systems that need to be analyzed and modeled have become in complex systems in terms of interdependencies, and accordingly, traditional modeling tools may not be as applicable as they once were; *(ii)* ABMs present an answer for those systems that always have been too complex to be represented (i.e., economic models); *(iii)* the collection process is finer now (i.e., individual-based simulations); and *(iv)* computational power is advancing rapidly. Nowadays, it is possible to compute large-scale microsimulation models that would not have been plausible just a few years ago.

3. The e-Grocery Demand Analysis in the City of Pamplona (Spain)

The interest of analysing the e-grocery demand in a medium sized city is three-fold. Firstly, the e-grocery penetration is lower and customers' characteristics heavily differ from those in large cities [46]. Secondly, the transportation infrastructure is usually poorer than in large cities, which makes transportation activities less efficient [47]. Thirdly, the literature review has revealed a lack of research focused on small and medium cities, being large cities the center of attention in most of the research. Therefore, the geographical scope of our experiment is Pamplona area in Northern Spain, which includes a population of about 250,000 inhabitants. Figure 1 shows the location of the city in Spain and demand and supply points, where purple dots stand for demand locations and hexagon marks stand for the selected supermarkets for the experiments.

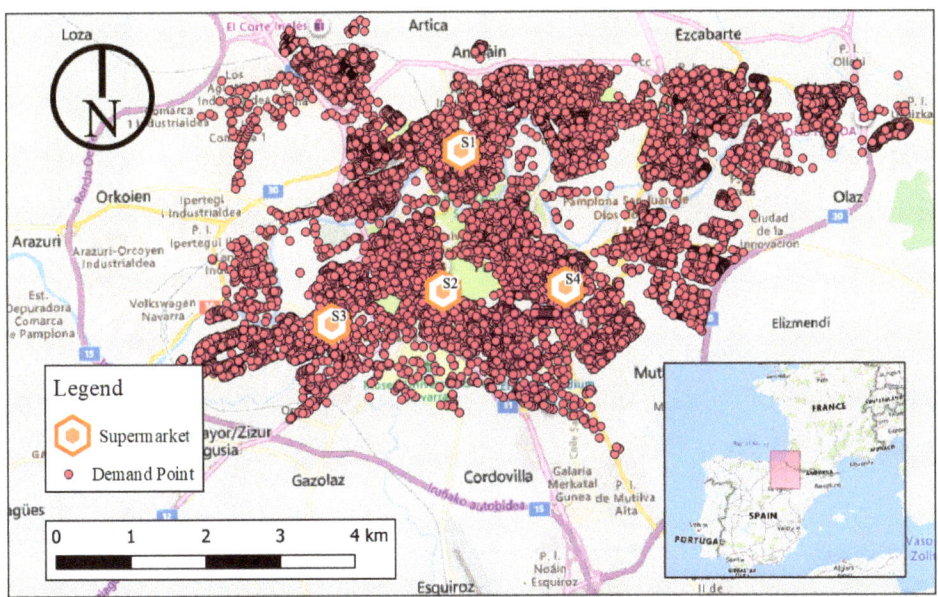

Figure 1. Survey geographical scope, customer and supermarket agents, and Pamplona location in Spain.

A survey was distributed in the area for gathering e-grocery demand information in the time period from 1 February 2020 to 31 March 2020. The questionnaire was compounded by three blocks of questions. An introductory section, aimed at collecting socio-economic information such as age, gender, and economic status, among others. This section is particularly interesting because it introduces the topic to analyse and focuses the survey on e-groceries. Therefore, the main objective of that section is to clarify what we refer to the e-grocery demand. The second section is intended to gather the e-grocery information. It contains questions related to the supermarket preference, the type of product, the frequency of shopping online groceries, and the expense made on e-grocery. Finally, the third section is focused on the logistic part of the e-grocery service. Therefore, the questions here referred to the day of the week, as well as the preferred time window for the delivery. The selection procedure was based on simple random sampling using the e-mail. For this purpose, different mail distribution lists, for example, from the Council and the Public University of Navarra, were used for reaching the participants. All in all, we accounted for 182 observations.

Analysing carefully the survey, we can highlight the main aspects related to the e-grocery demand patterns in Pamplona. Firstly, there are four main supermarkets for ordering online. They are detailed in Table 1. Thus, we will use these four supermarkets for our simulation model. Secondly, most of the participants do not usually order groceries online. About a 25% of the total order e-groceries at least once a month. The frequency of ordering is provided in Figure 2. Third, delivery preferences are basically during the weekdays at the 19-22 h time window. The detailed delivery preferences are provided in Figure 3.

Table 1. Preference for e-grocery supermarkets.

Supermarket	Nickname	Preference	Webpage
Eroski	S1	17.60%	https://www.eroski.es/
Mercadona	S2	9.10%	https://www.mercadona.es/
Carrefour	S3	7.50%	https://www.carrefour.es/
Dia	S4	4.80%	https://www.dia.es/

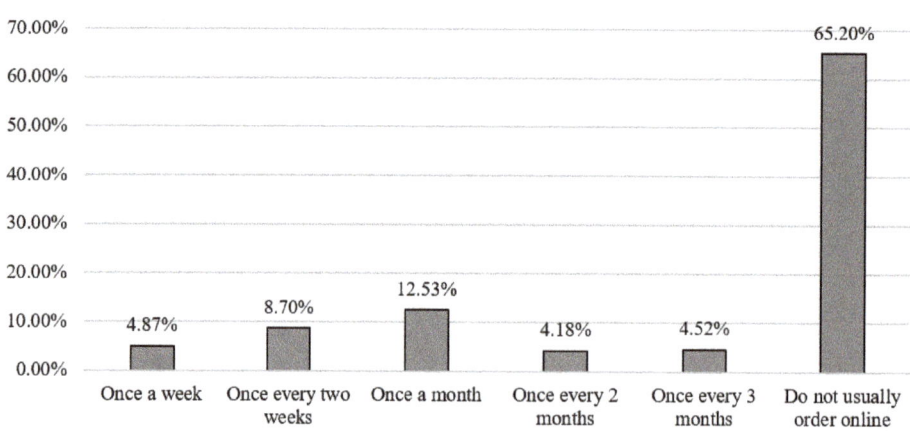

Figure 2. E-groceries frequency ordering.

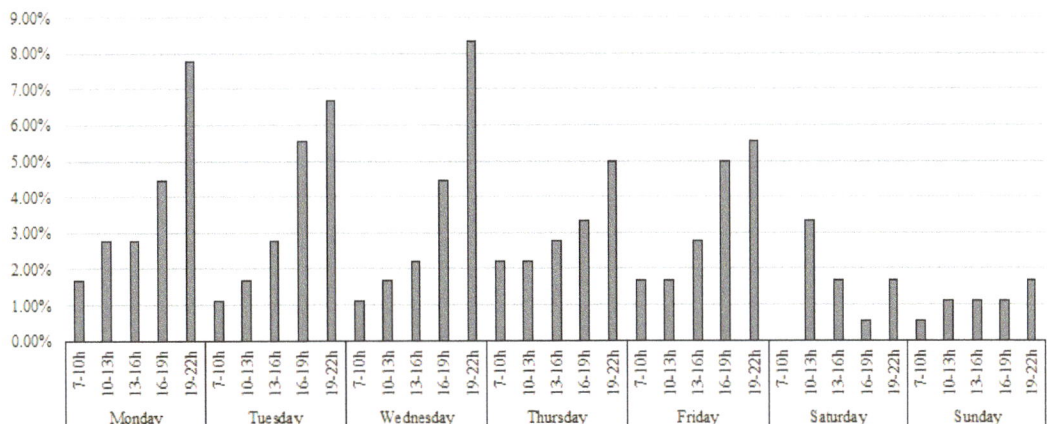

Figure 3. E-grocery delivery preferences per day of the week.

With the information previously obtained, we can estimate the expected demand, that is, number of orders, for the considered supermarkets. These estimations, shown in Table 2, are the main input for our simulation model. In particular, we first computed the expected weekly demand at the last row. These figures were obtained by using the information in Table 1 and Figure 2. Since those computations and experiments have been calculated on a weekly basis, we use a discrete random variable, for computing weekly demands, associated to the customers ordering frequency as it is shown in Figure 2. The possible values of that random variable are: 1 for purchasing once a week, 0.5 for purchasing once every two weeks, 0.25 for purchasing once a month, 0.125 for purchasing once every two months, 0.0625 for purchasing once every three months, and 0 for not ordering online. Additionally, we assume the study area accounts for 100,000 households. We consider this a good approximation due to the fact that the Pamplona metropolitan area has around 250,000 inhabitants and the average household size is around 2.5 people [48]. Therefore, the expected weekly demand for any supermarket is obtained as the product of the random variable, its probability distribution function, and the number of households. Afterwards, the expected weekly demand is distributed among the time windows according to estimated probabilities drawn from the information in Figure 3.

Table 2. Expected demand (number of orders) per time window and day of the week.

Day of the Week	Time Window	S1	S2	S3	S4
Monday	7–10 h	38.88	20.10	16.57	10.60
	10–13 h	64.79	33.50	27.61	17.67
	13–16 h	64.79	33.50	27.61	17.67
	16–19 h	103.67	53.60	44.18	28.27
	19–22 h	181.42	93.80	77.31	49.48
Tuesday	7–10 h	25.92	13.40	11.04	7.07
	10–13 h	38.88	20.10	16.57	10.60
	13–16 h	64.79	33.50	27.61	17.67
	16–19 h	129.58	67.00	55.22	35.34
	19–22 h	155.50	80.40	66.27	42.41
Wednesday	7–10 h	25.92	13.40	11.04	7.07
	10–13 h	38.88	20.10	16.57	10.60
	13–16 h	51.83	26.80	22.09	14.14
	16–19 h	103.67	53.60	44.18	28.27
	19–22 h	194.38	100.50	82.83	53.01
Thursday	7–10 h	51.83	26.80	22.09	14.14
	10–13 h	51.83	26.80	22.09	14.14
	13–16 h	64.79	33.50	27.61	17.67
	16–19 h	77.75	40.20	33.13	21.20
	19–22 h	116.63	60.30	49.70	31.81
Friday	7–10 h	38.88	20.10	16.57	10.60
	10–13 h	38.88	20.10	16.57	10.60
	13–16 h	64.79	33.50	27.61	17.67
	16–19 h	116.63	60.30	49.70	31.81
	19–22 h	129.58	67.00	55.22	35.34
Saturday	7–10 h	0.00	0.00	0.00	0.00
	10–13 h	77.75	40.20	33.13	21.20
	13–16 h	38.88	20.10	16.57	10.60
	16–19 h	12.96	6.70	5.52	3.53
	19–22 h	38.88	20.10	16.57	10.60
Sunday	7–10 h	12.96	6.70	5.52	3.53
	10–13 h	25.92	13.40	11.04	7.07
	13–16 h	25.92	13.40	11.04	7.07
	16–19 h	25.92	13.40	11.04	7.07
	19–22 h	38.88	20.10	16.57	10.60
Expected weekly demand		2332.53	1206.02	993.98	636.14

4. Methodology

For analyzing the impacts of horizontal cooperation on the urban e-grocery distribution we have developed an agent-based simulation model. This simulation model accounts for two populations of agents (i.e., the *customers* and the *supermarket*) who interact in the Pamplona metropolitan physical environment. Additionally, the coalition of supermarkets is also included as an agent. This coalition agent includes the supermarket agents and the different cooperative protocols, including the non cooperative setting in which the supermarkets act independently. Thus, each generated entity, as agent in the simulation model, has its own parameters, variables and rules that describe its behavior in the environment. Actually, we chose an agent-based simulation approach because it allows to easily deal with complexity and interdependencies between *customers* and *supermarkets* in cooperative and non cooperative settings [45]. As it is described in forthcoming subsections, the idea behind the simulation model is that *customers* place orders to their preferred *supermarket* choosing the time to receive their products inside a *time window*. Afterwards, the *supermarkets* have to fulfill the orders using the cooperative policies or not, depending on the running settings. This simulation model takes the backbone of the previous work performed by Serrano-Hernandez et al. [49] and Serrano-Hernandez et al. [50] and adapts it to our research requirements. Thus, Serrano-Hernandez et al. [49] test horizontal cooperation for a number of geographical distribution settings for last-mile urban distribution in the city of Vienna (Austria). Similarly, Serrano-Hernandez et al. [50] investigate some trust-related issues when some coalitions between supermarkets chains are created. The main differences of our work in relation to the previous papers lie on the geographical scope, the real-life based input data, the definition of horizontal cooperation policies, and the solving algorithms for the resulting Vehicle Routing Problems.

The rest of this section is organised as follows. The key performance indicators for our simulation are described in Section 4.1. The particularities of the agent are further described in Sections 4.2 and 4.3 for *customers* and *supermarkets*, respectively. Section 4.4 describes the rules for the cooperative settings and Section 4.5 shows the simulation flow.

4.1. Key Performance Indicators

We used a bidimensional performance for evaluating the impact of horizontal cooperation. The first dimension is an economic indicator whereas the second one is related to service quality. They are further described in Figure 4.

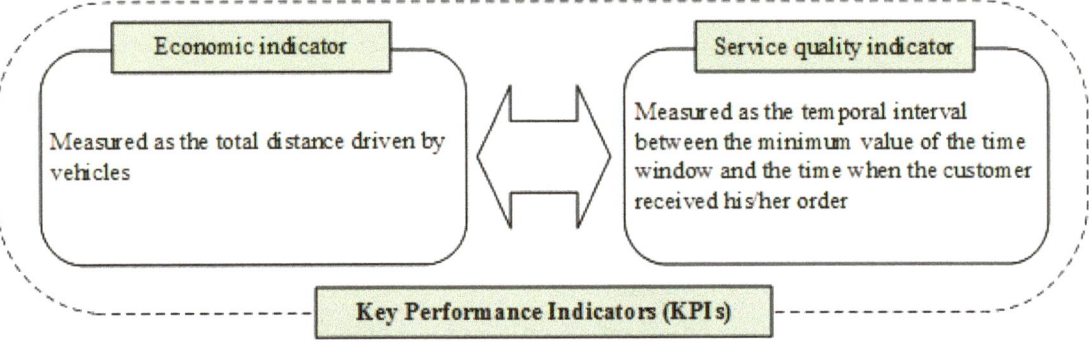

Figure 4. Key Performance Indicators for evaluating horizontal cooperation.

4.2. The Customer Agents

Customers are represented by the cadastral information in the area using a geographical information system (GIS). They are the purple dots in Figure 1, which provide the location for each building of the 12,000 constructions in the metropolitan area of Pamplona (Spain). Knowing the population of the city and the size of each household (its average is 2.5 [48]), we assume that each building lodges 8 households. Therefore, in our simulation model, each demand point is replicated 8 times. Parameters and variables associated to each of the roughly 96,000 demand points in the simulation model are related to the nature of the buyer, that is, whether it is an e-grocery buyer, and, if so, the preferred supermarket, the preferred time windows and day of the week for e-grocery deliveries, and the lead time from the beginning of the selected time window and the moment at which the products are delivered. Additionally, we assume that each customer has a service time of 3 min, where this time is considered as the temporal interval of making the physical delivery between the last mile distribution vehicle and the customer home.

4.3. The Supermarket Agents

We consider the top four e-grocery *supermarkets* in Navarre, region where Pamplona is located in Spain, for our experiments, that is, Eroski ($S1$), Mercadona ($S2$), Carrefour ($S3$), and Dia ($S4$). Recall Table 1 for additional details. They are popular supermarket chains in Spain and offer a wide range of online groceries, including fresh vegetables and fruits. The locations of these supermarkets are shown in Figure 1. The parameters and variables associated to each supermarket consist in the list of customers to serve each day and time window, distance driven, and available fleet. The fleet is a critical part in the logistics performance of the company. At this manner, we assumed that each supermarket owns an homogeneous fleet with a capacity of 20 orders. Likewise, the size of the fleet has been determined with the expected weekly demand per time window, which is shown in Table 2. Considering all the submitted orders to the supermarkets per day, we have obtained an average value of 100.36, 51.89, 42.77, and 27.37 orders for the supermarkets $S1$, $S2$, $S3$, and $S4$, respectively. Hence, knowing the aforementioned demand values, we assume that the fleet size is 4 vehicles for $S1$, 2 for $S2$ and $S3$, and 1 for $S4$. The purpose behind this assumption is to have a fleet size correlated to the number of orders at each supermarket.

4.4. The Cooperative Protocols and the Routing Algorithms

We consider three scenarios based on the degree of cooperation. Each of them features an algorithm to solve the problem. They are described in the following subsections.

4.4.1. No Cooperation Scenario

If cooperation is not enabled, each supermarket will serve its customers in an independent way. Consequently, each supermarket has to solve as many Vehicle Routing Problems (VRP) [51] as time window slots it offers to design the orders distribution plans. We have implemented a heuristic algorithm to solve each VRP, which is based on a biased randomization solution procedure of Clarke and Wright's Savings algorithm [52,53]. Thus, we have followed the instructions given in Grasas et al. [54] and Juan et al. [52] to design our own algorithm to solve the corresponding VRP. In this sense, we use the value 0.2 for the skewed distribution (a truncated geometrical distribution) mentioned by Grasas et al. [54] with 1000 iterations as stopping criterion. The flowchart of the proposed algorithm is shown in Figure 5.

4.4.2. Limited Cooperation Scenario

In the intermediate scenario of limited cooperation, companies in the coalition are allowed to share a given proportion of their customers for each logistic service, that is, each time window and day. The cooperative mechanism consists of creating a pool of customers that may be served from other companies in the coalition. We fix the quota for transferring customers to a 50%. Note that, it is based on time-distance (time to make the delivery in the real situation of traffic in a fixed time) to the chosen supermarket. Then, the customers are iteratively assigned to the closest supermarket until the pool of customers is empty. This process is illustrated in Figure 6 for a given time window, where companies transfer a total of 30 customers to the common pool. The initial contributions of each company in the example are 3 customers from $S1$, 15 from $S2$, 4 from $S3$ and 8 from $S4$. Then, customers are transferred at different rounds until the pool of customers is empty. In this case, there are 3 rounds for assigning the customers. In the first round, the percentage of customers the biggest contributor (supermarket having the greatest number of orders in one day) may pick is bounded by the percentage corresponding to the smallest contributor. Since there are 3 rounds, the smallest contributor is assigned a 33% of customers per round, which means that each company should receive a 33% of their given customers per round. That gives 5 customers to the first picker, that is, $S2$. Recall that customers assignment is based on time-distance. Therefore, the 5 closest customers in the pool are assigned to $S2$. If the aforementioned proportions do not produce an integer number, as it is the case for $S4$ and $S3$, then the number of assigned customers is rounded up. This process is repeated until all the customers are assigned in forthcoming rounds. Then, the resulting VRP is solved using the biased randomization procedure described in Figure 5. Finally, when customers are served, they are reassigned to the chosen supermarket and this process is restarted for the next time window.

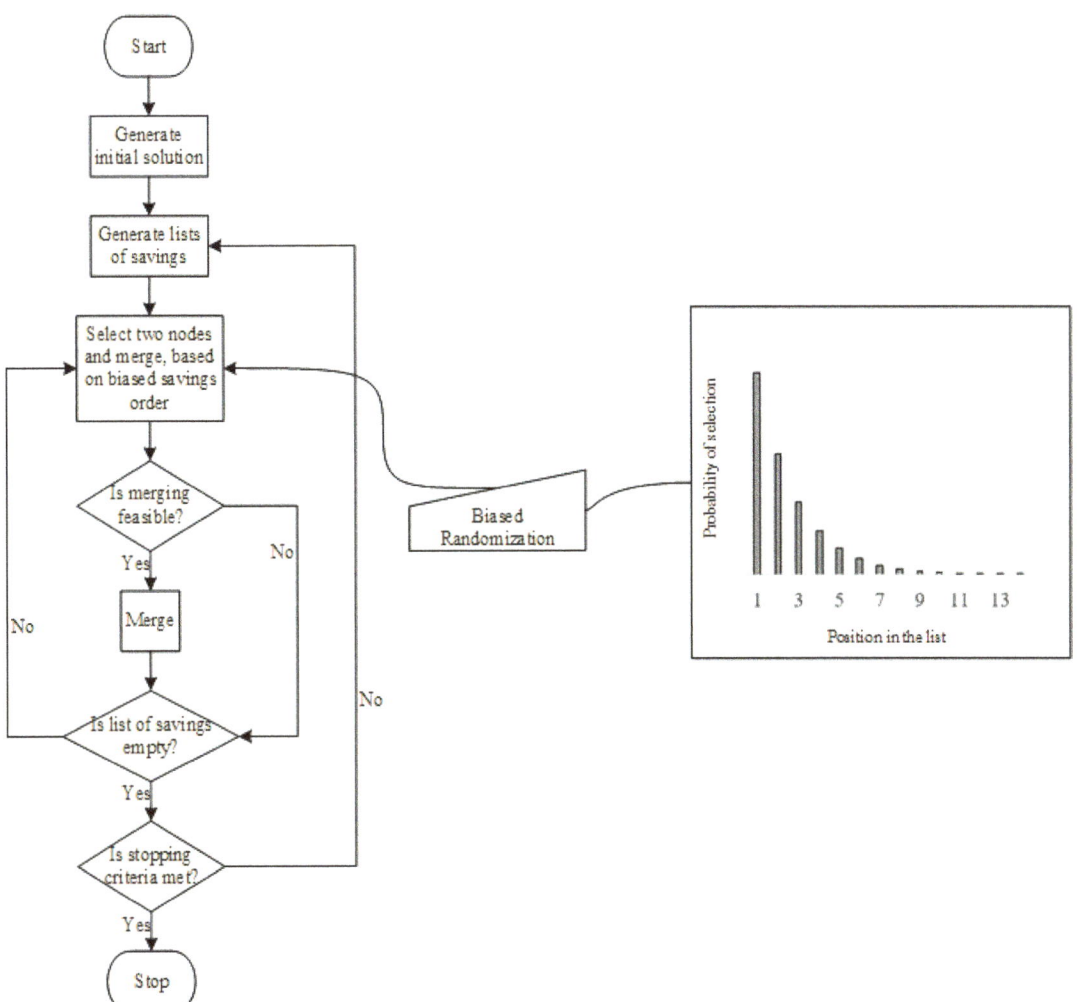

Figure 5. Flowchart of the proposed algorithm for solving the Vehicle Routing Problems (VRPs).

4.4.3. Full Cooperation Scenario

In full cooperative settings all *supermarkets* serve conjointly all *customers*. That is, the four supermarket chains make a coalition which sets a delivery problem for the demanded orders. This problem must be solved considering a number of Multi Depot Vehicle Routing Problems (MDVRP) [55] according to the time window slots we have. Consequently, we implemented a heuristic MDVRP following the recommendations described in Juan et al. [56]. The solution procedure starts sorting the *supermarkets* to each *customer* based on time-distances. Then, each customer is randomly assigned to a supermarket using a biased randomization procedure [56]. That is, closer supermarkets to the customers have greater probabilities to be chosen. Once all customers are assigned, the same biased-randomization procedure previously described in the VRP is applied to obtain a complete solution (see Figure 5). Finally, this solution is saved and a percentage of customers (50% in our experiments) are unassigned from their supermarkets and reassigned using the biased-randomized assignment procedure. Then, the MDVRPs are again solved. This process is repeated a number of iterations (150 in our case study) and the best solution so far is reported. The flowchart of the proposed algorithm for the MDVRP is shown in Figure 7.

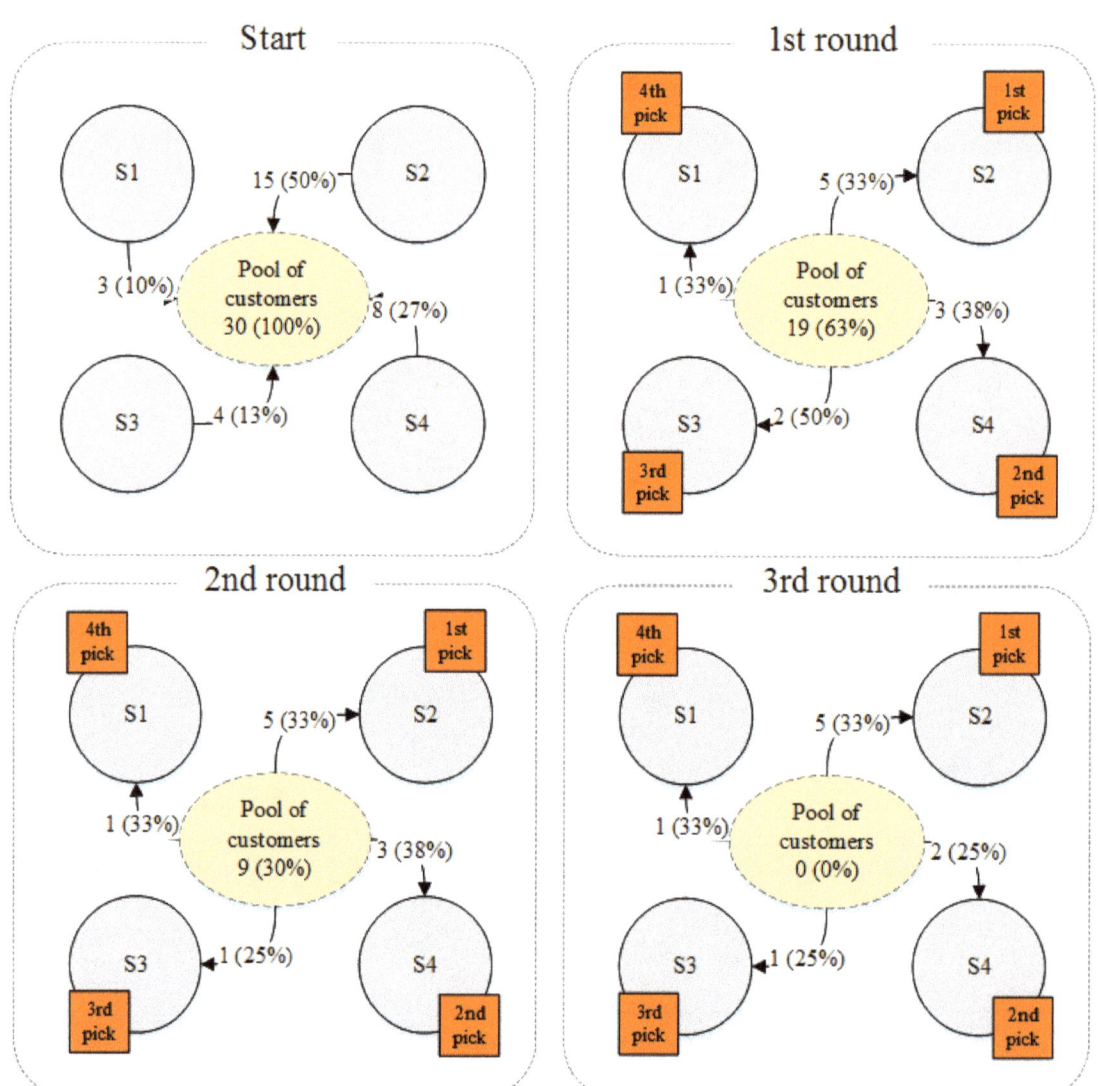

Figure 6. Example of the limited cooperation mechanism.

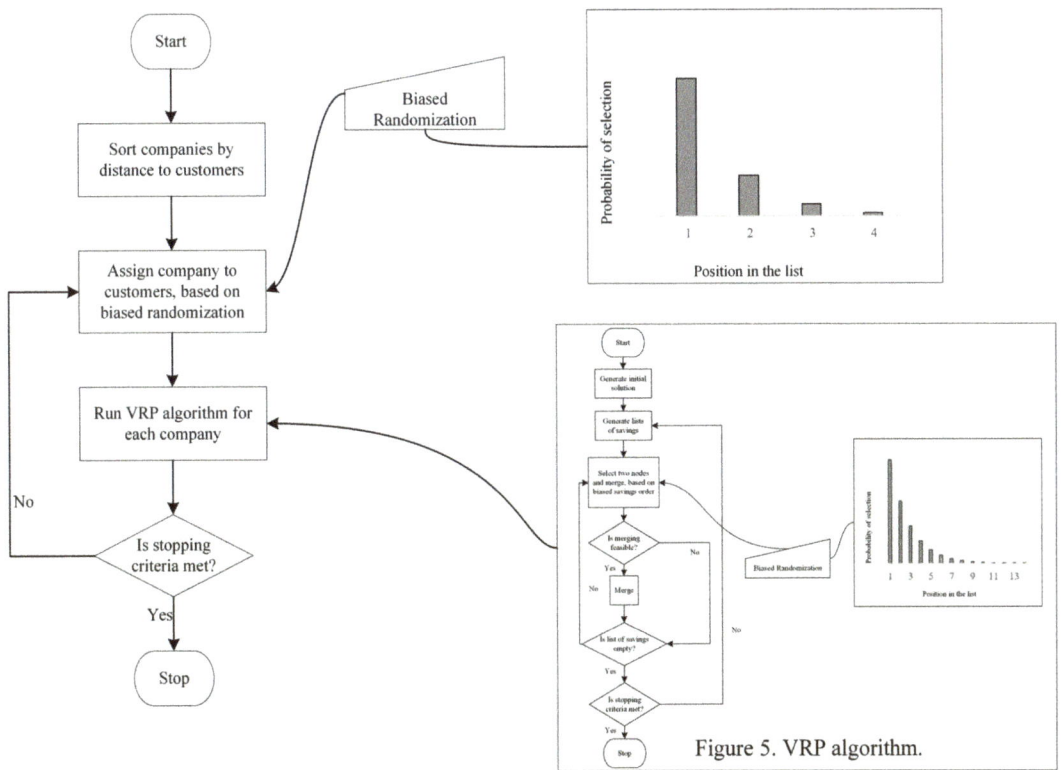

Figure 7. Flowchart of the proposed algorithm for solving the Multi Depot VRPs (MDVRP).

4.5. Dynamics of the Simulation

All parameters related to *customer* and *supermarket* agents are set at each simulation replication. That is, according to the input data, the *customers* place their e-groceries orders to their preferred *supermarket* to be served at a specific time window on a day-week. Note that customers are randomly assigned to a supermarket following the probability distribution function (that is, the preferences) given in Table 1. Then, the three cooperation settings are tested, following the next protocol: firstly, the non-cooperative settings; secondly, the limited cooperation protocol; and finally, the full cooperation policy. The simulation model starts on *Monday* with the non-cooperative settings. Orders are delivered following a sequential policy according to time windows. That is, all the supermarkets start their deliveries at 7*am* using the solution reported by the VRP algorithm described in Figure 5. Note that, the routes finish once all customers have been served, which implies that violating a time window will delay the starting time for the deliveries in the following time windows. This is repeated for the rest of the week. Once the non-cooperative scenario is solved, the key performance indicators are returned, and the limited cooperation protocol is evaluated following the procedure described in Section 4.4.2. Notice that, we maintain the parameters set at the beginning of the replication for these settings. Similarly, once limited cooperation is evaluated, the process is repeated for the full cooperation policy and the KPIs are reported. In total, we run 100 simulation replications. This simulation dynamics overview is shown in Figure 8.

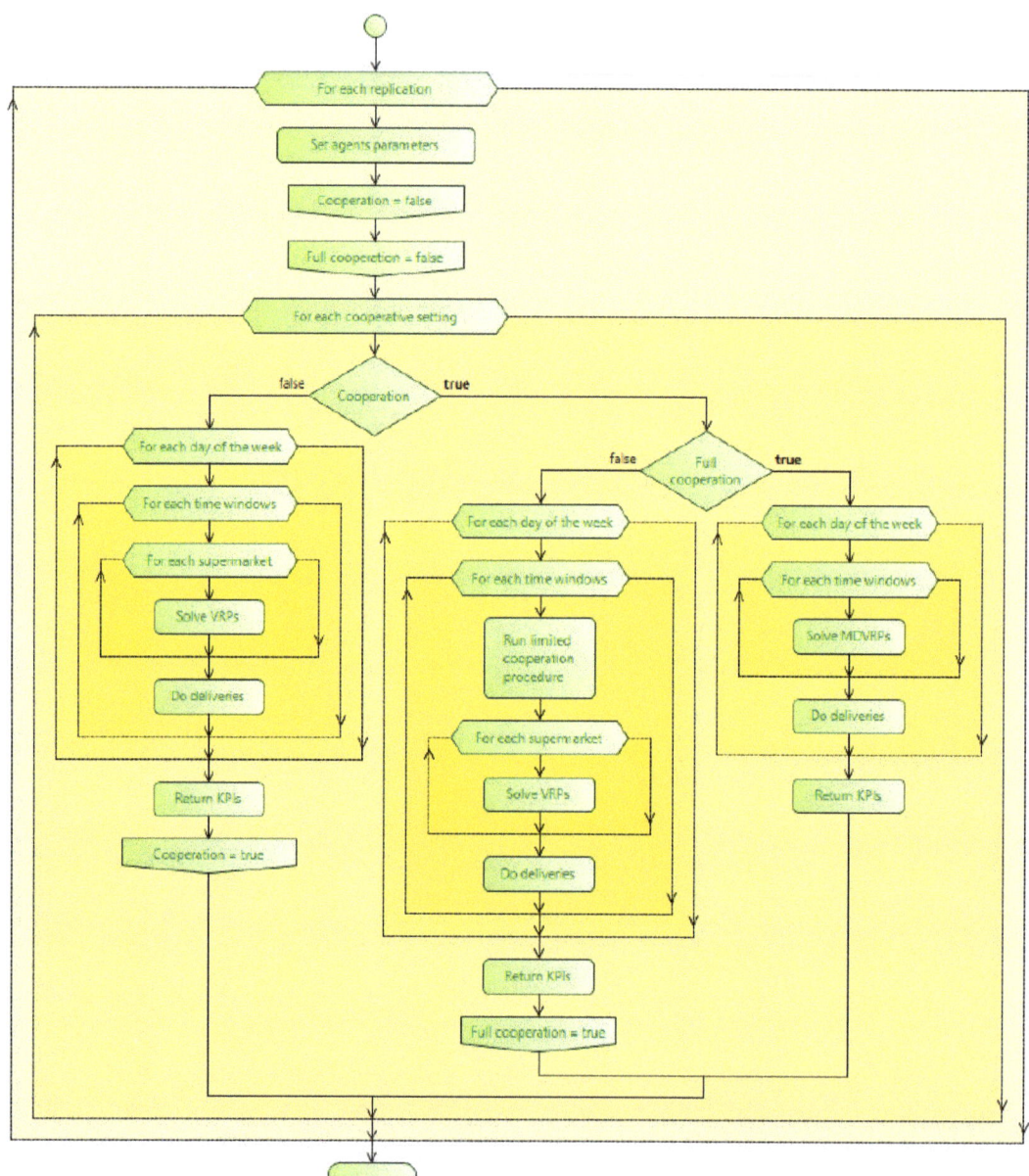

Figure 8. Simulation dynamics overview.

5. Experimental Results

The simulation model and the algorithms were implemented in AnyLogic 8.6.0 [57] software, and run in a standard desktop with an Intel® Core™ i7- 9700K CPU @3.60 GHz and 16 GB RAM. This section firstly describes the main results when running the simulation for different cooperation settings. Secondly, we analyse the general effects of an unexpected increase on demand figures.

The main results are depicted in Figures 9 and 10. They show the boxplots of average distances driven and lead times (which are defined as the temporal distances between the minimum value of the time window and the time when the customer received his or her order) of the 100 simulation replications, respectively. Tables 3 and 4 display average distance driven (in km) and average lead times (in minutes), respectively, for each supermarket and cooperation settings. They also show the percentage variation in the averages for non- and limited cooperation and limited and full cooperation strategies. Note that the last row in Table 3 shows the total distance driven by all supermarkets during a week, whereas the last row in Table 4 shows the average lead time a customer has to be waiting, independently from the chosen supermarket.

Table 3. Average distance driven (km) in the 100 replications for non-, limited, and full cooperation settings for each supermarket.

	No Cooperation	Limited Cooperation	% Change	Full Cooperation	% Change
S1	694.79	511.16	−26.43%	352.43	−49.27%
S2	357.24	297.21	−16.80%	210.68	−41.03%
S3	299.92	257.12	−14.27%	184.28	−38.56%
S4	192.27	166.04	−13.64%	133.48	−30.58%
Total	1544.21	1231.53	−20.25%	880.87	−42.96%

Table 4. Average lead times (minutes) in the 100 replications for non-, limited, and full cooperation settings for each supermarket.

	No Cooperation	Limited Cooperation	% Change	Full Cooperation	% Change
S1	166.69	126.74	−23.97%	80.36	−51.79%
S2	147.77	115.58	−21.78%	84.97	−42.50%
S3	134.14	106.41	−20.67%	80.19	−40.22%
S4	112.27	90.00	−19.84%	73.17	−34.83%
Average	149.74	115.99	−22.54%	80.55	−46.21%

As it can be observed, horizontal cooperation significantly improves the logistics performance of the e-grocery distribution. First of all, the total distance driven is reduced by a 20.25% when the limited cooperation mechanism is activated; and by a 42.96% when full cooperation is achieved, on average. Nevertheless, this effect clearly depends on the size of the supermarket (in terms of expected demand). Reductions are greater for large supermarkets (up to 49.27%) and much lower for smaller supermarkets (up to 30.58%). Secondly, service quality, measured as the lead time, is also benefited from the application of horizontal cooperation in a similar way. Actually, average lead time is reduced by a 22.54% and a 46.21%, on average, for limited and full cooperation, respectively. Here, the size of the supermarket also determines the horizontal cooperation impacts amplitude. Finally, we can observe how boxplots ranges and interquartile ranges clearly get reduced for all supermarkets when cooperation is implemented. Therefore, the KPIs, that is, distances and lead times, gain stability while uncertainty is mitigated.

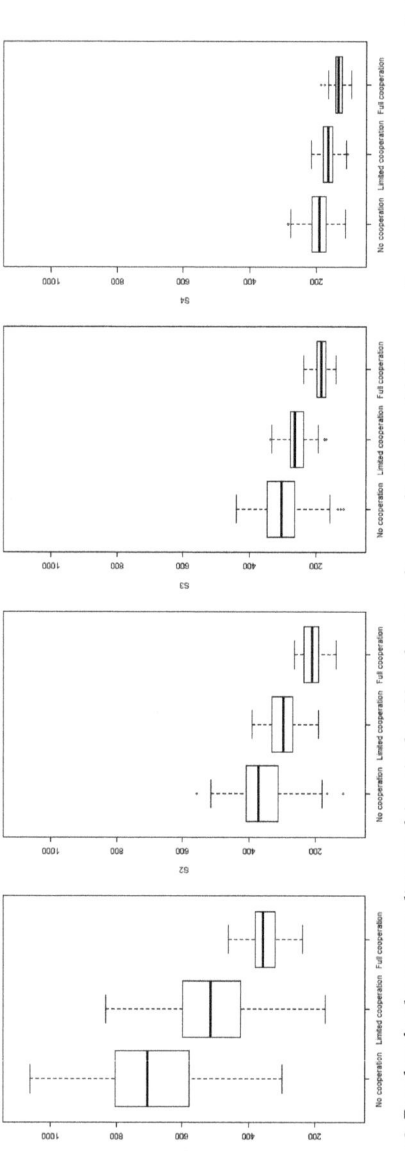

Figure 9. Boxplots for the average distance driven in the 100 replications for non-, limited, and full cooperation settings for each supermarket.

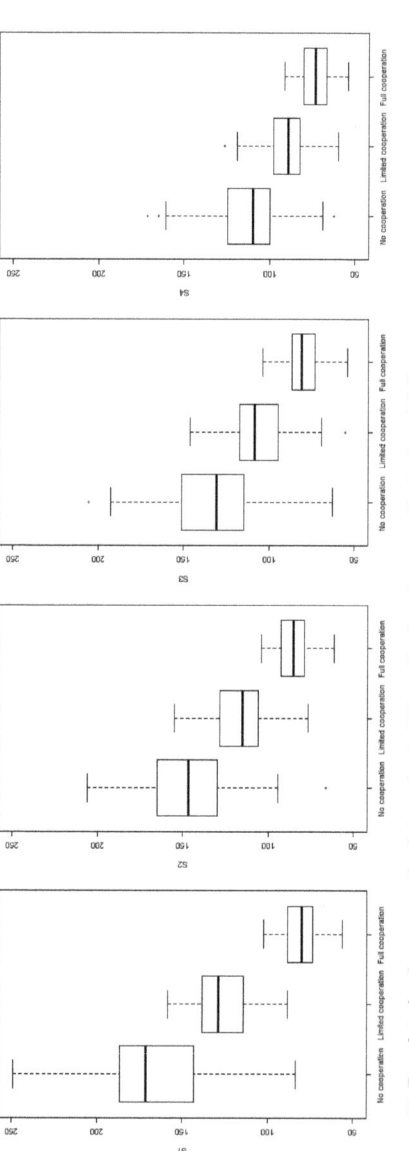

Figure 10. Boxplots for the average lead times in the 100 replications for non-, limited, and full cooperation settings for each supermarket.

Furthermore, additional scenarios have been analysed in order to demonstrate the robustness of the presented approach, featuring increases on the demand figures. Our aim is showing that the horizontal cooperation benefits are kept when we depict a wide range of scenarios. We consider three demand scenarios. Firstly, the base scenario, which has been already analysed and whose demand is estimated in Section 3. Secondly, a scenario featuring an increase of a 25% on demand figures. Finally, a scenario in which the number of orders increase a 50%. The fleet size is kept fixed for all the scenarios according to the description made in Section 4.3. Tables 5 and 6 show the KPIs obtained from the results in the mentioned scenarios, that is, distance driven and lead times, respectively. The first row in the tables show the scenarios to be addressed, the second one the cooperative strategy to be employed, the next four rows show the average results for each of the four supermarkets, and the last row the overall average results. As expected, an increase on demand levels produces increments on both the distance driven and the lead times. Nevertheless, it must be highlighted that those increments feature different patterns depending on the cooperation settings. Actually, as it can be observed in Figure 11, the greater the increase on demand figures is, the greater the positive effects on distances are. This is particularly noticeable in the no cooperation settings, where the distance driven increases a 29% and a 65% when demand increases a 25% and a 50%, respectively. However, these increments are lower in the full cooperation environment, a 20% and a 51%, respectively. That is, the slope (i.e., the negative effects) is softer when cooperation is implemented, which leads to a better response to unexpected demand increases. Similar insights can be obtained when analysing the effects on leading times in Figure 12.

Table 5. Average distance driven (km) in the 100 replications for non-, limited, and full cooperation settings for each supermarket by demand increase scenario.

	Base			25% Demand Increase			50% Demand Increase		
	No Coop	Limited	Full	No Coop	Limited	Full	No Coop	Limited	Full
S1	694.79	511.16	352.43	920.92	672.00	437.60	1,170.52	823.10	537.42
S2	357.24	297.21	210.68	453.13	366.93	249.79	589.85	481.62	324.80
S3	299.92	257.12	184.28	383.76	317.32	220.14	502.50	423.37	285.92
S4	192.27	166.04	133.48	235.53	199.21	152.93	280.24	235.75	185.27
Total	1544.21	1231.53	880.87	1993.34	1555.46	1060.45	2543.11	1963.84	1333.41

Table 6. Average lead times (minutes) in the 100 replications for non-, limited, and full cooperation settings for each supermarket by demand increase scenario.

	Base			25% Demand Increase			50% Demand Increase		
	No Cooperation	Limited	Full	No Coop	Limited	Full	No Coop	Limited	Full
S1	166.69	126.74	80.36	220.94	166.62	99.78	280.82	204.08	122.54
S2	147.77	115.58	84.97	187.44	142.69	100.74	243.99	187.29	130.99
S3	134.14	106.41	80.19	171.64	131.33	95.79	224.75	175.21	124.42
S4	112.27	90.00	73.17	137.53	107.98	83.83	163.64	127.79	101.56
Total	149.74	115.99	80.55	717.55	548.61	380.15	913.20	694.38	479.51

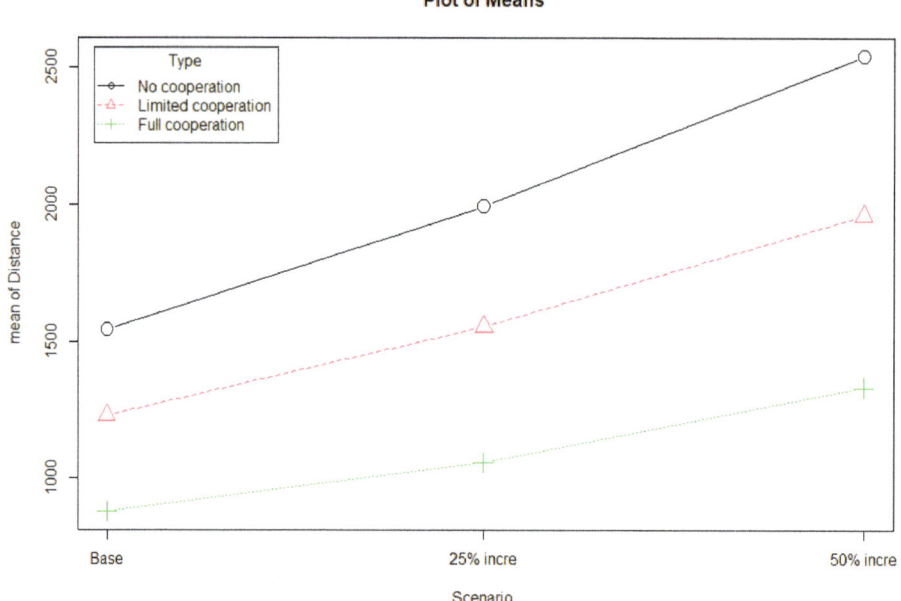

Figure 11. Mean plots by demand scenario and cooperative setting for total distances.

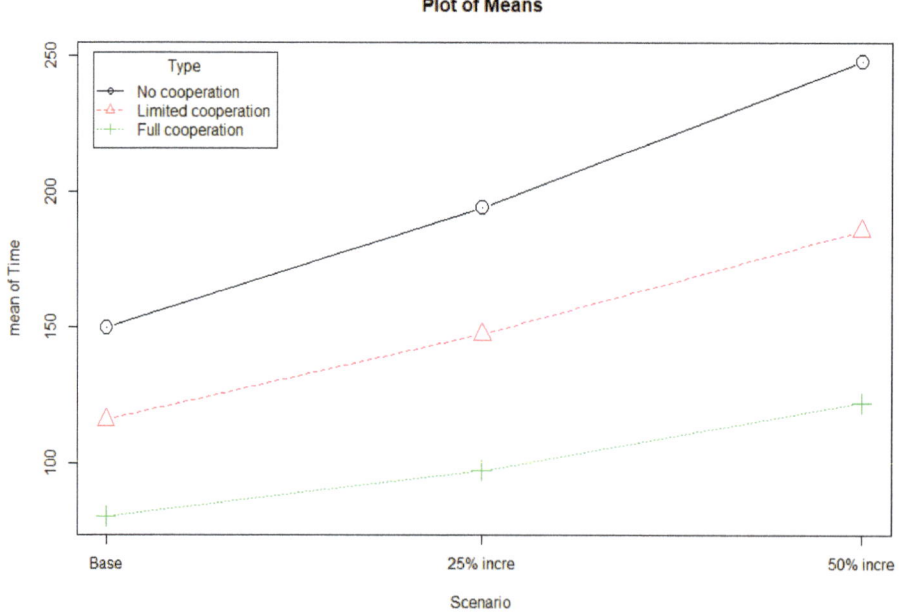

Figure 12. Mean plots by demand scenario and cooperative setting for average lead times.

6. Conclusions, Limitations, and Future Research

This work presents the use of horizontal cooperation as a way to gain competitiveness in the e-grocery delivery sector. For testing the convenience of using horizontal cooperation, we develop an agent-based simulation model in the city of Pamplona (Spain). We evaluate the effects on the economic and service quality sides of the logistics operations for different scenarios which consist on distribution of online demand orders at supermarkets. Two degrees of horizontal cooperation for performing the deliveries are tested, while distribution plans are determined by the implementation of a biased randomization algorithm. As a result, the use of horizontal cooperation clearly improves the economic and service quality performance of the e-grocery distribution. Furthermore, the distribution becomes more robust to unexpected demand increases when the coalition is able to absorb the new demand more efficiently than the actors independently.

Nevertheless, there are a number of assumptions made during the modeling process that imply some limitations to our work. Firstly, we assume all the orders contain products available at all supermarkets. Therefore, we are assuming that customers order products that are identical in the different supermarkets in the coalition, such as top brand products and fresh vegetables and fruits. Nonetheless, note that in our simulation experiments, the customers do not change the preferred supermarket, they still order to their preferred supermarket but it is the coalition that internally makes efficient assignments and then the order is supplied, or not, by a different supermarket or, even, by a third party logistic service provider. Secondly, we are considering that supermarkets will accept all orders they receive. That means there are no limitations for dispatching any order at any time window. Thirdly, we are assuming each supermarket owns an homogeneous fleet. This means that all the fleets are composed of vehicles of identical capacity, which does not resemble reality, as many different vehicle types may exist in a flotilla. Finally, we assume there are cooperation agreements as exposed. Actually, horizontal cooperation may adapt many different forms in terms of time frame, amplitude, stamina, and the involved organizational levels [58].

Regarding future research, two new clear scopes can be considered. On the one hand, there are opportunities to develop more complex simulation models. This involves the access to high resolution data to better estimate demand patterns and supermarket characteristics. Additionally, the ad-hoc definition of horizontal cooperation policies that are currently running on logistics-related services would allow the calibration and validation of forthcoming simulation-based researches. On the other hand, practical issues should be analysed and integrated in the optimization models. This refers to the way in which benefits and risks are shared in the coalition; as well as how the coalition should evolve during time.

Author Contributions: Conceptualization, A.S.-H. and J.F.; methodology, A.S.-H.; writing–original draft preparation, A.S.-H. and R.d.l.T.; writing—review and editing, L.C. and J.F. All authors have read and agreed to the published version of the manuscript.

Funding: This work has been partially supported by the Spanish Ministry of Science, Innovation, and Universities (RED2018-102642-T; PID2019-111100RB-C22/AEI/10.13039/501100011033) and the SEPIE Erasmus+ Program (2019-I-ES01-KA103-062602). We also want to acknowledge the support received from the CAN Foundation in Navarre, Spain (Grant ID 903 100010434 under the agreement LCF/PR/PR15/51100007).

Institutional Review Board Statement: Not applicable.

Informed Consent Statement: Not applicable.

Data Availability Statement: Data are available upon reasonable request to the corresponding author.

Conflicts of Interest: The authors declare no conflict of interest.

References

1. Kämäräinen, V.; Punakivi, M. Developing cost-effective operations for the e-grocery supply chain. *Int. J. Logist.* **2002**, *5*, 285–298. [CrossRef]
2. Olsson, J.; Hellström, D.; Pålsson, H. Framework of last mile logistics research: A systematic review of the literature. *Sustainability* **2019**, *11*, 7131. [CrossRef]
3. Fredriksson, A.; Liljestrand, K. Capturing food logistics: A literature review and research agenda. *Int. J. Logist. Res. Appl.* **2015**, *18*, 16–34. [CrossRef]
4. Williams, J.; Memery, J.; Megicks, P.; Morrison, M. Ethics and social responsibility in Australian grocery shopping. *Int. J. Retail. Distrib. Manag.* **2010**, *38*, 297–316. [CrossRef]
5. Teller, C.; Holweg, C.; Reiner, G.; Kotzab, H. Retail store operations and food waste. *J. Clean. Prod.* **2018**, *185*, 981–997. [CrossRef]
6. Fikar, C. A decision support system to investigate food losses in e-grocery deliveries. *Comput. Ind. Eng.* **2018**, *117*, 282–290. [CrossRef]
7. Rodríguez, S.V.; Plà, L.M.; Faulin, J. New opportunities in operations research to improve pork supply chain efficiency. *Ann. Oper. Res.* **2014**, *219*, 5–23. [CrossRef]
8. Sawik, B.; Faulin, J.; Pérez-Bernabeu, E. Multi-criteria optimization for fleet size with environmental aspects. *Transp. Res. Procedia* **2017**, *27*, 61–68. [CrossRef]
9. Schaltegger, S.; Burritt, R.; Varsei, M.; Soosay, C.; Fahimnia, B.; Sarkis, J. Framing sustainability performance of supply chains with multidimensional indicators. *Supply Chain. Manag. Int. J.* **2014**, *19*, 242–257. [CrossRef]
10. Soosay, C.A.; Hyland, P. A decade of supply chain collaboration and directions for future research. *Supply Chain. Manag. Int. J.* **2015**, *20*, 613–630. [CrossRef]
11. Wang, X.; Kopfer, H. Collaborative transportation planning of less-than-truckload freight. *OR Spectrum* **2014**, *36*, 357–380. [CrossRef]
12. Arlbjørn, J.S.; Wallenburg, C.M.; Raue, J.S. Conflict and its governance in horizontal cooperations of logistics service providers. *Int. J. Phys. Distrib. Logist. Manag.* **2011**, *41*, 385–400.
13. Cruijssen, F.; Dullaert, W.; Fleuren, H. Horizontal cooperation in transport and logistics: A literature review. *Transp. J.* **2007**, *46*, 22–39.
14. Fraser, J.; Fraser, N.; McDonald, F. The strategic challenge of electronic commerce. *Supply Chain. Manag. Int. J.* **2000**, *5*, 7–14. [CrossRef]
15. da Silveira, G.J. Towards a framework for operations management in e-commerce. *Int. J. Oper. Prod. Manag.* **2003**, *23*, 200–212. [CrossRef]
16. Emeç, U.; Çatay, B.; Bozkaya, B. An adaptive large neighborhood search for an e-grocery delivery routing problem. *Comput. Oper. Res.* **2016**, *69*, 109–125. [CrossRef]
17. Hübner, A.H.; Kuhn, H.; Wollenburg, J.; Towers, N.; Kotzab, H. Last mile fulfilment and distribution in omni-channel grocery retailing: A strategic planning framework. *Int. J. Retail. Distrib. Manag.* **2016**. [CrossRef]
18. Wilson-Jeanselme, M.; Reynolds, J. Understanding shoppers' expectations of online grocery retailing. *Int. J. Retail. Distrib. Manag.* **2006**, *34*, 529–540. [CrossRef]
19. Ellinger, A.E.; Keller, S.B.; Hansen, J.D. Bridging the divide between logistics and marketing: facilitating collaborative behavior. *J. Bus. Logist.* **2006**, *27*, 1–27. [CrossRef]
20. Seidel, S.; Mareï, N.; Blanquart, C. Innovations in e-grocery and logistics solutions for cities. *Transp. Res. Procedia* **2016**, *12*, 825–835.
21. Boyer, K.K.; Prud'homme, A.M.; Chung, W. The last mile challenge: evaluating the effects of customer density and delivery window patterns. *J. Bus. Logist.* **2009**, *30*, 185–201. [CrossRef]
22. Fikar, C.; Mild, A.; Waitz, M. Facilitating consumer preferences and product shelf life data in the design of e-grocery deliveries. *Eur. J. Oper. Res.* **2019**. [CrossRef]
23. Hornstra, R.P.; Silva, A.; Roodbergen, K.J.; Coelho, L.C. The vehicle routing problem with simultaneous pickup and delivery and handling costs. *Comput. Oper. Res.* **2020**, *115*, 104858. [CrossRef]
24. Figliozzi, M.; Saenz, J.; Faulin, J. Minimization of urban freight distribution lifecycle CO2e emissions: Results from an optimization model and a real-world case study. *Transp. Policy* **2020**, *86*, 60–68. [CrossRef]
25. Zissis, D.; Aktas, E.; Bourlakis, M. Collaboration in urban distribution of online grocery orders. *Int. J. Logist. Manag.* **2018**. [CrossRef]
26. Calleja, G.; Corominas, A.; Martínez-Costa, C.; de la Torre, R. Methodological approaches to supply chain design. *Int. J. Prod. Res.* **2018**, *56*, 4467–4489. [CrossRef]
27. Bahinipati, B.K.; Kanda, A.; Deshmukh, S. Horizontal collaboration in semiconductor manufacturing industry supply chain: An evaluation of collaboration intensity index. *Comput. Ind. Eng.* **2009**, *57*, 880–895. [CrossRef]
28. Lambert, D.M.; Emmelhainz, M.A.; Gardner, J.T. Building successful logistics partnerships. *J. Bus. Logist.* **1999**, *20*, 165.
29. Cao, M.; Zhang, Q. Supply chain collaborative advantage: A firm's perspective. *Int. J. Prod. Econ.* **2010**, *128*, 358–367. [CrossRef]
30. Nooteboom, B. *Inter-Firm Collaboration, Learning And Networks: An Integrated Approach*; Routledge, Taylor and Francis Group: New York, NY, USA, 2004.
31. Tidström, A. Causes of conflict in intercompetitor cooperation. *J. Bus. Ind. Mark.* **2009**, *27*, 506–518. [CrossRef]

32. Rindfleisch, A. Organizational trust and interfirm cooperation: an examination of horizontal versus vertical alliances. *Mark. Lett.* **2000**, *11*, 81–95. [CrossRef]

33. Jackson, J.C.; Rand, D.; Lewis, K.; Norton, M.I.; Gray, K. Agent-based modeling: A guide for social psychologists. *Soc. Psychol. Personal. Sci.* **2017**, *8*, 387–395. [CrossRef]

34. Garcia, R. Uses of agent-based modeling in innovation/new product development research. *J. Prod. Innov. Manag.* **2005**, *22*, 380–398. [CrossRef]

35. Macal, C.M.; North, M.J. Agent-based modeling and simulation. In Proceedings of the 2009 Winter Simulation Conference (WSC), Austin, TX, USA, 13–16 December 2009; pp. 86–98.

36. Macy, M.; Flache, A. *The Oxford Handbook of Analytical Sociology; Chapter Social Dynamics from the Bottom Up: Agent-Based Models of Social Interaction*; Oxford University Press: Oxford, UK, 2002; pp. 245–268.

37. Macal, C. Everything you need to know about agent-based modelling and simulation. *J. Simul.* **2016**, *10*, 144–156. [CrossRef]

38. Tesfatsion, L.; Judd, K.L. *Handbook of Computational Economics: Agent-Based Computational Economics*; Elsevier: Amsterdam, The Netherlands, 2006.

39. Bruch, E.; Atwell, J. Agent-based models in empirical social research. *Sociol. Methods Res.* **2015**, *44*, 186–221. [CrossRef] [PubMed]

40. Cederman, L.E. Computational models of social forms: Advancing generative process theory. *Am. J. Sociol.* **2005**, *110*, 864–893. [CrossRef]

41. Wooldridge, J.M. Cluster-sample methods in applied econometrics. *Am. Econ. Rev.* **2003**, *93*, 133–138. [CrossRef]

42. Liu, R.; Jiang, D.; Shi, L. Agent-based simulation of alternative classroom evacuation scenarios. *Front. Archit. Res.* **2016**, *5*, 111–125. [CrossRef]

43. Bonabeau, E. Agent-based modeling: Methods and techniques for simulating human systems. *Proc. Natl. Acad. Sci. USA* **2002**, *99*, 7280–7287. [CrossRef] [PubMed]

44. O'Sullivan, D.; Haklay, M. Agent-based models and individualism: is the world agent-based? *Environ. Plan. A* **2000**, *32*, 1409–1425. [CrossRef]

45. Macal, C.; North, M. Introductory tutorial: Agent-based modeling and simulation. In Proceedings of the Winter Simulation Conference 2014, Savanah, GA, USA, 7–10 December 2014.

46. Mkansi, M.; de Leeuw, S.; Amosun, O. Mobile application supported urban-township e-grocery distribution. *Int. J. Phys. Distrib. Logist. Manag.* **2019**, *50*, 26–53. [CrossRef]

47. Alvarez, P.; Serrano-Hernandez, A.; Faulin, J.; Juan, A. Using Modelling Techniques to Analyze Urban Freight Distribution. A Case Study in Pamplona (Spain). *Transp. Res. Procedia* **2018**, *33*, 37–74. [CrossRef]

48. Spanish Institute of Statistics. Continuous Household Survey. 2019. Available online: https://www.ine.es/dyngs/INEbase/en/operacion.htm?c=Estadistica_C&cid=1254736176952&menu=ultiDatos&idp=1254735572981 (accessed on 20 April 2020).

49. Serrano-Hernandez, A.; Hirsch, P.; Faulin, J.; Fikar, C. The role of horizontal cooperation to improve service quality in last-mile distribution. *Int. J. Simul. Process. Model.* **2018**, *13*, 299–309. [CrossRef]

50. Serrano-Hernandez, A.; Faulin, J.; Hirsch, P.; Fikar, C. Agent-based simulation for horizontal cooperation in logistics and transportation: From the individual to the grand coalition. *Simul. Model. Pract. Theory* **2018**, *85*, 47–59. [CrossRef]

51. Mor, A.; Speranza, M. Vehicle routing problems over time: A survey. *4OR* **2020**. [CrossRef]

52. Juan, A.; Faulin, J.; Ruiz, R.; Barrios, B.; Caballé, S. The SR-GCWS hybrid algorithm for solving the capacitated vehicle routing problem. *Appl. Soft Comput. Journal* **2010**, *10*, 215–224. [CrossRef]

53. Juan, A.A.; David Kelton, W.; Currie, C.S.M.; Faulin, J. Simheuristics Applications: Dealing with Uncertainty in Logistics, Transportation, and other Supply Chain Areas. In Proceedings of the 2018 Winter Simulation Conference (WSC), Gothenburg, Sweden, 9–12 December 2018; pp. 3048–3059. [CrossRef]

54. Grasas, A.; Juan, A.; Faulin, J.; de Armas, J.; Ramalhinho, H. Biased randomization of heuristics using skewed probability distributions: A survey and some applications. *Comput. Ind. Eng.* **2017**, *110*, 216–228. [CrossRef]

55. Ramachandiran, R.; Suresh Joseph, K.; Ravisasthiri, P.; Victer Paul, P. A comprehensive study on the recent variants of the VRP and its solving methodologies. *Int. J. Appl. Eng. Res.* **2015**, *10*, 43635–43644.

56. Juan, A.; Pascual, I.; Guimarans, D.; Barrios, B. Combining biased randomization with iterated local search for solving the multidepot vehicle routing problem. *Int. Trans. Oper. Res.* **2015**, *22*, 647–667. [CrossRef]

57. AnyLogic. Available online: https://www.anylogic.com/1 (accessed on 20 September 2020).

58. Serrano-Hernández, A.; Juan, A.; Faulin, J.; Perez-Bernabeu, E. Horizontal collaboration in freight transport: Concepts, benefits, and environmental challenges. *Stat. Oper. Res. Trans.* **2017**, *41*, 1–22.

Article

An Algorithm for Efficient Generation of Customized Priority Rules for Production Control in Project Manufacturing with Stochastic Job Processing Times

Mathias Kühn *, Michael Völker and Thorsten Schmidt

Institute of Material Handling and Industrial Engineering, Technische Universität Dresden, 01062 Dresden, Germany; michael.voelker@tu-dresden.de (M.V.); thorsten.schmidt@tu-dresden.de (T.S.)
* Correspondence: mathias.kuehn@tu-dresden.de

Received: 15 November 2020; Accepted: 11 December 2020; Published: 13 December 2020

Abstract: Project Planning and Control (PPC) problems with stochastic job processing times belong to the problem class of Stochastic Resource-Constrained Multi-Project Scheduling Problems (SRCMPSP). A practical example of this problem class is the industrial domain of customer-specific assembly of complex products. PPC approaches have to compensate stochastic influences and achieve high objective fulfillment. This paper presents an efficient simulation-based optimization approach to generate Combined Priority Rules (CPRs) for determining the next job in short-term production control. The objective is to minimize project-specific objectives such as average and standard deviation of project delay or makespan. For this, we generate project-specific CPRs and evaluate the results with the Pareto dominance concept. However, generating CPRs considering stochastic influences is computationally intensive. To tackle this problem, we developed a 2-phase algorithm by first learning the algorithm with deterministic data and by generating promising starting solutions for the more computationally intensive stochastic phase. Since a good deterministic solution does not always lead to a good stochastic solution, we introduced the parameter Initial Copy Rate (ICR) to generate an initial population of copied and randomized individuals. Evaluating this approach, we conducted various computer-based experiments. Compared to Standard Priority Rules (SPRs) used in practice, the approach shows a higher objective fulfilment. The 2-phase algorithm can reduce the computation effort and increases the efficiency of generating CPRs.

Keywords: simulation-based optimization; stochastic project scheduling; genetic algorithm; discrete event simulation; composite priority rules

---

1. Introduction

One of the challenges in industrial environments is the handling of a large number of product variants [1] (p. 46). In production, this trend is accompanied by shorter product life cycles and smaller batch sizes with simultaneously increased demands on the objective such as shorter delivery times [2] (p. 5). Short delivery times play a decisive role for the customer [3] (pp. 25–26). The resulting shorter time for product development as well as the prototype character of the products lead to an increase in fuzzy and missing process parameters. These circumstances result in additional requirements for Project Planning and Control (PPC), especially in complex assembly processes that are characterized by human work. Stochastic influenced job processing times are inherent in the process due to human error [4] (p. 31) and will therefore continue to exist in the future. Representative examples of the characteristics mentioned above include the final assembly of customer-specific machine tools and printing machines. An example for job processing time deviations in the considered industry is shown in Figure 1. In addition, each project has its own objectives. At present, neither centrally acting

Algorithms **2020**, *13*, 337; doi:10.3390/a13120337   www.mdpi.com/journal/algorithms

Manufacturing Execution Systems (MES) with integrated Advanced Planning and Scheduling Systems (APS-Systems) [5] (pp. 63–64) nor decentrally used Simple Priority Rules (SPRs, e.g., FIFO (First In–First Out)) can be used to control these requirements [6] (p. 8).

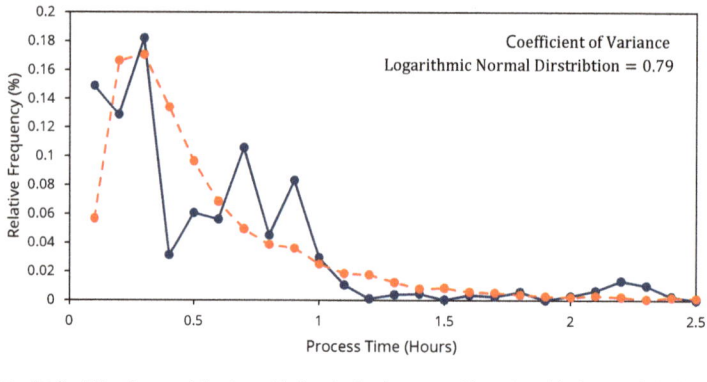

Figure 1. Example of job processing time deviations for a type representative in individual furniture assembly.

In sequence control performed by MES and APS, production follows a deterministic schedule that defines the next job [7] (p. 392). For the industrial domain under consideration, this approach is only suitable to a limited extent, since permanent rescheduling is necessary due to the fuzzy process parameters. Due to the lack of feedback on the processing status of individual work packages [8] (pp. 80–81), it is not clear whether a schedule is still valid or not. In short, the schedule can be obsolete after release. Furthermore, the necessary input of master and transaction data is often insufficient [9]. Sequencing with Priority Rules (PRs) means that a priority (e.g., shortest processing time) is assigned to each job. The priority determines the next job [10] (p. 111). However, the effect of SPRs on the objective values cannot be predicted in a dynamic production environment [11]. Moreover, project-specific objectives are not explicitly taken into account. Promising approaches consist in the combination of priority rules, the so-called Combined Priority Rules (CPRs). Here, different job attributes are combined, and thus, a priority index is calculated for determining the next job. In project manufacturing, CPRs are rarely used for decentralized control. On the one hand, the time for generation is very high; on the other hand, approaches for project-specific objectives are rare. In this paper, we take up the challenge of computational time for the generation of CPRs and develop a concept for project-specific objective fulfillment under stochastic influences.

In the presented paper, we generate project-specific CPRs by combining different individual job attributes with a weighted sum approach. These CPRs are assigned to the project jobs and used for short-term project scheduling. The proposed Genetic Algorithm (GA) used as a hyper-heuristic optimizes weight allocation of these individual attributes. For this purpose, we generate the CPRs by iterative simulation and evaluate the results with the Pareto dominance concept. Since the resulting optimized CPRs in deterministic condition do not necessarily lead to good results under stochastic conditions, we propose a 2-phase algorithm to determine the CPRs. The first phase serves to explore the solution space and to select the best individuals for the second stochastic phase. We validate the concept with computer-aided experiments on a software platform developed especially for this problem. As a simulation method, we use discrete event simulation combined with the theory of simulation-based optimization. Within the scope of the paper, we perform experiments on computation time and performance of the algorithm. In the context of the paper, we address the following research questions:

- Is it possible to improve mean value and standard deviation of project individual objectives by applying the generated CPRs?
- Is it possible to save computation time with the 2-phase algorithm?

The structure of the paper is as follows. Section 2 gives an overview of the state-of-the-art literature related to the possibilities of the automated generation of CPRs. Section 3 contains the model description. In Section 4, we describe the developed 2-phase algorithm. Furthermore, we present the developed software framework for experiment execution. In Section 5, we run experiments to investigate the computation time and performance of the approach. Section 6 provides a summary and outlook.

2. State-of-the-Art

2.1. Problem Definition: RCMPSP

The basic model of resource-constrained multi-project scheduling problem (RCMPSP) was developed by Pritsker et al. [12], Lova et al. [13], and Confessore et al. [14], among others. Based on the work by Confessore et al. [14], Homberger [15] (pp. 556–567) formulated some extensions with regard to decentralized control and developed a benchmark library [16] based on this model. The so-called Multi-Project Scheduling Problem Library (MPSPLIB) is a library with 140 different models differing in number of resources, projects, jobs, and network character. Solutions can be uploaded and checked for feasibility. The MPSPLIB is based on models of the Project Scheduling Problem Library (PSPLIB, [17]) which considers the RCPSP. The models differ mainly in terms of the number of projects ($|I| = 2, \ldots, 20$) and the number of jobs ($|J_i| = 30, \ldots, 120$). Furthermore, there are differences regarding the number of different instances of the individual projects ($iz = 1$: all projects have the same instances; $iz = 2$: each project has an individual instance). For mathematical modelling of the basic problem of the decentral resource constrained multi-project scheduling problem (DRCMPSP) [15] (pp. 556–557), the problem is briefly described as follows: A set of projects with individual objective functions has to be controlled in parallel in a production system. The production system consists of local (only used by project i) and global renewable resources (used by all projects $|I|$). Each project consists of a set of jobs with precedence constraints. The processing times of the jobs on the resources are stochastic. At the time of sequencing, only the expected value of the distribution and the coefficient of variation are known. The projects use both local and global renewable resources. Other project properties concern the earliest start time and due date. As Blasewicz et al. [18] proved, the resource-constrained project scheduling problem as a generalization of the job shop problem is one of the NP-hard (non-deterministic polynomial-time hardness) optimization problems. As a generalization of the resource-constrained project scheduling problem, the resource-constrained multi-project scheduling problem with specific extensions of the process time variations considered in this paper thus belongs to the NP-hard optimization problems [19] (p. 153). Exact procedures that lead to optimal results are largely suitable for generating benchmark solutions [20] (p. 149). The number of calculation steps and thus the calculation time increase with the problem size [21] (p. 38). Already from 60 jobs on, most problems cannot be solved with exact methods [22]. For practical problems, which usually involve considerably more jobs, heuristics are therefore indispensable in order to achieve good results in a shorter computation time. The application of the theory of simulation-based optimization, coupled with heuristics, is also more appropriate for complex models if complex relationships cannot be described simply with the help of mathematical formulas. Furthermore, the advantage is the clarity of simulation models (step-by-step event handling by discrete event simulation), which leads to a higher acceptance than with mathematical optimization models [21] (p. 30). For this reason, we use discrete event simulation as a simulation method. There are many software frameworks. With many of these software frameworks, the job-shop problem can be mapped. For modelling project scheduling problems, however, a high effort of customization is necessary.

2.2. Approaches for Decentralized Control of RCMPSP

In contrast to deterministic optimization, at least one parameter in stochastic optimization is subject to random events [23] (p. 45). Solutions, e.g., schedules or PRs, generated under deterministic conditions may be invalid in the stochastic environment [24] (p. 2); [10] (p. 111); [25] (pp. 21–23). The suitable methods for solving the stochastic optimization problem depend mainly on the dimension of the stochastic influences [19] (p. 249). If stochastic influencing variables can only be described by random variables, methods of stochastic optimization are suitable for scheduling [26] (p. 160). With a static approach, the PRs do not change during the observation period. In contrast, in a dynamic approach, the PRs are adapted during the production process. Thus, we focus on stochastic optimization with a static approach of PR since in the case study of the customized assembly of complex large products the job processing times are characterized by random variables of a logarithmic normal distribution and there are no possibilities for adaption of the PR during production.

PRs such as CPRs are suitable for the considered problem domain with similar functionality and application as SPRs. Simply stated, CPRs are attributes calculated according to a rule from the information on the product, process, resource, and system. The result of the calculation determines the job priority in the queue. A comprehensive review about CPRs and hyper-heuristics is given by Branke et al. [10]. Their paper proposes a taxonomy and guidelines for designing CPRs. As a hyper-heuristic, GAs or neuronal networks are mostly used. Multi-objective algorithms, such as the NSGA-III [27], are not used in the literature.

There are a lot of PPC approaches using CPRs for production control. The majority of existing approaches using CPRs focus on job-shop problems [10] (pp. 110–111), which are in general less complex (e.g., less complex precedence constraints and disjoint resources) compared to resource-constrained project scheduling problems (RCPSP). Kück et al. [28] developed a method based on real-time data to adapt the control model based on CPRs. For this purpose, a simulation is permanently carried out at the same time as actual production. If changes or disturbances occur, the simulation model and consequently the control model are adapted. Permanent data availability is necessary for concept implementation. Grundstein et al. [29] presented an approach to maintain planning reliability while simultaneously taking advantage of the benefits of autonomous control. Central planning provides information such as start and end times. Sequential decision trees determine job release, sequencing, and resource allocation. In addition to the information provided by central planning, these decision trees depend on extensive information on system status in production. Moreover, this concept requires an extensive database which is not available yet.

Decentralized approaches for solving the project scheduling problem focus mainly on agent-based auction and negotiation approaches [30] (pp. 695–704). Only Chand et al. [31] solves the control problem of project manufacturing with CPRs in a stochastic environment. Chand et al. [31] considers the stochastic RCPSP. Project-specific objectives are not considered. Hildebrandt et al. [32] also points out that a Pareto optimization (multi-criteria) is hardly considered.

Strategies that are mainly used in shop-floor production can also be implemented in project-oriented production and vice versa. In contrast with shop floor manufacturing with machines as the main resource, project controlled environments with human resources have less sophisticated data. Thus, it should not be assumed in such environments. While automatically generated CPRs are widely used in job-shop scheduling [10], applications of automatically generated CPRs for the solution of the RCPSP [31] and especially for the solution with a decentralized control of the stochastic RCPSP are rather rare in the literature. We can only guess the reasons for this: while the job-shop environment is traditionally stochastic, the RCPSP environment is also increasingly stochastic (Section 1). Classical solutions for RCPSP by generating a baseline schedule are no longer effective, and the interest in scheduling without a baseline schedule increases. One possibility for efficient scheduling without a baseline schedule are those CPRs. The challenge consists in the project-specific fulfilment of different individual objectives under stochastic influences.

2.3. Reducing Computation Time for Generating CPRs

Branke et al. [10] describe the challenge of computation time for CPRs in their work. We draw the following conclusions for our presented work: while sequencing with CPRs is comparatively fast, generating CPRs with hyper-heuristics (e.g., with evolutionary algorithm) is often very computationally intensive. If stochastic values are to be used as recommended during the generation of the CPRs (so-called training phase), the computational effort increases further. A first possibility to reduce computational effort is the representation of CPRs (Figure 2). The grammar-based tree representation is a composition of individual components to a configurable function based on mathematical operators. This representation has in theory no fixed length and is suitable for larger computational budgets [33]. The advantage of this representation is a large search space which fits the large computational budget [34]. Another variant is parameter-based representation, which is a configurable function with a defined format. The defined format means a fixed length and thus a calculable computational effort but, at the same time, a smaller search space.

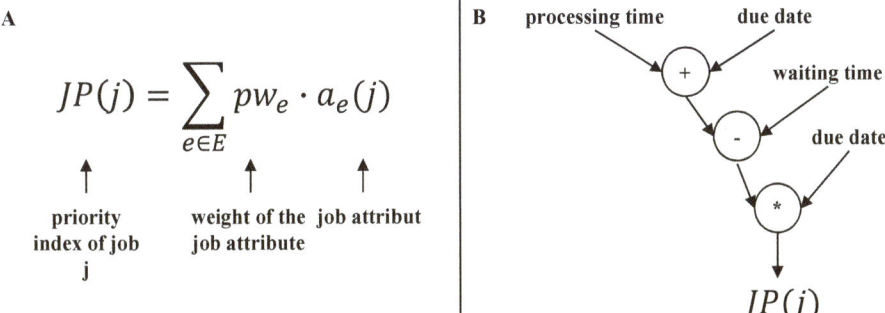

Figure 2. Combined Priority Rules (CPRs): (**A**) parameter-based representation and (**B**) grammar-based representation.

A further method to reduce computational effort is the generation of an optimized initial population, which is currently of minor interest [35]. Most researchers generate the initial population randomly (e.g., Werner [36]; Hildebrandt et al. [32]; Nguyen et al. [37]). Compared to a randomly generated population, the algorithm converges later than with an optimized diverse population. Thus, a decrease of simulation effort will be evolved with an optimized initial population. An approach for improvement consists for example in the use of existing PRs to form the initial population (e.g., Nguyen et al. [38]; Omar et al. [39]). However, research potential for the generation of good initial solutions is an ongoing issue which we address in our paper.

2.4. Contribution and Motivation

Based on the above study on the use of CPRs in project control, some of the differences in this paper compared to existing research are the following points:

- We consider the use of CPRs for short-term production control in an SRCMPSP environment. The CPRs are assigned to each project.
- We perform a Pareto optimization [40] (pp. 197–199) with the NSGA-III on project level, where the mean and standard deviation of delay and makespan of a single project are considered to evaluate the generated CPRs.
- A deterministic and stochastic optimization phase takes place for reducing computational effort. For the selection of deterministic solutions, we introduce the parameter Initial Copy Rate (ICR), which indicates how many solutions are copied and how many are randomized.
- We developed a software framework for generating CPRs and compared results with several different PRs.

3. Model Extensions of the Stochastic RCMPSP

In order to achieve the requirements of the project-specific objectives, a Pareto optimization is aimed as the multi-objective optimization method ($minimize(f_1(x), f_2(x), \dots, f_{zf}(x))$ with $zf > 2$ objective functions f_y).

Due to the stochastic influences, it is necessary to evaluate the individual objective values with statistical parameters. A stochastic scenario n is a realized random number of a specific distribution for job processing times (Section 2.1). The mean value and the standard deviation are considered. The mean value is an indicator for optimality of the solution. The standard deviation is an indicator for the robustness of the solution. A low standard deviation means that many solutions are close to the mean value and therefore stochastic influences are better compensated. The following objective functions are set up for the stochastic scenario.

For measuring the tardiness of project i of scenario n, the project delay PD_{in} is calculated by Equation (1):

$$f_y = PD_{in} = \max\left(0, \omega_{|J|in} - fz_i\right) \tag{1}$$

where $\omega_{|J|in}$ is the scheduled finish time of the last job j of project i of the stochastic scenario n and fz_i is the determined finish time of project i.

Another objective value is the makespan MS_{in}, which is calculated by Equation (2):

$$f_y = MS_{in} = \left(\omega_{|J|in} - \alpha_{1in}\right) \tag{2}$$

where α_{1in} is the starting time of the first job j of project i of the stochastic scenario n. The following objective functions are set up for statistic evaluation of the stochastic scenarios. Equation (3) calculates the mean of project delay M_PD_i of $|N|$ stochastic scenarios:

$$f_y = M\_PD_i = \frac{1}{|N|} \sum_{n \in N} PD_{in} \tag{3}$$

Equation (4) calculates the deviation of project delay M_PD_i of $|N|$ stochastic scenarios:

$$f_y = STD\_PD_i = \sqrt{\frac{1}{|N|} \sum_{n \in N} (PD_{in} - M\_PD_i)^2} \tag{4}$$

The corresponding statistical objective values for makespan MS_i are calculated in the same way as Equations (3) and (4) (STD_MS_i; M_MS_i). Statistical parameters for each objective value are assigned individually ($STD\_$ or $M\_$) or in combination ($STD\_$ and $M\_$), so that, in total, six objective functions are considered. For the objective makespan, the objective functions are given as an example. Minimize the average makespan of individual projects M_MS as in Equation (5):

$$f = M\_MS = (M\_MS_i, \dots, M\_MS_{|I|}) \rightarrow \min \tag{5}$$

Minimize the standard deviation makespan of individual projects STD_MS using Equation (6):

$$f = STD\_MS = (STD\_MS_i, \dots, STD\_MS_{|I|}) \rightarrow \min \tag{6}$$

Minimize the average and standard deviation of the makespan of individual projects M_STD_MS using Equation (7):

$$f = M\_STD\_MS = (STD\_MS_i, \dots, STD\_MS_{|I|}, M\_MS_i, \dots, M\_MS_{|I|}) \rightarrow \min \tag{7}$$

4. Proposed Algorithm for Generating CPR

4.1. Representation of CPR

As a sequence heuristic (SH), we use the basic approach of CPRs with weighting factors, the so-called linear representation of CPRs (Figure 2). Job attributes a_e are, for example, the expected processing time or the required completion date. The weightings can be determined either by an expert, randomly, or by an algorithm. As an extension to previous research work and in order to meet the requirement of project-specific objective fulfillment, weighting factors pw_{ie} are assigned individually to each project i. Thus, according to the individual objective function f_y and project characteristics, individual job attributes a_e can be preferred or disadvantaged.

The considered job attributes a_e are summarized in the tuple AA:

$$AA = (a_1, \ldots, a_e), \tag{8}$$

with $e \in E$, where $e \in \mathbb{N} [1 \ldots E]$. A project-specific weight set PSW_i is defined as follows and has the same length like AA:

$$PSW_i = (pw_{i1}, \ldots, pw_{ie}), \tag{9}$$

with

$$\sum_{e \in E} pw_{ie} = 1 \text{ where } pw_{ie} \in \mathbb{R} [0, 1] \tag{10}$$

For each job in a queue, the first step is to calculate the individual job priority according to the project-specific weight set and job attribute. Formally, the queue is a list of jobs with corresponding job attributes. Normalizing the values is necessary due to the different dimensions of the job attributes. After calculating the priority, the next step is sorting the jobs in descending order of priority. The job with the highest priority is executed next. Calculation of the job priority JP_{ji} of job j of project i is done with the following equation:

$$JP_{ji} (ji_e, max\, J_{I_e}) = PSW_i \cdot AA (ji_e, max\, J_{I_e}) = \sum_{e \in E} pw_{ie} \cdot \frac{a_e (ji_e)}{a_e (max\, J_{I_e})} \tag{11}$$

where with ji_e is the considered value of attribute a_e of the considered job j of project i and $max\, J_{I_e}$ is the maximum value of attribute a_e of all jobs J_I in the considered queue. The job attributes considered were based on locally determined attributes (here, among other things, information is obtained from the examples in MPSPLIB) and are oriented on the used information of the SPR (e.g., processing time, due date, starting time, work remain, and cumulative waiting time).

4.2. Two-Phase Genetic Algorithm for Generating CPRs

The parameterization of the weighting set poses a combinatorial problem with a large solution space. It is not possible to check all individual parameter combinations due to the high computational effort involved. To handle such large search spaces, evolutionary algorithms such as GAs are suitable. With regard to the problem of parameterizing the equation for determining job attributes, the GA corresponds to a hyper-heuristic. Therefore, they are suitable for the problem under consideration. Parallel computing can shorten computation time, especially in stochastic optimization. Computation time increases if the stochastic influences are already taken into account during the training phase. Since there is a correlation between the deterministic and stochastic solutions, we see potential in the combination of deterministic and stochastic training data for saving computation time. If the objective is to use this correlation, i.e., to generate a good quality initial population of solutions for a shorter computation time in the next phase, it is necessary to consider a multitude of deterministic solutions in the stochastic environment. We investigate the quantity and the best solutions for this purpose. Within the scope of the present research, a two-phase algorithm is proposed.

Phase one (Figure 3) starts with an initialization. This means that initial parameters of GA are selected along with the production model (planning task), and it is possible to define the attributes used for the CPRs. Next, initial solutions are generated randomly. Random numbers determine the weightings pw_{ie} of the attributes a_e. Based on the defined weightings for the respective attributes, the production is simulated (shop-floor simulation) with deterministic process times. The result is evaluated, and after a negative check of the stop criterion (unchanged objective values after a defined number of iterations), the weightings are changed by the GA. This process continues until the stopping criteria is reached. The result is a set of different weighting variations evaluated with respect to the objective value. In phase two, the corresponding weighting variants from phase one are firstly selected with the parameter initial copy rate ICR. An $ICR = 0.2$ means that the initial solution for stochastic optimization consists of 20% copied solutions from the first phase. The other 80% are random solutions. Then, in accordance with the theory of simulation-based optimization, GA adjusts weights until the stopping criteria is reached. Although the algorithm generated many schedules with different CPRs, the result is only the CPRs with which the best schedules were generated under stochastic conditions. Under stochastic conditions, the objective value will be identical when using this CPRs. The result of the training phase is therefore the result of the test phase.

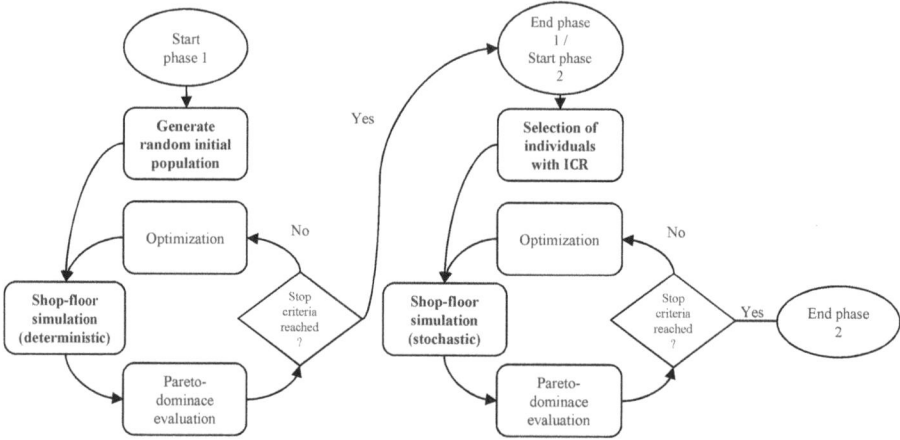

Figure 3. Two-phase genetic algorithm.

In accordance with the research aim of project-specific multi-objective optimization, the differentiated evaluation of the quality of solutions (solutions are the project-specific weight sets PSW_i, in the context of GA, an individual Ind) is carried out according to the Pareto dominance concept. Assuming two solution tuples A and B with zf objective functions f_y and the goal of minimizing the objective values $(f_y(a); f_y(b))$, solution A dominates solution B if $f_y(a) \leq f_y(b)$ applies for $y = 1, 2, \ldots, zf$ and for at least one y $f_y(a) < f_y(b)$.

Based on this rule, all individuals Ind of a population P_{gen} of generation gen can be compared in the current scenario. Non-dominated solutions are elements of a non-dominated solution front ($front = 1$). Since there are more than one solution in the Pareto front, we aggregate and normalize the individual objective to an overall objective value as a tiebreaker. The best solution gets the index $Best$. The formation of a new population P_{gen+1} is carried out with the NSGA-III. The algorithm was developed for multi-objective problems with $zf > 3$ objective functions f_y. The entire algorithm for generating the CPRs is called Genetic Algorithm Weighted Sum (GAWS).

4.3. Overall Concept for Using CPRs and Proposed Software-Framework

The presented concept (Figure 4) for decentralized sequencing is suitable for short-term sequencing at the operation level. For a short-term horizon, SHs are defined by how individual jobs are operatively sequenced on the shop floor. The result is therefore not an implemented schedule by the control system but evolved CPRs that are applied by the control system. The input to generate the CPRs is therefore a defined project pool with jobs or a predefined time horizon. The definition of the input is not part of the analysis but is taken as given in medium-term planning (e.g., MRP-II). Based on a project pool, the proposed algorithm for generating the CPRs is applied. The CPRs are transferred to production resources and applied for the defined validity period. This process is comparable to transfer of the production schedule to actual production. Various options are conceivable for technical implementation: In addition to the transfer to stationary computers at the workstations, the transfer to mobile devices (smartphones and handhelds) is also possible. A possible technical implementation of the CPRs with regard to job identification is for example barcode technology. The barcode contains all information about the projects. The stationary PC or handheld device contains CPRs for determining job priority. New incoming jobs can thus be added to the queue, and if renewable resources become available, the next job to be processed can be determined according to the CPRs. Thus, a rough status regarding finished jobs is known. Moreover, it is possible to share reconfiguration-relevant events (resource failure, etc.) through feedback and to initiate recalculation of CPRs based on the adjusted production parameters.

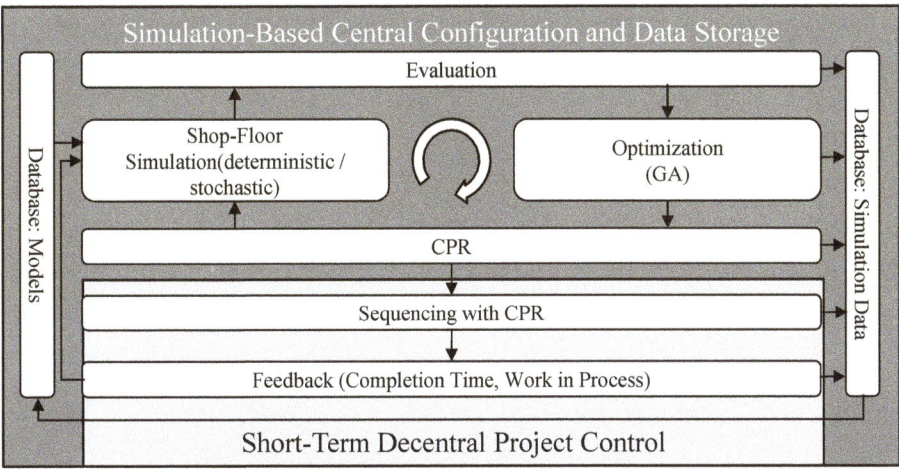

Figure 4. Concept hybrid Project Planning and Control (PPC).

We developed a software framework based on the Python programming language [41] called PyScOp (Python-Based Scheduling and Optimization Framework) to test the algorithm when generating the project-specific CPRs [42,43]. The developed software framework covers all functionalities from model generation to discrete-event simulation-based optimization and evaluation. To calculate the proposed CPRs in the form of weighting sets, the model is first imported. The standard format of MPSPLIB is used. The next step is parameterization of the model (definition of project-specific objectives) and the algorithm (stop criterion, etc.). With subsequent simulation and optimization, the project-specific CPRs are generated. In addition to the standard function for calculating CPRs, various options for evaluating the performance of the algorithm itself and the CPRs are integrated, which largely correspond to the experiments discussed in Section 5. For technical details, please refer to the method documentation within the software code. The software framework has a graphical user interface for simplified use by third parties. Intended tool tips make it easier for the first user to carry out experiments.

5. Results

5.1. Experiment Design for Concept Evaluation

As mentioned, we use benchmark problems from the MPSPLIB to evaluate the concept. We carried out preliminary investigations to determine the runtime of an optimization run (Intel® Xenon® Gold 6136 with 3.00 GHz CPU and 64 GB RAM). The average optimization takes about 12 h (average from small model $|J_i| = 30$, $|I| = 2$ to large model $|J_i| = 120$, $|I| = 5$). The number of experiments must be limited for this runtime. We chose a two-factor plan as the experimental plan for the model parameters. Each factor is assigned two levels and is combined. The levels should represent a low and a high level. This type of experimental design is chosen if many factors are to be investigated and experiments are highly computation intensive. To avoid process-inherent coincidences, the number of repetitions per single experiment is set to $|W| = 10$ [44] (p. 630); [45] (p. 593). The selected models of the MPSPLIB differ in the number of jobs $|J_i| = 30$ and 120, number of projects $|I| = 2$ and 5, and different instances (network character) $iz = 1$ and 2, so that a total of 8 models M are considered. The distribution of the process time is considered with $cv_{lognorm} = 0.1$ and 0.9. Other parameters are considered to be multifactorial and combined with the mentioned two-factor plan. These parameters are the objective functions f (6 factor stages) and the initial copy rate ICR (6 factor stages). These factor combinations are combined with the number of stochastic scenarios $|N|$. Standard values are assumed for the genetic operators by Schmidt et al. [43]. The population size is calculated according to Das et al. [46]. The number of stochastic scenarios for the evaluation of one CPR = GAWS is $|N| = 100$ (usually, in Freitag et al. [47], $|N| = 50$, while in Hildebrandt et al. [48], $|N| = 100$) with $n \in \mathbb{N}$.

5.2. Comparing Deterministic and Stochastic Solutions

For the comparison between deterministic and stochastic solutions, a deterministic optimization is performed first. Afterwards, the generated deterministic solutions ($f = PD$ and $f = MS$) are tested with stochastic values of the scenarios $|N|$. $f = M\_PD$, $f = STD\_PD$, $f = M\_MS$, and $f = STD\_MS$ are used as objective functions to evaluate the stochastic influences. The maximum number of generations is $gen = 100$. The deterministic optimization aborts after $gen = 20$ generations with an unchanged objective value. $Exp_{amt} = 2 \cdot cv_{lognorm} \cdot 8M \cdot 6f \cdot 10W = 960$ experiments were performed. To evaluate the correlation, the Pearson correlation coefficient $r(x, y)$ is calculated. For this purpose, the correlation between the deterministic solution (DET) and mean value (M) of the stochastic solution, the correlation between the deterministic solution and standard deviation (STD) of the stochastic solution, and the correlation between the mean value (M) and standard deviation (STD) of the stochastic solution are calculated. The results are shown in Figure 5 as a boxplot diagram and in Table 1 combined with the mean value and confidence interval $ki_{0.95}$.

Table 1. Statistical analysis coefficient of correlation.

$r(x,y)$	$\bar{x}$	$ki_{0.95}$
DET, M	0.47	± 0.08
DET, STD	0.18	± 0.07
STD, M	0.34	± 0.08

A high correlation exists between the deterministic solution (DET) and the mean value of the stochastic solution (M). Furthermore, there is a significant correlation between the mean value (M) and the standard deviation of the stochastic solution (STD). A low correlation exists between the deterministic solution (DET) and the standard deviation of the stochastic solution (STD). This reinforces the statement that deterministic solutions can be suitable as initial solutions for stochastic optimization. Therefore, setting the parameter initial copy rate *ICR* is of interest.

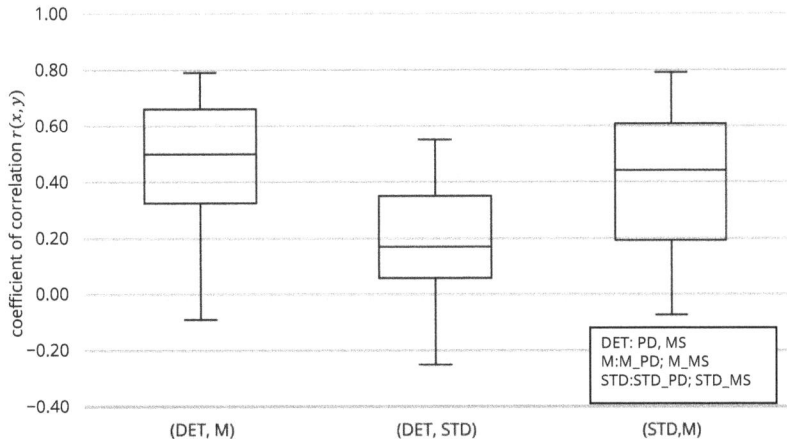

Figure 5. Boxplot correlation between the deterministic (DET) and stochastic (STD, M) solutions.

5.3. Comparing Computation Effort

In order to evaluate whether the simulation effort and thus the computational effort can be reduced with the presented 2-phase algorithm, a comparison of the simulation effort between the strategy for generating the initial population and the randomized generation of the initial population is necessary. The strategy for optimization of the initial population is called copied in the following, the strategy for the random generation of the initial population is called random. The simulation effort SA_{ICR} to generate the initial population with an initial copy rate of $ICR > 0.0$ is higher in contrast to the simulation effort of the randomized population SA_{rand} with an initial copy rate of $ICR = 0.0$. In order to equate the simulation effort $SA_{ICR} = SA_{rand}$, the following assumptions for calculation of the simulation effort are made and demonstrated using a calculation example: The deterministic simulation effort SA_{det} for the first phase of the 2-phase algorithm with $pop = 100$, generation amount $GA_{det} = 100$, and $|W| = 10$ repetitions is $SA_{det} = 100{,}000$ ($GA_{det} \cdot pop \cdot |W|$). Selection of the 100 best solutions with respect to the objective value out of 10 repetitions $|W|$ with subsequent stochastic simulation with $|N| = 100$ scenarios to generate the stochastic initial population leads to a further simulation effort of $SA_{init} = 100{,}000 (pop \cdot |N| \cdot |W|)$ simulations, so that the total simulation effort is $SA_{ICR} = 200{,}000 (SA_{det} + SA_{init})$. To compare the simulation effort, for example, more randomized solutions can be generated $SA_{init} = SA_{rand} = 200 pop \cdot 100|N| \cdot 10|W| = 200{,}000$. Another possibility is to leave the population size pop unchanged at $pop = 100$ $SA_{init} = 100 pop \cdot 100|N| \cdot 10|W| = 100{,}000$ and additionally to perform a generation step $GA_{stoch} = 1$ within the framework of stochastic optimization at $SA_{stoch} = 1 GA_{stoch} \cdot 100 pop \cdot 100|N| \cdot 10|W| = 100{,}000$, so that the simulation effort with the randomized initial population also corresponds to $SA_{rand} = 200{,}000 (SA_{init} + SA_{stoch})$. The latter option was chosen for comparison purposes, since it also uses the mode of action of the genetic algorithm, which requires a certain calculation time and thus makes the results more comparable. Figure 6 illustrates the performance of the different strategies for generating the initial population (randomized $ICR = 0.0$ and copied $ICR = 0.2$–1.0).

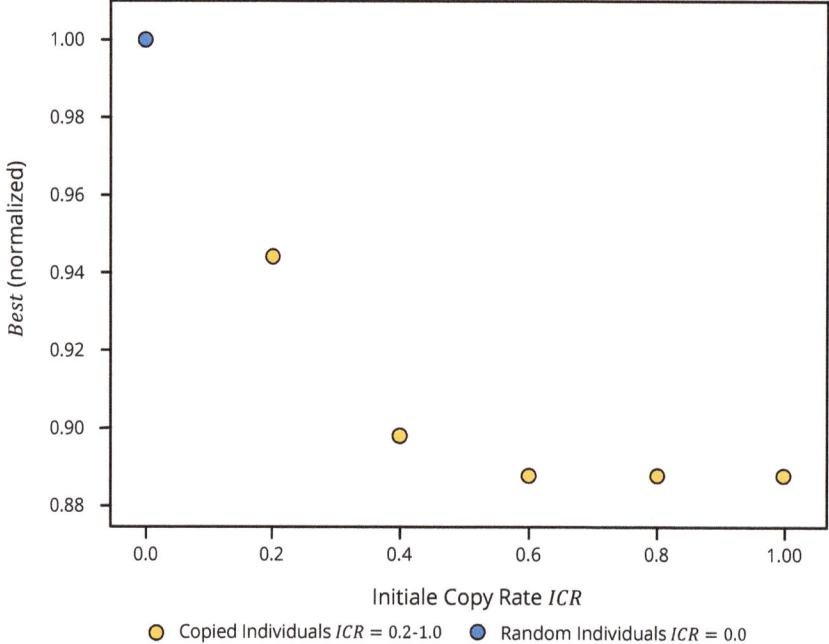

Figure 6. Example of how the initial copy rate works; worst value: $Best = 1.00$.

One possibility to evaluate the effectiveness of a copied initial population $ICR = 0.2$–1.0 is to compare the objective fulfillment of the best solution *Best* per experiment (Figure 7). A condensed evaluation is the relative frequency with which an ICR achieves the best value for the objective value *Best* per individual experiment. Of the 96 possible individual experiments ($2VarK_{lognorm} \cdot 8M \cdot 6f$), a copied initial population ($ICR = 0.2$–1.0) achieves the best objective value *Best* in 79.17% of the individual experiments. In 20.83% of the experiments, a randomized initial population achieves the best objective value ($ICR = 0.0$). The initial copy rate of $ICR = 0.4$ and $ICR = 0.6$ is more often used to achieve the best objective value *Best* (22.5%) than the initial copy rates $ICR = 0.2, 0.8$, and $1.0(12\%)$. The following conclusions can be drawn from the distribution of the frequency:

- An optimization of the initial population does not necessarily lead to the best result with respect to the objective value *Best*.
- A low and a too high initial copy rate lead less frequently to the best objective value *Best*. Therefore, it can be concluded that either too many randomized solutions ($ICR < 0.4$) or too many copied solutions ($ICR > 0.6$) do not sufficiently represent the correlation between deterministic and stochastic solution and that, therefore, for a diverse initial population, an equal ratio of copied and randomized solutions is most promising.

The relative saving $Best_{rel}$ between the copied population ($ICR = 0.2, 0.4, 0.6, 0.8$ and 1.0) compared to the randomized population ($ICR = 0.0$) is used to evaluate the performance of the initial copy rate ICR.

A positive value $Best_{rel}$ means a saving; a negative value $Best_{rel}$ is a loss. $Best_{rel}\%$ is calculated by the following:

$$Best_{rel}(\%) = \left(1 - \frac{Best(ICR = 0.2; \ 0.4; \ 0.6; \ 0.8; \ 1.0)}{Best(ICR = 0.0)}\right) \cdot 100 \tag{12}$$

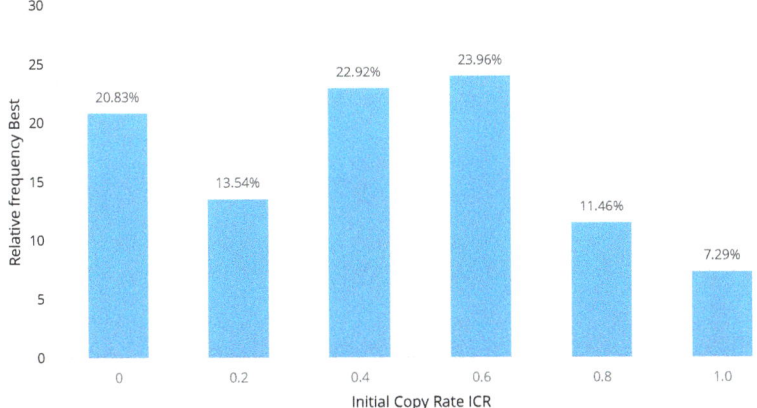

Figure 7. Comparison frequency *Best* between random and copied initial solutions.

With increasing initial copy rate *ICR*, the range of the relative saving potential $Best_{rel}$ increases (Table 2). From this, it can be concluded that, with initial copy rate *ICR*, the saving potential $Best_{rel}$ fluctuates significantly more and can be predicted less reliably. Thus, the initial copy rate *ICR* should be selected in such a way that the savings are maximized on average $\bar{x}(\%)$ with a high probability $ki_{0.95}(\%)$. When using the initial copy rate of *ICR* = 0.2–1.0, better results $Best_{rel}$ are obtained for 58.3% (*ICR* = 1.0) to 69.7% (*ICR* = 0.4) of the considered individual experiments than with an initial copy rate of *ICR* = 0.0. If the best initial copy rate ICR_{Best} was always selected, the results $Best_{rel}$ will be better in 79.17% of the individual experiments compared to randomized solutions (*ICR* = 1.0). In contrast, the results $Best_{rel}$ will be worse in 55.2% of the individual experiments if the worst initial copy rate ICR_{Worst} was selected. The average $\bar{x}$ best saving $Best_{rel}$ is achieved with an initial copy rate *ICR* = 0.6 ($\bar{x}$ = 0.42%), and the median $\tilde{x}$ best saving $Best_{rel}$ is achieved with an initial copy rate *ICR* = 0.4 ($\tilde{x}$ = 0.46%). These values should not be regarded as too low, since, as will be examined in Section 5.4, the overall optimization potential is approximately 4%. With both *ICR* = 0.4 and *ICR* = 0.6, the confidence interval is $ki_{0.95}$ = ±0.49%. Thus, there is no clear recommendation for the selection of an initial copy rate *ICR*, but *ICR* = 0.4 or *ICR* = 0.6 should be preferred. The following experiments uses *ICR* = 0.6.

Table 2. Relative saving potential initial copy rate for generating the copied population compared to randomized population.

Statistic	0.2	0.4	0.6	0.8	1.0	0.2–1.0	Best	Worst
Ant (%)	66.6	69.7	64.6	62.5	58.3	66.4	79.17	55.2
$\bar{x}$ (%)	0.28	0.39	0.42	0.26	0.05	0.26	0.66	−0.37
$\tilde{x}$ (%)	0.37	0.46	0.44	0.41	0.32	0.40	0.58	0.22
σ (%)	2.20	2.42	2.40	2.59	3.15	2.55	2.30	3.06
$ki_{0.95}$(%)	±0.45	±049	±0.49	±0.53	±0.64	±0.52	±0.47	±0.62

5.4. Evaluation of the Overall Quality of The Algorithm

To evaluate the performance of the overall concept, the objective value of the initial population is compared with the objective value of the last population of the optimization run. The maximum number of generations for deterministic and stochastic optimization is *gen* = 100 with a stop criterion of *gen* = 20 generations. The number of experiments is similar to that mentioned in Section 5.3. Since the results of the repetitions |*W*| do not differ significantly, |*W*| is set to |*W*| = 1 for the next experiments. With a coefficient of variation of $cv_{lognorm}$ = 0.9, the optimization potential is between

0–1% in about 50% of the experiments (Figure 8). For the remaining experiments, an optimization potential between 1–5% is achieved.

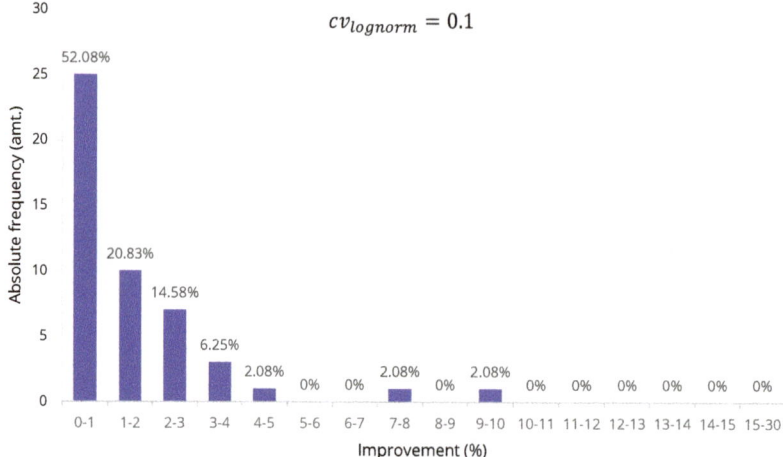

Figure 8. Performance of the genetic algorithm: comparison between best value initial population and best value last generation of optimization $cv_{lognorm} = 0.9$.

A higher optimization potential is achieved with a coefficient of variation of $cv_{lognorm} = 0.1$ (Figure 9). In about 50% of the experiments, the optimization potential is higher than 5%. It is remarkable that, in about 15% of the experiments, the optimization potential is between 15–30%. This represents that the optimization potential decreases with large stochastic influences, which represents that the actual process time deviates significantly from the expected value and that the solution is highly random. This corresponds almost to a complete lack of process knowledge so that an online optimization is probably more effective.

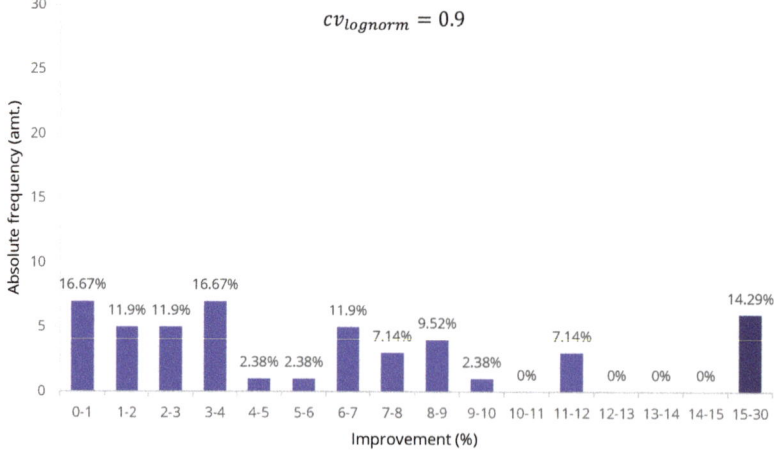

Figure 9. Performance of the genetic algorithm: comparison between best value initial population and best value last generation of optimization $cv_{lognorm} = 0.1$.

If we have a detailed look at the parameters (Figure 10), we see that there is a better improvement in general for the objective function project delay toward makespan. The model parameters have no significant influence. The influence of the coefficient of variation of the distribution is significant. In the median, an improvement of approximately 4% occurs independently of the parameters.

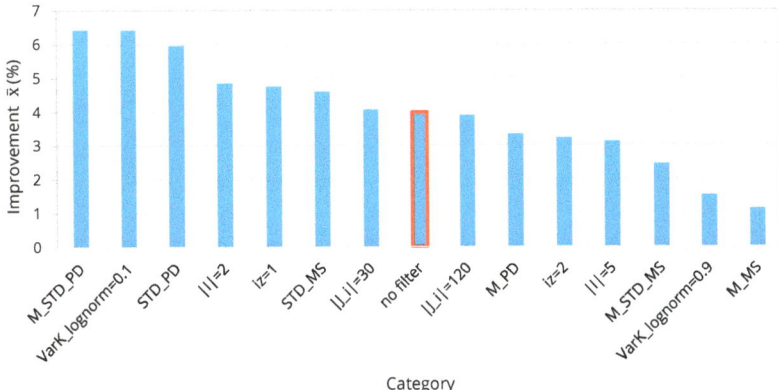

Figure 10. Performance of the proposed algorithm depending on the single parameters.

5.5. Comparison with Standard Priority Rules

For evaluation of the presented algorithm, we compare the performance of the $PR = GAWS$ with the $PR = SPR$ on 25 models M from the MPSPLIB, which essentially differ from the previously considered models by the instances. The experiments vary with respect to the coefficient of variance $cv_{lognorm}$ and the objective function f. The parameter initial copy rate ICR is still considered $ICR = 0.6$. The parameters of the GA are the same as in Section 5.4. Common SPRs serve as comparison criteria [49,50].

The presented algorithm achieves under stochastic influences without Pareto criterion in 50% better results than the considered SPR (Figure 11). The second best SPR MWRK (Most Work Remaining) achieves better results in 12% of the experiments, the third best SPR EDD (Earliest Due Date) achieves better results in 8% of the experiments, and the fourth best SPR FIFO achieves better results in 6% of the experiments. The remaining SPRs achieve the best results in 1% on average.

Looking at the three best PRs (GAWS, MWRK, and EDD) in Figure 12, it can be seen that all three PRs are represented on all ranks, with rank = 1 being the best PR and rank = 20 being the worst PR. GAWS is 95% among the 10 best PRs (sum of the relative frequency of GAWS from $rank = 1$ to $rank = 10$). SPR EDD is among the ten best SPRs in 70% of the experiments (sum of the relative frequency of EDD from $rank = 1$ to $rank = 5$). It is remarkable that the MWRK comes last $(rank = 20)$ in almost 10% of the experiments.

In the following, the saving potential is quantified if the CPR GAWS ranks first (Table 3). On average, there is a saving of 3.3% compared to $rank = 2$ regarding the objective value. Compared to the average performance, there is a saving of 10.8%, and compared to the worst SPR, there is a saving of about 25%.

If CPR GAWS does not occupy rank = 1, there is an average loss compared to $rank = 1$ of -10.6% regarding the objective value (Table 4). Compared to the medium performance of the other SPRs, an average saving of 3.63% is still achieved. Comparing CPR GAWS to the worst SPR, an average saving of 18.9% is achieved. In summary, the presented CPR can achieve an average improvement over a randomly selected SPR.

For complete evaluation of the presented CPR GAWS, it is necessary to assess the fulfillment of individual project objectives according to the Pareto criterion (Table 5). For this purpose, the solutions are divided into solution fronts (Section 4.2). CPR GAWS is on average in 90% of the experiments in the first front. There are no significant deviations when considering individual parameters. The only difference shows the parameter instance *iz*. A performance analysis of the other SPRs shows that no

SPR dominates another SPR with regard to its occurrence in the first front. The SPR FIFO is often in the first front. As far as frequency is concerned, no other SPR comes close to the presented CPR GAWS. This shows the real potential of CPR GAWS.

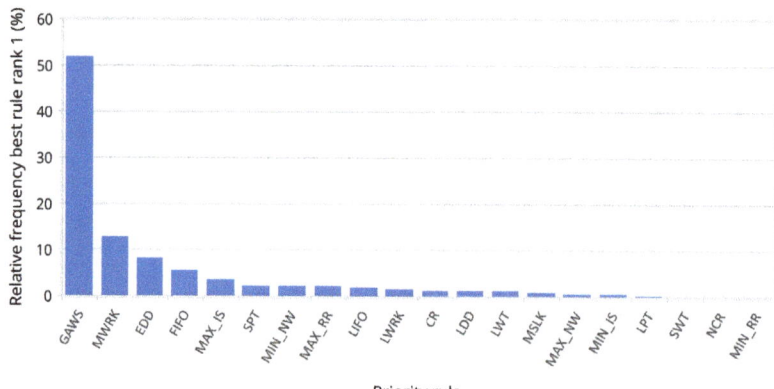

Figure 11. Performance of the proposed algorithm compared to Standard Priority Rules (SPRs): $MWRK$: Most Work Remaining; EDD: Earliest Due Date; $FIFO$: First In First Out; $MAXIS$: Maximum Immediate (Direct) Successors; $MAXRR$: Maximum Resource Request; $LIFO$: Last In First Out; $LWRK$: Least Work Remaining; CR: Critical Ration; NCR: None Critical Ratio; LDD: Least Due Date; LWT: Longest Wait Time; $MSLK$: Minimum Slack; $MAXNW$: Maximum Total Successors; $MINIS$: Minimum Immediate (Direct) Successors; LPT: Longest Processing Time; SWT: Shortest Wait Time (cumulative); NCR: None Critical Ration; $MINRR$: Minimal Resource Request.

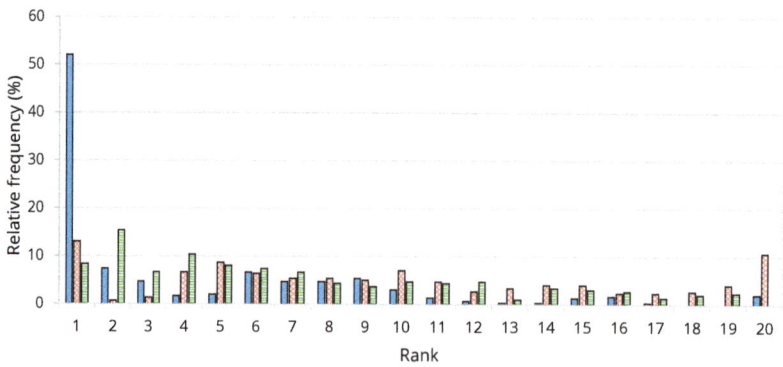

Figure 12. Comparison of the performance of the three priority rules.

Table 3. Improvement with GAWS = rank 1.

Comparing GAWS Rank = 1 to			
Statistic	Rank 2	MW Rank	Rank 20
$\bar{x}$ (%)	3.31	10.82	24.86
$\tilde{x}$(%)	2.66	8.49	17.64
σ (%)	2.88	7.56	20.65
$ki_{0.95}$ (%)	±0.46	±1.20	±3.27

Table 4. Deterioration with GAWS $\neq$ Rank 1.

Comparing GAWS Rank $\neq$ 1 to			
Statistic	Rank 2	MW Rank	Rank 20
$\bar{x}$ (%)	-10.60	3.63	18.90
$\tilde{x}$(%)	-3.22	2.91	14.68
σ (%)	19.15	5.43	15.66
$ki_{0.95}$ (%)	± 3.03	± 0.86	± 2.48

Table 5. Comparison of objective fulfillment with Pareto criterion.

Filter	GAWS = 1st Front (%)	2nd Best PR = 1st Front	2nd Best PR = 1st Front (%)
All experiments	91	FIFO	65
$cv_{lognorm} = 0.1$	95	FIFO	61
$cv_{lognorm} = 0.9$	88	FIFO	69
M_PD	94	FIFO	74
STD_PD	90	MSLK	42
$M\_PD\_STD\_PD$	92	FIFO	86
M_MS	92	FIFO	72
STD_MS	82	LWRK	42
M_MS_STD_MS	98	FIFO	88
$|I| = 2$	89	FIFO	55
$|I| = 5$	95	MAX_NW	88
$|J_i| = 30$	95	MAX_NW	64
$J_i| = 120$	89	FIFO	71
$iz = 1$	77	FIFO	72
$iz = 2$	100	MWRK	58

6. Conclusions and Outlook

In this paper, we present and study a 2-phase genetic algorithm for the efficient generation of project-specific composite priority rules for short-term production control of the stochastic resource-constrained multi-project scheduling problem. Computational results with our presented discrete-event simulation-framework PyScOp show that, with the same simulation effort, the proposed algorithm achieves better initial solutions compared to complete randomly generated initial solutions on average. The best initial population is based on half copied best and half randomly selected solutions. The experiments also show that, with our algorithm, the objective fulfillment compared to priority rules used in practice is much better. Our solutions are in 90% of the experiments in the Pareto front. The best priority rule FIFO is in about 65% of the experiments in the Pareto front. All experiments show that the performance of the algorithm depends on the model parameter.

We see further research in the parameter optimization of the GA to improve the generated composite priority rules. The computational effort can be further reduced if additional strategies for generating the initial population are applied. This includes generation of the start solution with known priority rules or with solutions from similar models. In general, the model-attribute-objective effects need to be further analyzed in order to set model-dependent parameters that can improve both computation time and objective values.

Author Contributions: Conceptualization, M.K.; methodology, M.K.; software, M.K.; writing—original draft preparation, M.K.; writing—review and editing, Michael Völker and T.S.; visualization, M.K.; supervision, M.V. and T.S.; project administration, T.S. All authors have read and agreed to the published version of the manuscript.

Funding: This work is funded by the German Research Foundation (DFG) within the projects Simulation-based generation of robust heuristics for self-control of manual production processes: A hybrid approach on the way to industry 4.0 (Project ID 418727532) https://gepris.dfg.de/gepris/projekt/418727532 and Sim4Pep (Project ID 439188616) https://gepris.dfg.de/gepris/projekt/439188616.

Conflicts of Interest: The authors declare no conflict of interest.

Abbreviations

The following abbreviations are used in this manuscript:

APS	Advanced Panning and Scheduling
CDR	Composite Dispatching Rule
CPR	Composite Priority Rule
CPPS	Cyber Physical Production System
GA	Genetic Algorithm
GAWS	Genetic Algorithm Weighted Sum
ICR	Initial Copy Rate
MES	Manufacturing Execution System
MPSPLIB	Multi-Project Scheduling Library
PPC	Project Planning and Control
PSPLIB	Project Scheduling Linrary
RCPSP	Resource Constrained Project Scheduling Problem
SH	Sequencing Heuristic
SPR	Simple Priority Rules
SRCMPSP	Stochastic Resource Constrained Multi-Project Scheduling Problem

References

1. Bischoff, J.; Taphorn, C.; Wolter, D.; Braun, N.; Fellbaum, M.; Goloverov, A.; Ludwig, S.; Hegmanns, T.; Prasse, C.; Henke, M.; et al. *Erschließen der Potenziale der Anwendung von Industrie 4.0 im Mittelstand*; BMWi: Berlin, Germany, 2015.
2. Huber, W. *Industrie 4.0 Kompakt—Wie Technologien Unsere Wirtschaft und Unsere Unternehmen Verändern*; Springer Fachmedien Wiesbaden: Wiesbaden, Germany, 2018; doi:10.1007/978-3-658-20799-1. [CrossRef]
3. Lödding, H. *Verfahren der Fertigungssteuerung: Grundlagen, Beschreibung, Konfiguration*; Springer: Berlin/Heidelberg, Germany, 2016.
4. Glonegger, M. *Berücksichtigung Menschlicher Leistungsschwankungen bei der Planung von Variantenfließmontagesystemen*; Forschungsberichte IWB; Utz, Herbert: München, Germany, 2014; Volume 292.
5. Marczinski, G. Einsatzgebiete von ERP-, APS- und MES-Lösungen. *ERP Manag.* **2008**, *2008*, 62–64.
6. Niehus, M.R. Adaptive Produktionssteuerung für Werkstattfertigungssysteme durch Fertigungsbegleitende Reihenfolgebildung. Ph.D. Thesis, Technische Universität München, München, Germany, 2016.
7. Hansmann, K.W. *Industrielles Management*; 8., völlig überarb. und erw. aufl. ed.; Oldenbourg: München, Germany, 2006.
8. Nyhuis, P.; Mayer, J.; Kuprat, T. Die Bedeutung von Industrie 4.0 als Enabler für logistische Modelle. In *Industrie 4.0*; Kersten, W., Ed.; Schriftenreihe der Hochschulgruppe für Arbeits- und Betriebsorganisation e.V. (HAB), Gito: Berlin, Germany, 2014; pp. 79–100.
9. Peßl, E. *Digitale Produktion: Studie über Status, Hemmnisse und Anforderungen österreichischer Produzierender Klein- und Mittelunternehmen und Analyse der Software-Hersteller von MES-Systemen*; Inst. Industrial Management/Industriewirtschaft FH JOANNEUM Kapfenberg: Kapfenberg, Austria, 2013.
10. Branke, J.; Nguyen, S.; Pickardt, C.W.; Zhang, M. Automated Design of Production Scheduling Heuristics: A Review. *IEEE Trans. Evol. Comput.* **2016**, *20*, 110–124. [CrossRef]
11. Hildebrandt, T.; Heger, J.; Scholz-Reiter, B. Towards improved dispatching rules for complex shop floor scenarios. In *Proceedings of the 12th Annual Conference on Genetic and Evolutionary Computation*; Pelikan, M., Branke, J., Eds.; ACM: New York, NY, USA, 2010; pp. 257–264. [CrossRef]
12. Pritsker, A.A.B.; Waiters, L.J.; Wolfe, P.M. Multiproject Scheduling with Limited Resources: A Zero-One Programming Approach. *Manag. Sci.* **1969**, *16*, 93–108. [CrossRef]
13. Lova, A.; Tormos, P. Analysis of Scheduling Schemes and Heuristic Rules Performance in Resource-Constrained Multiproject Scheduling. *Ann. Oper. Res.* **2001**, *102*, 263–286.:1010966401888. [CrossRef]
14. Confessore, G.; Giordani, S.; Rismondo, S. A market-based multi-agent system model for decentralized multi-project scheduling. *Ann. Oper. Res.* **2007**, *150*, 115–135. [CrossRef]
15. Homberger, J. A multi-agent system for the decentralized resource-constrained multi-project scheduling problem. *Int. Trans. Oper. Res.* **2007**, *14*, 565–589. [CrossRef]

16. Homberger, J. MPSPLIB: Multi Project Scheduling Problem Library. Hochschule für Technik Stuttgart. 2008. Available online: www.mpsplib.com (accessed on 17 October 2020).

17. Kolisch, R.; Sprecher, A. PSPLIB—A project scheduling problem library. *Eur. J. Oper. Res.* **1996**, *96*, 205–216. [CrossRef]

18. Blazewicz, J.; Lenstra, J.; Rinnooy Kan, A. Scheduling subject to resource constraints: Classification and complexity. *Discret. Appl. Math.* **1983**, *5*, 11–24. [CrossRef]

19. Ballestín, F. When it is worthwhile to work with the stochastic RCPSP? *J. Sched.* **2007**, *10*, 153–166. [CrossRef]

20. Kolisch, R.; Hartmann, S. Heuristic Algorithms for the Resource-Constrained Project Scheduling Problem: Classification and Computational Analysis. In *Project Scheduling: Recent Models, Algorithms and Applications*; Węglarz, J., Ed.; Springer US: Boston, MA, USA, 1999; pp. 147–178. [CrossRef]

21. März, L.; Krug, W.; Rose, O.; Weigert, G. *Simulation und Optimierung in Produktion und Logistik*; Springer: Berlin, Germany, 2011; Volume 1. [CrossRef]

22. Herroelen, W. Project Scheduling—Theory and Practice. *Prod. Oper. Manag.* **2005**, *14*, 413–432. [CrossRef]

23. Schade, K. Stochastische Optimierung. In *Stochastische Optimierung*; Schade, K., Ed.; Stochastic Programming, Vieweg+Teubner: Wiesbaden, Germany, 2012; pp. 45–72. [CrossRef]

24. Ashtiani, B.; Leus, R.; Aryanezhad, M.B. A Novel Class of Scheduling Policies for the Stochastic Resource-Constrained Project Scheduling Problem. *SSRN Electron. J.* **2008**. [CrossRef]

25. Stork, F. Stochastic Resource-Constrained Project Scheduling. Ph.D. Thesis, Technische Universitat Berlin, Berlin, Germany, 2001; doi:10.14279/DEPOSITONCE-398. [CrossRef]

26. Ashtiani, B.; Leus, R.; Aryanezhad, M.B. New competitive results for the stochastic resource-constrained project scheduling problem: Exploring the benefits of pre-processing. *J. Sched.* **2011**, *14*, 157–171. [CrossRef]

27. Deb, K.; Jain, H. An Evolutionary Many-Objective Optimization Algorithm Using Reference-Point-Based Nondominated Sorting Approach, Part I: Solving Problems With Box Constraints. *IEEE Trans. Evol. Comput.* **2014**, *18*, 577–601. [CrossRef]

28. Kück, M.; Broda, E.; Freitag, M.; Hildebrandt, T.; Frazzon, E.M. Towards adaptive simulation-based optimization to select individual dispatching rules for production control. In Proceedings of the 2017 Winter Simulation Conference (WSC), Las Vegas, NV, USA, 3–6 December 2017; pp. 3852–3863. [CrossRef]

29. Grundstein, S.; Freitag, M.; Scholz-Reiter, B. A new method for autonomous control of complex job shops—Integrating order release, sequencing and capacity control to meet due dates. *J. Manuf. Syst.* **2017**, *42*, 11–28. [CrossRef]

30. Fink, A.; Homberger, J. Decentralized Multi-Project Scheduling. In *Handbook on Project Management and Scheduling*; Schwindt, C., Zimmermann, J., Eds.; Springer International Publishing: Cham, Switzerland, 2015; Volume 1, pp. 685–706.

31. Chand, S.; Singh, H.; Ray, T. Evolving heuristics for the resource constrained project scheduling problem with dynamic resource disruptions. *Swarm Evol. Comput.* **2019**, *44*, 897–912. [CrossRef]

32. Hildebrandt, T.; Freitag, M. Bessere Prioritätsregeln für komplexe Produktionssysteme mittels multi-kriterieller simulationsbasierter Optimierung. In *Simulation in Production and Logistics 2015*; Rabe, M., Clausen, U., Eds.; Fraunhofer Verlag: Stuttgart, Germany, 2015; pp. 309–318.

33. Branke, J.; Hildebrandt, T.; Scholz-Reiter, B. Hyper-heuristic Evolution of Dispatching Rules: A Comparison of Rule Representations. *Evol. Comput.* **2015**, *23*, 249–277. [CrossRef]

34. Nguyen, S.; Zhang, M.; Tan, K.C. Surrogate-Assisted Genetic Programming With Simplified Models for Automated Design of Dispatching Rules. *IEEE Trans. Cybern.* **2017**, *47*, 2951–2965. [CrossRef]

35. Jorapur, V.S.; Puranik, V.S.; Deshpande, A.S.; Sharma, M. A Promising Initial Population Based Genetic Algorithm for Job Shop Scheduling Problem. *J. Softw. Eng. Appl.* **2016**, *9*, 208–214. [CrossRef]

36. Werner, F. A Survey of Genetic Algorithms for Shop Scheduling Problems. In *Heuristics: Theory and Application*; Siar, P., Ed.; Nova Science Publishers: Hauppauge, NY, USA, 2013; pp. 161–222.

37. Nguyen, S.; Zhang, M.; Johnston, M.; Tan, K.C. Automatic Design of Scheduling Policies for Dynamic Multi-objective Job Shop Scheduling via Cooperative Coevolution Genetic Programming. *IEEE Trans. Evol. Comput.* **2014**, *18*, 193–208. [CrossRef]

38. Nguyen, S.; Zhang, M.; Johnston, M.; Tan, K.C. A Computational Study of Representations in Genetic Programming to Evolve Dispatching Rules for the Job Shop Scheduling Problem. *IEEE Trans. Evol. Comput.* **2013**, *17*, 621–639. [CrossRef]

39. Omar, M.; Baharum, A.; Hasan, Y. A job-shop scheduling problem (JSSP) using genetic algorithm (GA). In Proceedings of the 2nd im TG T Regional Conference, Penang, Malaysia, 13–15 June 2006.

40. Goldberg, D.E. *Genetic Algorithm in Search, Optimization, and Machine Learning*; Addison-Wesley: Reading, MA, USA, 1989; Volume XIII.

41. Python Software Foundation. Python. 2019. Available online: www.python.org (accessed on 17 October 2020).

42. Kühn, M. PyScOp. 2019. Available online: https://tlscm.mw.tu-dresden.de/scm/git/PyScOp_2.0 (accessed on 17 October 2020).

43. Schmidt, T.; Kühn, M.; Genßler, P.R. Design of Project-oriented Calculation Models for Job Priorities by Using a Customized Genetic Algorithm. In *Simulation in Produktion und Logistik 2017*; Wenzel, S., Peter, T., Eds.; Kassel University Press: Kassel, Germany, 2017; pp. 99–108.

44. Law, A.M.; Kelton, W.D. *Simulation Modeling and Analysis*, 3rd ed.; internat. ed., [nachdr.] ed.; McGraw-Hill Series in Industrial Engineering und Management Science; McGraw-Hill: Boston, MA, USA, 2000.

45. Sexton, R.S.; Dorsey, R.E.; Johnson, J.D. Optimization of neural networks: A comparative analysis of the genetic algorithm and simulated annealing. *Eur. J. Oper. Res.* **1999**, *114*, 589–601. [CrossRef]

46. Das, I.; Dennis, J.E. Normal-Boundary Intersection: A New Method for Generating the Pareto Surface in Nonlinear Multicriteria Optimization Problems. *SIAM J. Optim.* **1998**, *8*, 631–657. [CrossRef]

47. Freitag, M.; Hildebrandt, T. Automatic design of scheduling rules for complex manufacturing systems by multi-objective simulation-based optimization. *CIRP Ann.* **2016**, *65*, 433–436. [CrossRef]

48. Hildebrandt, T.; Branke, J. On Using Surrogates with Genetic Programming. *Evol. Comput.* **2015**, *23*, 343–367. [CrossRef]

49. Haupt, R. A survey of priority rule-based scheduling. *Spektrum* **1989**, *11*, 3–16. [CrossRef]

50. Vanhoucke, M. *Integrated Project Management Sourcebook*; Springer International Publishing: Cham, Switzerland, 2016; doi:10.1007/978-3-319-27373-0. [CrossRef]

Publisher's Note: MDPI stays neutral with regard to jurisdictional claims in published maps and institutional affiliations.

Article

Applying Neural Networks in Aerial Vehicle Guidance to Simplify Navigation Systems

Raúl de Celis *, Pablo Solano and Luis Cadarso

Aerospace Systems and Transport Research Group, European Institute for Aviation Training and Accreditation (EIATA), Rey Juan Carlos University, Fuenlabrada, 28943 Madrid, Spain; pablo.solano@urjc.es (P.S.); luis.cadarso@urjc.es (L.C.)
* Correspondence: raul.decelis@urjc.es; Tel.: +34-914888775

Received: 12 November 2020; Accepted: 10 December 2020; Published: 11 December 2020

Abstract: The Guidance, Navigation and Control (GNC) of air and space vehicles has been one of the spearheads of research in the aerospace field in recent times. Using Global Navigation Satellite Systems (GNSS) and inertial navigation systems, accuracy may be detached from range. However, these sensor-based GNC systems may cause significant errors in determining attitude and position. These effects can be ameliorated using additional sensors, independent of cumulative errors. The quadrant photodetector semiactive laser is a good candidate for such a purpose. However, GNC systems' development and construction costs are high. Reducing costs, while maintaining safety and accuracy standards, is key for development in aerospace engineering. Advanced algorithms for getting such standards while eliminating sensors are cornerstone. The development and application of machine learning techniques to GNC poses an innovative path for reducing complexity and costs. Here, a new nonlinear hybridization algorithm, which is based on neural networks, to estimate the gravity vector is presented. Using a neural network means that once it is trained, the physical-mathematical foundations of flight are not relevant; it is the network that returns dynamics to be fed to the GNC algorithm. The gravity vector, which can be accurately predicted, is used to determine vehicle attitude without calling for gyroscopes. Nonlinear simulations based on real flight dynamics are used to train the neural networks. Then, the approach is tested and simulated together with a GNC system. Monte Carlo analysis is conducted to determine performance when uncertainty arises. Simulation results prove that the performance of the presented approach is robust and precise in a six-degree-of-freedom simulation environment.

Keywords: nonlinear-flight-mechanics; neural networks; guidance, navigation, and control; machine learning; model; matlab-simulink

1. Introduction

Global Navigation Satellite Systems (GNSS) signals are widely utilized for aerospace applications. However, reliability decreases as the requirement of the application for which it is designed increases. The main cause producing this effect is the reduced signal/noise relationship caused by the attenuation and loss of the GNSS signal. This basically means that independent sources of data for navigation are needed to ameliorate these negative effects and reduce interference. Inertial Navigation Systems (INS) are a good example of devices which are independent of external perturbations. Particularly, an inertial estimation unit (IMU) is an electronic gadget that measures and reports a body's specific force, angular rate, and orientation, utilizing a blend of accelerometers, gyroscopes, and sometimes magnetometers. IMUs are normally used in airplanes, including unmanned aeronautical vehicles (UAVs), and spacecraft. However, these systems also feature important lacks, such as frequent incorrect initialization, accelerometer and gyroscope imperfections, which are trigger for cumulative errors

Algorithms **2020**, *13*, 333; doi:10.3390/a13120333   www.mdpi.com/journal/algorithms

and imperfections in implemented dynamics model. Despite of this fact, Inertial Navigation Systems, when hybridized with GNSS receivers to minimize drift, are excellent for GNC data acquisition [1,2].

However, precision and cost are counterposed objectives. Reducing costs, while maintaining safety and accuracy standards, is key for development in aerospace engineering. Advanced algorithms for getting such standards while cutting down costs are are cornerstone. For example, to maintain an acceptable precision level while reducing costs, less precise devices may substitute expensive systems as long as GNSS signal is reachable and persistent to update the inertial system. However, many scenarios feature high uncertainty and alternatives are needed. An option to satisfy accuracy needs and budget limitations is to merge data of a few low cost sensors, which makes possible increases in accuracy levels.

The advantages of coordinated combination of information have appeared in numerous air applications [3]. For example, information combination strategies for six degrees of freedom rockets are depicted in [4]. The main issues in using various sorts of INS augmented with GNSS updates have been considered by [5]. Notwithstanding INS/GNSS hybridization, a set of nonlinear observers are presented by [6]. Note that, in case there are various sensors available, they may be additional contributions to a filter, e.g., the Kalman filter [1,2].

As it is shown in [1,2], the need to develop new Guidance, Navigation and Control (GNC) frameworks has fostered research on stability and controllability of aerospace vehicles. A novel guidance law is presented in [7], where only observations of line-of-sight angle and its rate of change coming from a seeker are employed. Ref. [8,9] present GNC cooperative techniques based on the conventional Proportional Navigation (PN). In [10] a target-follower engagement is considered, in which the target is followed while it tries to prevent interception. An attitude control-framework device for a spinning sounding rocket, which depends on a proportional, integral, and derivative (PID) controller, is created in [11]. Proportional-derivative GNC laws for the terminal phases of flight are proposed in [12,13]. In [14], a limited time concurrent sliding-mode GNC law is introduced. An overall scheme concerning the guidance and autopilot modules for a class of spin-stabilized balance controlled devices is introduced in [15].

Yet, even in GNSS/IMU hybrid devices, there exist negative influences, such as irregular estimations, which might be predominant during terminal guidance. Other methods, which are based on image recognition using multispectral cameras and other sensors, may be used in navigation for aerospace applications [16]. However, they usually feature high costs. Hence, advancement on new algorithms which may easily fulfill the required precision levels and budget limitations is a foundation in research. For instance, there are recent advances which consist of incorporating IMU, GPS, and laser guidance capacity, offering high accuracy and all-weather capacity [17,18].

Laser guidance may be provided by means of Semi Active Laser Kits (SAL). These devices are applied in many designing areas, such as calculating rotational speed of objects and estimating dynamics of laser spots [19,20]. The bonus of these kits is their favorable position during the last periods of the guidance, when they can provide high precision for GNC systems.

Therefore, it can be stated that sensor hybridization techniques [16,21] for viable and robust estimations are a current need when autonomy, accuracy, and minimal cost are to be achieved. However, also note that as the number of sensors to employed increases, the cost of system also increases. In this sense, Machine Learning (ML) techniques come onto the scene. They offer multitudinous options and innovative solutions of particular interest for GNC applications, where their foray is still latter and shallow, yet with no doubt promising. The utilization of ML strategies for the estimation of parameters dependent on the dynamics of aerial vehicles presents the bit of leeway that once the algorithm is calibrated or trained, it is not important to know the physical-mathematical establishments that rule the flight mechanics. Given the input signals, ML algorithms may restore the data that can later be utilized within the GNC system, such that the subsequent solutions will fit the genuine output [22,23]. Taking benefit of these facts, a reduced set of sensors may be selected to work together with ML algorithms, all while safety and accuracy standards are matched, and complexity and costs are decreased.

However, the application of these strategies to a wide set of scenarios, which may also include uncertain conditions, depends largely on the representativity and amount of input and output data employed for training ML algorithms. This fact implies that desired performance stability and convergence is to be restricted to the trained mission envelope. Other approaches, which could ensure convergence and stability parameters under the proposed uncertain conditions, might also be employed for this type of application. For instance, adaptive control that uses adaptation laws to online estimate unknown system parameter variations for various mission envelopes [24–26].

Altogether, the objective of this paper is to improve current guidance strategies applying a powerful hybridization approach, which also introduces ML to enable attitude determination with a reduced availability of sensors, namely GNSS, accelerometer and semiactive laser quadrant photo-detectors. In particular, neural networks (NN) are implemented to precisely estimate the gravity vector to be combined with velocity and line of sight vectors in order to determine the attitude or rotation of the vehicle without needing gyroscopes. Note that the mentioned vectors need to be obtained in two different reference frames because otherwise the attitude determination problem cannot be solved.

Contributions

The main contribution of this scientific research is the application of Machine Learning techniques, i.e., neural network (NN) algorithms, to hybridize GNSS, accelerometer and semiactive laser quadrant photo-detectors signals. The role of the neural networks is to predict the gravity vector to estimate the attitude of the vehicle. Consequently, the advantage of such a hybrid system over the traditional ones, which are usually based on GNSS and IMUs, is the capability of eliminating gyros, which may be expensive and too sensitive for high demanding maneuvers and not reliable at all during some stages of flight.

The presented approach relies on neural networks and training algorithms to predict the gravity vector in body fixed axes while the vehicle is flying. The three components of the acceleration of the vehicle in body fixed axes are the inputs for the NN. After that, the predicted gravity vector is processed together, by means of a hybridisation algorithm, with velocity and line of sight vector to determine body rotation or attitude.

To reproduce the flight dynamics of an aerial vehicle, a nonlinear mathematical model is proposed, which considers nonlinear aerodynamic forces and moments and that has been validated to build up realistic conditions for simulation experiments [1,2]. On top of that, a robust double-input double-output control algorithm is employed to manage coupling among the normal and lateral nonlinear dynamics.

Note that the presented approach depends on the amount of available data for training, which means stability and convergence may be restricted to the trained mission envelope. However, note that training has been performed for a wide variety of launching, flight, and destination point conditions to resemble realistic settings, i.e., for a comprehensive set of missions. Overall, the methodology results in good enough quality results, even including good response to uncertainty in several conditions and characteristics, i.e., showing good GNC performance. Therefore, the presented research poses a path for a generalized and systematic application of NN/Machine Learning in GNC systems.

The rest of this paper is organized as follows. In Section 2, the system modeling is described in detail. Section 3 describes the navigation, guidance and control algorithms. Section 4 exposes simulations results. Finally, discussion and conclusions are presented.

2. Vehicle Modeling

This section is dedicated to the vehicle description, the flight dynamics model, and sensor and actuation models.

2.1. Definition of the Vehicle

The proposed GNC approach is applied to an aerial vehicle which features a maneuvering system composed of four canard surfaces, which is roll-decoupled from the main body of the vehicle. The motivation for this aerodynamic configuration is deeply explained in [1]. Note a canard is a small winglike surface attached to an aircraft forward of the main wing to provide extra stability or control, usually replacing the tail. Here, canards are decoupled 2 by 2, to produce control force and its related torque (see [1] for more details on this).

Table 1 shows some characteristic parameters of the vehicle, including thrust typical parameter values, vehicle and fuel mass, inertia, and aerodynamic parameters. These parameters are obtained from fluid dynamics numerical simulations, experimental measurements, and wind tunnel verification (see [1] for clarifications). Note that, to keep continuity and derivability on aerodynamic coefficients and thrust, a cubic splines based interpolation method has been employed at intermediate points. According to the shown moments of inertia, the vehicle features planes of symmetry.

Table 1. Aerial vehicle parameters.

Parameter	Maximum Thrust		Initial Mass	
Value	29,160.00 N		62.40 kg	
Parameter	Fuel mass		I_{x0}	I_{y0}
Value	21.00 kg		0.19 kg m^2	18.85 kg m^2

M	C_{D_0}	$C_{D_{a2}}$	C_{L_a}	$C_{L_{a3}}$	C_{mf}	C_{Nq}
0.00	0.27	10.74	8.01	19.82	−0.59	50.81
0.40	0.25	10.88	8.17	19.55	−0.64	53.25
0.60	0.24	11.10	8.43	19.12	−0.70	57.43
0.70	0.24	11.24	8.60	18.83	−0.72	60.31
0.80	0.23	11.40	8.79	18.49	−0.75	63.80
0.90	0.23	11.45	8.98	17.28	−0.78	67.93
1.00	0.41	15.12	8.93	44.05	−0.81	71.38

M	C_{M_a}	$C_{M_{a3}}$	C_{M_q}	C_{mm}	C_{spin}	$C_{N\alpha_w}$
0.00	−35.58	−16.65	−225.73	3.02	−0.04	0.00
0.40	−35.72	−18.09	−232.75	3.29	−0.04	0.42
0.60	−36.00	−20.39	−245.32	3.57	−0.04	0.43
0.70	−36.21	−21.82	−254.10	3.71	−0.03	0.44
0.80	−36.51	−23.39	−264.85	3.84	−0.03	0.44
0.90	−36.57	−18.48	−276.57	3.98	−0.03	0.45
1.00	−35.99	15.39	−287.82	4.12	−0.03	0.45

2.2. Equations of Flight Mechanics

To construct the equations of flight, three reference frames are defined to project forces and moments: NED axes, working axes and body axes. NED axes, which are ground axes, are depicted by sub index NED. They are defined by x_{NED} pointing north, z_{NED} orthogonal to x_{NED} and pointing nadir, and y_{NED} yielding a clockwise trihedron. Working axes are represented by sub index w. They are given by x_w pointing to the destination point, y_w orthogonal to x_w and pointing apex, and z_w forming a clockwise trihedron. AZ_0 is the initial azimuth, i.e., the azimuth between x_e and x_w. Body axes are depicted by sub index b. x_b pointing forward and contained in the plane of symmetry of the vehicle, z_b orthogonal to x_b pointing down and contained in the plane of symmetry of the vehicle, and y_b shaping a clockwise trihedron. The origin of body axes is located at the gravity center of the vehicle and they are rigid coupled to the roll-decoupled control device. Figure 1 shows the previously defined axes systems.

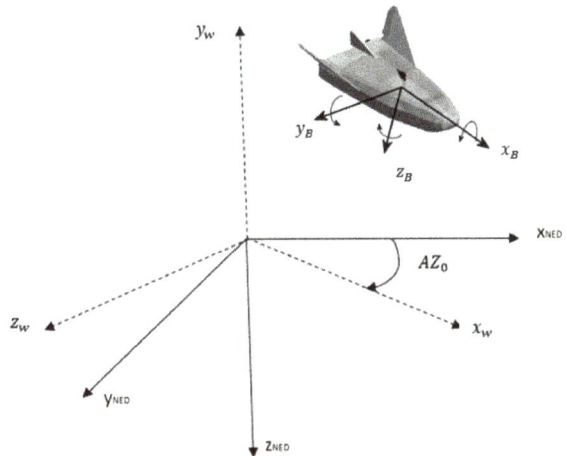

Figure 1. The three employed reference frames.

Next, flight dynamics equations are described. Note that these equations are compliant with the standard convention in [27]. Because the vehicle is assumed to be rigid, classical mechanics theory is employed. The Newton–Euler equations describe the combined translational and rotational dynamics of a rigid body. These laws, which are given by six equations, relate the motion of the center of gravity of a rigid body with the sum of forces and moments acting on the rigid body.

$$
\begin{bmatrix} \overrightarrow{F_{ext}} \\ \overrightarrow{M_{ext}} \end{bmatrix} = \begin{bmatrix} \overrightarrow{L} + \overrightarrow{D} + \overrightarrow{P} + \overrightarrow{M} + \overrightarrow{T} + \overrightarrow{W} + \overrightarrow{C} \\ \overrightarrow{P_M} + \overrightarrow{O} + \overrightarrow{M_M} + \overrightarrow{S} \end{bmatrix}, \tag{1}
$$

Equation (1) shows total external forces and moments acting on the vehicle: $\overrightarrow{L}$ is the lift force, $\overrightarrow{D}$ is the drag force, $\overrightarrow{P}$ is the pitch damping force, $\overrightarrow{M}$ is the Magnus force, $\overrightarrow{T}$ is the thrust force, $\overrightarrow{W}$ is the weight force, $\overrightarrow{C}$ is the Coriolis force, $\overrightarrow{P_M}$ the is pitch damping moment, $\overrightarrow{O}$ is the overturn moment, $\overrightarrow{M_M}$ is the Magnus moment, and $\overrightarrow{S}$ is the spin damping moment.

$$
\begin{bmatrix} \overrightarrow{L} \\ \overrightarrow{D} \\ \overrightarrow{P} \\ \overrightarrow{M} \\ \overrightarrow{T} \\ \overrightarrow{W} \\ \overrightarrow{C} \end{bmatrix} = -\frac{\pi}{8}d^2\rho \begin{bmatrix} \left(C_{L_\alpha}(M) \cdot \alpha + C_{L_{a3}}(M)\alpha^2\right)\left(\|\overrightarrow{v_w}\|^2\overrightarrow{x_w} - \left(\overrightarrow{x_w} \cdot \overrightarrow{v_w}\right)\overrightarrow{v_w}\right) \\ \left(C_{D_0}(M) + C_{D_{a2}}(M)\alpha^2\right)\|\overrightarrow{v_w}\|\overrightarrow{v_w} \\ -d\frac{C_{Nq}(M)}{I_y}\|\overrightarrow{v_w}\|^2\left(\overrightarrow{L_w} \times \overrightarrow{x_w}\right) \\ d\frac{C_{mf}(M)}{I_x}\left(\overrightarrow{L_w} \cdot \overrightarrow{x_w}\right)\left(\overrightarrow{x_w} \times \overrightarrow{v_w}\right) \\ T(t)\overrightarrow{x_w} \\ m\overrightarrow{g_w} \\ -2m\overrightarrow{\Omega} \times \overrightarrow{v_w} \end{bmatrix} \tag{2}
$$

For the computational experiments in this paper, the external forces in working axes are shown in expression (2), where C_{L_α} is the lift force linear coefficient, $C_{L_{a3}}$ is the lift force cubic coefficient, α is the total angle of attack, C_{D_0} is the drag force linear coefficient, $C_{D_{a2}}$ is the drag force square coefficient, $\overrightarrow{L_w}$ is the vehicle angular momentum in working axes, I_x *and* I_y are the vehicle inertia moments in body axes, C_{Nq} is the pitch damping force coefficient, C_{mf} is the Magnus force coefficient, $\overrightarrow{x_w}$ is vehicle pointing vector in working axes, $\overrightarrow{g_w}$ is the gravity vector in working axes, $\overrightarrow{\Omega}$ is earth's angular speed vector, $\overrightarrow{v_w}$ is vehicle velocity in working axes, d is the reference surface of the vehicle, ρ is the air density, and m is the mass of the vehicle. Note that, $\overrightarrow{x_w}$ is the unitary vector of the x_w axis, and $\overrightarrow{g_w}$ is the gravity vector in working axes. Be aware they are nonlinear functions of the variables describing the movement of the vehicle, such as aerodynamic speed, total angle of attack, Mach number, and aerodynamic parameters.

$$
\begin{bmatrix} \overrightarrow{P_M} \\ \overrightarrow{O} \\ \overrightarrow{M_M} \\ \overrightarrow{S} \end{bmatrix} = \frac{\pi}{8} d^3 \rho \begin{bmatrix} \frac{1}{T_y} C_{M_q}(M) \|\overrightarrow{v_w}\| \left(\overrightarrow{L_w} - \left(\overrightarrow{L_w} \cdot \overrightarrow{x_w} \right) \overrightarrow{x_w} \right) \\ \left(C_{M_\alpha}(M) + C_{M_{\alpha^3}}(M) \alpha^2 \right) \|\overrightarrow{v_w}\|^2 \left(\overrightarrow{v_w} \times \overrightarrow{x_w} \right) \\ -\frac{d}{T_x} C_{mm}(M) \left(\left(\overrightarrow{L_w} \cdot \overrightarrow{x_w} \right) \left((\overrightarrow{v_w} \cdot \overrightarrow{x_w}) \overrightarrow{x_w} \right) - \overrightarrow{v_w} \right) \\ \frac{d}{T_x} C_{spin}(M) \|\overrightarrow{v_w}\| \left(\overrightarrow{L_w} \cdot \overrightarrow{x_w} \right) \overrightarrow{x_w} \end{bmatrix}, \tag{3}
$$

Similarly, the equations in (3) show the mathematical expressions for the moments, including overturning, pitch damping, Magnus, spin damping, and variables and parameters. Here, C_{M_q} is the pitch damping moment coefficient, C_{M_α} is the overturning moment linear coefficient, $C_{M_{\alpha^3}}$ is the overturning moment cubic coefficient, C_{mm} is the Magnus moment coefficient and C_{spin} is the spin damping moment coefficient.

Control forces $(\overrightarrow{CF})$ and moments $(\overrightarrow{CM})$ are obtained from the maneuvering system, which is composed of four canard surfaces. Therefore, the contribution of each of them is summed to obtain the total control forces and moments.

$$
\begin{bmatrix} \overrightarrow{CF} \\ \overrightarrow{CM} \end{bmatrix} = \sum_{i=1}^{i=4} \begin{bmatrix} \frac{1}{8} d^2 \rho \pi \|\overrightarrow{v_b}\|^2 (C_{N\alpha_w}(M) \delta_i) \overrightarrow{n_{ci}} \\ \frac{1}{8} d^3 \rho \pi \|\overrightarrow{v_b}\|^2 (C_{M\alpha_w}(M) \delta_i) (\overrightarrow{x_b} \times \overrightarrow{n_{ci}}) \end{bmatrix} \tag{4}
$$

The expressions in (4) show the mathematical functions for control forces and moments, where $C_{N\alpha_w}$ and $C_{M\alpha_w}$ are the force and moments coefficients of the canard surface respectively, $\overrightarrow{n_{ci}}$ is the normal vector of each canard, and δ_i is the deflection angle of the canard surface. Here, $\overrightarrow{v_b}$ is vehicle velocity in body axes.

$$
\begin{bmatrix} \overrightarrow{CF} + \overrightarrow{F_{ext}} \\ \overrightarrow{CM} + \overrightarrow{M_{ext}} \end{bmatrix} = \begin{bmatrix} \frac{dm\overrightarrow{v_b}}{dt} + \overrightarrow{\omega_b} \times m\overrightarrow{v_b} \\ \frac{d\overrightarrow{L_b}}{dt} + \overrightarrow{\omega_b} \times \overrightarrow{L_b} \end{bmatrix} \tag{5}
$$

As stated before, a Newton-Euler approach is used to formulate the equations of motion of the aerial vehicle. These equations are in (5). Note that the body-fixed coordinate system (denoted by frame b) and the flat-Earth coordinate system (denoted by frame e) are related by Euler yaw (ψ), pitch (θ), and roll (ϕ) angles.

In Equations (5), $\overrightarrow{v_b}$ stands for vehicle speed expressed in body axes, $\overrightarrow{\omega_b}$ for angular speed of the vehicle in body axes, and $\overrightarrow{L_b}$ for the angular momentum also in body axes. Recall that control and external forces and control and external moments must be expressed in body axes also to be employed in Equations (5).

2.3. Sensors Models

As exposed in the introduction, this research aims at simplifying navigation systems. Here, this means reducing the need for complex and/or expensive sensors. A gyroscope is a device used for measuring orientation and angular velocity, and it is widely employed in navigation systems. However, their precision downgrades for high-dynamics aerial platforms meanwhile costs increase if performance is to be maintained. Therefore, the objective is to avoid them by fusing information from

GNSS sensors, accelerometers, and photo-detector signals to improve vehicle navigation performance in terms of accuracy. This section aims at describing the employed models for these sensors.

2.3.1. Global Navigation Satellite System (GNSS)

The GNSS sensor is modeled as a random noise and a bias added to the model calculated position. Note that these systems have typical accuracy of 3 m; therefore, the random noise and bias parameters have been adjusted to satisfy that performance. Because it is not the objective of this paper to model such a sensor, the reader is referred to [2,28] for more details on this.

These kind of sensors provide good performance during intermediate phases of flight and are employed to determine the line of sight vector expressed in NED axes. Note that GNSS sensors also provide velocity vector in NED axes. This vector is also modeled as a random noise and a bias of $0.1~\mathrm{ms}^{-1}$, which resembles real performance of these sensors.

2.3.2. Accelerometers

An accelerometer is a device that measures acceleration, i.e., the rate of change of velocity of the vehicle in its own instantaneous reference frame. They are modeled as a random noise and bias of $0.001~\mathrm{ms}^{-2}$ which resembles real performance of these sensors. Because they provide the acceleration vector expressed in body axes, velocity vector expressed in body triad can be obtained after integration of each of its components along time.

In addition, the magnitudes obtained from accelerometers will be used in the gravity vector estimation approach. As it is explained in the following sections, the velocity vector module is required to estimate it.

2.3.3. Semiactive Laser Kit

Laser guidance may be used to guide a vehicle to a target by means of a laser beam. With this method, a laser is kept pointed at the objective and the laser radiation bobs off the objective and is dispersed every which way. At the point when the vehicle is close enough for a portion of the reflected laser energy from the objective to arrive at it, a laser seeker detects which direction this energy is coming from and provides a signal to correct the trajectory towards the source. The device seeking the laser and providing the signal is a semiactive laser kit.

The signal provided by this sensor features the centroid of the laser footprint in the photo-detector of the kit, which is composed of four photodiodes that convert light into an electrical current. To estimate its coordinates, the produced electrical intensities in the photodiodes (I_1, I_2, I_3 and I_4) are employed, which rely upon the illuminated area. These coordinates can be determined as $[ln\frac{I_4}{I_2}, ln\frac{I_1}{I_3}]$ [17], and from them, it is possible to obtain the measured radial distance, r_{quad}. Notwithstanding, real coordinates differ from those calculated, although the transformation is conformal [17]. To obtain the real radial distance, r_c, the following mathematical functional relationship may be employed: $r_c = f(r_{quad})$. Then, cubic splines based interpolation is applied to obtain a continuous relationship. Equations (6) are utilized to estimate x_c and y_c (see [17] fore more details on this), which are the real spot center coordinates:

$$\begin{bmatrix} x_c \\ y_c \end{bmatrix} = R_{quad} \cdot \frac{r_c}{r_{quad}} \begin{bmatrix} ln\frac{I_4}{I_2} \\ ln\frac{I_1}{I_3} \end{bmatrix}, \tag{6}$$

where the physical radius of the photo-detector of the kit is given by R_{quad}. Consequently, the line of sight vector projected in body axes may be calculated from x_c and y_c and also from the distance of the photo-detector of the kit to the center of mass of the vehicle.

Note that the signal of this sensor is only available during the terminal phase of the flight. However, it is during final stages of flight when errors of 3 m in positioning target and vehicle induces enormous errors. In this way, an accurate terminal guidance sensor, for example, a semiactive laser kit, is suggested for these last flight stages. This semiactive laser sensor, in combination with GNSS and accelerometers, will provide an accurate determination of the line of sight, especially in the terminal phase. For that purpose, the signals of these sensors' must be hybridized.

Next, GNC algorithms are presented. At their kernel, neural networks are implemented to determine gravity vector in two reference frames in order to determine vehicle attitude. In addition, hybridization algorithms are applied to sensors' signals to improve precision.

3. Guidance, Navigation and Control (GNC) Algorithm Definition

This section details the proposed navigation, guidance and control algorithms. A scheme of the overall process is depicted in Figure 2. The navigation function determines the position and attitude of the vehicle by means of the information sensed by the sensors. The position is determined through the integration of the signals provided by the accelorometers and the hybridization of the signal from a GNSS device. The determination of attitude is the core of the research in this paper. From the information provided by the accelerometers and the GNSS, the neural network determines the gravity vector in two different axes systems. Then Euler angles are devised from a triad algorithm. The guidance function compares the information from the navigation function with a reference and computes a desired action to the control function. The control function processes this desired action and transforms it into a command to the actuators of the plant (i.e., the vehicle), which execute the action. The action taken is again measured by the sensors, which closes the loop.

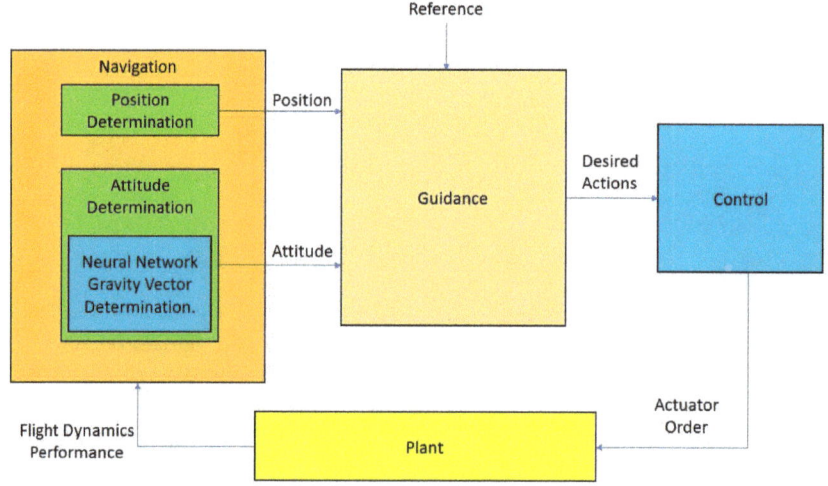

Figure 2. Scheme of the GNC process.

3.1. Navigation

Navigation refers to the determination during the flight, of the position and attitude of the vehicle, and target position.

Determining the position of the vehicle may consist of integrating accelerometers' measurements to be hybridized with GNSS sensor information. The details of these calculations are out of the scope of this paper, see [1,2,28,29] for details on this approach.

As it was mentioned before, determining attitude involves knowing two or more different vectors in two different reference systems. The velocity vector and the line of sight vectors can be the two needed vectors. If a GNSS sensor device is equipped on the aircraft, velocity vector can be directly obtained from sensor measurements in the NED triad, which can be expressed as shown in (7), where $v_{x_{NED}}, v_{y_{NED}}$ and $v_{z_{NED}}$ are the components of this velocity in NED axes.

$$\overrightarrow{v_{NED}} = [v_{x_{NED}}, v_{y_{NED}}, v_{z_{NED}}]^T \tag{7}$$

In parallel, the same velocity vector can also be calculated in body triad from a set of accelerometers, one on each of the axes. Integrating each of their measures along time, the velocity vector is obtained as shown in (8). Here, a_{x_B}, a_{y_B} and a_{z_B} are the components of the acceleration in body axes as measured by the accelerometers and $\overrightarrow{\omega_b}$ is the estimated angular speed expressed in body axes. Note that, at this point, $\overrightarrow{\omega_b}$ is unknown, and the algorithm for estimating it will be shown in the following sections.

$$\overrightarrow{v_B} = \int \left\{ [a_{x_B}, a_{y_B}, a_{z_B}]^T + \overrightarrow{\omega_b} \times \overrightarrow{v_B} \right\} dt \tag{8}$$

Similarly, the line of sight vector must be obtained in NED and body reference systems, $\overrightarrow{LOS_{NED}}$ and $\overrightarrow{LOS_B}$, respectively. $\overrightarrow{LOS_{NED}}$ can be easily obtained from GNSS sensor information. However, the semiactive laser kit is needed to derive $\overrightarrow{LOS_B}$, and this sensor signal is not available until the vehicle is close enough to the target. This means another vector is needed to successfully estimate the attitude of the vehicle during all the phases of flight.

The gravity vector poses as a natural candidate for such a challenge. Notice that determining the gravity vector in NED triad is straightforward. It is always parallel to $\overrightarrow{z_{NED}}$. Its expression is shown in (9), where g is the gravity acceleration, which is a fixed constant in this model (9.81 m/s^2). Note that precision may be increased using more sophisticated models, i.e., it can be made variable with longitude, latitude, and altitude.

$$\overrightarrow{g_{NED}} = g[0, 0, 1]^T \tag{9}$$

However, the gravity vector expressed in another reference system, i.e, body axes, is also needed. However, although there are multiple available approaches to obtain it, none of them is simple and/or require additional sensors. For example, it can be estimated determining the constant component of the measured acceleration employing a low pass filter, where Jerk in body axes is calculated by derivation of the acceleration; then, it is integrated to obtain the nonconstant component of acceleration and, by subtracting this nonconstant component from the measured acceleration, gravity vector may be estimated. However, this method is not valid when the aircraft rotates. Another method to obtain the gravity vector is to integrate the mechanization equations [30] to obtain it from the resulting expressions. However, gyros are needed to implement this method. Therefore, the keystone of the presented attitude determination method is determining gravity vector in body axes.

An estimation method for the gravity vector, which is valid for nonrotating and rotating aircraft and which is only based on accelerometers, is presented in the following subsection.

3.1.1. Neural Network Based Gravity Vector Estimation

Among the numerous applications that machine learning offers to exemplary and current GNC issues (see [23,31–34]), its potential to precisely estimate the gravity vector from sensor information is one of the main unexplored settings. The utilization of neural networks (NN) to understand the evolution of nonlinear equations has been demonstrated before [35], regardless of uncertainty. Scientifically, this infers NN will learn flight mechanics equations [36] and produce an equal outcome.

The gravity vector estimation method presented here depends on the aerial platform on which it will be employed. This means that the method must be adjusted for the aircraft of interest. Without loss of generality, the estimation method detailed in this section is particularized for a four canard controlled aerial vehicle. However, using the appropriate neural network training, it may be applied to other aircraft.

The estimated gravity vector may be expressed as shown in (10), where its components in body axes are displayed. The point is to recoup a high precision gravity vector by consolidating the estimations from the accelerometers and the potential offered by machine learning.

$$\vec{g}_B = [\widetilde{g_{x_B}}, \widetilde{g_{y_B}}, \widetilde{g_{z_B}}]^T \tag{10}$$

In order to prove the suitability of the proposed approach two different methods or strategies are proposed, as they can be visualized in Table 2:

- Method 1: it is based on a neural network which features two-layers with one hundred standard sigmoid hidden neurons and the usual linear output neuron [35]. The input vector is composed of three components constructed from a_{x_B}, a_{y_B} and a_{z_B}. The outputs of the neural networks are the components of the gravity vector expressed in body axes ($\vec{g}_B$).
- Method 2: this method is the same as method 1, but the number of neurons in the hidden layer is 50.

Table 2. Neural network schemes for the two different methods or strategies.

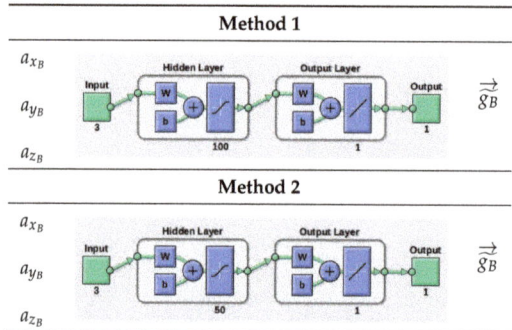

The choice of the number and shape of neurons as well as the amount of training and validation data selected for the presented two strategies is a result of the literature review (specially from [35]) and a performed hyperparametric study. This study provided two points of interest: around 100 neurons and 50 neurons. Increasing the number or neurons or layers translated only into an increase of computation time for a limited improvement in terms of error of approximation. A further and detailed hyperparametric study will be performed in future work to precisely determine the optimal working point but is not the objective of this research to formalize this statement. The preliminary results of this hyperparametric study suggest that there is a limit number of neurons in the intermediate layer (estimated at about 100 neurons), and over this limit, results do not get improved.

Then, neural networks are trained replicating the flight dynamics problem. Two examples of the available $3 \cdot 10^8$ rows of data, which are obtained from 12,000 simulations, are showed in Table 3.

Table 3. Neural network input and target values.

Accelerometer Inputs			Target		
a_{x_B}	a_{y_B}	a_{z_B}	$\widetilde{g_{x_B}}$	$\widetilde{g_{y_B}}$	$\widetilde{g_{z_B}}$
−17.68	−0.004	9.761	−0.614	−0.002	9.791
−6.019	5.605	0.1891	5.838	−0.093	7.883
...	...	...	...	...	...

Regarding the training process, three different backpropagation algorithms are employed: Scaled Conjugate Gradient (SCG) [37], Bayesian regularization (BR) [38,39], and Levenberg-Marquardt backpropagation (LM) [40,41]. The choice of these algorithms is a result of literature study. The percentage of data employed in this training is 70%. As it is common practice, a representative amount of sensor data and its corresponding gravity vector are left aside for validation purposes. In this case, a 15% of the available data corresponds to validation data. Note that the total amount of methods and training algorithms provide six different combinations which are analyzed next.

The performance of each of the six approaches can be quantified by means of the Mean Squared Error (MSE) and the Regression (R) parameter values. The MSE is the average squared difference between outputs and targets. Lower value means lower error. Zero means no error. R values measure the correlation between outputs and targets. An R value of 1 means a close relationship and 0 a random relationship. Other kind of error indicators (such as Mean Average Error, MAE) may also be used to monitor and validate the training to avoid overfitting.

For each of the the training processes, a maximum number of 1000 iterations has been established. As it is common practice in the field, classified by epochs. For the LM and SCG algorithms, training automatically stops when generalization stops improving, as indicated by an increase in the MSE of the validation samples. In the case of the BR algorithm, training stops according to adaptive weight minimization (regularization). In both cases the MAE is controlled as usual to avoid overfitting.

In addition, the trained NN is tested with the independent data (15% of the collected data), and MSE and R values are also calculated to validate the presented strategies.

Table 4 summarizes the obtained results for the training, validation and tests. It shows the values for the MSE and the R parameters. In the first column, the "Set" of data is defined, i.e., train (70%), validation (15%), or test (15%) data. The second column displays the employed training algorithm. The third and forth columns present the MSE and R values for the methods 1 and 2 showed in Table 2.

Table 4. MSE and R values for neural network based gravity vector estimator.

Set	Alg.	Method 1		Method 2	
		MSE	R	MSE	R
Train	SCG	5.81×10^{-3}	7.22×10^{-1}	5.82×10^{-3}	7.24×10^{-1}
Validation	SCG	5.89×10^{-3}	7.21×10^{-1}	5.98×10^{-3}	7.25×10^{-1}
Test	SCG	5.94×10^{-3}	7.18×10^{-1}	5.85×10^{-3}	7.21×10^{-1}
Train	BR	6.95×10^{-5}	9.98×10^{-1}	9.83×10^{-4}	9.55×10^{-1}
Validation	BR	6.92×10^{-5}	9.98×10^{-1}	9.80×10^{-4}	9.54×10^{-1}
Test	BR	6.95×10^{-5}	9.97×10^{-1}	9.81×10^{-4}	9.56×10^{-1}
Train	LM	5.63×10^{-5}	9.98×10^{-1}	7.31×10^{-4}	9.60×10^{-1}
Validation	LM	5.61×10^{-5}	9.98×10^{-1}	7.21×10^{-4}	9.72×10^{-1}
Test	LM	5.70×10^{-5}	9.97×10^{-1}	7.32×10^{-4}	9.65×10^{-1}

Analyzing the results in Table 4, it may be concluded that the best results are obtained for the combination of Method 1 and LM algorithm, which yields a MSE value of $5.63 \cdot 10^{-5}$ and a Regression value of 0.998. Additionally, the combinations of Method 2 and LM and BR algorithms also result in acceptable values for MSE and R values, they are of the same order of magnitude. Consequently, we may conclude that Methods 1 and 2 provide good results when the LM and BR training algorithms are used. Nevertheless, the SCG training algorithm is not appropriate for this application, as the best results for this algorithm are 2 orders of magnitude worse as compared to the the the rest of the algorithms.

Next, the attitude determination algorithm is presented. It is based on the estimated gravity vector by the neural networks (NN). In addition, note that, because there is information regarding two additional vectors during terminal flight, i.e., the speed vector and the line of sight vector, a hybridization approach is also presented to improve performance.

3.1.2. Attitude Determination Algorithm

Attitude determination can be determined by solving a classical Wahba's problem [42]. An orthonormal base must be defined in both axes systems, B and NED. This orthonormal base is defined for intermediate phases of flight, when signal of the photo-detector is not available and for the terminal phase of flight, when it is available, by unitary vectors $\vec{i}, \vec{j}$ and $\vec{k}$ expressed in both bases. For the intermediate phases, these unitary vectors are calculated using the speed vector and the gravity vector. Furthermore, for the terminal flight, the line of sight vector and the gravity vector are to be employed. For the intermediate phases, fl, the unitary vectors are defined by expressions (11) and (12).

$$\overrightarrow{i_{NED_{fl}}} = \frac{\overrightarrow{v_{NED}}}{\left\|\overrightarrow{v_{NED}}\right\|}, \quad \overrightarrow{j_{NED_{fl}}} = \frac{\overrightarrow{v_{NED}} \times \overrightarrow{g_{NED}}}{\left\|\overrightarrow{v_{NED}} \times \overrightarrow{g_{NED}}\right\|}, \quad \overrightarrow{k_{NED_{fl}}} = \frac{\overrightarrow{i_{NED_{fl}}} \times \overrightarrow{j_{NED_{fl}}}}{\left\|\overrightarrow{i_{NED_{fl}}} \times \overrightarrow{j_{NED_{fl}}}\right\|} \tag{11}$$

$$\overrightarrow{i_{B_{fl}}} = \frac{\overrightarrow{v_B}}{\left\|\overrightarrow{v_B}\right\|}, \quad \overrightarrow{j_{B_{fl}}} = \frac{\overrightarrow{v_B} \times \overrightarrow{g_B}}{\left\|\overrightarrow{v_B} \times \overrightarrow{g_B}\right\|}, \quad \overrightarrow{k_{B_{fl}}} = \frac{\overrightarrow{i_{B_{fl}}} \times \overrightarrow{j_{B_{fl}}}}{\left\|\overrightarrow{i_{B_{fl}}} \times \overrightarrow{j_{B_{fl}}}\right\|} \tag{12}$$

During the terminal guidance phase, tf, when the photo-detector is receiving information, a new set of unitary vectors is obtained by Equations (13) and (14).

$$\overrightarrow{i_{NED_{tf}}} = \frac{\overrightarrow{LOS_{NED}}}{\left\|\overrightarrow{LOS_{NED}}\right\|}, \quad \overrightarrow{j_{NED_{tf}}} = \frac{\overrightarrow{LOS_{NED}} \times \overrightarrow{g_{NED}}}{\left\|\overrightarrow{LOS_{NED}} \times \overrightarrow{g_{NED}}\right\|}, \quad \overrightarrow{k_{NED_{tf}}} = \frac{\overrightarrow{i_{NED_{tf}}} \times \overrightarrow{j_{NED_{tf}}}}{\left\|\overrightarrow{i_{NED_{tf}}} \times \overrightarrow{j_{NED_{tf}}}\right\|} \tag{13}$$

$$\overrightarrow{i_{B_{tf}}} = \frac{\overrightarrow{LOS_B}}{\left\|\overrightarrow{LOS_B}\right\|}, \quad \overrightarrow{j_{B_{tf}}} = \frac{\overrightarrow{LOS_B} \times \overrightarrow{g_B}}{\left\|\overrightarrow{LOS_B} \times \overrightarrow{g_B}\right\|}, \quad \overrightarrow{k_{B_{tf}}} = \frac{\overrightarrow{i_{B_{tf}}} \times \overrightarrow{j_{B_{tf}}}}{\left\|\overrightarrow{i_{B_{tf}}} \times \overrightarrow{j_{B_{tf}}}\right\|} \tag{14}$$

Note that to determine the attitude of a vehicle with respect to a reference frame, the direction cosine matrix (DCM) must be determined. It represents the attitude of the body frame (B) relative to the reference frame (NED). It is specified by a 3×3 rotation matrix, where the columns represent unit vectors in the body axes projected along the reference axes. Therefore, the expression to determine the DCM is as shown in Equation (15), where $\left[\overrightarrow{i_{B_i}}, \overrightarrow{j_{B_i}}, \overrightarrow{k_{B_i}}\right]$ is a 3×3 square matrix composed of orthonormal vectors in body triad, $\left[\overrightarrow{i_{NED_i}}, \overrightarrow{j_{NED_i}}, \overrightarrow{k_{NED_i}}\right]$ expresses the same concept in NED triad, and DCM_{B,NED_i} is the director cosine matrix that transforms NED triad into body triad. Notice that depending on the phase of flight, i.e., intermediate (fl) or terminal (tf), the matrix may be calculated with different inputs.

$$\left[\overrightarrow{i_{B_i}}, \overrightarrow{j_{B_i}}, \overrightarrow{k_{B_i}}\right] = DCM_{B,NED_i} \left[\overrightarrow{i_{NED_i}}, \overrightarrow{j_{NED_i}}, \overrightarrow{k_{NED_i}}\right] \forall i \in \{tf, fl\} \tag{15}$$

The DCM matrix can be solved from Equation (15) as it is shown in Equation (16). Employing an orthonormal base simplifies the calculation of the inverse matrix as it is the transposed matrix.

$$DCM_{B,NED_i} = \left[\overrightarrow{i_{B_i}}, \overrightarrow{j_{B_i}}, \overrightarrow{k_{B_i}}\right] \left[\overrightarrow{i_{NED_i}}, \overrightarrow{j_{NED_i}}, \overrightarrow{k_{NED_i}}\right]^T \forall i \in \{tf, fl\} \tag{16}$$

After obtaining the two different director cosine matrices, which will be essentially similar matrices, the rotation is characterized. The most suitable method to express this rotation is through quaternions, as they avoid any possible singularities on the poles of rotation. It is widely known that quaternions themselves are enough to express rotations without singularities, but it is also known that conceptually they are difficult to be visualized. An easier manner to define these rotations is by means of Euler angles. Concretely, the most common aeronautical rotation is defined by roll (ϕ_i), pitch (θ_i), and yaw (ψ_i) angles for $i \in \{tf, fl\}$. A method to obtain a quaternion solution is explained in [2]. Note that two different values for each quaternion are obtained, $i \in \{tf, fl\}$. This fact requires an hybridization between them in order to only obtain one value for each quaternion.

Hybridization Algorithm

The Euler angles (or their corresponding quaternions) values obtained for $i \in \{tf, fl\}$ are hybridized applying the recursive algorithm described in (17) and (18):

$$
\left\{\overrightarrow{Eul}\right\}\Big|_{n} = \begin{cases} \left\{\overrightarrow{Eul}\right\}\Big|_{n-1} + \kappa\big|_{n}\left[\left\{\overrightarrow{Eul_{fl}}\right\}\Big|_{n} - \left\{\overrightarrow{Eul}\right\}\Big|_{n-1}\right] & \text{if } \not\exists \left\{\overrightarrow{Eul_{tf}}\right\}\Big|_{n} \\ \left\{\overrightarrow{Eul}\right\}\Big|_{n-1} + \kappa\big|_{n}\left[\left\{\overrightarrow{Eul_{tf}}\right\}\Big|_{n} - \left\{\overrightarrow{Eul}\right\}\Big|_{n-1}\right] & \text{if } \exists \left\{\overrightarrow{Eul_{tf}}\right\}\Big|_{n} \end{cases}
\tag{17}
$$

$$
\kappa\big|_{n} = \Gamma \cdot [\Gamma + \Lambda]^{-1},
\tag{18}
$$

where $\overrightarrow{Eul}$ are the Euler angles (ϕ, θ, ψ), and Γ and Λ are the error covariance matrices for $i = tf$ and for $i = fl$ measurements, which are set to $1.3 \cdot 10^{-6}$ and $0.95 \cdot 10^{-3}$, respectively. Those values were determined empirically.

The Euler angles obtained in (17) may be used to characterize rotations and angular speeds in navigation, guidance, and control algorithms. This basically means that $\overrightarrow{\omega_b}$ is now known. Furthermore, from these Euler angles, the hybridized director cosine matrix ($DCM_{B,NED}$) may be calculated.

3.2. Guidance Law

Guidance is given in two stages. The first comprises of a constant angle glide trajectory, while the second one is based on a modified proportional law.

3.2.1. Constant Angle Glide Trajectory

Equation (19) proposes a law which is chosen to increase range. It adjusts the longitudinal axis of the vehicle (x_b) with a vertical flight plane, orthogonal to ground, parallel to the line joining the gravity center of the vehicle and the destination target and containing the gravity center of the vehicle. The line of sight is expressed in working axes is given by vector $\overrightarrow{LOS_w} = [LOS_{1_w}, LOS_{2_w}, LOS_{3_w}]$. x_b in working axes is represented by vector $\overrightarrow{x_{b_w}} = [x_{b1_w}, x_{b2_w}, x_{b3_w}]$. Consequently, the lateral correction to be applied (ψ_{dem}) is calculated by the first component of Equation (19), while the correction in the vertical plane (θ_{dem}) with respect to a constant glide angle trajectory given by C_1 [1] is given by the second component. Note that guidance effectively starts after apogee, which is determined by the pitch angle (θ) and after fuel burn time.

$$
\begin{bmatrix} \psi_{dem} \\ \theta_{dem} \end{bmatrix} = \begin{cases} \begin{bmatrix} \left(atan\dfrac{LOS_{3_w}}{LOS_{1_w}} - atan\dfrac{x_{b3_w}}{x_{b1_w}}\right) \\ C_1 \end{bmatrix} & \text{if } t > 5 \text{ and } \theta \leq 0 \\ \begin{bmatrix} 0 \\ 0 \end{bmatrix} & \text{else} \end{cases}
\tag{19}
$$

3.2.2. Modified Proportional Law

The guidance for the terminal phase of flight is formulated as a modified proportional law ruled by expression (20). Equation (21) calculates time to target, t_{go}. Guidance is activated only when the vertical coordinate of the line of sight vector is greater than a given constant (C_2) [1].

$$
\begin{bmatrix} \psi_{dem} \\ \theta_{dem} \end{bmatrix} = \begin{cases} \dfrac{\overrightarrow{LOS_w} - \overrightarrow{v_w} t_{go}}{t_{go}^2} \cdot \begin{bmatrix} \overrightarrow{k_w} \\ -\overrightarrow{i_w} \end{bmatrix} & \text{if } atan\dfrac{LOS_{3_{NED}}}{\sqrt{LOS_{1_{NED}}^2 + LOS_{2_{NED}}^2}} \leq C_2 \\ \begin{bmatrix} 0 \\ 0 \end{bmatrix} & \text{else} \end{cases}
\tag{20}
$$

$$t_{go} = max \begin{bmatrix} \frac{1}{g}\left(\overrightarrow{v_w} \cdot \overrightarrow{j_w} + \sqrt{(\overrightarrow{v_w} \cdot \overrightarrow{j_w})^2 + 2gLOS_{2_w}} \right) \\ \frac{1}{g}\left(\overrightarrow{v_w} \cdot \overrightarrow{j_w} - \sqrt{(\overrightarrow{v_w} \cdot \overrightarrow{j_w})^2 + 2gLOS_{2_w}} \right) \end{bmatrix}$$ (21)

Here, $\overrightarrow{i_w}$, $\overrightarrow{j_w}$, and $\overrightarrow{k_w}$ represent the orthonormal basis of the working axes, and $\overrightarrow{LOS_w} = [LOS_{1_w}, LOS_{2_w}, LOS_{3_w}]^T$ and $\overrightarrow{LOS_{NED}} = [LOS_{1_{NED}}, LOS_{2_{NED}}, LOS_{3_{NED}}]^T$ are the vectors of the line of sight and its components in working and NED axes, respectively.

3.3. Control System

The control law presented in [29] is employed in the current research. Two control conditions are presented in the actuation device: the modulus and the angle for the control force. Control is computed by a double loop feedback system. The inner loop aims at augmenting the stability of the vehicle. Equation (22) characterizes modulus (τ_c) and angle (ϕ_c) of the control force. Its inputs are pitch (θ_{dem}) and yaw (ψ_{dem}) errors. K_i, K_d and K_p are the integral, derivative and proportional constants of the controller, K_{mod} is a constant to adjust force module and $L1$ and $L2$ are experimental gains. The procedure to decide these constant values, which appear in Table 5, is clarified in [1]. Note that the acceleration, without accounting for gravity, of the vehicle in body axes is defined by $[acc_{xb}, acc_{yb}, acc_{zb}]$. Euler angles as introduced before are represented by $[\phi, \theta, \psi]$.

$$\begin{bmatrix} \phi_c \\ \tau_c \end{bmatrix} = \begin{bmatrix} K_p\,(E1 - E2) + K_i \int (E1 - E2)\,dt + K_d\frac{d}{dt}\,(E1 - E2) + E1 \\ K_{mod}\sqrt{(\theta_{dem} - L_1\theta)^2 + (L_2(\psi_{dem} - L_1\psi))^2} \end{bmatrix}$$

$$\text{where} \begin{cases} E1 = atan\frac{\theta_{dem} - L_1\theta}{L_2(\psi_{dem} - L_1\psi)} \\ E2 = atan\frac{acc_{zb}}{acc_{yb}} \end{cases}$$ (22)

Table 5. Values for the constants of the control systems for each flight phase.

Constant / Phase of Flight	C_1	C_2	K_i	K_p	K_d	K_{mod}	L_1	L_2
Intermediate phases	−7.5 deg	−21 deg	0	0.5	0	0.08	0.01	100
Terminal phase	−7.5 deg	−21 deg	1	0.25	0.05	0.08	0.01	1

Summarizing, the control law works as follows. The controller determines the required pointing angle of the aerodynamic force. This is calculated obtaining the arc-tangent of the quotient of the pitch and yaw error, which provides an angle, in the $y_b - z_b$ plane, at which the aerodynamic force should point to reach the objective. However, due to gyroscopic effects, the response of the vehicle is hard to govern, i.e., pointing the control force upwards may not make the vehicle to react upwards. Consequently, knowing the acceleration of the vehicle, without accounting for gravity, is a must. Similarly, the difference between ϕ_c and the angle the projection of the aerodynamic force in the $y_b - z_b$ plane forms with y_b needs to be determined [1].

The aforementioned parameters of control are transformed into canard surface deflections, i.e., $\delta_1, \delta_2, \delta_3$ and δ_4, which are ruled by two different actuators, as it is shown in Equation (23).

$$\begin{bmatrix} \delta_1 \\ \delta_2 \\ \delta_3 \\ \delta_4 \end{bmatrix} = \tau_c \begin{bmatrix} sin\phi_c \\ cos\phi_c \\ sin\phi_c \\ cos\phi_c \end{bmatrix}$$ (23)

4. Numerical Simulations

The described nonlinear dynamics are integrated forward in time utilizing a fixed time step Runge–Kutta method of fourth grade to get a single flight path. [1] shows the validation of this modeling and solving approach for aerial platforms. To demonstrate the precision of the novel methodology introduced in this research, which is based on neural networks, the obtained results are compared to the obtained outcomes in [29]. The methodology in [29] features a Kalman based hybridization [43,44] of GNSS, IMU and semiactive laser quadrant photo-detector sensors. To integrate the equations of motion and their interactions with GNC system and environment, MATLAB/Simulink R2020a on a personal computer with a processor of 2.8 Ghz and 32 GB RAM is used.

The remainder of this section is separated in two subsections. The first one presents the noncontrolled trajectories to which the developed navigation, guidance, and control algorithms will be applied. The second one performs Monte Carlo simulations of ballistic flights, Kalman hybridization based controlled flights, and neural networks based controlled flights. Moreover, an ideal controller without induced errors in the line of sight is also developed to compare results with ideal results.

4.1. Noncontrolled Trajectories

Three nominal trajectories are established to test the developed approach. Each one differs in its initial pitch angle: 20°, 30° and 45°. Destination points are at 18,790 m, 23,007 m, and 26,979 m, respectively. In order to compensate Coriolis and gyroscopic forces, initial lateral correction is set to 0.15°, 0.19° and 0.31°, respectively. Figure 3 shows many of these trajectories in a 3D setting for different settings.

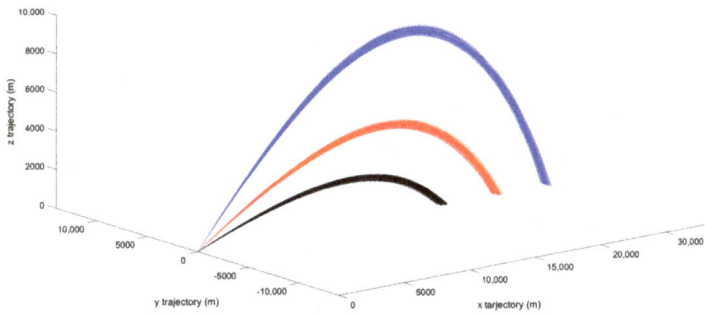

Figure 3. Noncontrolled flights for 20° (black), 30° (red) and 45° (blue) initial pitch angles.

4.2. Monte Carlo Simulations

Noncontrolled flights have been validated against real data provided by the Spanish air force. Monte Carlo simulations are performed to calculate closed-loop performance over a full range of uncertainty settings, which have been defined with the support of the Spanish air force. These settings model the potential uncertainty that can arise in aspects such as initial conditions, sensor information procurement, weather conditions, and thrust properties. Note that, details on uncertainty models for sensors are given in the previous sections. Table 6 shows mean and standard deviation for the rest of the considered uncertain parameters.

A set of 2000 flights is performed for each of the following approaches: noncontrolled flights, Kalman hybridization based controlled flights, neural network based controlled flights, and ideally controlled flights. Simulations are run for each of the initial pitch angles. Note that the previously used data for neural network training is different from the data employed in the simulations in this section.

Table 6. Monte Carlo simulation parameters.

Parameter (deg)	Initial ϕ	Initial Pitch	Wind Speed	Wind Direction	Thrust	Initial Azimuth
Mean	0°	Nom.	10 m/s	0°	T(t)	Nom.
Standard Deviation	20°	0.01°	5 m/s	20°	10 N	0.01°

4.3. Discussion

Results for noncontrolled trajectories are shown in Figure 3, which depicts destination point dispersion patterns. This figure shows the ballistic trajectory that the vehicle follows for three different launch angles without using the control system at all, that is, it shows the flight of the system before implementing the improvements provided by the GNC system. The circular error probable (CEP), which is defined as the radius of a circle, centered on the mean, whose boundary is expected to include the landing points of 50% of the flights. The CEP is employed as a quality check parameter at the final step of the simulation as it is a valid reference for any utilized method. Indeed, the lower the CEP is the better the global GNC device is.

Table 7 displays the CEP for noncontrolled flights, Kalman hybridization based controlled flights and ideally controlled flights for each of the initial pitch angles.

Table 7. The CEP for noncontrolled flights, Kalman hybridization based controlled flights and ideally controlled flights for 20°, 30° and 45° initial pitch angles.

Initial Pitch Angle (deg)	Noncontrolled CEP (m)	Kalman Based CEP (m)	Ideal CEP (m)
20	169.34	1.28	1.18
30	239.37	1.18	1.06
45	281.59	0.98	0.83

Analyzing Table 7, it may be concluded that the CEP increases with target distance for noncontrolled flights, as expected. However, it almost remains constant for either Kalman based or ideally controlled flights, which means the use of an appropriate GNC device eliminates the correlation between the CEP and the distance to the objective. Recall, the main purpose is to show that these results are reproducible when employing machine learning and when reducing the availability of sensors.

Table 8 shows again the CEP for different trajectories, now as obtained by the novel presented approach. Each row, excluding the first one, which shows the headings of the columns, displays the resulting CEPs for every combination of trajectory and NN training algorithm. The first column in the table identifies the trajectory, the second one the training algorithm, the third one the CEP for the NN architecture in method 1, and the last one the CEP for the NN architecture in method 2. One of the main conclusions drawn from Table 8 is that the results for the SCG training algorithm present an unacceptable big CEP, which means low accuracy when reaching destination. Consequently, this training algorithm should be discarded in this case. Indeed, we recover results equivalent to a defective GNC system, even showing worse performance than ballistic flights. Several tests and a hyperparametric analysis were conducted, and it is observed that these kinds of errors were systematic, concluding that this training algorithm does not match well with the fed data to the NN. However, the results from BR and LM training algorithms show a good behavior throughout the trajectory, which means level of accuracy at destination is high. Diving into the numerical results in Table 8, it can be stated that the presented novel approach, which relaxes sensor requirements, is even able of outperforming the Kalman hybridization based approach. It can also be observed that the results are coherent with the training results depicted in Table 4. For example, the poor MSE and R values for the SCG training algorithm are reflected in the unacceptable GNC device results. Comparing the obtained CEPs to what it was obtained in [1,22,29], it can be concluded that the results here are of the same order of magnitude and that the NN algorithms are viable for these type of applications.

As a summary, results for ballistic trajectories and comparisons between different approaches are shown in Figure 4. It is composed of four columns and three rows of subfigures. Each row features a different initial pitch angle. The first column of subfigures compares ballistic flights against Kalman hybridization assisted flights, the second one compares Kalman hybridization against neural network hybridization, the third one neural network hybridization against ideal controller, and the last one ballistic flights against neural network hybridization assisted flights. Note that, even with an ideal controller, which features perfect information on the attitude angles, there are still errors associated to the aerodynamic response of the vehicle.

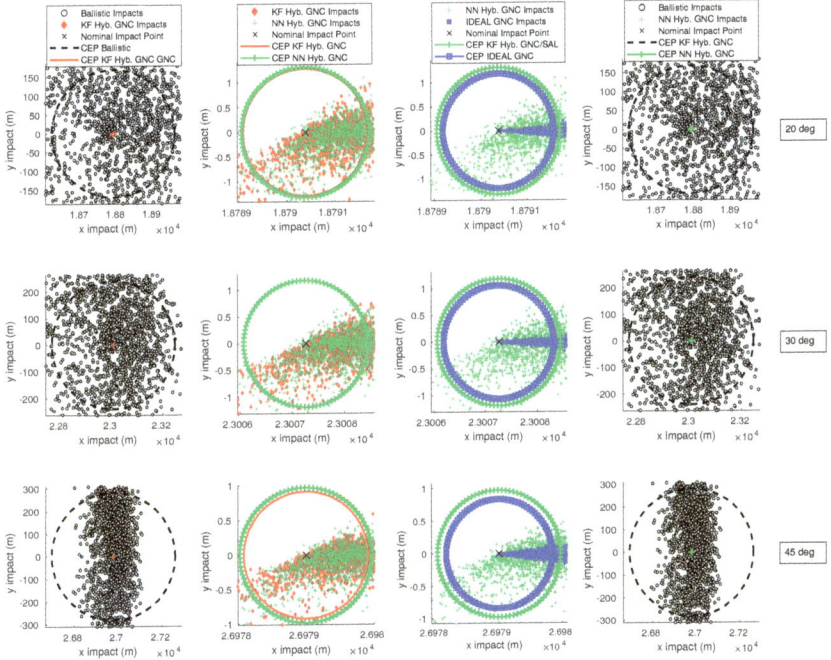

Figure 4. Detailed shots for different algorithms.

Table 8. The CEP in neural network based controlled flights for the different methods and training algorithms for 20°, 30° and 45° initial pitch angles.

Init. Ang. (deg)	Alg.	CEP	
		Method 1	Method 2
20	SCG	2211.93	2115.80
30	SCG	2174.67	2369.82
45	SCG	2565.99	2285.93
20	BR	1.23	1.33
30	BR	1.19	1.25
45	BR	0.99	1.15
20	LM	1.22	1.31
30	LM	1.17	1.26
45	LM	0.95	0.97

5. Conclusions

A novel methodology, which depends on an innovative hybridization among several sensor signals, has been proposed. At the core of the approach, neural networks are employed to get estimations of the gravity vector, which allows avoiding the use of gyroscopes. Traditional GNSS/IMU frameworks feature little errors of up to one meter, which may imply huge mistakes in line of sight vector computation when separation to the objective is small. With the proposed approach the exactness of line of sight calculation can be improved during the terminal GNC, enhancing the accuracy at the destination point, while sensor needs are lowered.

The proposed approach employs information gathered from GNSS, acceloremeters, and a semiactive laser kit. With that information, two different neural network architectures are applied to estimate the gravity vector in order to determine the attitude of the vehicle. Three training algorithms have been addressed to tune the parameters in the neural networks. In total, six different strategies are developed for estimating the gravity vector along the trajectory. In addition, because the methodology allows for determining attitude in two ways, the information is hybridized with the aim of augmenting precision.

This innovative methodology is integrated into a two-phase guidance algorithm for aerial vehicles, which provides the required input data for the GNC system. The guidance law is founded on a constant glide angle and on a modified proportional law. The control algorithm is based on a robust and effective but simple double-input double-output device. Overall, the resulting GNC system presents excellent values regarding dispersion at the destination objective, significantly increasing the precision for noncontrolled flights, as expected, but also matching accuracy as provided by other GNC systems requiring more sensors on-board. Note that results also show good behavior of the system under uncertainty conditions. Summarizing, the developed approach, which is based on neural networks, shows that precision levels can be matched or improved as compared to other methodologies.

Future research will address the increase of the use of neural networks in other modules of GNC algorithms to further simplify the overall architecture.

Author Contributions: Conceptualization, R.d.C.; methodology, R.d.C. and L.C.; software, L.C.; validation, R.d.C.; formal analysis, R.d.C. and P.S.; investigation, R.d.C. and P.S.; resources, L.C.; data curation, R.d.C. and P.S.; writing–original draft preparation, L.C.; writing–review and editing, R.d.C.; visualization, R.d.C. All authors have read and agreed to the published version of the manuscript.

Funding: This research was funded by Project Grant F663—AAGNCS by the "Dirección General de Investigación e Innovación Tecnológica, Consejería de Ciencia, Universidades e Innovación, Comunidad de Madrid" and "Universidad Rey Juan Carlos".

Acknowledgments: The authors would like to thank Lieutenant Colonel Jesús Sánchez (NMT) of the National Institute for Aerospace Technology (INTA) for the solid modeling of the concept.

Conflicts of Interest: The authors declare no conflict of interest.

References

1. De Celis, R.; Cadarso, L.; Sánchez, J. Guidance and control for high dynamic rotating artillery rockets. *Aerosp. Sci. Technol.* **2017**, *64*, 204–212. [CrossRef]
2. De Celis, R.; Cadarso, L. Hybridized attitude determination techniques to improve ballistic projectile navigation, guidance and control. *Aerosp. Sci. Technol.* **2018**, *77*, 138–148. [CrossRef]
3. Waltz, E.L.; Buede, D.M. Data fusion and decision support for command and control. *IEEE Trans. Syst. Man Cybern.* **1986**, *16*, 865–879. [CrossRef]
4. Nguyen, N.V.; Tyan, M.; Lee, J.W. Efficient Framework for Missile Design and 6DoF Simulation using Multi-fidelity Analysis and Data Fusion. In Proceedings of the 17th AIAA/ISSMO Multidisciplinary Analysis and Optimization Conference, Washington, DC, USA, 13–17 June 2016; p. 3365.
5. Schmidt, G.T.; Phillips, R.E. INS/GPS Integration Architecture Performance Comparisons. Available online: https://www.semanticscholar.org/paper/INS%2FGPS-Integration-Architecture-Performance-Schmidt-Phillips/1cb8e282e25d90048c1232778f3fbb21eb4c9de8 (accessed on 12 November 2020).

6. Bryne, T.H.; Hansen, J.M.; Rogne, R.H.; Sokolova, N.; Fossen, T.I.; Johansen, T.A. Nonlinear observers for integrated INS\/GNSS navigation: Implementation aspects. *IEEE Control Syst. Mag.* **2017**, *37*, 59–86.

7. Gaudet, B.; Furfaro, R.; Linares, R. Reinforcement learning for angle-only intercept guidance of maneuvering targets. *Aerosp. Sci. Technol.* **2020**, *99*, 105746. [CrossRef]

8. Zhao, J.; Zhou, R. Unified approach to cooperative guidance laws against stationary and maneuvering targets. *Nonlinear Dyn.* **2015**, *81*, 1635–1647. [CrossRef]

9. Creagh, M.A.; Mee, D.J. Attitude guidance for spinning vehicles with independent pitch and yaw control. *J. Guid. Control. Dyn.* **2010**, *33*, 915–922. [CrossRef]

10. Shalumov, V. Cooperative Online Guide-Launch-Guide Policy in a Target-Missile-Defender Engagement using Deep Reinforcement Learning. *Aerosp. Sci. Technol.* **2020**, *104*, 105996. [CrossRef]

11. Lee, H.I.; Sun, B.C.; Tahk, M.J.; Lee, H. Control design of spinning rockets based on co-evolutionary optimization. *Control Eng. Pract.* **2001**, *9*, 149–157. [CrossRef]

12. Lechevin, N.; Rabbath, C.A. Robust discrete-time proportional-derivative navigation guidance. *J. Guid. Control. Dyn.* **2012**, *35*, 1007–1013. [CrossRef]

13. Wang, X.; Wang, J.; Gao, G. Partial integrated missile guidance and control with state observer. *Nonlinear Dyn.* **2015**, *79*, 2497–2514. [CrossRef]

14. Zhang, Y.; Sun, M.; Chen, Z. Finite-time convergent guidance law with impact angle constraint based on sliding-mode control. *Nonlinear Dyn.* **2012**, *70*, 619–625. [CrossRef]

15. Theodoulis, S.; Gassmann, V.; Wernert, P.; Dritsas, L.; Kitsios, I.; Tzes, A. Guidance and control design for a class of spin-stabilized fin-controlled projectiles. *J. Guid. Control. Dyn.* **2013**, *36*, 517–531. [CrossRef]

16. Safari, S.; Shabani, F.; Simon, D. Multirate multisensor data fusion for linear systems using Kalman filters and a neural network. *Aerosp. Sci. Technol.* **2014**, *39*, 465–471. [CrossRef]

17. De Celis, R.; Cadarso, L. Spot-Centroid Determination Algorithms in Semiactive Laser Photodiodes for Artillery Applications. *J. Sens.* **2019**, *2019*, 7938415. [CrossRef]

18. Zhang, X.; Yang, Z.; Sun, T.; Yang, H.; Han, K.; Hu, B. Optical system design with common aperture for mid-infrared and laser composite guidance. In Proceedings of the Second International Conference on Photonics and Optical Engineering, Xi'an, China, 14–17 October 2016; International Society for Optics and Photonics: Bellingham, WA, USA, 2017; Volume 10256, p. 102560S.

19. Zeng, X.; Zhu, Z.; Chen, Y. Remote evaluation of rotational velocity using a quadrant photo-detector and a DSC algorithm. *Sensors* **2016**, *16*, 587. [CrossRef]

20. Esper-Chaín, R.; Escuela, A.M.; Fariña, D.; Sendra, J.R. Configurable quadrant photodetector: An improved position sensitive device. *IEEE Sens. J.* **2015**, *16*, 109–119. [CrossRef]

21. Razmi, H.; Afshinfar, S. Neural network-based adaptive sliding mode control design for position and attitude control of a quadrotor UAV. *Aerosp. Sci. Technol.* **2019**, *91*, 12–27. [CrossRef]

22. Solano-López, P.; de Celis, R.; Fuentes, M.; Cadarso, L.; Barea, A. Strategies for high performance GNSS/IMU Guidance, Navigation and Control of Rocketry. In Proceedings of the 8th European Conference for Aeronautics and Space Sciences, Madrid, Spain, 1–4 July 2019; Volume 1, pp. 1–8. [CrossRef]

23. Mohamed, M.; Dongare, V. Aircraft neural modeling and parameter estimation using neural partial differentiation. *Aircr. Eng. Aerosp. Technol.* **2018**, *90*, 764–778. [CrossRef]

24. Ferreres, G.; Hardier, G.; Seren, C. Adaptive control of a civil aircraft through on-line parameter estimation. In Proceedings of the 2016 3rd Conference on Control and Fault-Tolerant Systems (SysTol), Barcelona, Spain, 7–9 September 2016; IEEE: Piscataway, NJ, USA, 2016; pp. 798–804.

25. Hardier, G.; Ferreres, G.; Sato, M. On-line parameter estimation for indirect adaptive flight control: A practical evaluation of several techniques. In Proceedings of the 2020 IEEE Conference on Control Technology and Applications (CCTA), Montreal, QC, Canada, 24–26 August 2020; IEEE: Piscataway, NJ, USA, 2020; pp. 180–187.

26. Ignatyev, D.I.; Shin, H.S.; Tsourdos, A. Two-layer adaptive augmentation for incremental backstepping flight control of transport aircraft in uncertain conditions. *Aerosp. Sci. Technol.* **2020**, *105*, 106051. [CrossRef]

27. North Atlantic Treaty Organization, N. Standardization Agreement (STANAG 4355). In *The Modified Point Mass Trajectory Model*; NATO Headquarters: Brussels, Belgium, 1992.

28. De Celis, R.; Cadarso, L. Attitude determination algorithms through accelerometers, GNSS sensors, and gravity vector estimator. *Int. J. Aerosp. Eng.* **2018**, *2018*, 5394057. [CrossRef]

29. De Celis, R.; Cadarso, L. GNSS/IMU laser quadrant detector hybridization techniques for artillery rocket guidance. *Nonlinear Dyn.* **2018**, *91*, 2683–2698. [CrossRef]
30. Britting, K.R. *Inertial Navigation Systems Analysis*; NASA: Washington, DC, USA, 1971.
31. Yu, J.Y.; Zhang, Y.A.; Gu, W.J. An approach to integrated guidance/autopilot design for missiles based on terminal sliding mode control. In Proceedings of 2004 International Conference on Machine Learning and Cybernetics (IEEE Cat. No. 04EX826), Shanghai, China, 26–29 August 2004; IEEE: Piscataway, NJ, USA, 2004; Volume 1, pp. 610–615.
32. Jankovic, M.; Paul, J.; Kirchner, F. GNC architecture for autonomous robotic capture of a non-cooperative target: Preliminary concept design. *Adv. Space Res.* **2016**, *57*, 1715–1736. [CrossRef]
33. Yu, Y.; Yao, H.; Liu, Y. Aircraft dynamics simulation using a novel physics-based learning method. *Aerosp. Sci. Technol.* **2019**, *87*, 254–264. [CrossRef]
34. Villa, J.; Taipalmaa, J.; Gerasimenko, M.; Pyattaev, A.; Ukonaho, M.; Zhang, H.; Raitoharju, J.; Passalis, N.; Perttula, A.; Aaltonen, J.; et al. aColor: Mechatronics, Machine Learning, and Communications in an Unmanned Surface Vehicle. *arXiv* **2020**, arXiv:2003.00745.
35. Yadav, N.; Yadav, A.; Kumar, M. *An Introduction to Neural Network Methods for Differential Equations*; Springer: Berlin/Heidelberg, Germany, 2015.
36. Tatar, M.; Masdari, M. Investigation of pitch damping derivatives for the Standard Dynamic Model at high angles of attack using neural network. *Aerosp. Sci. Technol.* **2019**, *92*, 685–695. [CrossRef]
37. Møller, M.F. *A Scaled Conjugate Gradient Algorithm for Fast Supervised Learning*; Aarhus University, Computer Science Department: Aarhus, Denmark, 1990.
38. MacKay, D.J. Bayesian interpolation. *Neural Comput.* **1992**, *4*, 415–447. [CrossRef]
39. Foresee, F.D.; Hagan, M.T. Gauss-Newton approximation to Bayesian learning. In Proceedings of International Conference on Neural Networks (ICNN'97), Houston, TX, USA, 12 June 1997; IEEE: Piscataway, NJ, USA, 1997; Volume 3, pp. 1930–1935. [CrossRef]
40. Moré, J.J. The Levenberg-Marquardt algorithm: Implementation and theory. In *Numerical Analysis*; Springer: Berlin/Heidelberg, Germany, 1978; pp. 105–116.
41. Kanzow, C.; Yamashita, N.; Fukushima, M. Withdrawn: Levenberg–marquardt methods with strong local convergence properties for solving nonlinear equations with convex constraints. *J. Comput. Appl. Math.* **2005**, *173*, 321–343. [CrossRef]
42. Wahba, G. A least squares estimate of satellite attitude. *SIAM Rev.* **1965**, *7*, 409–409. [CrossRef]
43. Borkowski, P.; Pietrzykowski, Z.; Magaj, J.; Mąka, M. Fusion of data from GPS receivers based on a multi-sensor Kalman filter. *Transp. Probl.* **2008**, *3*, 5–11.
44. Jaroś, K.; Witkowska, A.; Śmierzchalski, R. Data fusion of GPS sensors using particle Kalman filter for ship dynamic positioning system. In Proceedings of the 2017 22nd International Conference on Methods and Models in Automation and Robotics (MMAR), Miedzyzdroje, Poland, 28–31 August 2017; IEEE: Piscataway, NJ, USA, 2017; pp. 89–94.

Publisher's Note: MDPI stays neutral with regard to jurisdictional claims in published maps and institutional affiliations.

Article

A Simulation-Based Optimization Method for Warehouse Worker Assignment

Odkhishig Ganbold *, Kaustav Kundu, Haobin Li and Wei Zhang *

Department of Industrial Systems Engineering and Management, Faculty of Engineering, National University of Singapore, Singapore 117576, Singapore; isekk@nus.edu.sg (K.K.); li_haobin@nus.edu.sg (H.L.)
* Correspondence: iseog@nus.edu.sg (O.G.); isezw@nus.edu.sg (W.Z.)

Received: 30 September 2020; Accepted: 1 December 2020; Published: 4 December 2020

Abstract: The general assignment problem is a classical NP-hard (non-deterministic polynomial-time) problem. In a warehouse, the constraints on the equipment and the characteristics of consecutive processes make it even more complicated. To overcome the difficulty in calculating the benefit of an assignment and in finding the optimal assignment plan, a simulation-based optimization method is introduced. We first built a simulation model of the warehouse with the object-oriented discrete-event simulation (O2DES) framework, and then implemented a random neighborhood search method utilizing the simulation output. With this method, the throughput and service level of the warehouse can be improved, while keeping the number of workers constant. Numerical results with real data demonstrate the reduction of discrepancy between inbound and outbound service level performance. With a less than 10% reduction in inbound service level, we can achieve an over 30% increase in outbound service level. The proposed decision support tool assists the warehouse manager in dealing with warehouse worker allocation problem under conditions of random daily workload.

Keywords: discrete-event simulation; simulation-based optimization; assignment problem; neighborhood search; warehouse

---

1. Introduction

Workforce planning has been reported to be a persistent problem for a variety of process-centered industries [1]. These include healthcare operations—in particular, emergency departments, service industries, and warehouse management—whose performances are dependent on swift and even flows of resources and customers [2–4]. As the theory of swift and even flow suggests, the bottleneck management and process standardization are key to the speed and variance of the process flow [2]. The productivity of any process increases with the speed at which the materials (or information) flow through the process [5]. This indicates the importance of workforce planning for improving productivity.

Warehousing is a vital component of the supply chain, where the optimal planning of its workforce is a prerequisite towards achieving its global efficiency [6]. In a warehouse, a sequence of multiple processes is performed, starting from shipment arrivals and ending in shipment releases. These processes are usually constrained by space and workforce capacity. The main focus of the current study is the workforce planning system implemented in a warehouse. As the labor resources represent a significant cost item in a labor-short country such as Singapore; this poses new challenges for cost minimization and efficiency improvements via innovations in workforce planning and optimization. The preliminary analysis of the warehouse operations, and specifically worker allocation, revealed an unbalanced utilization of workers across different warehouse activities. It was identified that one of the critical bottlenecks affecting overall service level of the warehouse was the need to optimize worker assignment to each task/workstation while balancing the workload of each workstation.

Algorithms **2020**, *13*, 326; doi:10.3390/a13120326   www.mdpi.com/journal/algorithms

In the traditional assignment optimization problem, the benefit can be directly calculated given a fixed worker–task pairing. Even with this assumption, the assignment problem is NP-hard [7]. The problem in the warehouse is more complicated due to the precedence constraints, whereby the succeeding activity cannot start until the preceding activity is completed. Another related problem is the assembly line balancing, which considers the precedence constraints. However, oftentimes such problems do not consider worker capability and capacity factors, which are critical to human resource allocation problems [8].

Discrete-event simulation (DES) is one of the popular modeling techniques in which a model changes only at a discrete random set of time points [9]. Nowadays, many commercial simulation software packages such as Arena integrate optimization techniques with DES [10,11]. Although such commercial software packages are designed to provide users with functionality to create their desired simulation models based on processes, oftentimes the users are not allowed to customize the event logic, which is an integral part of each DES model [10]. In this study, we adopt the object-oriented discrete-event simulation (O2DES in C#) framework developed by Li et al. [12]. This novel framework features a flexible simulation modeling environment, which allows the user to customize the event logic, configure simulation parameters, and incorporate add-on algorithms, including optimization models.

Our research aim was to develop a simulation-based optimization method to improve the warehouse service level, i.e., daily productivity, by optimally allocating warehouse workers into inbound and outbound activities, while at the same time considering all operational constraints of the warehouse's operation. In addressing this aim, a warehouse manpower planning tool was developed based on the simulation-based optimization method, which combines the O2DES simulation framework and a random neighborhood search method. Our study is the first in the operations research domain to introduce a decision support tool for warehouse worker allocation using a simulation-based optimization method.

The manpower allocation tool was tested in a warehouse located at Singapore. It is now used to support the warehouse managers' decisions on a weekly and/or daily basis.

The rest of the paper is organized as follows. In Section 2, a literature review on the related topics is presented. Next, the worker assignment problem in the warehouse is described in Section 3. Section 4 outlines the simulation-based optimization method. The O2DES framework and the warehouse simulation model are introduced in Section 5, followed by the simulation-based optimization algorithm specifications in Section 6. Section 7 presents the numerical results.

2. Literature Review

Customer satisfaction via effective resource utilization, the shipment of the right product in good condition and within the target shipment time, is the key objective of warehousing [13–16]. Warehousing aims to address the differences in time and space between suppliers and customers, while adapting to the fluctuating market conditions [17]. Warehouses execute a broad range of process-based functions, including temporary storage, protecting goods, service support in customer order fulfillment, goods packaging, after sales service support, quality inspections, testing, assembly, and repairs [18,19].

In the current global economic environment, the warehouses face an unprecedented level of competitive and economic pressures [20], including a high level of uncertainty and risk of supply chain disruptions due to the COVID-19 pandemic [21,22]. The pressures from competitors and customers result in the reduction of profit margins [23,24]. Under this situation, efficient resource utilization becomes more critical than ever.

Humans are the central and most critical elements of the resource base in warehousing [25]. Due to the high fluctuations (both predictable and unexpected) in workload demand [18], research has advocated the need for the implementation of manpower planning strategies [20,26]. For example, Edwards et al. [27] distinguishes three phases of manpower planning, which include the prediction of manpower demand, the prediction of the future supply of manpower, and reconciliation of the discrepancies between supply and demand via workforce scheduling and staffing. Considering the above, workforce scheduling—and specifically personnel work assignments that deal with the allocation of personnel to tasks and work stations—is crucial to warehouse operational efficiency [6,28,29]. Optimal staffing, or allocation of workers to tasks, is the key to tackling the challenges of high demand fluctuations on a daily basis. In the warehouse, this problem is dependent on workers; qualifications, i.e., skill sets, which are very specific to each employee.

The most relevant problem to our topic is the mixed-model assembly line balancing problem (MALBP), which tries to assign the tasks of different models to the workstations. It is called a mixed-model as multiple models are assembled on the same assembly line. As summarized in Becker et al. [8], there are three types of MALBP problems, categorized according to the constraint and objective:

1. MALBP-I: given the cycle time to minimize the number of workstations;
2. MALBP-II: given the number of workstations to minimize the cycle time;
3. MALBP-III: minimize both the cycle time and the number of workstations.

However, our target is to maximize the service level, i.e., the ratio between the number of completed tasks and the number of arriving tasks, given a fixed number of workers. Our research problem is different from the above-mentioned three problems by Becker et al. [8], except for the MALBP-II which can be considered the most relevant to our problem. The major points that differentiate our problem are:

- In our problem, each worker is only capable of performing a subset of operations.
- The processing time of each task is stochastic.
- The objective is to maximize the service level.

In Dou et al. [30], a machine deployment problem is considered, where the objective is to minimize the cost of setting up all the machines, while satisfying the precedence and space constraints. This involves also assignments of the machines to the tasks, and a GA-based optimization approach was designed to identify a set of best solutions. The machines in Dou et al.'s [30] model can be considered as workers in our model. However, in our problem the number of workers is fixed, while the objective is to maximize the service level. In contrast, in Dou et al.'s [30] model the number of machines in different stages (tasks) are independent.

Simulation-based optimization has been used for a number of decades for problem solving in logistics. For example, Azadivar [31] showed that the discrete rack systems can be better optimized through simulations rather than approximating with mathematical models. Later on, Ding et al. [32] extended this idea to the supply chain context. They developed a simulation-based optimization method for the selection of potential suppliers. To obtain an optimal design of the cold supply chain, Saif and Elheldhli [33] developed an innovative simulation-based optimization approach to minimize the total cost that includes the logistics costs and the global warming impact. More recently, Ghasemi and Khalili-Damghani [34] developed a novel simulation-based optimization approach to solve a multi-period inventory planning problem for the supply chain of a company in Iran.

3. Problem Description

Warehouses typically handle a variety of stock-keeping units (SKUs), which require a range of activities to be executed. Different products may require different activities. Considering the space and workforce constraints, the warehouse aims to maximize its productivity with via appropriate worker assignment. As warehouse workers may have different skills, it is not only the number of the workers that count, but also every specific worker–activity pairing becomes critical. Under the conditions of high fluctuations in daily workload, it is important for the warehouse planner to obtain an optimal worker assignment in a rather short period of time. To address this problem, a simulation-based optimization method was developed. Specifically, the optimal worker assignment to warehouse activities/tasks should be achieved while satisfying all operational and worker skill set constraints.

In our showcase, the following operational assumptions are considered:

- Product types: We chose to consider all product types, i.e., franchises, that the warehouse handles. There are in total nine franchises being handled in the warehouse. Different franchises require different processing times for different activities. More details are provided in Section 5.

- Inbound activities: Inbound activities start with the arrival of shipments at the warehouse. Immediately after the dock-in, the products in pallets are unloaded at the inbound staging area and later moved to the sorting workstation. After manual counting and checking for defects and damage, the products are moved to the goods receipt (GR) workstation. At the GR station, workers scan the barcode on each item and register the items in the warehouse management system (WMS), while putaway slips with storage bins are generated for each pallet load. After the GR, they are ready for putaway to the storage area(s). The putaway worker puts away the pallet in its designated storage area following the storage bin information printed on the putaway slip. Putaway activity is denoted as the terminal inbound activity. Figure 1 shows the entity flow diagram for inbound shipments.

- Outbound activities: Outbound activities start when order information arrives into the WMS and a pick slip is generated. One order is assigned to one picker. After the order picking is completed, depending on the labeling requirements, the items need to be labeled before scanning starts. Otherwise, the picked items are sent to the scanning station. There are two types of scanning, each for a certain type of product, i.e., manual scanning and scanning via auto-scanning tunnel (AST). The scanning activity makes sure that all the items are picked against the order lists, and it generates slips that denote items which need to be packed together based on pallet or case dimension constraints. Then the items are packed into pallets and cases accordingly. A release worker moves the order to the outbound staging, from where the order is shipped out with an outbound truck. Figure 2 describes the outbound entity flow diagram.

- Three types of storage areas: There are three storage areas in the warehouse, i.e., racking, long-span shelving (LSS), and vertical lift modules (VLMs). Racking is designed to store SKUs in full pallets, LSS contains SKUs in loose boxes, and VLMs are for loose boxes. Each storage type is dedicated to one or more product types.

- Shift configuration and working days: There are two shifts operating during business days (excluding weekends and holidays): the morning shift operates from 8:00 a.m. to 6:00 p.m. with a one-hour break during 12:00–1:00 p.m., and the night shift operates from 9:00 p.m. to 7:00 a.m. (next day) with a one-hour break during 1:00–2:00 a.m.

- Worker numbers and shift assignment: The total number of workers is fixed (31 workers in total). Worker numbers assigned to each shift are pre-fixed; 21 workers are assigned to the morning shift and 5 workers are assigned to the night shift. Additionally, 5 outsourced workers are assigned to value-added service (VAS) activity for labeling upon request.

- Worker skill set matrix: We assume that each worker has his/her own unique skill set. If the worker is trained to conduct an activity, "yes" is put in the respective activity cell. Table 1 shows the worker skill set matrix assumed in our model.

- Workload demand for one-week period is known upfront.

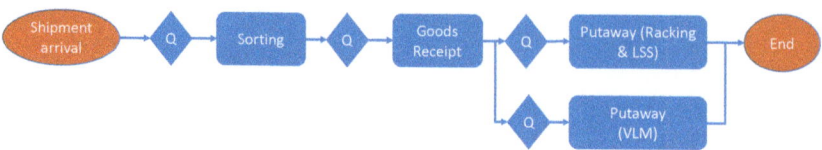

Figure 1. Inbound entity flow diagram.

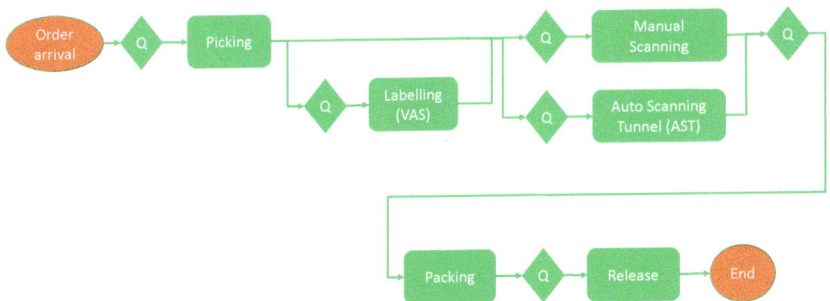

Figure 2. Outbound entity flow diagram.

Table 1. Worker skill set.

Worker id	Shift	Sorting	GR	Putaway	VLM	Picking	AST	Scanning	Packing	Release	VAS
Worker 1	Shift 1	Yes	Yes	Yes	Yes				Yes		
Worker 2	Shift 1	Yes	Yes		Yes				Yes		
Worker 3	Shift 1	Yes	Yes	Yes	Yes				Yes		
Worker 4	Shift 1	Yes	Yes	Yes	Yes				Yes		
Worker 5	Shift 1	Yes	Yes	Yes	Yes				Yes		
Worker 6	Shift 1	Yes	Yes	Yes	Yes				Yes		
Worker 7	Shift 1	Yes	Yes	Yes	Yes				Yes		
Worker 8	Shift 1	Yes	Yes	Yes	Yes			Yes	Yes		
Worker 9	Shift 1	Yes	Yes	Yes	Yes				Yes		
Worker 10	Shift 1	Yes	Yes	Yes	Yes	Yes	Yes	Yes	Yes	Yes	
Worker 11	Shift 1	Yes			Yes				Yes		
Worker 12	Shift 2	Yes	Yes	Yes	Yes	Yes			Yes		
Worker 13	Shift 2	Yes	Yes	Yes	Yes	Yes	Yes	Yes	Yes		
Worker 14	Shift 2	Yes		Yes	Yes	Yes	Yes		Yes		
Worker 15	Shift 2	Yes		Yes	Yes	Yes	Yes	Yes	Yes		
Worker 16	Shift 2	Yes	Yes	Yes	Yes	Yes	Yes	Yes	Yes		
Worker 17	Shift 1	Yes			Yes	Yes	Yes	Yes	Yes		
Worker 18	Shift 1				Yes			Yes	Yes	Yes	
Worker 19	Shift 1				Yes	Yes			Yes	Yes	
Worker 20	Shift 1			Yes	Yes	Yes	Yes	Yes	Yes	Yes	
Worker 21	Shift 1				Yes	Yes	Yes	Yes	Yes		
Worker 22	Shift 1			Yes	Yes		Yes	Yes	Yes	Yes	
Worker 23	Shift 1	Yes	Yes	Yes	Yes		Yes	Yes	Yes	Yes	
Worker 24	Shift 1			Yes	Yes	Yes	Yes	Yes	Yes	Yes	
Worker 25	Shift 1				Yes	Yes	Yes		Yes	Yes	
Worker 26	Shift 1	Yes	Yes	Yes	Yes	Yes			Yes	Yes	
Worker 27	Shift 1										Yes
Worker 28	Shift 1										Yes
Worker 29	Shift 1										Yes
Worker 30	Shift 1										Yes
Worker 31	Shift 1										Yes

To tackle the problem, the constraints on the workforce should be dealt with. These constraints may be worker-specific, such as the skill set, or arise from the resource limits and operational rules in the warehouse. For example, due to the warehouse equipment capacity, there is an upper bound on the number of workers allowed to be assigned to some activities. Namely, there is a limited amount of the material handling equipment (MHE) and a limited number of scanning computers at a workstation, thereby determining the maximum number of workers allowed to work at each workstation or activity at the same time. In our showcase in Section 7, it is assumed that GR allows up to two workers, putaway three workers, VLM two workers, picking six workers, AST either two or zero workers, and scanning up to three workers. However, we do not impose any constraints on sorting, packing, and release activities regarding the maximum number of workers, as such activities do not require any specific equipment. Moreover, following the warehouse operation requirements, we assume that the night shift can perform only putaway, picking, scanning, and packing activities.

Worker skill set is an important constraint in the assignment problem, which is also considered here. As shown in Table 1, each worker owns a distinct set of skills that allows the worker to perform the corresponding warehouse activities. If the worker is not trained to perform an activity, that worker cannot be considered as a candidate for assignment to this activity.

Nonetheless, we do not impose any constraints on warehouse storage capacity, working areas, and buffer zones between activities.

In the following sections, we will show how the simulation-based optimization method can be used to solve this problem. As the situation in reality may vary day by day, and also from one warehouse to another, our tool will provide the solution for the specific settings of the warehouse, including flexibility of both products and workers.

First of all, inbound and outbound workload information should be defined. For example, the inbound shipment arrival and/or outbound order start time-stamp, product name, workload in terms of number of pallets, and target completion time-stamp information, are all handled by the warehouse planners. This information is dependent on the forecast or expectation. Hence, this information may vary. Moreover, we allow the model to capture the pending workload from the previous day in pallet quantity, and by each type of inbound and outbound activity. Besides, the more detailed information, such as the product type and processing time for each activity, can also be customized by the user. Here we specify product name, designated storage area, whether the product requires AST for scanning or not, and per-pallet processing time (mean, standard deviation) by all inbound and outbound activities needed by each product type.

The tool also allows variability in the worker parameters. The number of workers assigned to a shift and the shift duration can vary. As an example, we consider two shifts in the showcase of Section 7, i.e., morning and night, operating from 8 am to 6 pm and from 9 pm to 7 am (next day), respectively, with a one-hour break in each shift. Besides, the information on national holidays can also be captured by our tool to specify the non-working days.

The worker skill set matrix is another important parameter. As defined in Table 1, each worker has a skill set ("Yes" if the worker owns the skill for the activity) with respect to each type of activity conducted in the warehouse.

To measure the performances of different worker assignment options in the warehouse, the hourly and daily KPIs are generated. The hourly KPIs include worker utilization by each activity in each hour, inbound and outbound throughput in terms of the number of completed pallets by each hour, and overall inbound and outbound team utilization rate by each hour. Overall daily KPIs include inbound and outbound team overall daily utilization, total work-in-progress (WIP) pallet quantity in inbound and outbound activities, total quantity of completed pallets by inbound and outbound teams, inbound and outbound service levels, and per-worker average productivity rate in terms of number of completed pallets.

To express the KPIs formally, we define the following notation:

- w_{occ}: number of occupied workers;
- w_{ava}: total number of available workers;
- p_{com}: number of completed pallets;
- p_{arr}: number of arrived pallets;
- p_{incom}: number of completed inbound pallets;
- p_{outcom}: number of completed outbound pallets;
- w_{in}: number of inbound workers;
- w_{out}: number of outbound workers.

We define $avg(\cdot)$ as the average function over the simulation days. The KPIs can be calculated with the following formula:

$$\text{Utilization rate by activities and overall utilization rate} = avg\left(\frac{w_{occ}}{w_{ava}}\right) \tag{1}$$

$$\text{Daily service level} = \frac{p_{com}}{p_{arr}} \tag{2}$$

$$\text{Daily per-worker productivity for Inbound} = \frac{p_{incom}}{w_{in}} \tag{3}$$

$$\text{Daily per-worker productivity for Outbound} = \frac{p_{outcom}}{w_{out}} \tag{4}$$

In our simulation-based optimization model we consider service level as the target KPI, as communicated by the warehouse team. The warehouse operations team measures their service level performance as the ratio of total number of completed pallets (output) to total number of arrived pallets (input) on a given day, which is oftentimes denoted as throughput productivity in the warehouse literature. Additionally, it is considered to be one of the frequently used direct warehouse performance indicators [35,36].

For the purpose of parsimony, we further concentrate on the service level performance as per our target optimization objective of the simulation-based optimization tool.

4. Methodology

Ladier et al. [6] considered the staff scheduling in the warehouse on both weekly and daily granularity levels. They built three mixed integer programming (MIP) models and solved the models to obtain the optimal staff assignment and shift pattern. Their objective was to minimize the cost, while assuming that all the tasks should be completed by hiring sufficient number of staff. However, in the daily operations of the warehouse, the number of available workers may not be enough to complete all the tasks. In this situation, the objective is to finish as many tasks, with an optimal worker assignment.

The selected warehouse in this study serves as a distribution center with variations in product types and demands. There are different teams working on different activities. The warehouse operates as one single processing unit, which consists of sequence of activities. The major concern of the warehouse is to assign the optimal number of workers to each team. Moreover, under uncertainty in demand and processing time, this may require reallocation of worker(s) to other teams. This adds an additional layer of complexity to the problem and requires a methodology that can solve the problem. Given these requirements, following Amorim et al. [37], we devised a simulation–based optimization model that explores both simulation and optimization methods to improve the service level performance, by suggesting appropriate manpower assignment to different activities. First of all, the discrete-event simulation model was developed, considering the relationship between different activities. Then, the processing time of each activity was defined along with an initial assignment of manpower. Due to uncertainty in daily workload, the initial solution is not always optimal. Therefore, additional effort is required to optimally assign the manpower. As the assignment of workers to different activities is a complex task, a heuristic algorithm instead of exact algorithm was developed to find the optimal worker assignment. With each iteration, the new assignment of workers is input to the simulation model until the model output achieves the highest service level performance.

5. O2DES Framework and Warehouse Simulation

For the worker assignment problem in the warehouse, it is difficult to obtain a direct calculation for the worker assignment problem. In this case the simulation comes into play. With the simulation modeling of the warehouse, we can replicate the real system in a computer environment. The systems performance can be evaluated in a simulation, and additional features of system can be tested before its deployment. The simulation outcome allows the decision maker to fine tune a set of parameters to improve the operational performance. However, configuring these parameters for a complex system, such as warehouses, can be challenging. Therefore, the simulation-based optimization approach, which integrates the best of optimization with discrete-event simulation (DES) techniques, can be used to handle this complexity.

The object-oriented discrete-event simulation (O2DES) was adopted from Li et al. [12] and implemented as a core simulation engine in our simulation-based optimization tool to achieve the main objective of our research, i.e., the development of a decision support tool that can optimally assign workers to the warehouse activities.

5.1. O2DES

The main features of O2DES are as follows:

1. Events are described in modules and they interact with each other.
2. Simplified syntax for:

    (a) Event execution;
    (b) Event scheduling;
    (c) Input/output event interfacing.

3. Automated warm-up induction.

5.2. Simulation Modeling

Any process system consists of a sequence of steps, i.e., activities. Entities move through the activities. Similarly, in the simulation modeling, the real life situation can be represented using an entity flow diagram (EFD), a logical flow diagram of entities between the activities. The resources required for the different activities are mapped in the EFD.

As described in Section 3, the warehouse operations consist of two main types, i.e., inbound and outbound, while the pallet is the entity that flows through inbound and outbound activities. To build the simulation model, an EFD based on the warehouse operational processes needs to be developed, as shown in Figure 3.

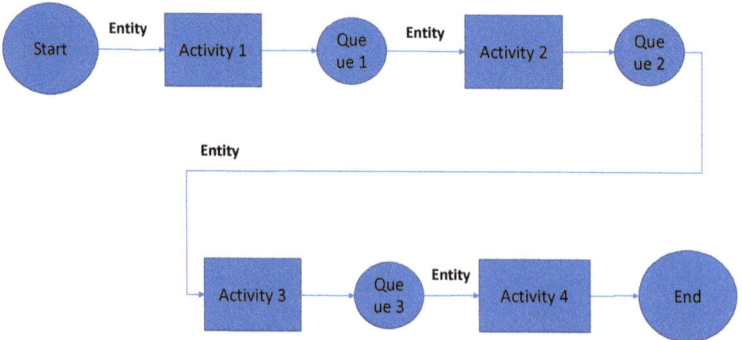

Figure 3. Entity flow diagram (EFD).

With certain assumptions, the simulation model was built using these EFDs in C# code and simple heuristics integrated with simulation were used to assign the manpower.

Input information on inbound and outbound workload has been provided by the warehouse for simulation. On top of incoming inbound shipment load and customer order volume, leftover workload information was also considered.

Due to possible uncertainties in warehouse operations, we assumed the processing time of each activity follows a gamma distribution. The characteristics and advantages of gamma distribution can be found in several previous studies [38–41]. For example, in a study by Song [39], the Poisson distribution was considered to be inappropriate to describe the lead time, as the uncertainty may arise due to several reasons, which makes a more centralized distribution like the gamma distribution a preferred method.

The values of mean μ and standard deviation σ for each activity are calculated based on the time-motion study conducted in the warehouse. Gamma distribution can be characterized by α and λ, where the density probability function:

$$f(x;\alpha,\lambda) = \frac{\lambda^\alpha x^{\alpha-1} e^{-\lambda x}}{\Gamma(\alpha)}, \tag{5}$$

with $\Gamma(\alpha) = (\alpha-1)!$ As the mean $\mu = \frac{\alpha}{\lambda}$ and squared deviation $\sigma^2 = \frac{\alpha}{\lambda^2}$, we can derive α and λ as following:

$$\lambda = \frac{\mu}{\sigma^2}, \alpha = \mu\lambda. \tag{6}$$

Table 2 shows the processing time data used in the simulation model.

Table 2. Processing times of different franchises and processes. GR represents goods receipt; VAS value added service.

Franchise Name	Storage Type	AST	Sorting		GR		Putaway		Picking		Scanning		Packing		Release		VAS	
			μ	σ	μ	σ	μ	σ	μ	σ	μ	σ	μ	σ	μ	σ	μ	σ
Product 1	LSS	Y	48.9	23.4	13.3	1	77.4	1.8	77.6	1.5	30.1	2.6	67.6	6.3	1	0.2	289	13
Product 2	Racking	N	23.4	2.2	6.5	1	6.4	1.5	4.7	1.5	27.3	2.7	67.6	6.3	1	0.2	482	22.5
Product 3	Racking	N	19.9	3.3	3.3	1.2	6.4	1.5	4.7	1.5	13.3	2.7	67.6	6.3	1	0.2	482	22.5
Product 4	VLM	N	72	11.6	26.3	0.2	54.6	0.7	75.1	1.3	20.4	2.8	67.6	6.3	1	0.2	482	22.5
Product 5	LSS	N	40.4	2.6	16.1	1.1	77.4	1.8	77.6	1.5	15.5	7.5	67.6	6.3	1	0.2	482	22.5
Product 6	LSS	N	40.4	2.6	16.1	1.1	77.4	1.8	77.6	1.5	15.5	7.5	67.6	6.3	1	0.2	482	22.5
Product 7	LSS	N	40.4	2.6	16.1	1.1	77.4	1.8	77.6	1.5	15.5	7.5	67.6	6.3	1	0.2	482	22.5
Product 8	LSS	N	40.4	2.6	16.1	1.1	77.4	1.8	77.6	1.5	15.5	7.5	67.6	6.3	1	0.2	482	22.5
Product 9	LSS	N	40.4	2.6	16.1	1.1	77.4	1.8	77.6	1.5	15.5	7.5	67.6	6.3	1	0.2	482	22.5

All simulation experiments were performed on an Intel Core™ i7-8550U CPU 1.80 GHz 1.99 GHz with 16 GB RAM and a 64-bit operating system. First of all, it was necessary to determine the simulation settings: initial conditions, warm-up length, and number of replications [10]. Preliminary tests were performed to evaluate the simulation duration and the number of replications necessary to achieve the steady-state results. Upon the initiation, the simulation tool reads input data and adjusts for the real simulation start time by running a single replication. As a warm-up, this process does not generate any statistics. Using real forecast data of the workload with arrival times, the simulation results indicate that one replication is sufficient to achieve steady output.

Once the model was validated, simulation iterations were run for each possible scenario, in combination with the optimization algorithm. This will be explained in the next section.

6. Simulation-Based Optimization

The objective is to maximize service level for both inbound and outbound operations, where service level= $\frac{p_{com}}{p_{arr}}$.

Considering the constraints, the model is defined as follows:

$$\max \quad f_{nn} + \lambda f_{out} \tag{7}$$

$$s.t. \quad x_{ij} \leq a_{ij} \tag{8}$$

$$\sum_i x_{ij} \leq m_j, \forall j. \tag{9}$$

where f_{in} and f_{out} represent inbound and outbound service levels, respectively; λ is a weight factor to control the trade-off between inbound and outbound. X is an assignment matrix, where $x_{ij} = 1$ means that the worker i is assigned to the activity i, otherwise $x_{ij} = 0$. $a_{ij} = 1$ indicates that worker i has the skill j. In practice, the outbound service level performance is considered to be of a high priority as it is directly related to the customer satisfaction. Hence, a higher weight λ is set for the outbound service level f_{out}.

The constraint part of the model is an assignment problem, where multiple workers can be assigned to the same task. As the objective is not an explicit function of the assignment scheme, but some metric given by the simulation output, it is not easy to solve the problem by an exact algorithm. In the context of a similar problem, i.e., the assembly line worker assignment, the neighborhood search method was shown to be effective in Polat et al. [42] and to outperform other heuristic methods. Motivated by this, we adopted a neighborhood search method in our model.

For a binary vector of matrix, the Hamming distance is the number of bit positions in which the two corresponding bits are different. For two assignment matrices X_1 and X_2; $D(X_1, X_2)$ is denoted as the Hamming distance between them. For each worker w_i, if the worker is assigned to different tasks in X_1 and X_2, the difference will be two in row i. Thus X_1 is called a c-neighbor of X_2 if $D(X_1, X_2) = 2c$. In our problem, due to predetermined upper bounds for the number of workers in each activity, a c-neighbor may not be feasible.

We propose a random neighborhood search algorithm to solve the problem, which is described in Algorithm 1. Accordingly, every time a 1-neighborhood X' of the current solution is built randomly. If the new solution is feasible, the simulation will run with this assignment and generate the output statistics. The metric used for our objective is the service level. If the service level of the new solution is better than the incumbent solution, we will update the incumbent as this new solution. Usually, a random 1-neighborhood is not feasible, in the sense that the number of workers assigned to a task may be larger than M_j. In this case, a 1-neighborhood of X' will be built and checked again. This procedure will be repeated until a feasible solution is found, or the number of solutions we have generated is larger than a determined threshold.

Note that our method is different from the 1-step neighborhood search. Before a new feasible solution is found, several workers may have been reassigned to other task(s). This can help to avoid the local optimum. As the random search is in a broader neighborhood, the probability of reaching a global optimum is higher. From the practical perspective, the number of new solutions and the number of simulation runs are both bounded, to make the total time reasonable for the industry application.

Algorithm 1: The random neighborhood search algorithm.

Data: the workload
Result: an optimal assignment
initialization: find a feasible assignment X_0, set $Y_0 = X_0$, $s_{opt} = s = 0$, $loop = iteration = 0$;
while $loop<m_1$ and $iteration<m_2$ **do**
    if $s > s_{opt}$ **then**
        set $s_{opt} = s$;
        set $Y_{iteration} = X_{loop}$
    end
    repeat
        repeat
            randomly select a worker i ;
            randomly select a task j ;
            modify X_{loop} by assigning worker i to task j, resulting in X_{loop+1} ;
            loop++;
        until *worker i can do task j;*
    until X_{loop} *satisfy all the constraints;*
    run simulation and update s as the output value ;
    iteration++;
end

---

7. Numerical Results

Using the simulation-based optimization method, the software tool was developed. The graphical user interface (GUI) design of the software is shown in Figure 4. The warehouse planner can select the workload data as an input and run the tool. The output includes the service level, along with other metrics.

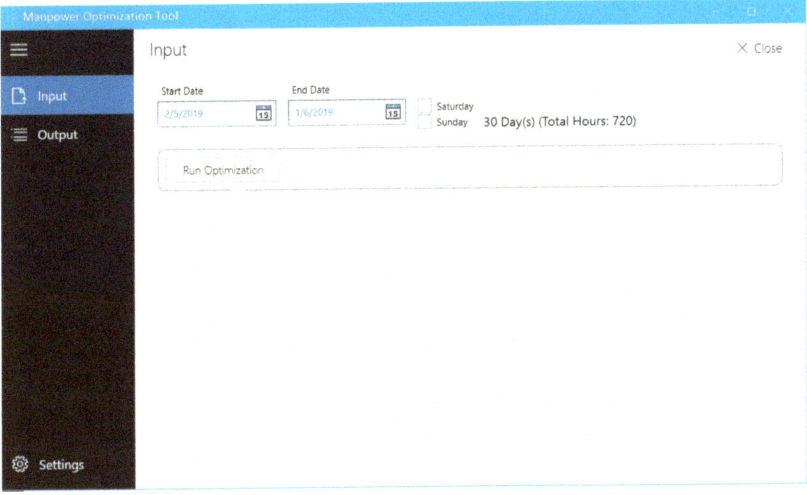

Figure 4. The GUI of the manpower allocation tool.

In a set of experiments, we tested different values of λ for inbound and outbound service levels, with the input data sampled from different months of years 2018 and 2019. The simulation-based optimization was run with different values of the coefficient λ.

We used the historical data provided by the warehouse. Specifically, inbound shipment arrival and outbound shipment order information for the following months were chosen: July 2018, January 2019 and March 2019. For each month, we conducted the assignment optimization week by week, and calculated the summation over all weeks of the month. The value of coefficient λ ranges from 1.0 to 2.0, with a step of 0.1. Data analyses of historical workload demand suggest that the outbound order volume generally prevails the inbound one. To diversify our sample pools, the sampling was done in the following way:

1. In July 2018, the outbound pallet number was nearly 5% less than inbound pallet number;
2. In January 2019, the outbound pallet number was nearly 13% larger than the inbound one;
3. In May 2019, the outbound pallet number was nearly 29% larger than the inbound one.

For the warehouse, outbound service level is considered to be more critical than the inbound service level. As shown in Figures 5–7, the results suggest that the optimized worker assignment can always achieve a better performance for the outbound service level, compared to the current assignment shown in Table 3. Regarding the inbound service level, the performance may be better when the value of λ is relatively small, that is, when the priority of outbound service level performance is not considered to be so high. Generally, with a decrease of less than 10% for the inbound service level, an increase of more than 30% can be obtained in the outbound service level performance. This indicates that our assignment can achieve a higher utilization of workers and a higher level of customer satisfaction.

As seen from the reported results, when the value of λ increases, the outbound service level increases, while the inbound service level decreases. This indicates that the parameter λ can be used to control the trade-off between inbound and outbound service level performance metrics.

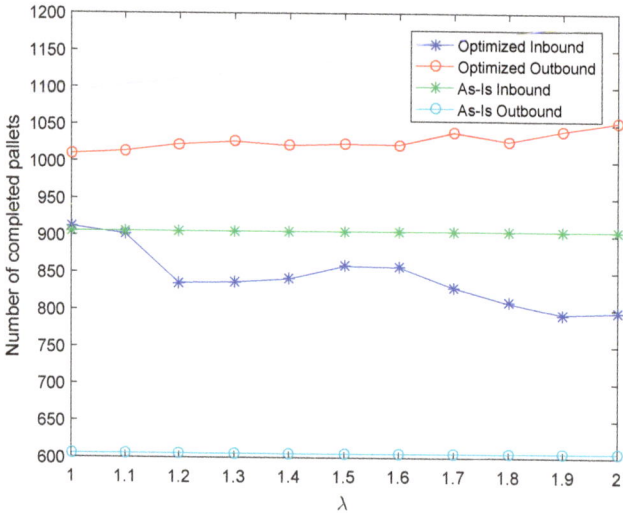

Figure 5. Numerical results for January 2019 data, given the total numbers of inbound/outbound pallets of 1508/1702, and the numbers of completed pallets with the current worker allocation are 906/606.

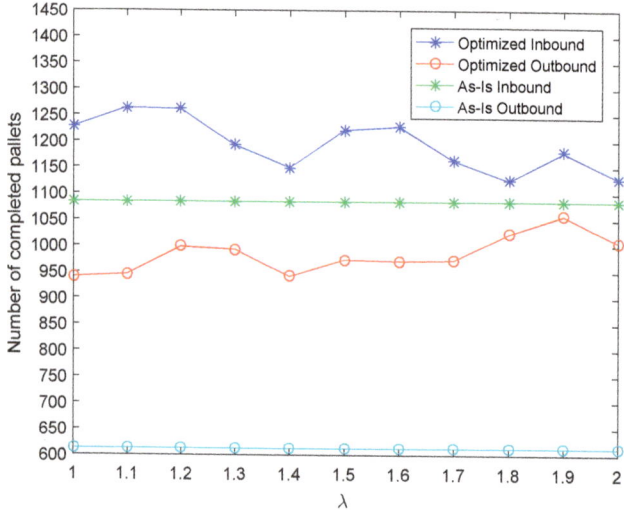

Figure 6. Numerical results for May 2019 data, given the numbers total inbound/outbound pallets of 1541/1981, and the numbers of completed pallets with the current worker allocation are 1085/613.

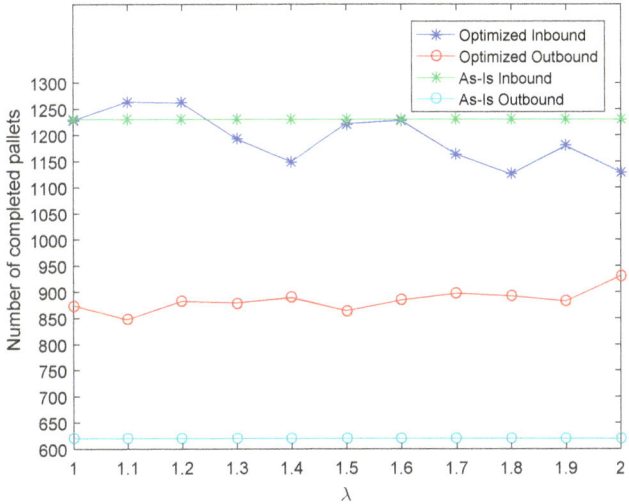

Figure 7. Numerical results for July 2018 data, given the total numbers of inbound/outbound pallets of 1656/1529, and the numbers of completed pallets with the current worker allocation are 1231/621.

Table 3. The current assignment used in the warehouse.

Sorting	GR	Putaway	VLM	Picking	AST	Scanning	Packing	Releasing
6	2	2	1	2	2	2	3	1

To demonstrate the improvements via the simulation-based optimization method, we generated additional service level outputs for a benchmark worker allocation case under the same workload scenarios. This benchmark worker allocation refers to the worker allocation matrix previously used by the warehouse manager prior to the implementation of our simulation-based optimization tool. In generating the service level statistics for the benchmark worker allocation, we preset the worker allocation and conducted simulations without any optimization. The comparisons of performance outputs from the optimized and non-optimized (benchmark) manpower allocations are shown in Figures 5–7, indicating that with less than 10% decrease for the inbound service level, on average, the outbound service level can be increased by 30% across all three scenarios considered.

8. Conclusions

As a real-life complex system, the warehouse is characterized by high variability in workload arrival. Thus, the optimal worker assignment in such a dynamic system is a non-trivial task. Since the workload may vary on a daily basis, it is important for the warehouse planner to have a decision support tool that can optimally assign workers to different activities. As the exact method is impossible for this problem, we proposed the simulation-based optimization method, which combines the O2DES framework with a random neighborhood search method. Under dynamic daily workload conditions, the random neighborhood search model was shown to efficiently identify an improved manpower assignment strategy based on the simulation output. A decision support tool based on the proposed method was then verified and validated using the real data from a warehouse located in Singapore. The results show that with a slight decrease of the inbound service level, we can improve the outbound service level by more than 30%.

This study provides a practical contribution to the problem of workforce planning in a warehouse. Warehouse planners and managers can benefit from the use of such a manpower allocation tool. The managers or users of the tool will need to provide the upcoming workload forecast as the input, while the tool automatically generates the optimal manpower allocation to activities.

On the theoretical side, although the literature has advocated the need for implementation of strategies for manpower planning [20,26], the reported solutions have not been numerous. One of the few examples is from Ladier et al. [6], who proposed a two-step mixed integer linear programming model which optimizes worker allocation to activities and different shifts daily. Said optimization model does not capture the arrival time of the daily workload, and assumes that the human resources are always sufficient. Hence, such a model is not capable pf effectively accounting for the industry circumstances. In contrast, our simulation-based optimization model accounts for the workload arrival and queuing, and allows one to achieve a higher service level with the available manpower.

Future studies may further improve the flexibility of the proposed method by integrating a better selection of initial solution to accelerate the neighborhood search. This method can also be applied to other resource allocation problems in supply chains and logistics.

Author Contributions: Conceptualization, H.L. and O.G.; methodology, K.K. and W.Z.; software, H.L. and K.K.; validation, O.G.; resources, H.L.; data curation, O.G.; writing–original draft preparation, O.G., K.K., and W.Z.; writing–review and editing, O.G. and K.K.; visualization, W.Z. and O.G. All authors have read and agreed to the published version of the manuscript.

Funding: This research has been made possible by the funding support from the Centre for Next Generation of Logistics (C4NGL), Department of Industrial Systems Engineering and Management, Faculty of Engineering, National University of Singapore. The work has been also supported by Singapore A*STAR IAF-PP fund (Grant No. A1895a0033) under the project "Digital Twin for Next Generation Warehouse". The authors appreciate our researchers for their great contributions to the centre and projects.

Conflicts of Interest: The authors declare no conflict of interest. The funders had no role in the design of the study; in the collection, analyses, or interpretation of data; in the writing of the manuscript, or in the decision to publish the results.

References

1. Schmenner, R.W. Looking ahead by looking back: Swift, even flow in the history of manufacturing. *Prod. Oper. Manag.* **2001**, *10*, 87–96. [CrossRef]
2. Fredendall, L.D.; Craig, J.B.; Fowler, P.J.; Damali, U. Barriers to swift, even flow in the internal supply chain of perioperative surgical services department: A case study. *Decis. Sci.* **2009**, *40*, 327–349. [CrossRef]
3. Devaraj, S.; Ow, T.T.; Kohli, R. Examining the impact of information technology and patient flow on healthcare performance: A Theory of Swift and Even Flow (TSEF) perspective. *J. Oper. Manag.* **2013**, *31*, 181–192. [CrossRef]
4. Garn, W.; Aitken, J.; Schmenner, R. Smoothly Pass the Parcel: Implementing the Theory of Swift, Even Flow. *ResearchGate* **2020**. [CrossRef]
5. Schmenner, R.W. Service businesses and productivity. *Decis. Sci.* **2004**, *35*, 333–347. [CrossRef]
6. Ladier, A.L.; Alpan, G.; Penz, B. Barriers to swift, Joint employee weekly timetabling and daily rostering: A decision-support tool for a logistics platform. *Eur. J. Oper. Res.* **2014**, *234*, 278–291. [CrossRef]
7. Nauss, R.M. Solving the generalized assignment problem: An optimizing and heuristic approach. *INFORMS J. Comput.* **2003**, *15*, 249–266. [CrossRef]
8. Becker, C.; Scholl, A. A survey on problems and methods in generalized assembly line balancing. *Eur. J. Oper. Res.* **2006**, *168*, 694–715. [CrossRef]
9. Burinskiene, A.; Lorenc, A.; Lerher, T. A simulation study for the sustainability and reduction of waste in warehouse logistics. *Int. J. Simul. Model.* **2018**, *17*, 485–497. [CrossRef]
10. Kelton, W.D.; Sadowski, R.P.; Sadowski, D.P. *Simulation with Arena*; McGraw-Hill: New York NY, USA, 1998.
11. Muller, D. Automod™-providing simulation solutions for over 25 years. In Proceedings of the 2011 Winter Simulation Conference (WSC), Phoenix, AZ, USA, 11–14 December 2011; pp. 39–51.

12. Li, H.; Zhu, Y.; Chen, Y.; Pedrielli, G.; Pujowidianto, N.A. The object-oriented discrete event simulation modeling: A case study on aircraft spare part management. In Proceedings of the 2015 Winter Simulation Conference (WSC), Huntington Beach, CA, USA, 6–9 December 2015; pp. 3514–3525.

13. Frazelle, E. The title of the cited contribution. In *Supply Chain Strategy: The Logistics of Supply Chain Management*; McGraw-Hill: New York, NY, USA, 2002.

14. Abushaikha, I.; Salhieh, L.; Towers, N. Improving distribution and business performance through lean warehousing. *Int. J. Retail. Distrib. Manag.* **2018**, *46*, 780–800. [CrossRef]

15. Guthrie, B.; Parikh, P.J.; Kong, N. Evaluating warehouse strategies for two-product class distribution planning. *Int. J. Prod. Res.* **2017**, *55*, 6470–6484. [CrossRef]

16. Ahmed, D.; Hyder, M. Improving Distribution and Business Performance through Lean Warehousing. *Int. J. Bus. Stud.* **2020**, *1*, 35–37.

17. De Koster, R.; Le-Duc, T.; Roodbergen, K.J. Design and control of warehouse order picking: A literature review. *Eur. J. Oper. Res.* **2007**, *182*, 481–501. [CrossRef]

18. Van Den Berg, J.P. *Integral Warehouse Management*; Management Outlook Publications: Utrecht, The Netherlands, 2007.

19. Heragu, S.S.; Du, L.; Mantel, R.J.; Schuur, P.C. Mathematical model for warehouse design and product allocation. *Int. J. Prod. Res.* **2005**, *43*, 327–338. [CrossRef]

20. De Leeuw, S.; Wiers, V.C.S. Warehouse manpower planning strategies in times of financial crisis: Evidence from logistics service providers and retailers in The Netherlands. *Prod. Plan. Control* **2015**, *26*, 328–337. [CrossRef]

21. Ivanov, D. Predicting the impacts of epidemic outbreaks on global supply chains: A simulation-based analysis on the coronavirus outbreak (COVID-19/SARS-CoV-2) case. *Transp. Res. Part E Logist. Transp. Rev.* **2020**, *136*, 101922. [CrossRef]

22. Nikolopoulos, K.; Punia, S.; Schäfers, A.; Tsinopoulos, C.; Vasilakis, C. Forecasting and planning during a pandemic: COVID-19 growth rates, supply chain disruptions, and governmental decisions. *Eur. J. Oper. Res.* **2020**. [CrossRef]

23. Klaus, P. The assessment of competitive intensity in logistics markets. *Logist. Res.* **2011**, *3*, 49–65. [CrossRef]

24. Rebitzer, D.W. The European logistics market. In *Europe Real Estate Yearbook*; Real Estate Publishers BV: VC Den Haag, The Netherlands, 2007. Available online: www.europe-re.com (accessed on 18 November 2020).

25. Graham Douglas, D. Warehouse of the future. *Frontline Solut.* **2003**, *4*, 20–26.

26. Pooya, A.; Pakdaman, M. A new continuous time optimal control model for manpower planning with promotion from inside the system. *Oper. Res.* **2018**, 1–16. [CrossRef]

27. Edwards, J.S. A survey of manpower planning models and their application. *J. Oper. Res. Soc.* **1983**, *34*, 1031–1040. [CrossRef] [PubMed]

28. Parker, S.C.; Malstrom, E.J.; Usmani, T. Computer-assisted warehouse personnel scheduling. *Intell. Robot. Comput. Vis. Algorithms Tech. Int. Soc. Opt. Photonics* **1992**, *1607*, 636–645.

29. Sanders, N.R.; Ritzman, L.P. Using warehouse workforce flexibility to offset forecast errors. *J. Bus. Logist.* **2004**, *25*, 251–269. [CrossRef]

30. Dou, J.; Dai, X.; Meng, Z. A GA-based approach for optimizing single-part flow-line configurations of RMS. *J. Intell. Manuf.* **2011**, *22*, 301–317. [CrossRef]

31. Azadivar, F. A simulation optimization approach to optimum storage and retrieval policies in an automated warehousing system. In Proceedings of the 1984 Winter Simulation Conference (WSC), Dallas, TX, USA, 28–30 November 1984; pp. 207–214.

32. Ding, H.; Benyoucef, L.; Xie, X. A simulation-optimization approach using genetic search for supplier selection. In Proceedings of the 2003 Winter Simulation Conference (WSC), New Orleans, LA, USA, 7–10 December 2003; pp. 1260–1267.

33. Saif, A.; Elhedhli, S. Cold supply chain design with environmental considerations: A simulation-optimization approach. *Eur. J. Oper. Res.* **2016**, *252*, 274–287. [CrossRef]

34. Ghasemi, P.; Khalili-Damghani, K. A robust simulation-optimization approach for pre-disaster multi-period location–allocation–inventory planning. *Math. Comput. Simul.* **2021**, *179*, 69–95. [CrossRef]

35. De Marco, A.; Mangano, G. Relationship between logistic service and maintenance costs of warehouses. *Facilities* **2011**, *29*, 411–421. [CrossRef]

36. Staudt, F.H.; Alpan, G.; Di Mascolo, M.; Rodriguez, C.M.T. Warehouse performance measurement: A literature review. *Int. J. Prod. Res.* **2015**, *53*, 5524–5544. [CrossRef]

37. Amorim-Lopes, M.; Guimarães, L.; Alves, J.; Almada-Lobo, B. Improving picking performance at a large retailer warehouse by combining probabilistic simulation, optimization, and discrete-event simulation. *Int. Trans. Oper. Res.* **2020**, *28*, 687–715. [CrossRef]

38. Zhang, C.W.; Xie, M.; Liu, J.Y.; Goh, T.N. A control chart for the Gamma distribution as a model of time between events. *Int. J. Prod. Res.* **2007**, *45*, 5649–5666. [CrossRef]

39. Song, D.P. Optimal integrated ordering and production policy in a supply chain with stochastic lead-time, processing-time, and demand. *IEEE Trans. Automat. Contr.* **2009**, *54*, 2027–2041. [CrossRef]

40. Guasch, A.; Piera, M.A.; Figueras, J. Automatic warehouse modelling and simulation. *Int. J. Simul. Process. Model.* **2011**, *6*, 288–296. [CrossRef]

41. Andriansyah, R.; Etman, P.; Rooda, J. Simulation model of a single-server order picking workstation using aggregate process times. In Proceedings of the First International Conference on Advances in System Simulation, Porto, Portugal, 20–25 September 2009; pp. 23–31.

42. Polat, O.; Kalayci, C.B.; Mutlu, Ö.; Gupta, S.M. A two-phase variable neighbourhood search algorithm for assembly line worker assignment and balancing problem type-II: An industrial case study. *Int. J. Prod. Res.* **2016**, *54*, 722–741. [CrossRef]

Publisher's Note: MDPI stays neutral with regard to jurisdictional claims in published maps and institutional affiliations.

Article

Combining Optimization and Simulation for Designing a Robust Short-Sea Feeder Network

Carl Axel Benjamin Medbøen, Magnus Bolstad Holm, Mohamed Kais Msakni *, Kjetil Fagerholt and Peter Schütz

Department of Industrial Economics and Technology Management,
Norwegian University of Science and Technology, 7491 Trondheim, Norway;
camedboe@stud.ntnu.no (C.A.B.M.); magnusbh@stud.ntnu.no (M.B.H.); kjetil.fagerholt@ntnu.no (K.F.);
peter.schutz@ntnu.no (P.S.)
* Correspondence: kais.msakni@ntnu.no

Received: 5 October 2020; Accepted: 16 November 2020; Published: 20 November 2020

Abstract: Here we study a short-sea feeder network design problem based on mother and daughter vessels. The main feature of the studied system is performing transshipment of cargo between mother and daughter vessels at appropriate locations at sea. This operation requires synchronization between both types of vessels as they have to meet at the same location at the same time. This paper studies the problem of designing a synchronized feeder network, explicitly accounting for the effect of uncertain travel times caused by harsh weather conditions. We propose an optimization-simulation framework to find robust solutions for the transportation system. The optimization model finds optimal routes that are then evaluated by a discrete-even simulation model to measure their robustness under uncertain weather conditions. This process of optimization simulation is repeated until a satisfactory condition is reached. To find even better solutions, we include different performance-improving strategies by adding robustness during route generation or exploiting flexibility in sailing speed to recover from delays. We apply the solution method to a case based on realistic data from a Norwegian shipping company. The results show that the method finds near-optimal solutions that offer robustness against schedule perturbations due to harsh weather. They also highlight the importance of considering uncertainty when designing a short-sea feeder network with transshipment at sea.

Keywords: maritime transportation; liner network design; synchronization; weather uncertainty; optimization simulation

---

1. Introduction

Maritime transportation is one of the most efficient (per cargo ton-mile) transportation modes to transport large volumes of cargo over long distances [1,2]. Over short distances, however, competing with road-based transportation is more challenging. Truck-based door-to-door deliveries are often less expensive compared to other shipping solutions and offer frequent and reliable departures [3,4].

The demand for cargo transportation in Norway is expected to grow by 40% (in tonne-kilometers) until 2030 [5]. This predicted increase i is met by the political ambition to shift more goods from road to sea [6]. Still, new and innovative solutions need to be developed to substantially improve the competitiveness of short-sea shipping and support the transition of cargo from road-based to waterborne transportation. The Short Sea Pioneer (SSP) logistics system is a new suggested solution to improve competitiveness, proposing a new transshipment mode for short-sea feeder networks [7]. The proposed system is inspired by the ship-to-ship cargo transfer method currently

Algorithms **2020**, *13*, 304; doi:10.3390/a13110304

used to transfer petroleum products and bulk cargo between seagoing vessels. In the SSP system, a mother (large) vessel can be connected to a daughter (small feeder) vessel at a suitable location at sea to transship containerized cargo using a specialized handling cargo system (see [8] for an illustration). One advantage of this system is to reduce the number of port calls, which reduces the operational cost of the shipping system. Indeed, cargo-related port costs can account for up to 30% of the turnover of a smaller short-sea shipping company [9]. Besides, it becomes possible to serve small ports that large vessels cannot visit, for example, due to physical limitations.

The SSP logistics system is composed of one main route sailed by mother vessels that transport cargo between the European continent and large ports located at the Norwegian west coast. Small daughter vessels operate feeder routes serving smaller Norwegian ports. Due to size or location, these ports may only be served by the smaller daughter vessels. Potential candidate transshipment locations will be in sheltered locations (e.g., inside a fjord or inshore) such that harsh weather does not affect the transshipment operation. An example is illustrated in Figure 1.

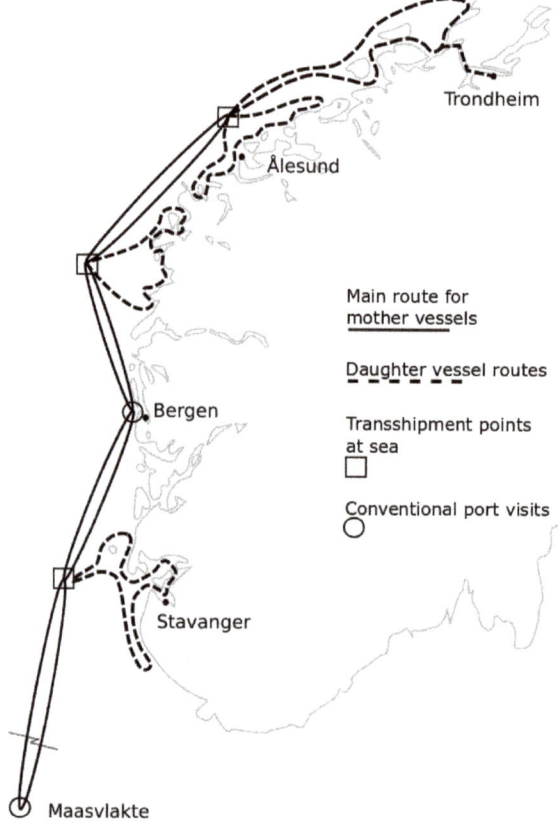

Figure 1. An example of the short sea pioneer (SSP) logistics system [10] composed of one main route and three daughter routes. The main route serves the continental port, Maasvlakte, a large Norwegian port in Bergen, and three ocean hubs. All daughter routes depart from ocean hubs and serve local Norwegian ports.

While potentially having considerable economic benefits, transshipment at sea also raises many technical challenges. Among others, the system requires synchronizing the main route sailed by the mother vessel with all routes sailed by the daughter vessels. Conversely, Weather conditions are known to impact sailing times and can cause considerable delays [2]. Thus, the synchronization operation can be subject to disruptions that may cause additional waiting times at the transshipment location and can propagate through the system for the subsequent periods. To function correctly, the routes for both mother and daughter vessels need to be robust to potential delays, i.e., they have to account for uncertainty in weather conditions.

Traditionally, the literature on liner shipping network design problems has been focusing on deterministic deep-sea (long-haul) shipping networks. These problems usually determine the optimal set of routes to be served by a heterogeneous fleet of vessels while satisfying demand, transshipment, and frequency requirements (see, e.g., Brouer et al. [11]). The following publications are recent examples, discussing different variants of the traditional liner network design problem. Meng and Wang [12] include the repositioning of empty containers in the shipping operations when determining the optimal network design. Reinhardt and Pisinger [13] consider more advanced route structures, such as butterfly routes, because they allow for better use of vessel resources. Brouer et al. [11] study one of the largest networks operated by a major liner-shipping company, where cargo can be transshipped several times to take more than one route to be delivered. Karsten et al. [14] extend this problem to include transit time restrictions. Balakrishnan and Karsten [15] incorporate limitations on number of transshipments for the cargo. For the short-sea shipping, Msakni et al. [16] study the impact of different network designs for a local liner shipping company. Fadda et al. [17] address the problem of a roll-on roll-off liner service that operates using a hub-and-spoke network design. Akbar et al. [18] provide an economic analysis of introducing autonomous vessels in short-sea shipping. For a more detailed overview of the literature on liner shipping network design, please also see the surveys by Meng et al. [19], Brouer et al. [1] and Christiansen et al. [20].

Synchronization has received relatively little attention in the literature on maritime transportation. Cargo is usually transshipped in ports, often requiring a sequence of arrivals or specifying a time window. The work of Agarwal and Özlem Ergun [21] is one of the fewest papers to address synchronization directly. The problem considers a combined vessel scheduling and cargo routing problem, where transshipment of cargo is only possible when two routes meet at the same port on the same day. In another work, Andersson et al. [22] study a problem from project shipping where different cargoes may require a synchronized delivery. In land-based transportation, synchronization issues are more common. The reader is referred to Drexl [23] for an overview of the literature on VRPs with multiple synchronization constraints.

The research on uncertainty in maritime service networks mainly distinguishes between two types of uncertainty. The first type is uncertainty in service times, usually port times or sailing times, whereas the second type considers uncertainty in demand. When considering uncertainty in operations, the research focuses on keeping a designed schedule, i.e., satisfy frequency requirements or pickup and delivery time windows. As an example of this work line, the problem examined by Wang and Meng [24] of designing liner vessel routes with uncertainty in port operation times. The uncertainty is related to sailing times as a consequence of making up for the delays. In Song et al. [25], a multi-objective liner shipping service problem with uncertain port times is studied. One of the objectives is to minimize schedule unreliability, which is the probability of the vessels arriving after the scheduled time windows. Conversely, Li et al. [26] study how vessels can recover from delays caused by regular uncertainties and unexpected disruptions. In their work, regular uncertainties may happen both at sea and in port, and their characteristics can be estimated using historical data. When it comes to demand uncertainty, the research usually focuses on designing a maritime transportation system such that demand can be served. For example, Ng and Lin [27] study the problem of fleet deployment under incomplete demand information. Lo et al. [28] present a model for designing a ferry network given uncertain demand. An and Lo [29] study the design of more general transit networks under uncertain demand. However, none of these studies consider uncertainty in service times.

One approach to deal with the uncertainty is to combine simulation and optimization models to provide robust solutions. Fischer et al. [30] use simulation and optimization to evaluate the robustness of tactical fleet deployment plans for roll-on roll-off liner shipping with respect to random disruptions at the operational level. Castilla-Rodríguez et al. [31] study the quay crane scheduling problem in a port terminal and consider the uncertainty from the availability of some delivery vehicles and disruptions in quay crane operations. The authors use simulation-optimization to produce robust quay crane schedules. Layeb et al. [32] develop a simulation-optimization method for multimodal freight transportation systems where the uncertainty is related to demand and travel times. Poeting et al. [33] combine a metaheuristic with a discrete-event simulation to provide robust solutions at the operational level in parcel transshipment terminals.

This paper considers the first type of uncertainty, more specifically uncertain sailing times due to harsh weather conditions. However, in contrast to the papers mentioned above, it studies a short-sea liner network instead of a deep-sea network. A common assumption in papers on deep-sea liner network design with uncertain port times is that vessels can make up for delays by increasing their speed between ports (see, e.g., Wang and Meng [24]). This can be reasonable when legs between ports are long. However, for short-sea networks, the sailing legs are short, and weather conditions may prevent the vessel from reducing or even eliminating a delay.

The problem presented in this paper is an extension to the deterministic Short-sea Liner Network Design Problem with Transshipment at Sea (SLNDP-TS) introduced by Holm et al. [10]. It contributes to the research literature on liner shipping network design in three ways. Firstly, we take into account uncertain sailing times due to harsh weather in the network design problem. Secondly, we consider transshipments at sea, which requires that the synchronization of routes to ensure that mother and daughter vessels are at the same location at the same time. Thirdly, we apply an iterative solution approach combining optimization with discrete event simulation to handle both uncertainties in sailing times and synchronization requirements.

Our solution method is based on the hybrid optimization-simulation method proposed by Acar et al. [34] with the difference of using a discrete-event model instead of an optimization model for the simulations. Unlike commonly used probabilistic models, we use wave height from historical weather data to adequately capture the effect of harsh weather conditions on sailing speed. The simulation model links wave height to vessel speed and evaluates the impact on the synchronization operations. The simulation results are returned to the optimization model to select routes that are less likely to generate delays. Additionally, we develop and test different performance-improving strategies to enhance the solutions' robustness to possible delays. The computational study results show that our approach provides more robust solutions than deterministic ones without a significant increase in costs.

The remainder of this paper is structured as follows. In Section 2, the problem is described in more detail. Section 3 outlines the solution approach. The optimization and simulation models are presented in more detail in Section 4. Results from the computational study are presented in Section 5. We conclude in Section 6.

2. Problem Description

The problem of designing a short-sea liner network with transshipment at sea has been introduced by Holm et al. [10]. The authors provide a deterministic problem formulation as well as a solution method based on a priori route generation. In this section, we first present the problem before discussing the impact of weather conditions on shipping operations in such a network.

2.1. Network Design Problem

The shipping company serves each port on a weekly basis. The Norwegian ports are classified according to their size. Small ports are only served by daughter vessels, whereas large ports can be visited by either a mother or a daughter vessel. All mother vessels start their voyage at a European continental main port. Transshipment of cargo between mother and daughter vessels occurs at the so-called ocean hubs, which are suitable locations along the Norwegian coast and offer enough stability for vessels to perform transshipment at sea. For presentation and modeling purposes, each ocean hub is artificially split into a north-going and a south-going ocean hub. A mother vessel serves a north-going ocean hub during its northbound journey and a south-going ocean hub on its southbound journey.

The feeder routes taken by daughter vessels are referred to as daughter routes. Each daughter route is served by one daughter vessel. These routes have a maximum duration of one week to ensure weekly port visits. The route served by the mother vessel is referred to as main route. Since the duration of the main route is typically more than one week, the number of deployed mother vessels is equal to the number of weeks rounded up to the nearest integer, thus ensuring weekly service.

The major activity of the shipping company case is to transport cargo between the main continental port and Norwegian ports. There is also some local demand between Norwegian ports, but can be considered as negligible in this study. The aim is to determine the optimal main and daughter routes and the optimal fleet of mother and daughter vessels to be deployed. This problem is at a tactical level, where the established routes last for typically four to 12 months, and, therefore, the weekly demand is assumed to be known and constant.

Transshipment of cargo between mother and daughter vessels is only possible at ocean hubs. During its northbound journey, mother and daughter vessels meet at a north-going ocean hub where cargo is delivered to the daughter vessel. The same mother and daughter vessels meet again at the corresponding south-going ocean hub during the southbound journey of the mother vessel to transship cargo from the daughter vessel. In the case an ocean hub is the northernmost point of the main route, there is no artificial distinction between north- and south-going ocean hub, and the ocean hub is therefore only visited once.

A solution to the problem consists of a set of main and daughter routes serving the ports and an allocation of vessels to routes (as illustrated in Figure 1). This also includes determining the number of deployed mother and daughter vessels. The mother vessels are considered to have enough capacity to transport all cargo. The size of the daughter vessels can be selected from a given set of available capacities. The problem is separable in the size of the daughter vessel because all daughter vessels must have the same capacity due to the technical requirements of the SSP design. The objective is to minimize the weekly operating costs, including weekly time charter costs for each vessel in the selected fleet, bunker, port, and cargo handling costs.

2.2. Impact of Harsh Weather

A transshipment in an ocean hub requires that both the mother vessel and the daughter vessel have to be present at the same location at the same time. The meeting point is selected in a sheltered location, such that harsh weather will not affect the transshipment operation. However, harsh weather conditions will affect sailing operations as they may force vessels to slow down, causing delays in the vessels' schedules. We refer to the situation of a mother vessel waiting for a daughter vessel in an ocean hub as a synchronization violation. Synchronization violations delay the waiting vessel, potentially delaying later synchronizations and affecting other vessels in the system.

If a vessel is delayed by too much, it might be unable to complete its route within the maximum allowed duration. This is called a duration violation. Duration violations prevent a weekly port visit frequency because the delay is transferred into the next week. For a logistics system with transshipment at sea to be viable in practice, duration violations must be kept at a minimum.

Figure 2 illustrates synchronization and duration violations. Consider a logistics system consisting of a mother vessel, M, and two daughter vessels, D1 and D2. Daughter vessel D1 visits the north- and south-going ocean hubs, 1n and 1s, respectively. The mother vessel and Daughter vessel D2 meet at ocean hub 2 for picking-up and delivering cargo because ocean hub 2 is the northernmost point. For simplicity, Norwegian ports and the continental main ports are not shown.

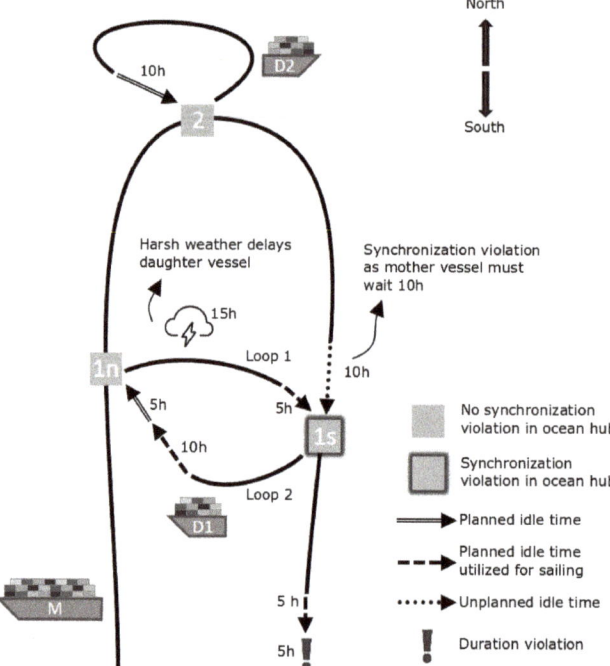

Figure 2. An example to show duration and synchronization violations due to harsh weather. The mother vessel has to wait for 10 h in ocean hub 1s, causing a synchronization violation and a duration violation of five hours.

In the example, the mother vessel is sailing north from the continental main port. In ocean hub 1n, she meets with daughter vessel D1, and after the transshipment, both vessels depart as scheduled. Neither of the vessels is delayed at this point. The mother vessel continues north to ocean hub 2 without any delay. Daughter vessel D2 is not delayed either, and thus both vessels can synchronize as planned in ocean hub 2. In this example, daughter vessel D2 has 10 h of planned idle time before the arrival of the mother vessel. It could, therefore, be up to 10 h delayed and still synchronize with the arriving mother vessel as scheduled.

After leaving ocean hub 2, the mother vessel starts its southbound journey and sails towards ocean hub 1s to synchronize again with daughter vessel D1. However, harsh weather has caused a delay for daughter vessel D1 after departing from ocean hub 1n. Despite arriving on time in ocean hub 1s, the mother vessel has to wait for daughter vessel D1 and experiences a synchronization violation.

The schedule for daughter vessel D1 has planned idle time of five hours in ocean hub 1s before the arrival of the mother vessel. As the vessel is delayed by as much as 15 h, the mother vessel has to wait for 10 h. As the mother vessel only has five hours of planned idle time in its schedule, the next departure from the continental main port is five hours of delay. The synchronization violation in ocean hub 1s has caused a duration violation of five hours for the mother vessel.

Note that daughter vessel D1 does not incur a duration violation, even though it is 10 h delayed when leaving ocean hub 1s. This is because there is enough planned idle time when sailing between ocean hub to 1s and ocean hub 1n to make up for the delay.

3. Solution Approach

Our iterative solution method is based on the hybrid optimization simulation framework proposed by Acar et al. [34]. The solution method combines an optimization model (also referred to as the master problem) and a simulation model. The role of the optimization model is to select routes for mother and daughter vessels from a set of a priori generated routes, while the simulation is a discrete event simulation model that evaluates the robustness of solutions (a solution is a combination of routes) with respect to uncertain weather conditions. The simulation model results are used to update the costs of the simulated solutions and then faded back to the optimization model. Alternating between optimization and simulation models is repeated until no new improved solution is found. The proposed solution method is illustrated in Figure 3. According to the classification of Crainic et al. [35], the proposed approach is within the alternate simulation-optimization category.

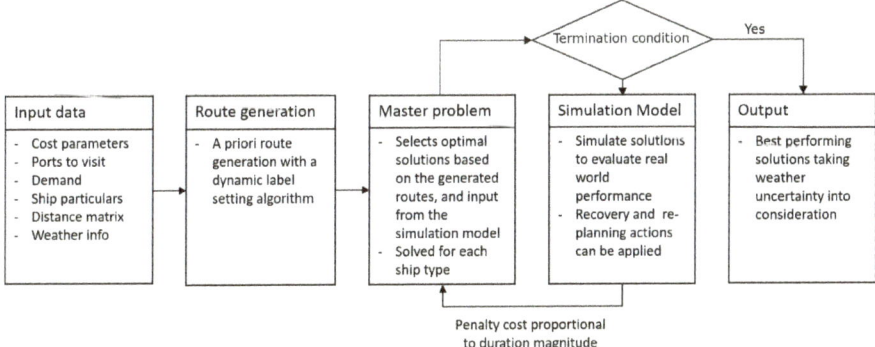

Figure 3. An overview of the optimization-simulation framework. From input data, the routes are generated. The master problem and the simulation model are iteratively solved until no new solution is found.

A static set of routes for the mother and daughter vessels is generated using the provided input data. For each of the daughter vessel types, the master problem then selects the cost-minimizing routes from this set by solving an integer programming model (described in more detail in Section 4.1). Afterwards, the combination of routes chosen by the master problem is simulated using historical weather data to estimate the solution's real-world performance (described in more detail in Section 4.2).

As explained in Section 2.2, a duration violation is caused by harsh weather conditions that lead to a delay long enough to prevent the vessel from completing its round trip within its scheduled duration. Synchronization violations can amplify delays as they may transfer the delay of one vessel to another. A duration violation will automatically lead to an initial disruption when starting the next round trip. The magnitude of a duration violation is defined as the number of hours by which a vessel is late compared to the allowed duration of one round trip.

We add a penalty cost based on the magnitude of duration violations from the simulation to the costs of the selected combination of routes. This additional penalty cost makes solutions (or route combinations) prone to duration violations less attractive in subsequent iterations of solving the master problem. When the master problem is solved again with updated route costs, it might choose a new solution with lower costs. The iterations between the master problem and the simulation model continue until all of the selected solutions have been simulated, and no new improving solutions are found. This feedback approach between the master problem and the simulation model allows generating good solutions based on the trade-off between operational costs and robustness (i.e., penalty costs).

Different strategies to provide robustness against disruptions due to harsh weather and/or synchronization violations can be included in the optimization and/or simulation model (discussed more in Section 4.3). Thus, the framework can also be used to evaluate the potential benefit of introducing performance-improving strategies, for example, permitting speed-ups in case of a delay (see, e.g., Fischer et al. [30], Brouer et al. [36]).

4. Optimization and Simulation Model

This section provides a more detailed description of the optimization and the simulation models used in the proposed solution method. The optimization model is described in Section 4.1, while the simulation model is presented in Section 4.2. Possible performance-improving strategies that can be evaluated using our solution methods are described in Section 4.3.

4.1. Optimization Model

The optimization model is based on the approach developed by Holm et al. [10] and consists of a route generation procedure and a master problem. The difference is that, in this study, the optimization model incorporates updated costs from the simulation model. For an efficient route generation, a label-setting algorithm (see, e.g., Irnich [37]) is used to generate a priori the routes for mother and daughter vessels. After the routes are generated, the daughter routes are grouped in subsets according to which main route they can be synchronized with.

The label setting algorithm is used to limit the set of routes introduced to the optimization model. Only non-dominated routes are retained, which means that similar routes composed of the same ports but in a different order and with higher operational costs are eliminated. The route generation assumes that vessels sail at their design sailing speed, i.e., no speed-up is allowed. Here, it should be pointed out that some of the deterministically dominated routes might perform better in our setting with uncertain travel time, e.g., due to a sequence of port visits that allows avoiding harsh weather conditions. However, identifying these routes during the route generation procedure is, in general, too computationally expensive.

Before formulating the optimization model, let us first introduce the following notation:

Sets

$\mathcal{P}^{OH}$	set of ocean hubs,
$\mathcal{P}^{CD}$	set of Norwegian small ports,
$\mathcal{P}^{CM}$	set of Norwegian main ports,
$\mathcal{R}^M$	set of all non-dominated main routes,
$\mathcal{R}^D$	set of all non-dominated daughter routes,
$\mathcal{R}^M_p$	subset of main routes, for which port p is served, $\mathcal{R}^M_p \subseteq \mathcal{R}^M$,
$\mathcal{R}^D_p$	subset of daughter routes, for which port p is served, $\mathcal{R}^D_p \subseteq \mathcal{R}^D$,
$\mathcal{R}^D_{pm}$	subset of daughter routes that can be synchronized to a main route m at ocean hub p, $\mathcal{R}^D_{pm} \subseteq \mathcal{R}^D_p \subseteq \mathcal{R}^D$,
S	set of simulated solutions. If the set is empty, no solutions have been simulated. The size of the set increases for every new solution that is simulated.

Parameters

C^M_m	total operational cost of main route m, which includes the weekly time charter cost of mother vessels sailing m, bunker costs and port costs,
C^D_d	operational cost of daughter route d, which includes the weekly time charter cost of daughter vessel sailing d, bunker costs and port costs,
C^S_s	penalty cost of simulated solution s,
M^{OH}	upper limit on the number of daughter vessels that can perform transshipment at an ocean hub,
M^S	a value that is marginally larger than ε,
S^D_{ds}	is equal to 1 if daughter route d belongs to simulated solution s, and 0 otherwise,
S^M_{ms}	is equal to 1 if main route m belongs to simulated solution s, and 0 otherwise,
S_s	number of routes which belong to solution s. This can be expressed as follows: $S_s = \sum_{m \in \mathcal{R}^M} S^M_{ms} + \sum_{d \in \mathcal{R}^D} S^D_{ds}$, for each simulated solution s,
ε	auxiliary parameter used to express a less than relation as a less than or equal relation. The value can be as small as possible as long as $\varepsilon > 0$.

Binary decision variables

x_m equals to 1 if main route m is selected, and 0 otherwise,
z_d equals to 1 if daughter route d is selected, and 0 otherwise,
y_s takes value 1 if a simulated solution is included in the optimal solution, and 0 otherwise.

The deterministic optimization problem can be formulated as follows:

$$\min \sum_{m \in \mathcal{R}^M} C_m^M x_m + \sum_{d \in \mathcal{R}^D} C_d^D z_d + \sum_{s \in \mathcal{S}} C_s^S y_s \tag{1}$$

subject to

$$\sum_{m \in \mathcal{R}^M} x_m = 1, \tag{2}$$

$$\sum_{d \in \mathcal{R}_p^D} z_d - M^{OH} \sum_{m \in \mathcal{R}_p^M} x_m \leq 0, \qquad\qquad p \in \mathcal{P}^{OH}, \tag{3}$$

$$\sum_{d \in \mathcal{R}_{pm}^D} z_d - \sum_{d \in \mathcal{R}_p^D} z_d \geq M^{OH}(x_m - 1), \qquad\qquad p \in \mathcal{P}^{OH}, m \in \mathcal{R}_p^M, \tag{4}$$

$$\sum_{d \in \mathcal{R}_{pm}^D} z_d - x_m \geq 0, \qquad\qquad p \in \mathcal{P}^{OH}, m \in \mathcal{R}_p^M, \tag{5}$$

$$\sum_{m \in \mathcal{R}_p^M} x_m + \sum_{d \in \mathcal{R}_p^D} z_d = 1, \qquad\qquad p \in \mathcal{P}^{CM}, \tag{6}$$

$$\sum_{d \in \mathcal{R}_p^D} z_d = 1, \qquad\qquad p \in \mathcal{P}^{CD}, \tag{7}$$

$$\sum_{m \in \mathcal{R}^M} S_{ms}^M x_m + \sum_{d \in \mathcal{R}^D} S_{ds}^D z_d - S_s + \varepsilon \leq M^S y_s, \qquad\qquad s \in \mathcal{S}, \tag{8}$$

$$x_m \in \{0,1\}, \qquad\qquad m \in \mathcal{R}^M, \tag{9}$$

$$y_s \in \{0,1\}, \qquad\qquad s \in \mathcal{S}, \tag{10}$$

$$z_d \in \{0,1\}, \qquad\qquad d \in \mathcal{R}^D. \tag{11}$$

The objective function (1) minimizes the total weekly cost of the shipping system. The first and second terms of (1) are related to the costs of mother and daughter vessels deployed in the system. The last term represents the penalty cost of a solution.

Equation (2) forces the optimal solution to select only one main route. Constraints (3) to (5) are the synchronization constraints, ensuring that selected daughter routes can synchronize with the main route at an ocean hub visited by both routes. The reader is referred to Holm et al. [10] for a more detailed description of how synchronization is taken care of through these constraints. Further, Equation (6) ensure that a main port is visited by either a mother or a daughter vessel. Equations (7) ensure that each small Norwegian port is served by a daughter route. Constraints (8) set the indicator variable y_s. If the master problem selects a route combination that constitutes a previously simulated solution, $y_s = 1$ and the penalty cost is added to the objective. Lastly, Constraints (9)–(11) restrict the variables to take binary values.

4.2. Simulation Model

The optimal solution of the master problem assumes that the shipping system runs under perfect weather conditions, and both mother and daughter vessels sail at design speed. The simulation model evaluates the proposed solution under real-world operating conditions. Harsh weather conditions may force vessels to slow down, affecting the sailing times. In such a situation, synchronization and duration violations can occur.

The simulation model adjusts the sailing speed based on wave height. To this end, we divide a route into legs connecting two consecutive ports. For a given leg, waypoints are defined and mark a change in the vessel's travel direction. The segment between two successive waypoints is defined as a sub-leg. The simulation model updates the sailing speed of a vessel at specific points of a leg. Such a point is called an observation point and is defined (i) at a departure port and (ii) after sailing a certain distance, called step distance.

Figure 4 shows an example of a route between two ports. There are three sub-legs defined by the ports and waypoints. The observation points are equally separated by the step distance, which is set to be five nautical miles in this example. The background of Figure 4 shows the gridded weather data points.

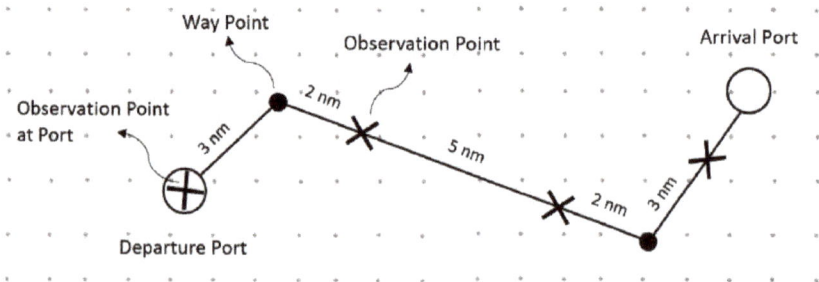

Figure 4. Illustration of a leg. The vessel changes direction at the waypoints and the speed is updated at every observation point.

To determine the speed of a vessel, we use historical weather data composed of a grid of data points that contain significant wave height. The parameter 'significant wave height' is often used to describe the weather in maritime navigation and is defined as the average height of the highest one-third waves [38]. At each observation point, we extract the significant wave height from the closest data point.

Estimating the vessel speed in open water requires detailed information about the vessel, e.g., regarding hull design and loading conditions, to carry out accurate hydrodynamic calculations. Such information is often not available at an early stage of designing feeder networks. Therefore, we use a simplified approximation of the hydrodynamic relationship between wave height and vessel speed in our simulation model. We assume that vessels are often designed to be operated at a particular propulsion power for which the engines run efficiently, and they sail with constant design power that is maintained throughout the route. Since the vessel speed is a function of propulsion power and total resistance, and given that the propulsion power is assumed to be constant, higher waves and winds due to harsh weather cause an increase in total resistance, which results in a decrease of vessel speed. In our model, resistance from waves is calculated according to the STAwave-1 method [39].

The flow chart in Figure 5 shows the overall simulation process. The input to the simulation model is one (or more) feasible solution(s) from the master problem. In Step 1, the simulation model chooses a solution from the master problem. The week to simulate is chosen in Step 2. In Steps 3–5, all routes in the solution are simulated. Once all routes in the solution are simulated for the given week, synchronization and duration violations are calculated in Step 6. Note that these violations are system-specific, i.e., dependent on the set of routes in the given solution and not only on each route individually. If any violations occur, penalty costs are added to the solution in Step 7. Step 8 checks whether the solution has been simulated for all weeks. Finally, Step 9 ensures that all solutions provided by the optimization model are simulated.

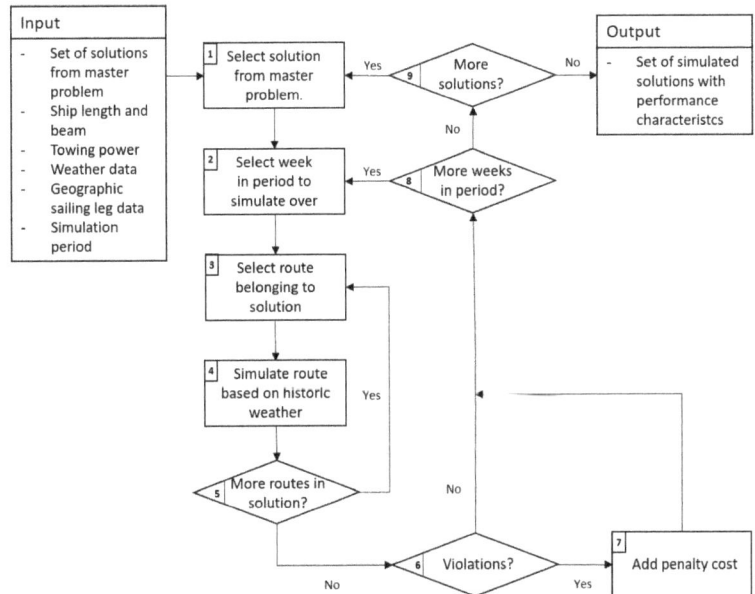

Figure 5. Flow chart of the simulation model. The solutions provided by the master problem are simulated week-by-week over a long period using historical data. When a violation is detected, a penalty cost is added to the operational costs of the solution.

An important element of the simulation model is to penalize duration and synchronization violations. The total penalty cost for a simulated solution is the accumulated penalty costs for all vessels for each week of the simulation period. Hence, route compositions that often incur duration or synchronization violations are receiving a high penalty cost and are less likely to be chosen by the master problem in subsequent iterations.

4.3. Performance-Improving Strategies

Penalizing synchronization and duration violations helps select more robust routes for both mother and daughter vessels, but does not necessarily reflect real-world operations of a feeder network service. In our optimization-simulation model, duration violations propagate from one week to another. In contrast, real-world vessel operators would try to either avoid a delay (e.g., by using more robust routes) or recover from the delay (e.g., by speeding up) before it causes any violations. To further improve the quality of the solutions, we propose two types of performance-improving strategies that mimic real-world operations and are integrated into the solution approach: enhancing the robustness of the routes and recovery from delays.

4.3.1. Enhancing Route Robustness

The first type of strategy tries to enhance the routes' robustness during the route generation procedure, i.e., before starting the optimization-simulation process. Additional slack (or idle time) is added to some or all of its legs when generating routes. By doing so, a vessel might still be able to synchronize in an ocean hub, even if it has to slow down due to harsh weather. Conversely, adding too much slack can cause excessive waiting times and, as such, increase the operational cost for the vessels. Therefore, determining the amount and place of additional slack while ensuring a sufficient robustness level is an important trade-off to assess. This strategy is comparable to the current practice of airlines where delayed routes can recover at night when no flights are scheduled and the network resets [36].

Similarly, the robustness of the routes can be enhanced by considering seasonality in the schedules. Due to the difference in weather conditions between summer and winter, it might be beneficial to operate dedicated routes for each season. However, the system needs to operate the same fleet of mother and daughter vessels during the whole year, regardless of the season.

4.3.2. Recovery from Delays

The second type of strategy tries to exploit operational flexibility to recover from delays. If weather permits, a vessel can increase its speed to reduce or even eliminate a delay. Fischer et al. [30], for example, show that speed-up can be used as a recovery action when considering disruptions in planning fleet deployment in roll-on roll-off liner shipping. Though speeding-up allows recovering from delays in some cases, it requires increased power output, which in turn will increase fuel consumption and thus bunker costs. The ability to speed-up is limited by the maximum propulsion power of the vessels.

5. Computational Study

The route generation procedure and the simulation model have been implemented in MATLAB R2016b. The master problem is formulated and solved using FICO Xpress 7.9. All computations have been carried out on a PC with a 3.4 GHz Intel Core i7 processor and 32 GB RAM.

5.1. The Short Sea Pioneer Logistics System

The selection of ports is based on the ports currently served by the case shipping company NorthSea Container Line (NCL), which operates a line for container transportation between the Norwegian west coast and the European continent port located at Maasvlakte in the Netherlands. The candidate hub locations are selected close to major local ports and inshore to have stable weather conditions for the cargo transshipment. The port locations of this case study are illustrated in Figure 6.

The weekly number of containers transported to and from the European continent is based on the number of containers imported and exported in ports along the Norwegian west coast during the first quarter 2016 data [40]. The numbers have been corrected according to NCL's market share to approximate realistic transportation demand. We refer to Holm et al. [10] for detailed input data.

The possible capacities for the daughter vessels are 100, 200, and 300 twenty-foot-equivalent units (TEU). The capacity of the mother vessels is 2500 TEU, which is sufficient to transport the cargo of the whole system. The design speed for all vessels is set to 12 knots.

The relationship between speed and wave height for the mother and three candidate daughter vessel types considered in this experiment is shown in Figure 7. We can see from Figure 7a that at design power, the sailing speed significantly decreases as waves become higher, especially for the daughter vessels. Figure 7b illustrates the same relationship, but for speed-up power that can be used to recover from delays. The power output for speed-up is set to be 125% of design power.

The legs between ports required to simulate sailing speed have been discretized according to container vessel AIS data available from the Norwegian Coastal Administration. Historical wave height data from both the Norwegian Meteorological Institute (MET.no) and the European Centre for Medium-Range Weather Forecasts (ECMWF) is used in the simulations. These data sets provide weather data with a time increment of six hours. Figure 8 shows a visualization of the data grid for both data sources. The data from ECMWF has a resolution of $0.75° \times 0.75°$, which is sufficient for the zone between Europe and Norway but not detailed enough for vessels sailing the Norwegian coastline. The data from Norwegian Meteorological Institute offers a better resolution, i.e., $0.3° \times 0.15°$ and is used for latitudes higher than $57.5°$ N. Please note that no wave height data is available inside fjords or very close to land. If a vessel is within these areas, it is assumed to sail at design speed, i.e., 12 knots.

In our simulations, we use data of two successive years (2000 and 2001). To make the simulation by weeks easier, we assume that the length of each month is exactly four weeks, resulting in a total of 96 weeks to simulate. The winter season is defined as lasting from October to March, and the summer season lasts from April to September.

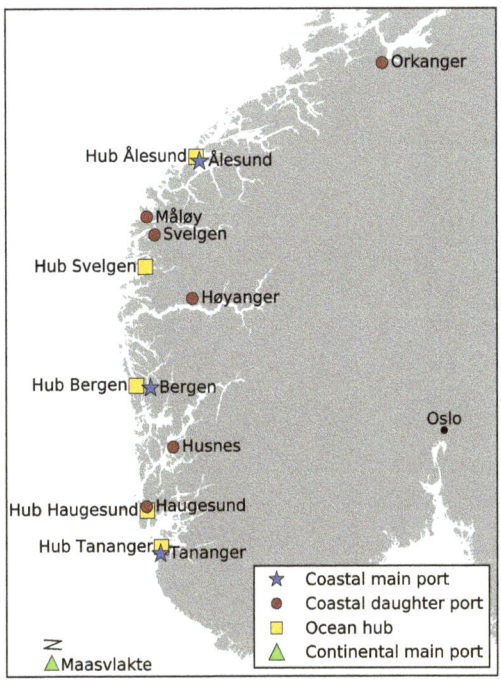

Figure 6. A map showing ports considered in the case study. The possible ocean hubs are represented with yellow squares.

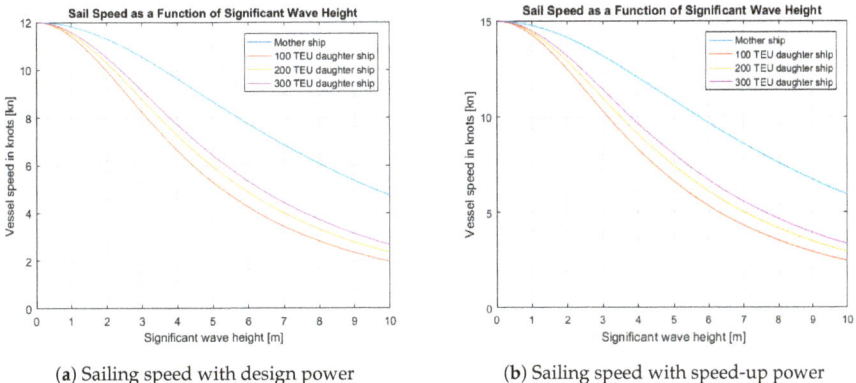

(**a**) Sailing speed with design power   (**b**) Sailing speed with speed-up power

Figure 7. Impact of significant wave heights on the sailing speed for the fleet of vessels considered in the experimentation.

(**a**) European Centre for Medium-Range Weather Forecasts (ECMWF) data used south of a latitude of 57.5°N

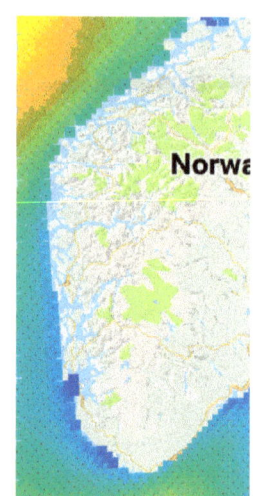

(**b**) Data from MET.no used north of 57.5°N

Figure 8. Data grid with time series observation on each cell used for the weather simulation.

5.2. Runtime Considerations

The runtime of the optimization-simulation framework mainly depends on the number of iterations needed for the framework to converge to a solution. To speed up this process, we can reduce the number of times to run the optimization model by returning multiple feasible solutions for simulation instead of only the optimal solution. This has the advantage of possibly simulating the solution that performs best under uncertainty at early iterations. On the other hand, extracting too many solutions implies simulating solutions that may never be needed. Thus, it would be interesting to study the trade-off between the number of solutions extracted in each iteration and the number of iterations of the optimization-simulation framework.

We extract the n best solutions found while solving the master problem. The results for the convergence speed of the solution method for different values of n are presented in Table 1. The first column indicates the maximum number of extracted solutions n in each iteration. The column Itr. needed states how many times the master problem has been solved, i.e., the number of iterations. The third column, Route Gen. Time, is the time needed to generate the routes. Note that this time is constant, as the routes are only generated once. The total time spent by Xpress to solve the master problems is given in column Opt. Time, whereas the total time used by MATLAB to simulate the solutions is given in column Sim. Time. Column Total Time shows the total runtime spent by the solution approach. The last column, Solutions Simulated, contains the total number of simulated solutions.

As can be seen from Table 1, the number of iterations of solving the master problem decreases with higher values of n. In contrast, the time needed to simulate all solutions increases by n. For our case, we select $n = 20$ for which the best total time is obtained. Finally, we point out that the approach is not sensitive to n when considering the solution quality. The same best solution is found for all different values of n.

Table 1. Runtime (in seconds) for the solution approach with different values of n.

n	Itr. needed	Route Gen. Time	Opt. Time	Sim. Time	Total Time	Solutions Simulated
1	75	94	2855	131	3080	75
5	19	94	771	149	1014	89
10	13	94	510	182	786	113
20	9	94	390	246	**730**	157
50	7	94	405	473	972	297
100	6	94	393	573	1060	494

5.3. Determining Global Estimated Optimal Routes

In this section, we analyze the route networks obtained using the solution method. We first describe the different performance-improving strategies, before discussing the solutions produced by our method.

5.3.1. Performance-Improving Strategies

We combine the optimization-simulation solution method with different performance-improving strategies to impose additional robustness and exploit operational flexibility. The different strategies are listed in Table 2 and are explained in more detail below.

Table 2. List of applied performance-improving strategies.

Strategy	Category	Description
None	-	No performance-improving strategy is applied.
Slack 10%	Route robustness	10% slack is added on each sailing leg.
Realistic	Route robustness	Simulated sailing times with additional 5% extra slack.
Seasonal	Route robustness	Tailor-made winter and summer schedules are used.
Speed-up	Recovery	vessels can speed-up to reduce delays.
Combined	Route robustness & recovery	Realistic, Speed-Up, and Seasonal strategies are applied.

We test three different performance-enhancing strategies for enhancing the robustness of the routes and one strategy for recovery from delays. The Slack 10% and the Realistic strategies are implemented as part of the route generation procedure. The Slack 10% strategy is characterized by calculating the sailing time along a leg (based on design speed) and then adding 10% additional sailing to immunize the route against delays. While adding robustness to a route, this strategy may result in considerable amounts of unnecessary idle time in the schedule. The Realistic strategy tries to account for the fact that particular sailing legs are more likely to be subject to delays than others. Sailing speeds along the different legs are first simulated using weather data from 1998 to 2000. To further improve robustness, the resulting average sailing time on each leg is then increased by an additional 5%.

With the Seasonal strategy, the routes sailed by the vessels are allowed to change for each season. We distinguish here between the summer season and winter season. The seasonal routes are obtained by solving the simulation-optimization framework for each season with a set of routes based on design speed. Note that the same fleet has to be used in all seasons.

The Speed-up strategy is part of the simulation model. This strategy allows delayed vessels to increase their speed by increasing their power output. Mother and daughter vessels speed-up independently according to their routes, but the conditions for when they do so are slightly different. A mother vessel will try to speed-up once it is more than one hour delayed compared to its generated route. Increased speed will be maintained until the vessel is no longer delayed. Daughter vessels usually have a certain amount of idle time included in their schedules, e.g., waiting for the mother vessel to arrive in an ocean hub. The daughter vessel starts to speed-up as soon as the remaining idle time falls below a given threshold (for the case study, this is set to one hour) and will continue to sail at increased speed until it has up to two hours idle time available. However, a daughter vessel will never speed-up to get more than its original amount of idle time.

The Combined strategy applies realistic, speed-up, and seasonal strategies simultaneously. The realistic sailing times used in the combined strategy are calculated separately for each season during the preliminary simulation of sailing time. This implies that more absolute slack will be added in the winter season than in the summer season.

5.3.2. Best Routes with and without Weather Uncertainty

We first solve the problem deterministically and use its solution as a benchmark when comparing the solutions considering weather uncertainty. For the deterministic case, the solution using daughter vessels with a capacity of 300 TEU has the lowest total weekly cost with an objective function value of 457,800 USD. Two mother vessels and two daughter vessels are deployed in this optimal solution, as shown in Figure 9. In particular, the main route visits two ocean hubs at Tananger and Haugesund, as well as the main port at Tananger. The hub Haugesund is the northernmost port served by the main route and is therefore visited only once. The mother vessel is more expensive in terms of bunker cost and port visits, which causes the model to select a short main route.

Figure 9. The optimal routes for the Short Sea Pioneer (SSP) deterministic version. The mother route visits two hub ports that are connected to two daughter routes.

We then solve the network design problem using our optimization-simulation method, applying each of the performance-improving strategies separately. In all best solutions, two mother vessels and two daughter vessels are deployed. However, the solution without the performance-improving strategy deploys smaller daughter vessels than other solutions. Table 3 summarizes the results for the different performance-improving strategies. The cost of the best solutions is compared to the cost of the best deterministic solution, where 100% representing the cost of the deterministic solution. In this comparison, the penalty costs added by the simulation model are excluded as they are fictional and only used to identify low-performing solutions. However, the increased costs due to speeding up are included. This comparison facilitates evaluating the solution quality since the deterministic solution is obtained under ideal weather conditions and, thus, can be considered as a lower bound. Table 3 also shows important performance characteristics for the different solutions, such as the total number and accumulated time (in hours) of both duration and synchronization violations. It also reports the total amount of planned idle time included in the selected routes and how much time this idle time is used to recover from incurred delays. The last column indicates the daughter vessel size of the solutions.

Table 3. Performance characteristics for the different solutions.

Strategy	Cost [%]	Dur. Viol.	Dur. Mag.	Sync. Viol.	Sync. Mag.	Idle Time	Idle Use [%]	Vessel Size
None	102.1	0	0	200	1958	219	14.8	200
Slack 10%	101.4	4	18.7	61	450	171	3.9	300
Realistic	101.4	4	17.1	52	319	162	2.5	300
Seasonal	101.5	3	4.3	204	1859	180	17.3	300
Speed-up	102.8	2	4.1	125	927	188	8.9	300
Combined	101.2	1	0.7	21	192	160	1.8	300

All obtained solutions result in a slight increase in operational costs compared to the deterministic solution, where the Combined strategy gives the lowest operational cost with an increase of only 1.2%. Only one duration violation occurs with a negligible magnitude. The number of synchronization violations and the related magnitude is also significantly lower than for other strategies. The utilization of idle time is also low, implying that the vessels usually keep the estimated arrival times set up in the route generation procedure. As such, the solution obtained when using the combined performance-improving strategy is quite robust without increasing the cost level by much. Note that the solution resulting from not using a performance-improving strategy does not incur any duration violation but is exposed to many synchronization violations. The solution includes a lot of idle time, a large share of which needs to be used for sailing to recover from delays.

Figure 10 shows the optimal seasonal routes for the Combined strategy. The solid red line is the main route that continues further south to Maasvlakte port. The blue and pink dashed lines are daughter routes 1 and 2, respectively. The corresponding ocean hubs are marked as squares.

As seen in Figure 10, the main route extends further north in the winter than during the summer season. Compared to a daughter vessel, a mother vessel is more expensive in terms of bunker and port costs. By having a mother vessel sailing further north, the daughter vessels can reduce their total sailing distance, resulting in planned idle time. This is beneficial during the winter season since the weather conditions are rougher, and a greater buffer against delays is needed to avoid duration violations. Conversely, during the summer season, the weather conditions are better, resulting in a shorter main route with corresponding longer daughter routes to reduce operational cost.

5.3.3. Analyzing the Best Deterministic Solution

The best deterministic solution is slightly cheaper than all solutions found by the solution triggered feedback approach. However, these cost savings come at the expense of a lack of robustness for harsh weather conditions. Table 4 provides the performance characteristics for simulating the optimal deterministic solution under weather conditions without any performance-improving strategy.

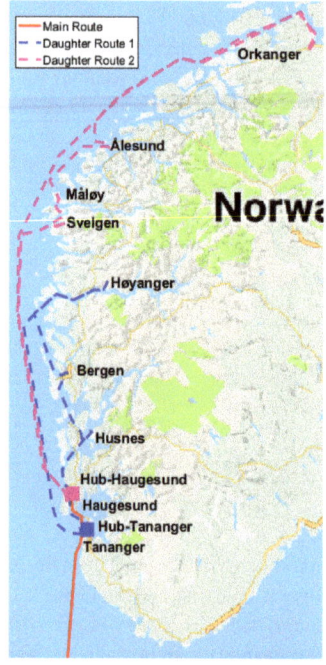 

(**a**) Routes for the summer season (**b**) Routes for the winter season.

Figure 10. The difference between the summer and winter solutions when using the combined strategy. The main route sails further north in the winter season due to rough weather conditions.

Table 4. Performance characteristics for the best deterministic solution.

Cost [%]	Dur. Viol.	Dur. Mag.	Sync. Viol.	Sync. Mag.	Idle Time	Idle Use [%]	Vessel Size
100	277	45,429	194	14,332	192	82.5	300

In particular, the high number of duration violations renders the best deterministic solution infeasible in practice. While almost all of the planned idle time is used for sailing to mitigate delays, the system is still unable to recover. The poor performance of the optimal deterministic solution clearly shows the importance of taking into account weather uncertainty. All solutions found the using optimization-simulation approach (see Table 3) perform significantly better, while being less than 3% more expensive. The solution from the Combined strategy for example, reduces the number of duration violations from 277 to 1 and the duration magnitude from 45,429 h to 0.7 h, while the costs only increase by 1.2%.

Pushing the analysis further, we simulate the best deterministic solution with the Speed-up strategy. This combination results in a cost increase of 2.2%, which is due to the higher fuel consumption from the required speed-ups. However, the number of duration violations is reduced from 277 to 28, and the number of synchronization violation is reduced from 194 to 181. Even though these are significant improvements, the solution still performs much worse than the solutions found by the optimization-simulation method.

In another analysis, we consider another criterion of a well-performing solution. It consists of measuring the stability of arrival times, which translates directly into predicting future arrivals and maintaining a given schedule. For the Combined-strategy solution, the arrival times for the summer and winter routes are presented in Figures 11 and 12. The mother vessels are scheduled to depart from the main continental port at time zero. The arrival times for all vessels refer to this departure time.

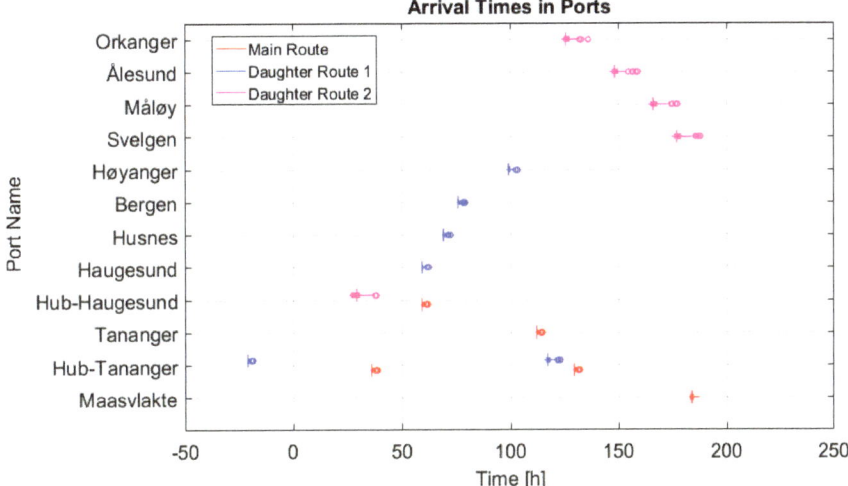

Figure 11. A box and whisker plot of the arrival times for the summer season of the Combined-strategy solution.

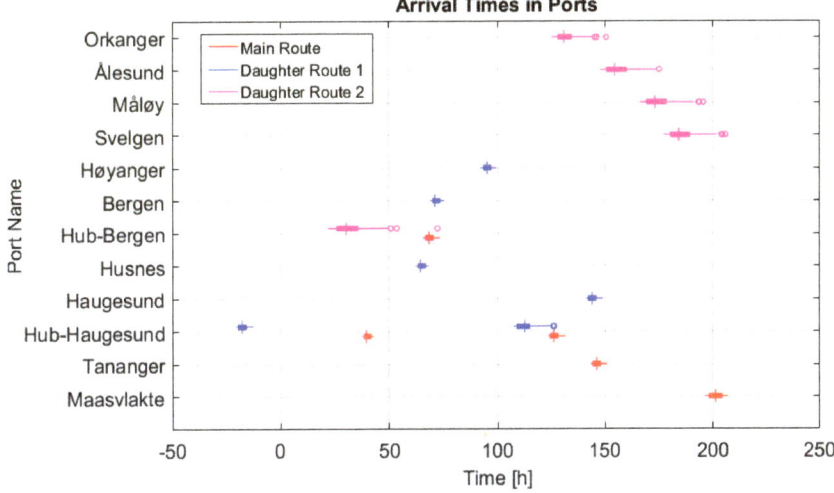

Figure 12. A box and whisker plot of the arrival times for the winter season of the Combined-strategy solution.

The small vertical line represents the median arrival time. The width of each box corresponds to the interquartile range (IQR) defined by the first and third quartile, and accounts for 50% of all port arrivals in the simulation period. The left and right whiskers capture all arrival times within $1.5 \cdot IQR$. Arrival times outside this range are considered outliers and represented with circles.

For both seasons, arrival times are mostly within relatively small intervals, particularly for the main route and daughter route 1. The longer daughter route 2 is slightly more prone to variations in arrival time, especially during the winter season, although this route is considerably shortened during this season (see Figure 10). Still, these varying arrival times do not affect synchronization with the mother vessel at ocean hubs (except Bergen) because daughter vessel 2 always arrives first anyway (with one exception).

Figure 13 presents the arrival times for the deterministic solution. Here, we observe much wider intervals for different arrival times. For example, about 50% of all arrivals at the main continental port in Maasvlakte happen approximately 48 h around the median arrival time. This median arrival time of the mother vessel is also about 100 h after the end of the planned two-week route due to a large number of duration violations. Moreover, Figure 13 shows that the deterministic solution is very sensitive to weather uncertainty, causing arrival times to vary a lot. Therefore, the deterministic solution is not applicable in a real-world setting and should be discarded in favor of the solution from the Combined-strategy. These results highlight once more the need for considering the weather uncertainty in designing the short-sea feeder network considered in this paper.

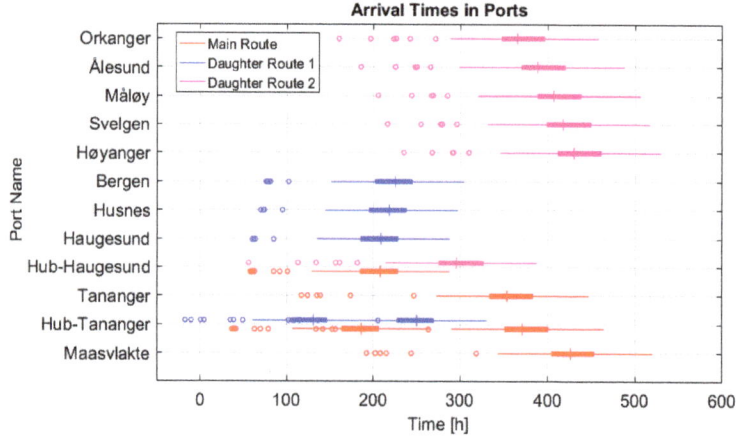

Figure 13. A box and whisker plot of the arrival times of deterministic solution.

6. Concluding Remarks

In this paper, we study the problem of designing a short-sea liner network with transshipment at sea under uncertain weather conditions and propose an iterative solution method that combines optimization and simulation. In the deterministic optimization step, we select routes for both mother and daughter vessels that minimize the cost of operating the logistics system. These routes are then evaluated using a discrete event simulation model. Solutions that are not performing well in the simulations are penalized in the objective function in subsequent iterations of the optimization model to reduce their attractiveness. The steps of selecting routes in the optimization model and simulating them continue until no new (not simulated) solution is selected. The computational study performed on a case based on real-world data shows that our solution method provides solutions for the system with a good trade-off between operational cost and robustness.

The results show that weather uncertainty can severely impact the synchronization of the routes and should be taken into account in the design phase of the logistics system. The optimization-simulation approach, especially when using different performance-improving strategies, finds robust solutions at only a small operational cost increase. The solution method has been applied to a short-sea feeder network design problem in this paper, but it should be straightforward to apply to other related problems.

Author Contributions: Conceptualization, K.F. and P.S.; methodology, C.A.B.M., M.B.H., K.F. and P.S.; software, C.A.B.M. and M.B.H.; validation, C.A.B.M., M.B.H., K.F. and P.S.; formal analysis, C.A.B.M. and M.B.H.; investigation, C.A.B.M. and M.B.H.; writing—original draft preparation, C.A.B.M. and M.B.H.; writing—review and editing, M.K.M., K.F. and P.S.; visualization, C.A.B.M. and M.B.H.; supervision, K.F. and P.S.; project administration, K.F. and P.S. All authors have read and agreed to the published version of the manuscript. Authors contributed equally to this work.

Funding: This research received no external funding.

Conflicts of Interest: The authors declare no conflict of interest.

References

1. Brouer, B.D.; Karsten, C.V.; Pisinger, D. Optimization in liner shipping. *4OR* **2017**, *15*, 1–35. [CrossRef]
2. Christiansen, M.; Fagerholt, K.; Nygreen, B.; Ronen, D. Maritime Transportation. In *Transportation*; Elsevier: Amsterdam, The Netherlands, 2007; pp. 189–284. [CrossRef]
3. Haram, H.K.; Hov, I.B.; Caspersen, E. Potensiale og Virkemidler for Overføring av Gods Fra Veg- Til Sjøtransport. Available online: https://www.toi.no/getfile.php?mmfileid=41079 (accessed on 27 July 2020).
4. Goel, A. A roadmap for sustainable freight transport. In *Methods of Multicriteria Decision Theory and Applications*; Shaker: Maastricht, Germany, 2009; pp. 47–56.
5. Norwegian Ministry of Transport and Communications. Nasjonal Transportplan 2014–2023. Available online: https://www.regjeringen.no/no/dokumenter/meld-st-26-20122013/id722102/ (accessed on 27 July 2020).
6. Norwegian Ministry of Transport and Communications. Nasjonal Transportplan 2018–2029. Available online: https://www.regjeringen.no/no/dokumenter/meld.-st.-33-20162017/id2546287/ (accessed on 27 July 2020).
7. NCE Maritime Clean Tech. Short Sea Pioneer the New Way of Transporting Goods at Sea. Available online: https://maritimecleantech.no/wp-content/uploads/2017/01/SSP-folder.pdf (accessed on 27 July 2020).
8. NCE Maritime Clean Tech. Short Sea Pioneer. Available online: https://maritimecleantech.no/project/short-sea-pioneer-2 (accessed on 27 July 2020).
9. Stensvold, T. Slik skal ny 2-i-1-løsning Flytte Mer Gods Fra Vei Til Sjø. Available online: http://www.tu.no/artikler/slik-skal-ny-2-i-1-losning-flytte-mer-gods-fra-vei-til-sjo/223103 (accessed on 27 July 2020).
10. Holm, M.B.; Medbøen, C.A.B.; Fagerholt, K.; Schütz, P. Shortsea liner network design with transhipments at sea: A case study from Western Norway. *Flex. Serv. Manuf. J.* **2018**, *31*, 598–619. [CrossRef]
11. Brouer, B.D.; Alvarez, J.F.; Plum, C.E.M.; Pisinger, D.; Sigurd, M.M. A Base Integer Programming Model and Benchmark Suite for Liner-Shipping Network Design. *Transp. Sci.* **2014**, *48*, 281–312. [CrossRef]
12. Meng, Q.; Wang, S. Liner shipping service network design with empty container repositioning. *Transp. Res. Part E Logist. Transp. Rev.* **2011**, *47*, 695–708. [CrossRef]
13. Reinhardt, L.B.; Pisinger, D. A branch and cut algorithm for the container shipping network design problem. *Flex. Serv. Manuf. J.* **2012**, *24*, 349–374. [CrossRef]
14. Karsten, C.V.; Brouer, B.D.; Pisinger, D. Competitive Liner Shipping Network Design. *Comput. Oper. Res.* **2017**, *87*, 125–136. [CrossRef]
15. Balakrishnan, A.; Karsten, C.V. Container shipping service selection and cargo routing with transshipment limits. *Eur. J. Oper. Res.* **2017**, *263*, 652–663. [CrossRef]
16. Msakni, M.K.; Fagerholt, K.; Meisel, F.; Lindstad, E. Analyzing different designs of liner shipping feeder networks: A case study. *Transp. Res. Part E Logist. Transp. Rev.* **2020**, *134*, 101839. [CrossRef]
17. Fadda, P.; Fancello, G.; Mancini, S.; Pani, C.; Serra, P. Design and optimisation of an innovative two-hub-and-spoke network for the Mediterranean short-sea-shipping market. *Comput. Ind. Eng.* **2020**, *149*, 106847. [CrossRef]
18. Akbar, A.; Aasen, A.K.A.; Msakni, M.K.; Fagerholt, K.; Lindstad, E.; Meisel, F. An economic analysis of introducing autonomous ships in a short-sea liner shipping network. *Int. Trans. Oper. Res.* **2020**. [CrossRef]
19. Meng, Q.; Wang, S.; Andersson, H.; Thun, K. Containership routing and scheduling in liner shipping: overview and future research directions. *Transp. Sci.* **2014**, *48*, 265–280. [CrossRef]
20. Christiansen, M.; Hellsten, E.; Pisinger, D.; Sacramento, D.; Vilhelmsen, C. Liner shipping network design. *Eur. J. Oper. Res.* **2019**. [CrossRef]
21. Agarwal, R.; Ergun, Ö. Ship Scheduling and Network Design for Cargo Routing in Liner Shipping. *Transp. Sci.* **2008**, *42*, 175–196. [CrossRef]

22. Andersson, H.; Duesund, J.M.; Fagerholt, K. Ship routing and scheduling with cargo coupling and synchronization constraints. *Comput. Ind. Eng.* **2011**, *61*, 1107–1116. [CrossRef]

23. Drexl, M. Synchronization in Vehicle Routing—A Survey of VRPs with Multiple Synchronization Constraints. *Transp. Sci.* **2012**, *46*, 297–316. [CrossRef]

24. Wang, S.; Meng, Q. Liner ship route schedule design with sea contingency time and port time uncertainty. *Transp. Res. Part B Methodol.* **2012**, *46*, 615–633. [CrossRef]

25. Song, D.P.; Li, D.; Drake, P. Multi-objective optimization for planning liner shipping service with uncertain port times. *Transp. Res. Part E Logist. Transp. Rev.* **2015**, *84*, 1–22. [CrossRef]

26. Li, C.; Qi, X.; Song, D. Real-time schedule recovery in liner shipping service with regular uncertainties and disruption events. *Transp. Res. Part B Methodol.* **2016**, *93*, 762–788. [CrossRef]

27. Ng, M.; Lin, D.Y. Fleet deployment in liner shipping with incomplete demand information. *Transp. Res. Part E Logist. Transp. Rev.* **2018**, *116*, 184–189. [CrossRef]

28. Lo, H.K.; An, K.; Lin, W. Ferry service network design under demand uncertainty. *Transp. Res. Part E Logist. Transp. Rev.* **2013**, *59*, 48–70. [CrossRef]

29. An, K.; Lo, H.K. Two-phase stochastic program for transit network design under demand uncertainty. *Transp. Res. Part B Methodol.* **2016**, *84*, 157–181. [CrossRef]

30. Fischer, A.; Nokhart, H.; Olsen, H.; Fagerholt, K.; Rakke, J.G.; Stålhane, M. Robust planning and disruption management in roll-on roll-off liner shipping. *Transp. Res. Part E Logist. Transp. Rev.* **2016**, *91*, 51–67. [CrossRef]

31. Castilla-Rodríguez, I.; Expósito-Izquierdo, C.; Melián-Batista, B.; Aguilar, R.M.; Moreno-Vega, J.M. Simulation-optimization for the management of the transshipment operations at maritime container terminals. *Expert Syst. Appl.* **2020**, *139*, 112852. [CrossRef]

32. Layeb, S.B.; Jaoua, A.; Jbira, A.; Makhlouf, Y. A simulation-optimization approach for scheduling in stochastic freight transportation. *Comput. Ind. Eng.* **2018**, *126*, 99–110. [CrossRef]

33. Poeting, M.; Rau, J.; Clausen, U.; Schumacher, C. A combined simulation optimization framework to improve operations in parcel logistics. In Proceedings of the 2017 Winter Simulation Conference (WSC), Las Vegas, NV, USA, 3–6 December 2017. [CrossRef]

34. Acar, Y.; Kadipasaoglu, S.N.; Day, J.M. Incorporating uncertainty in optimal decision making: Integrating mixed integer programming and simulation to solve combinatorial problems. *Comput. Ind. Eng.* **2009**, *56*, 106–112. [CrossRef]

35. Crainic, T.G.; Perboli, G.; Rosano, M. Simulation of intermodal freight transportation systems: A taxonomy. *Eur. J. Oper. Res.* **2018**, *270*, 401–418. [CrossRef]

36. Brouer, B.D.; Dirksen, J.; Pisinger, D.; Plum, C.E.; Vaaben, B. The Vessel Schedule Recovery Problem (VSRP)—A MIP model for handling disruptions in liner shipping. *Eur. J. Oper. Res.* **2013**, *224*, 362–374. [CrossRef]

37. Irnich, S. Resource extension functions: Properties, inversion, and generalization to segments. *OR Spectr.* **2008**, *30*, 113–148. [CrossRef]

38. DNV GL. Environmental Conditions and Environmental Loads. Recommended Practice DNV-RP-C205. Available online: https://rules.dnvgl.com/docs/pdf/dnv/codes/docs/2010-10/rp-c205.pdf (accessed on 2 April 2020).

39. Van den Boom, H.; Van der Hout, I.; Flikkema, M. Speed-power performance of ships during trials and in service. In Proceedings of the SNAME, Athens, Greece, 17–18 September 2008.

40. Statistics Norway. Maritime Transport. Available online: https://www.ssb.no/en/statbank/table/03648/ (accessed on 27 July 2020).

Publisher's Note: MDPI stays neutral with regard to jurisdictional claims in published maps and institutional affiliations.

Article

Scheduling Algorithms for a Hybrid Flow Shop under Uncertainty

Christin Schumacher * and Peter Buchholz

Informatik 4—Modeling and Simulation, Department of Computer Science, TU Dortmund University,
D-44221 Dortmund, Germany; peter.buchholz@cs.tu-dortmund.de
* Correspondence: christin.schumacher@tu-dortmund.de

Received: 30 September 2020; Accepted: 27 October 2020; Published: 31 October 2020

Abstract: In modern production systems, scheduling problems have to be solved in consideration of frequently changing demands and varying production parameters. This paper presents a approach combining forecasting and classification techniques to predict uncertainty from demands, and production data with heuristics, metaheuristics, and discrete event simulation for obtaining machine schedules. The problem is a hybrid flow shop with two stages, machine qualifications, skipping stages, and uncertainty in demands. The objective is to minimize the makespan. First, based on the available data of past orders, jobs that are prone to fluctuations just before or during the production phase are identified by clustering algorithms, and production volumes are adjusted accordingly. Furthermore, the distribution of scrap rates is estimated, and the quantiles of the resulting distribution are used to increase corresponding production volumes to prevent costly rescheduling resulting from unfulfilled demands. Second, Shortest Processing Time (SPT), tabu search, and local search algorithms are developed and applied. Third, the best performing schedules are evaluated and selected using a detailed simulation model. The proposed approach is validated on a real-world production case. The results show that the price for a very robust schedule that avoids underproduction with a high probability can significantly increase the makespan.

Keywords: scheduling; uncertainty; discrete event simulation; hybrid flow shop; scrap; local search; tabu search; machine qualifications; clustering; shortest processing time

---

1. Introduction

In complex production environments in the automotive industry, machine schedules have to be calculated by taking into account frequently changing customer demands and potential failures or unanticipated delays. The calculation of high quality schedules in such an environment is a challenge because the scheduling problem itself usually has significant complexity, tight time restrictions are given, and uncertainty occurs in various production parameters. Even by neglecting uncertainty, the resulting optimization problems are NP-hard and can only be solved exactly with acceptable computation times of some minutes for small and unrealistic configurations. More applicable solution methods for practical problem instances are heuristics and metaheuristics, because they require less computation time and allow one to approximate the optimal schedule with deterministic models, even for larger configurations. However, the parameters of the model have to be set according to the current situation. This means that data from the running production are used to define the actual scheduling problem; a statistical evaluation of past data allows for the determination of safety margins to compensate for scrap or unplanned demands. Before schedules, which were calculated by deterministic optimization methods, should be applied to a production with its statistical effects, they should be tested in stochastic simulation models.

Algorithms **2020**, *13*, 277; doi:10.3390/a13110277   www.mdpi.com/journal/algorithms

The objective of this paper is to provide combined solutions to various problems at the machine scheduling level for a real application example from a supplier in the automotive industry, which describes a two-stage scheduling problem with parallel machines per stage with uncertainty in several parameters. The system layout of the application case can be found in Figure 1. The production includes 11 unrelated parallel machines in the first stage. In the second stage, there are two identical parallel machines. The restrictions and characteristics of the basic scheduling problem are machine qualifications, i.e., not every job can be produced on every machine, jobs might skip stages, and the production data show several uncertainties in demands and different production parameters, which need to be handled to provide usefully applicable schedules that perform in production with as few makespans as possible. A composition of forecasting, classification, discrete event simulation, metaheuristic, and heuristic algorithms is developed to identify demand fluctuations, including scrap rates, and to approve schedules for their use in a production environment. So, in contrast to common scheduling approaches, various problems at the machine scheduling level have to be considered in combination. First, based on the available data of past orders, risky jobs that are prone to fluctuations just before or during the production phase are identified by clustering algorithms and corresponding demands are adjusted. Furthermore, the distributions of scrap rates are estimated, and the quantiles of the resulting distribution are used to increase quantities of produced items to avoid costly losses due to unfulfilled demands. Second, we show how deterministic methods solving the described optimization problem are developed from the scheduling problem and how parameters are derived from the available data. Third, a detailed simulation model of the production has been built (see Figures 2 and 7) using the software AnyLogic 8.5 [1]. By means of simulation, it is possible to evaluate and improve schedules before they are applied in a real production environment.

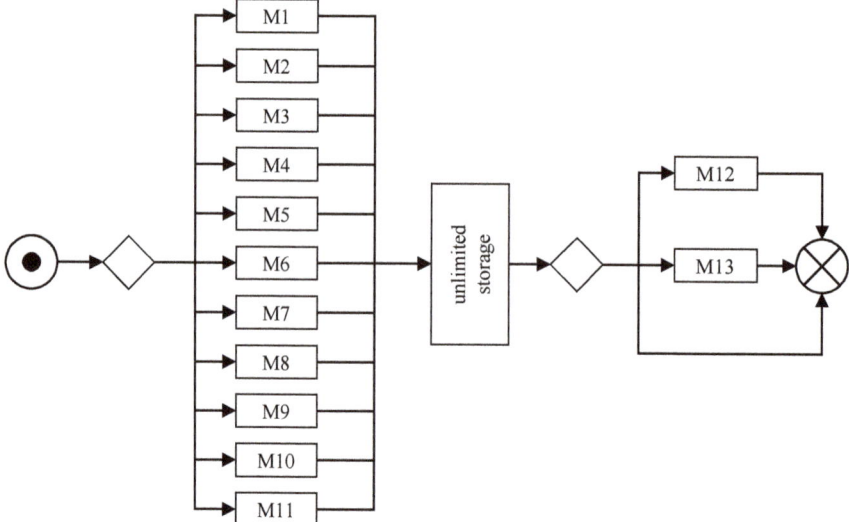

Figure 1. System layout of the hybrid flow shop in the application case.

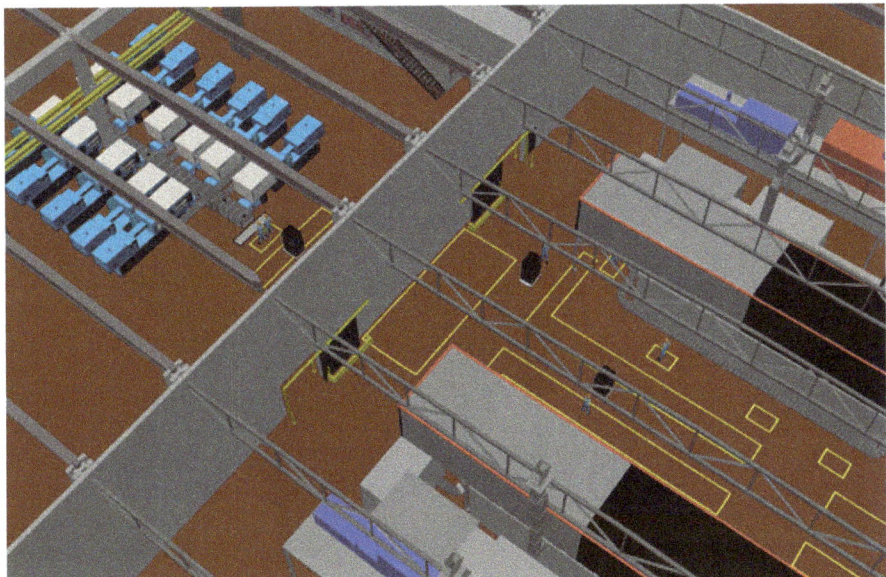

Figure 2. Production flow of the application case in AnyLogic 8.5.

The structure of the paper is as follows. In the next section, we present a detailed description of the two-stage hybrid flow shop problem with its restrictions. Related work is summarized afterwards. Section 4 introduces several metaheuristic and heuristic algorithms to compute schedules for the hybrid flow shop problem. Afterwards, in Sections 5 and 6, the available data from the production are described and methods are presented to estimate all parameters of the optimization problem and to calculate the appropriate production volume from the data. Then in Section 7, a detailed analysis of the schedules, using simulation and the structure of the simulation model, are introduced. In Section 8, results of example runs are presented, evaluating makespans and order fulfilment as key indicators. Our findings are summarized in the conclusions, which also outline some steps for future research.

2. Description of the Basic Model

The problem analyzed in this paper is a two-stage hybrid flow shop ($FH2$), in which a set of jobs $N = \{1, \ldots, n\}$ has to be completed. To produce the components, there are two production stages i, with $i \in M$ with $M = \{1, 2\}$, through which each job $j \in N$ follows the same route. At each stage i a job is processed by at most one machine l, with $l \in M_i = \{1, \ldots, m_i\}$, where $m_i \geq 1$.

As far as possible, we set the parameters according to Ruiz et al. [2] and de Siqueira et al. [3], to support a more homogeneous notation for machine scheduling studies. The following assumptions hold for our model. In brackets, descriptions of the assumptions from the notation in the paper by Graham et al. [4] are added.

1. In the first stage, all jobs are available at time zero.
2. Jobs that are to be produced in the first and last stage can only start in the second stage, after the job has been finished completely in the first stage.
3. Each machine can only handle one job at the same time.
4. Processing of a job on a machine is not interrupted, i.e., preemption is not allowed.
5. The problem contains machine qualifications (M_j), i.e., each job can only be processed on certain machines at each stage, where the set of eligible machines is E_{ij}, with $1 \leq |E_{ij}| \leq m_i$.
6. Some jobs visit only one of the stages (*skip*). The set of stages to be visited is F_j, where $1 \leq |F_j| \leq 2$.

7. Jobs do not need to be dispatched in the same order in all stages. Thus, no fix permutation is considered.

8. There are infinite buffers in front, between and at the end of the two stages.

9. Processing times p_{ilj} of one product of job j are described by independent stochastic distributions separated by machine, stage and job, i.e., machines are unrelated. Especially in the first stage, processing times differ by machine ($RM^{(1)}$), in the second stage, they are machine-independent ($PM^{(2)}$).

10. For setup times s_i, stochastic distributions over all machines and jobs per stage are available.

11. For scrap rates r_{ij}, job- and stage-related stochastic distributions are available for both stages. Scrap parts are those parts which do not pass the quality check.

12. Available parts on stock $stock_{ij}$ are included to fulfill the demand.

13. The objective is to minimize the makespan C_{max}, where C_{max} is the maximum completion time and C_{ij} defines the completion time of a job j on stage i, where $C_{max} = \max\limits_{i \in M, j \in N} C_{ij}$.

14. Order quantities of the job's *demand$_{ij}$* underlie uncertainty and may change even during the week when the job is produced, which results in varying production volumes *productionvolume$_{ij}$*. The needed processing time for one job is the *productionvolume$_{ij}$* $* p_{ilj}$.

According to Pinedo [5] and Ruiz and Vázquez-Rodríguez [6], this problem can be formalized in the Graham et al. [4] notation as $FH2$, $(RM^{(1)}, PM^{(2)}) \mid M_j, skip \mid C_{max}$. In addition, several uncertainties in the model parameters as listed above have to be included, which are not formalized in Graham et al. [4] notation.

In addition, these other parameters of the Graham et al. [4] notation are needed in the following sections:

- S_{sd}: sequence-dependent setup times
- *avail*: block times for machines
- *rm*: block times for machines at the start of the production time
- *lag*: overlapping or gaps between the processing of jobs in successive stages
- *prec*: priority relationships between jobs, i.e., one jobs needs to begin production before another job can be started

Following Ruiz et al. [2] and to support a more homogeneous notation for machine scheduling studies, the variables x_{iljk} and x are introduced. With these variables, the schedules can be described to their fullest extent with $x = (x_{iljk})_{i \in M, l \in M_i, j, k \in N}$. The binary variable for the precedence relations x_{iljk} is defined as

$$x_{iljk} \quad := \quad \begin{cases} 1, & \text{if job } j \text{ precedes job k on machine } l \text{ at stage } i, \\ 0, & \text{otherwise.} \end{cases}$$

Furthermore, *PrioList* is a permutation of jobs. Exemplarily, if jobs should be scheduled to released machines in the order of j_2, j_3, j_1, they are saved as $PrioList = (j_2, j_3, j_1)$.

3. Related Work

A large number of papers on scheduling in hybrid flow shops are available. Overviews can be found in Ruiz and Vázquez-Rodríguez [6], Ribas et al. [7], and Komaki et al. [8]. In the following, a selected number of studies that deal with problems related to our problem (see Section 2) are discussed.

Jabbarizadeh et al. [9] test three constructive heuristics for the problem FHM, $((PM^{(k)})_{k=1}^c) \mid M_j, S_{sd}, avail \mid C_{max}$. Based on Kurz and Askin [10], they assign the jobs in the processing stages $i > 1$ in the order of completion times of the previous stage. They evaluate that Shortest Processing Time (SPT) provides better results than Longest Processing Time (LPT).

A heuristic based on the algorithm of Johnson [11] gave the best results in their study. In the field of metaheuristics, a version of simulated annealing, which is a local search algorithm with the acceptance of setbacks, outperforms a genetic algorithm. In each step, the position of a randomly selected job in the first stage is changed. In the following processing steps, the jobs are dispatched according to the Earliest Completion Times (ECT) using the completion times of the previous step.

Ruiz et al. [2] present a study dealing with an enormous number of realistic components in the problem FHM, $((RM^{(k)})_{k=1}^{c}) \mid M_j$, S_{sd}, rm, lag, $prec$, $skip \mid C_{max}$. Yet the study only compares constructive heuristics and finds that NEH, a heuristic first published for flow shops by Nawaz et al. [12], provides the best solutions.

Low et al. [13] compare for $FH2$, $(RM^{(1)}, 1^{(2)}) \mid M_j \mid C_{max}$ sixteen combinations of heuristics. They do not consider skipping stages. To form a production sequence for the first stage, Low et al. [13] use the following methods: random sequence, SPT using processing times of the first stage, LPT using process times of the second processing stage, and Johnson's algorithm. Once the queue is created, for each method, the jobs are assigned to the machines of the second processing stage with four different rules. They find that the modified Johnson, rule by planning the second stage according to the Earliest Completion Times (ECT) of the first stage, C_{1j} performs best.

For FHM, $((PM^{(k)})_{k=1}^{c}) \mid S_{sd}$, $skip \mid C_{max}$ Naderi et al. [14] conduct job sequencing and machine assignment in the same step. All stages i are scheduled according to the Earliest Completion Times (ECT) of the stage i itself and they take the arrival times at the stages into account, if $i > 1$, which result from C_{i-1j}. In comparison to other constructive algorithms for their problem and for their test data, this constructive algorithm gives the best results. The paper also uses Iterated Local Search, which outperforms the other tested metaheuristics, like genetic algorithms, up to a number of 80 jobs. Since their problem takes sequence-dependent processing times into account, the problem in combination with applying these algorithms corresponds to unrelated machine problems.

In Burdett and Kozan [15], several constructive heuristics are compared with simulated annealing (SA) and a genetic algorithm (GA) for the computation of schedules for flow shops with non-unique jobs. Again, SA and GA outperform constructive heuristics but GA does not, in general, do better than SA. Burdett and Kozan [16] analyze flow shops with resource constraints where limited resources have to be assigned and a schedule has to be computed simultaneously. They show that an evolutionary algorithm gives good results for this class of scheduling problems. The models in the papers differ from our models in several aspects, e.g., they do not consider machine qualification, stochastic demands and scrap.

Dios et al. [17] compare 24 constructive heuristics for FHM, $((PM^{(k)})_{k=1}^{c}) \mid skip \mid C_{max}$ and the evaluation of their experiments shows that two SPT-based and one LPT-based heuristic generate the best schedules according to C_{max}. They do not take unrelated machines into account.

Logendran et al. [18] use tabu search for FFM, $((PM^{(k)})_{k=1}^{c}) \mid batch$, $skip \mid C_{max}$. Since the study works with *batch*, the algorithm contains many details that cannot be used for this work.

Kaczmarczyk et al. [19] apply tabu search to FFM, $((PM^{(k)})_{k=1}^{c}) \mid block$, $skip \mid C_{max}$. For their sequence of jobs, they swap two jobs in each iteration. The positions of the two exchanged jobs are saved in the tabu list. To schedule the created sequence, the earliest available machine on every stage is chosen for the job and the stages on which the job has to be produced.

De Siqueira et al. [3] modify a variable neighbourhood search of Geiger [20] for the problem FHM, $((RM^{(k)})_{k=1}^{c}) \mid M_j$, $skip \mid C_{max}$. To change the solutions, one of the six neighborhood strategies is applied randomly:

- swapping two jobs on one machine;
- swapping three jobs on one machine;
- shifting the position of a job on one machine;
- swapping of two jobs in the schedule (jobs can be scheduled on the same or different machines);
- shifting a job within a processing stage;

- relocating of a block of three consecutive jobs to a new position in a processing stage.

Thus, no study provides local search and tabu search algorithms for the problem of our paper, which is specified in Section 2. Furthermore, the above mentioned approaches are all based on a fully parametrized deterministic model. One way to optimize stochastic models is the use of sample average approximations, which are used by Almeder and Hartl [21] with variable neighborhood search to optimize a two-stage flow shop problem describing a real world production process in the metalworking industry. In contrast to our problem, the number of machines is smaller, machine qualification and setup times are not required, and the behavior of orders seems to be more homogeneous. In this case, production data are not used to determine model parameters. Instead, the sampling averaging of simulation results is used to determine the parameters of the optimization problem, which are analyzed with similar methods to the ones that we apply, but tabu lists do not seem to be used.

Burdett and Kozan [22] studied buffering in the area of machine scheduling for a parallel machine environment with one stage. They add idle times to the schedule, which depend on the variance of the processing times of the jobs. Uncertainties regarding demand are taken into account by limiting the number of jobs that can be produced in a given production period or by completely blocking resources for unexpected demand. Their study differs from our study since the variance of the processing times in our application case plays a minor role, whereas scrap rates have high influence on the demand. In addition, we can use significant historical data of demand developments to adjust the demand according to the articles through clustering.

Our approach is also related to approaches that combine simulation and optimization [23]. Regarding the different possibilities in this area to combine optimization and simulation, our study is allocated in the category of first computing a schedule for a deterministic model, which is evaluated afterwards in the detailed simulation model. In a further step, schedules can be enhanced based on the simulation results. Juan et al. [24] introduced this technique as simheuristics.

In application scenarios, the model has to be built, i.e., parameters have to be estimated and demands have to be forecasted. For parameter estimation and modeling from available data, standard methods of input modeling, as summarized, for example, in Law [25], may be applied. Classification of products according to their future demands is more demanding. Murray et al. [26] have examined an application case of order classification in production planning, but they use k-means clustering in order to group customers into segments. The main difference to the problem analyzed in this paper is in the position in the supply chain. Customers are the first layer in a supply chain because they are causing the demand for orders. The demand becomes more distorted and volatile when customers' order quantities are planned through the different stages of the supply chain [27]. We consider a problem which is more at the end of a supply chain, so the so-called bullwhip effect can be intense. To forecast demands, regression or time series can be applied. There is no one method with an optimal parameter set that is best to predict demand in different settings; instead, algorithms are developed to select good parameters Kück and Scholz-Reiter [28] or to even select the optimal prediction method together with the parameters, as carried out by Scholz-Reiter et al. [29]. According to our results and in order to generate a robust schedule, it is sufficient to oversupply the demand for high-risk jobs, which are identified by clustering algorithms.

Although we do not develop new optimization techniques, the originality of our study is that, to the best of our knowledge, it combines the statistical analysis of production data with heuristic and metaheuristic optimization methods to the specific problem of this paper and the subsequent detailed simulation of a real production problem. The experiments give insights into the behavior of different local search metaheuristics and indicate as expected that local search metaheuristics are able to improve the makespan significantly compared to schedules resulting from simple heuristics like SPT. Moreover, local search and tabu search metaheuristics to the best of our knowledge have not been adapted to the specific problem of this paper in the literature before.

4. Computation of Schedules

Taking the findings of Section 3 into account, we choose to apply SPT, local searches and tabu searches, and ECT schedules the jobs for the basic model described in Section 2. We also apply algorithms for the restriction of machine qualifications, skipping stages, and unrelated machines. At first, the first stage is scheduled with one of the algorithms, which then is combined with ECT in each case to schedule the second stage. Thus, we obtain Algorithms 1–4, which were already presented in our conference paper Schumacher et al. [30].

To create an initial solution, we generate feasible schedules with SPT (Algorithm 1), which uses ECT (Algorithm 2). With Algorithm 1, jobs are ordered according to their increasing average processing times in stage 1 and after that they are scheduled successively to stage 1 on the machines, which becomes available. When the scheduling of all jobs to stage 1 is finished, stage 2 is scheduled with Algorithm 2 according the job completion times of stage 1.

Algorithm 1: Shortest Processing Time, SPT

---

1. Order jobs j according their increasing average processing times in stage 1 ($productionvolume_{1j} \cdot p_{1j}$) and save the queue in *PrioList*.
2. Whenever a machine in stage 1 becomes available, select next unscheduled job j of *PrioList* that is qualified for the given machine and schedule j on the available machine.
3. Execute Algorithm 2 (ECT).
4. **return** schedule x with $C_{max}(x)$.

Algorithm 2: Earliest Completion Time, ECT

---

1. Order jobs on stage 2 according to their completion times C_{1j}. If a job is not processed on stage 1, set $C_{1j} := 0$. Of course, if a job should not be processed on stage 2, the job is not in the sequence for stage 2. If two jobs have the same completion time C_{1j}, order these jobs alphanumerically. Save queue in *PrioList*.
2. Whenever a machine in stage 2 becomes available, select next unscheduled job j of *PrioList* that is qualified for the given machine and schedule j on the available machine.

Based on this initial solution, six algorithms of Algorithms 3 and 4 optimize the solution. Both can be computed with one of the variants "shift" or "swap". With "shift", one randomly selected job in each iteration is positioned elsewhere in the existing schedule. In contrast, "swap" exchanges the positions of two randomly selected jobs. After one of these moves and the consideration of the eligibility restrictions for machines and stages, the resulting new schedule is compared with the old schedule and checked for improvement by computing and comparing makespans. Random Descent generates a new solution out of the existing one and if this solution performs better, regarding C_{max}, the new solution is the starting point for the new testing of solutions. In contrast, Steepest Descent first tests for one job j the solutions in the neighborhood of the current solution, which are created by shifting or swapping that job to all the other machines that are eligible for that job. Furthermore, Algorithm 4 can be executed with or without tabu list ($tabu \in \{true, false\}$). If tabu list is used, the algorithms avoid testing a solution x again which has already been tested and is currently part of the tabu list. So, the tabu list contains elements x, which have been tested before. If there is no improvement in the makespan within a predefined amount of iterations, Algorithms 3 and 4 terminate. By choosing all possible combinations of $method \in \{shift, swap\}$ and $tabu \in \{true, false\}$ in Algorithm 4, we have four variants of that algorithm. By computing the two possibilities $method \in \{shift, swap\}$

in Algorithm 3, we have two further algorithms to evaluate. So, in total, with SPT, we get seven different optimization algorithms for the basic model of Section 2.

Algorithm 3: Local Search—Random Descent

---

1. Given a feasible initial solution x with makespan $C_{max}(x)$.

   Choose parameter *iterations* > 0 and set *termination* $:= iterations$.

   Choose parameter *method* $\in \{shift, swap\}$.

2. **while** *termination* $\neq 0$

   (a) Duplicate $x_n := x$.

   (b) Randomly choose a job j on stage $i = 1$. For this job $\exists! x_{ilkj} = 1$. According to $x_{ilkj} = 1$ define l and k.

   (c) Randomly choose a machine $l_n \in E_{ij}$.

   (d) **if** *method* $= shift$

        i. Shift job j to machine l_n and choose randomly a position to insert job j on this machine l_n.

   (e) **if** *method* $= swap$

        i. Choose randomly a job j_s on selected machine l_n. For this job $\exists! x_{il_nk_nj} = 1$. According to $x_{il_nk_nj} = 1$ define k_n.

        ii. Exchange positions of selected jobs j and j_s with setting $x_{ilkj} = 0$, $x_{il_nk_nj_s} = 0$, $x_{ilkj_s} = 1$, and $x_{il_njk_n} = 1$.

   (f) Save solution in x_n, execute Algorithm 2 (ECT) and compute makespan $C_{max}(x_n)$.

   (g) **if** $C_{max}(x_n) < C_{max}(x)$

        $x := x_n$, $C_{max}(x) := C_{max}(x_n)$.
        termination $:= iterations$.

        else

        termination $:= termination - 1$.

3. **return** x with $C_{max}(x)$.

Algorithm 4: Tabu and Local Search—Steepest Descent

---

1. Given a feasible initial solution x with makespan $C_{max}(x)$.

   Choose parameter *iterations* and set *termination* := *iterations*.

   Choose parameter *method* $\in \{shift, swap\}$.

   Choose parameter *tabu* $\in \{true, false\}$.

2. **if** *tabu* = *true*

   > Initialize tabu set $T := \{x\}$.
   > Choose parameter $t > 0$.

   else

   > Initialize tabu set $T := \{\}$.

3. **repeat** *termination* $\neq 0$

   (a) Duplicate $x_n := x$.

   (b) Initialize set $S := \{\}$.

   for all jobs j on stage 1.

   > For the selected job $\exists! x_{ilkj} = 1$. According to $x_{ilkj} = 1$ define l and k.
   > **for all** $l_n \in E_{ij}$
   >
   > > **if** *method* = *shift*
   > >
   > > > Shift job j to machine l_n and choose random a position to
   > > > insert job j on this machine l_n.
   > > > Save solution in x_n, execute Algorithm 2 (ECT) and compute
   > > > makespan $C_{max}(x_n)$.
   > > > **if** $x_n \notin T$
   > > > $\quad S = S \cup \{x_n\}$.
   > >
   > > **if** *method* = *swap*
   > >
   > > > **for all** j_s on the selected machine l_n
   > > > According to $x_{il_n k_n j_s} = 1$ define k_n.
   > > > Exchange positions of jobs j and j_s with $x_{ilkj} = x_{il_n k_n j_s} = 0$, $x_{ilkj_s} = x_{il_n k_n j} = 1$.
   > > > Execute Algorithm 2 (ECT).
   > > > Save solution in x_n and compute makespan $C_{max}(x_n)$.
   > > > **if** $x_n \notin T$
   > > > $\quad S = S \cup \{x_n\}$.
   > >
   > > **if** *tabu* = *true*
   > >
   > > > $T = T \cup S$.
   > > > **if** $|T| > t$
   > > >
   > > > > Delete the $|T| - t$ elements from T, which are
   > > > > added earliest.

   if $S = \{\}$

   > Set *termination* := 0.

   for all schedules $x_n \in S$.

   > **if** $C_{max}(x_n) < C_{max}(x)$
   >
   > > $x := x_n, C_{max}(x) := C_{max}(x_n)$.
   > > *termination* := *iterations*.
   >
   > **else**
   >
   > > *termination* := *termination* $- 1$.

4. **return** x with $C_{max}(x)$.

In the following, the algorithms of [30] are presented.

5. Parameter Uncertainty

All algorithms presented in the previous section are assumed to have full access to the information about the problem. However, this is rarely found in practical scenarios. Usually, information about a system includes uncertainty and some parameters like processing times underlie statistical fluctuation. Some of the parameters can be described by statistical models like distributions or stochastic processes, whereas for other parameters like machine breakdowns only very little information is available.

If uncertainty is modeled by stochastic distributions, a stochastic optimization problem can be formulated; see Van Hentenryck and Bent [31]. The complexity of solving stochastic optimization problems is higher than the complexity of solving the related deterministic models. For realistic stochastic hybrid flow shop problems, even the analysis of a single configuration cannot be evaluated analytically with exact methods. Instead, for optimization of such models, stochastic discrete event simulation has to be coupled with metaheuristic optimization methods; see Juan et al. [32]. Stochastic simulation needs a lot of computation time for function evaluation and metaheuristic optimization methods often need numerous function evaluations. Therefore, the computation of nearly optimal schedules and the evaluation with simulation in every iteration with a random initial schedule can exceed available computation time in production planning of mostly only a few minutes. In order to decrease the computation time, it is more efficient to compare different near-optimal schedules from deterministic optimization models using a detailed simulation model. Furthermore, any model approximates the real system, so that the best solution for the simulation model or deterministic model is not automatically the best schedule for the real-world system. Finding a high-quality schedule which is robust against small changes in the parameters or the description of the random variables is more important.

In production systems, a large amount of data from business information systems are often available. These data can be utilized to model uncertainty. We have to differentiate between internal parameters of the production system on the one hand, like processing times, setup times, scrap rates, and the availability of machines and external parameters, which are mainly described by the varying demand, on the other. We begin with the internal parameters that, to some extent, are under the control of the company and can be measured in the production system. This, of course, does not imply that uncertainty can be deleted from the system but it is often possible to apply standard methods from input modeling to generate a distribution that appropriately models the field data or to use the cleaned data as an empirical distribution.

The availability and quality of production data vary considerably. In Table 1, we analyzed scenarios where data are available in different levels of detail, and show how these data can be used in deterministic and stochastic models. Another issue to consider are effects of outliers. Due to their high values, it is more realistic for models to use the median instead of the mean for processing times and setup times to compute more realistic schedules by using the deterministic optimization model. In contrast, for scrap rates, it is recommended to use the mean value or some quantile to avoid underproduction. If the needed data are available, the highest category of detail of Table 1 should be used for the models. It is possible that job-related and machine-related distributions, even for machines of the same type, like in our application case, differ significantly. Differences result from detailed machine conditions even if machines are nearly identical. For example, in Figure 3, the processing times of similar jobs on different machines of one type are presented.

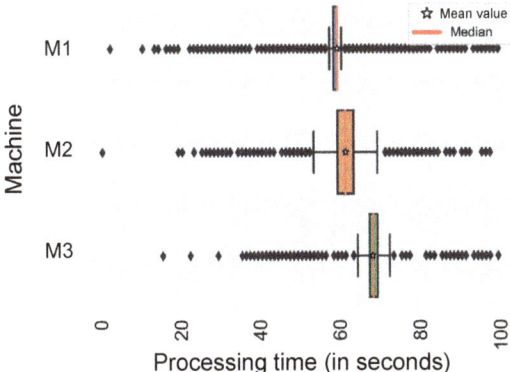

Figure 3. Boxplot for processing times for one exemplar of similar jobs *j* on different machines at stage 1 of the same machine type.

Table 1. Data concept for scheduling parameters in optimization and simulation.

Scenario	Processing Times p_{ilj} and Setup Times s_i		Scrap Rate r_{ij}	
	Optimization	Simulation	Optimization	Simulation
data on dedicated machine available	median per job and machine	random value from distribution per job and machine	mean value or value from quantile per job and machine	random value from distribution per job over all machines
no data on dedicated machines available for the job, but job data at the stage available	median per job over all machines	random value from distribution per job over all machines	mean value or value from quantile per job over all machines	random value from distribution per job over all machines
no job-related and machine-related data available, but estimates for job data are available from external sources (e.g., expert knowledge)	estimated data for the job at the stage	estimated data for the job at the stage	-	-
no job-related and machine-related data available, but data for all jobs at the stage available	median over all machines for all jobs	random value from distribution over all machines for all jobs	mean value or value from quantile over all machines for all jobs	random value from distribution over all machines for all jobs

External uncertainty, which is part of the problem in this paper, caused by varying demands, is out of the control of the producer. Future demands can be predicted based on historical data. In particular, at the first levels of a longer supply chain, uncertainty in demands grow in volatility and amount throughout the levels [27]. Figure 4 gives an example of demands over twelve weeks of one specific job and the same production date from a supplier in the automotive industry. The value in the last week in each time series shows the demand that has to be finally supplied to the customer. The other observations illustrate the development of the previously mentioned amount from the customer for the same date.

In the example of Figure 4, the demand grows in the last week considerably. Thus, if a schedule has been computed with the data of one week in advance, the production will produce less than is needed. Moreover, during the planned week itself, changes occur for high-risk jobs. Fluctuation in demands is, of course, job specific and it is not necessary or possible to model every job in detail. Hence, we first perform a cluster analysis based on historical data to distinguish between low, medium and high-risk jobs. A high-risk job changes its demand often and significantly in the weeks before and in the week of production, whereas for low-risk jobs, ordered quantities and final demand are very similar. For high-risk jobs, we use over-provisioning to avoid situations where the demand cannot be satisfied. The method is specified in the next section.

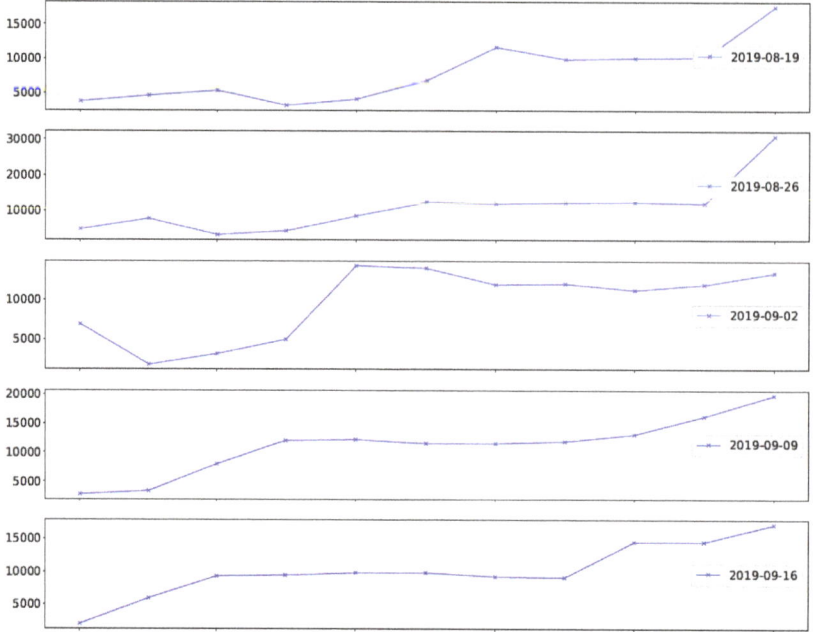

Figure 4. Time series of demands of a high-risk job.

6. Clustering and Forecasting in the Application Case

In order to allocate the appropriate production volume (*productionvolume$_{ij}$*) per job and stage and to meet the final customer demand volume, scrap and customer ordering behavior have to be considered. Therefore, the currently known demand per job and stage (*demand$_{ij}$*) as well as historical data of scrap and demand are used. The procedure of including these factors is described in the following and finally results in Equation (1).

The clustering procedure was first mentioned in Schumacher et al. [30]. For clustering demand data and identifying high-risk jobs (see Figure 4), k-means++ is applied with three parameters and the result is shown in Figure 5. For k-means++, Arthur and Vassilvitskii [33] theoretically prove and show in their results the quality of the algorithm against k-means algorithms for clustering. The three parameters for clustering are namely:

- the probability that the demand of a job grows by 500 or more parts in the last week based on historical data (*emp_prob*);
- the average increase in demand per job (only counted if the demands are increased) (*mean_pos_diff*);
- and the variance of the variation coefficient for the demands of the last three observations of the previously ordered amount. (*var_vark_last_3*).

Following the elbow method, see Leskovec et al. [34], k-means should be applied for our application case with four clusters. After analyzing the data, we computed the four clusters as shown in Figure 5 and defined the jobs of cluster 3 and 4 (marked in light red in Figure 5) as high-risk jobs. The demand for high-risk jobs is multiplied with job-related safety factors, namely $SF2_{ij}$, where $1 \geq SF2_{ij} \geq 2$. The safety factor is used to keep the slot for the higher demand in the schedule reserved. Instead of only planning with the $\frac{demand_{ij}-stock_{ij}}{(1-r_{ij})}$ for high-risk-articles, the production volume for risky jobs is extended in this first step to $\frac{demand_{ij}-stock_{ij}}{(1-r_{ij})} \cdot SF2_{ij}$, where $SF2_{ij} \geq 1$ for high-risk jobs *j*.

The demands of non high-risk jobs are multiplied with $SF2_{ij} = 1$. These considerations are also finally included in Figure 6.

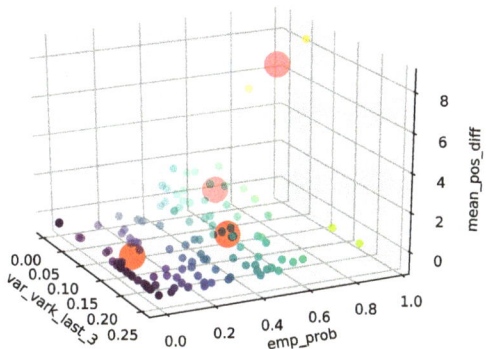

Figure 5. Clusters for identification of high-risk jobs (calculated with the method of [30]).

The same procedure of reserving slots for required higher amounts in the schedules can also be applied to other non high-risk job demands, e.g., if products are sensitive about producing less than the required demand. So, for these jobs, this method for overproduction compared to *demand$_{ij}$* can be applied. The demands can be multiplied with another safety factor, namely *SF1*. This bears the possibility to include the knowledge of experienced production planners, e.g., about sensitive demands. A production planner may decide which value to use for the safety factor. At this point, it is important to note that an earlier completion, which can be the cause of slots being reserved for too long in the schedule, is easy to handle with our algorithms presented in Section 2. Such a schedule causes, at most, only a slightly extended storage cost. In contrast, an unexpected longer slot for jobs would result in drastic delays in the schedule and elaborate rescheduling. With this method, changes in the demand and production quantities can be considered in optimization and simulation models for scheduling.

To choose the appropriate scrap rate per job and stage for our application case, different quantile values of the available empirical probability distribution per job and stage are considered. Figure 6 shows a histogram for the scrap rate of an exemplary job. For every job, we use the same quantile value. Afterwards, per job, the scrap rates r_{ij} are computed as a function of the quantile value and the probability distribution.

In practice, it is not realistic that the production volume *productionvolume$_{ij}$* is completely produced without failure. So, for every job, we have to increase the production volume to finally get the demand that is to be produced. All analyzed factors influencing the demand in the production process in our application case result in the following formula to calculate the appropriate production quantity *productionvolume$_{ij}$*:

$$productionvolume_{ij} = \frac{demand_{ij} - stock_{ij}}{(1 - r_{ij})} \cdot SF1_{ij} \cdot SF2_{ij} \tag{1}$$

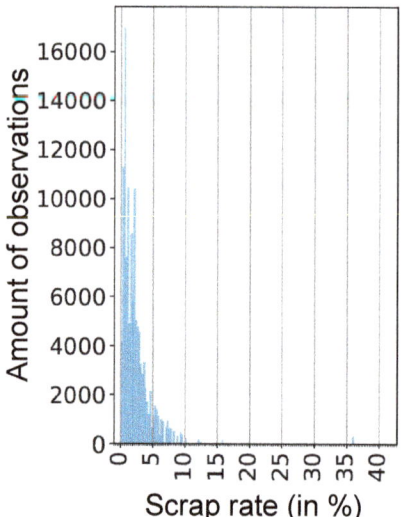

Figure 6. Scrap rate histogram for an exemplary product.

7. Scheduling under Uncertainty

Figure 7 shows the simulation architecture for our application case, which is built in Anylogic 8.5. In contrast to the deterministic optimization model, the discrete event simulation model uses random values, as mentioned in Table 1, for every produced part. Beyond that and the aspects that have already been considered in the optimization model, the following specific characteristics of production are included in the simulation model:

- In the first stage, there are two cranes and one crane needs to be used for every setup process of a machine. The first crane can only reach a defined group of machines in the first stage and the second crane can only reach the other machines. Therefore, the machines in the first stage in the model are divided into two different groups and only two machines can be set up at the same time if they do not belong to the same group, i.e., if they do not need the same crane for the setup process.
- Produced products, which are transported by conveyors to a quality check station in the first stage, can cumber each other. This can cause time losses in the production process.
- If there are not enough parts available from the first stage for producing the amount of the second stage, the production volume of the second stage has to be reduced.
- To transport the products, which were produced at the first stage, to the second stage, they are carried on small load carriers, where a certain number of produced parts fit in one small load carrier and a certain number of small load carriers fits on one trolley, which transports the products to the second stage. Both the packing and the logistics process flow between the two stages are considered.
- Detailed modeling of the connection of logistics and production between the first and second stages.
- Shift times: One of the two machines at the second stage does not produce at night and both machines at stage two do not produce on weekends.
- There are four quality checking stations, where scrap parts are identified. All stations are modeled in the simulation model with separate job-related distributions for scrap parts.

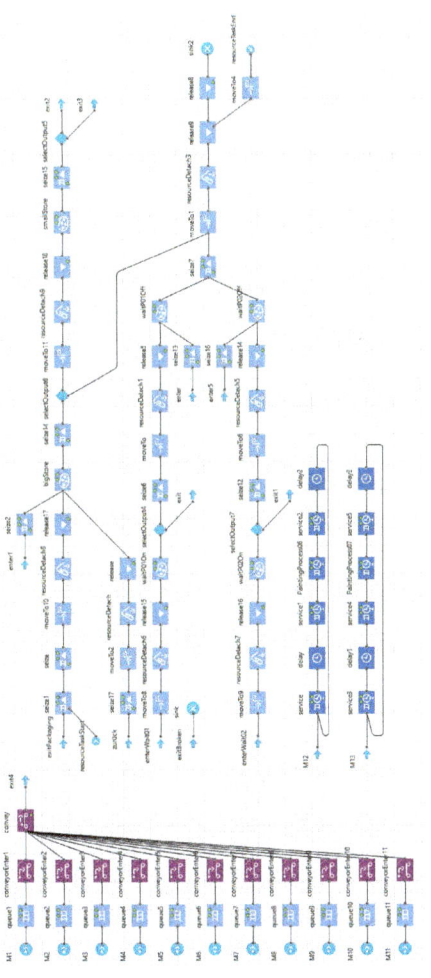

Figure 7. Structure of simulation model for the application case of the paper in AnyLogic 8.5.

Since the machine qualifications are already considered in the algorithms of Section 4, an additional validation in the simulation model is not needed.

For an almost realistic analysis of a schedule, simulation has to be used. However, a simulation run under realistic conditions is costly and should not be applied to evaluate clearly sub-optimal schedules that appear during optimization. Thus, schedules are first generated by the algorithms of Section 4 from the deterministic model and the best solutions from the deterministic model are subsequently analyzed with simulation. In a simulative analysis, several replications are performed to achieve confidence intervals of a predefined width for C_{max}. The variance of the estimator for C_{max} is also an indicator of the robustness of the schedule; a small variance indicates a predictable behavior, which is important in an industrial environment. Uncertainties resulting from scrap (see Section 5) are analyzed by counting the number of runs where the required demand is produced and the runs that fail to produce enough. The latter situation has to be avoided whenever possible in the given case study.

8. Results

To select one of the schedules created by the seven algorithms, described in Section 4, that should be applied in the application case and to select the most preferable algorithm for the application case over a defined time horizon, we derive all the algorithms with the historical demands and process data of the production. On the one hand, we evaluate the C_{max} values for the algorithms. On the other hand, we test different values for the quantile to reduce and evaluate the risk of producing less demands than the customer order (Sections 5 and 6) and simulate the calculated schedules with our simulation model, described in Section 7. For the evaluation of different security factor levels, e.g., for SF_{ij}, we refer to Schumacher et al. [30].

The specific characteristics of the evaluation data for the application case are as follows:

1. Every week, around 60 jobs are processed in the two-stage system.
2. In the first stage, there are 11 unrelated parallel machines. In the second stage, there are two identical parallel machines.
3. In both stages, stochastic distributions for p_{ilj} are available. The median at stage 1 is about 80 s per job and at stage 2 it is 4 s per job.
4. In stage 1, for setup times s_i, the stochastic distribution is available for all machines and products. The median at stage 1 is about 100 min. The median at stage 2 is about 4 min and the given data are deterministic because the second stage is a conveyor belt production stage with a constant flow rate.
5. For the scrap rate r_{ij}, job-related stochastic distributions are available for both stages.

We have applied the optimization algorithms on a computer with an Intel® Core™ i7-6920 2.9 GHz and 32 GB RAM and we have run the simulation on a Intel® Xeon™ E5-2699 v4 2.2 GHz and 64 GB RAM and an Intel® Core™ i5-4670 3.4 GHz and 16 GB RAM.

The first step for scheduling is to run the seven optimization algorithms that include deterministic processing times and setup times. Therefore, we compare the makespan resulting from the algorithms for six selected calendar weeks in the past. We run the six metaheuristics with the parameter value *iterations* = 1000 and their initial solution is given by SPT. After running the optimizations, for each week and each quantile value, each algorithm provides an objective value so that, for each algorithm, we get six data points per quantile. The analysis is illustrated in Figures 8–13.

In Schumacher et al. [30], we also analyzed the variation in objective function values caused by stochastic components in the metaheuristics for an exemplary week. Steepest Descent and tabu search algorithms provide the same objective value without variation over different runs. In contrast, the random descent algorithms provide more varying schedules. The majority of their values differ within about a quarter of a day, which means that the influence of the stochastic is relatively small in all of the developed metaheuristics of this paper.

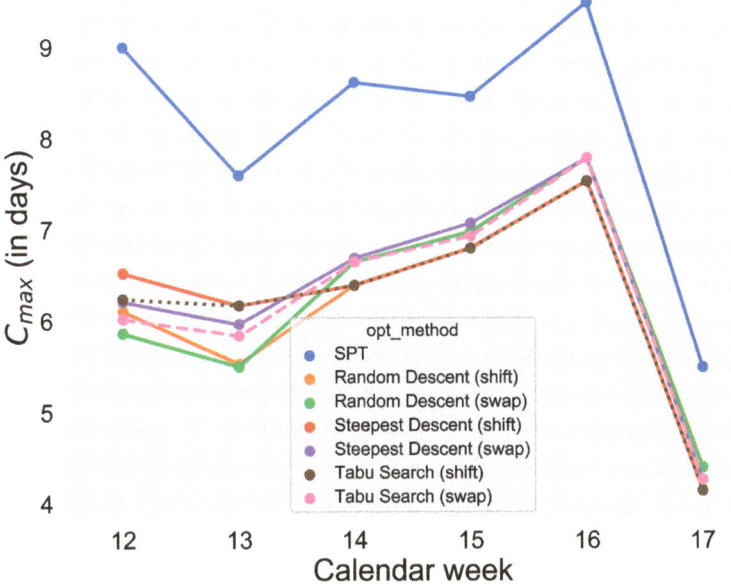

Figure 8. Optimization results for quantile 60%.

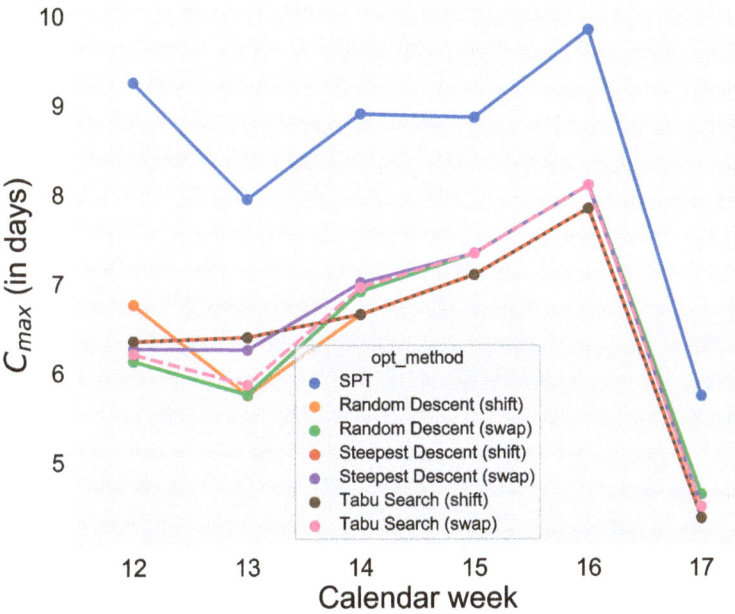

Figure 9. Optimization results for quantile 90%.

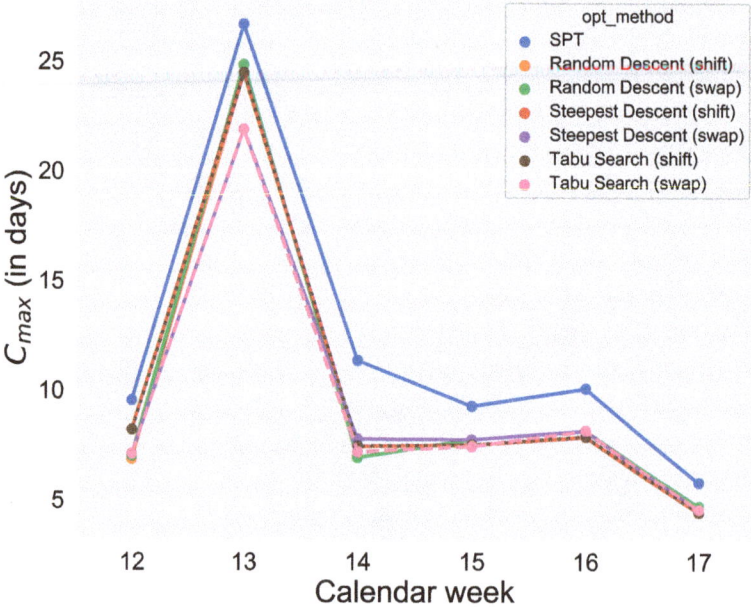

Figure 10. Optimization results for quantile 92%.

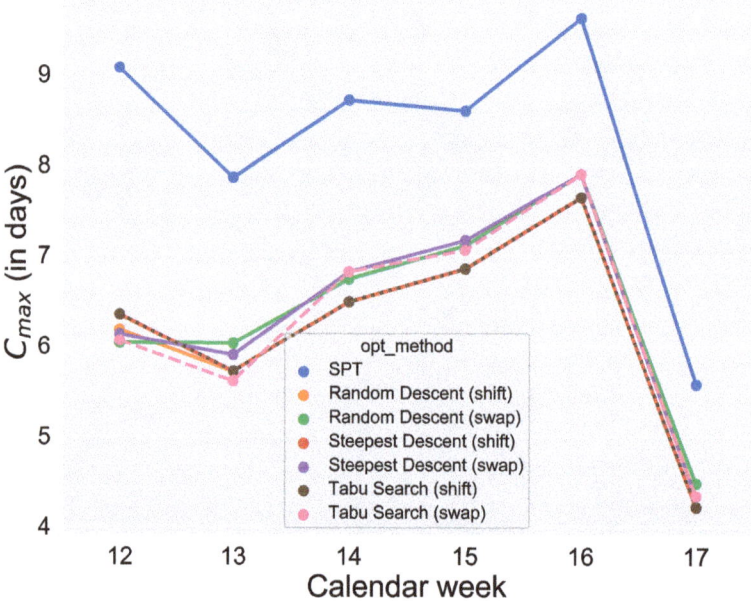

Figure 11. Optimization results for quantile 80%.

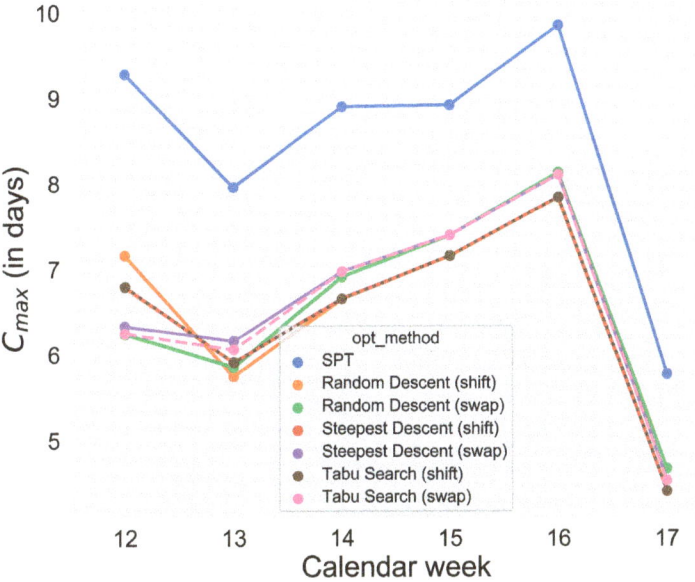

Figure 12. Optimization results for quantile 91%.

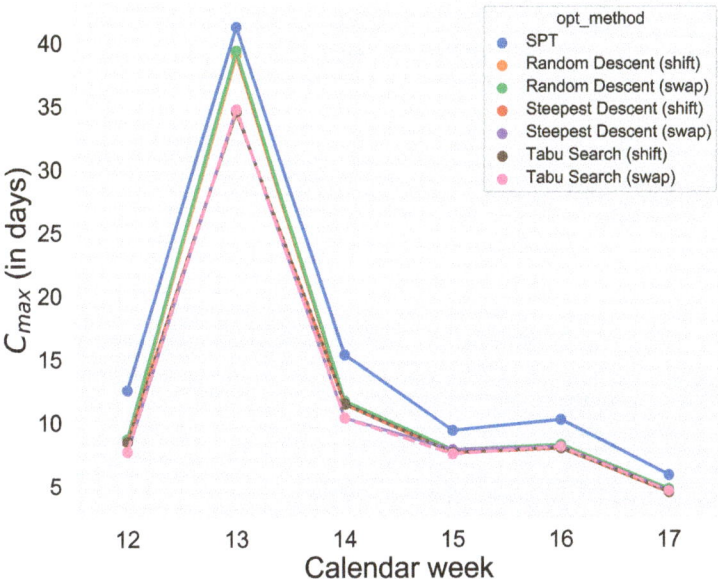

Figure 13. Optimization results for quantile 93%.

The largest computation time over all algorithms and weeks in optimization was about 4 min 45 s for a tabu search (swap) run and the minimum was less than 1 s for the calculation of SPT.

The results of C_{max} are visualized in Figures 8–13. Since the initial solution for the local search and tabu search algorithms is given by SPT, it is not surprising that, over all selected values for the quantile, the six metaheuristics provide better results than SPT. However, the difference between the C_{max} values and SPT is respectable. To show how the degree of usage for the machines increases in the production period by using metaheuristics rather than a static approach like SPT, Figure 14 compares one schedule of SPT and one schedule of a metaheuristic, namely the random descent (swap) exemplar for week 12. In contrast, the difference in makespan when comparing only the six metaheuristics for each week is minor. Hence, with this evaluation, we cannot determine which of the metaheuristics will perform best in the application case and which schedule should be applied in practice. Instead, we need simulation to see which solution of the metaheuristics is the most convenient and robust.

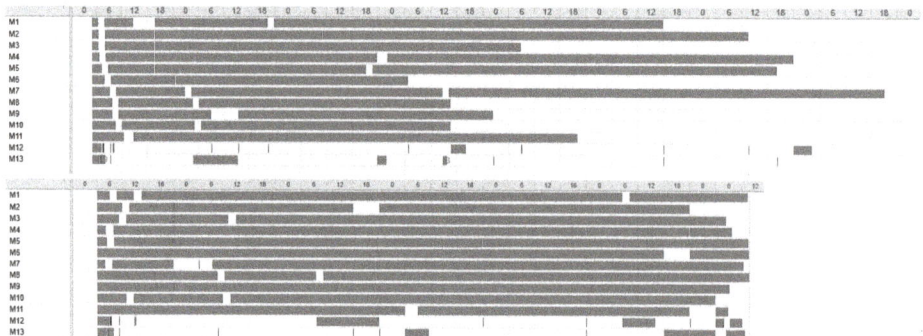

Figure 14. Comparison of schedules in MS Project for Shortest Processing Time (SPT) (**above**) and Random Descent swap (**below**) in calendar week 12 for quantile 91%.

Due to the high importance in our application case of fulfilling weekly demands as completely as possible, we also evaluate which quantile value for scrap performs best in optimization with regard to the makespan C_{max}. The results are also shown in Figures 8–13. It was found that the quantiles 60%, 80%, 90% and 91% provide similar good results for makespan. In contrast, comparing the C_{max} values of the 60%, 80%, 90% and 91% group of quantiles, and the 92% and 93% group shows large differences. The differences between 91% and 92% are also illustrated in an exemplary comparison of schedules in Figure 15. By increasing the value of the quantile by one percent in this exemplary week, the production volume *productionvolume*$_{ij}$ of one specific product increases from around 13 thousand parts to about 60 thousand parts and causes the extreme extension of the makespan shown in Figure 15. Considering the results of Figures 8–13, a production with a quantile higher than 91% seems uneconomical in this application case. To guarantee a sufficiently high degree of fulfilled orders and avoid extreme overproduction, we recommend the 91% quantile for the selected period of the application case.

Figure 15. Comparison of schedules in MS Project for quantile 91% (**above**) and quantile 92% (**below**) in calendar week 13 with tabu search swap.

For comparing the fulfillment of orders and evaluating the makespan under near-realistic conditions for the different quantile values, we use simulation. Figures 16–19 show the variation in four different key indicators of the simulation results per quantile. For each algorithm and each calendar week, we run the simulation 40 times so that, per data point, we take the average of up to 280 simulation runs. Accordingly, for every figure, 280 key indicators are extracted from the simulation per data point. Only for Figure 17 are the SPT results excluded, mainly in order to highlight the possible achievable C_{max} values.

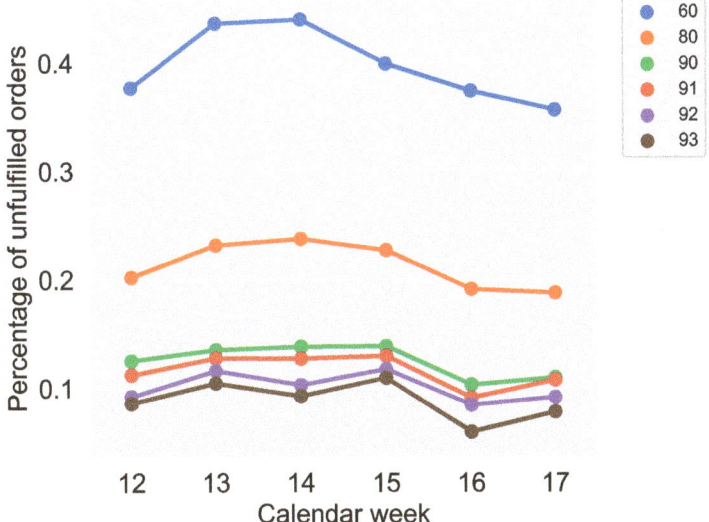

Figure 16. Average percentage of unfulfilled orders per quantile over all simulation runs.

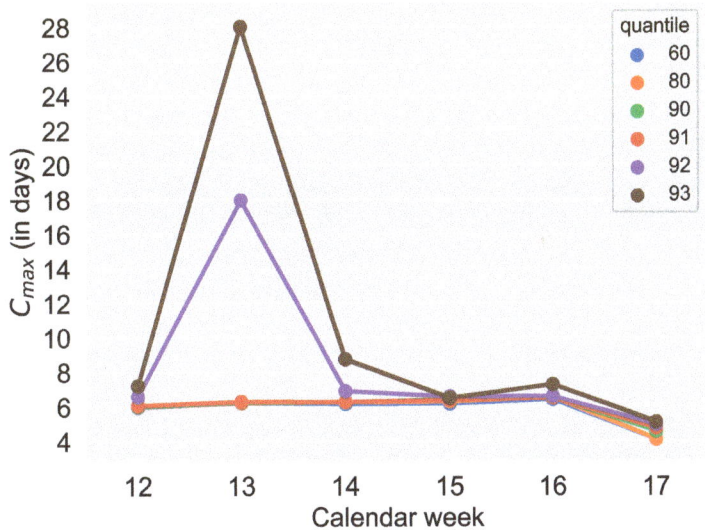

Figure 17. Average makespan of simulation runs over the six metaheuristics per quantile.

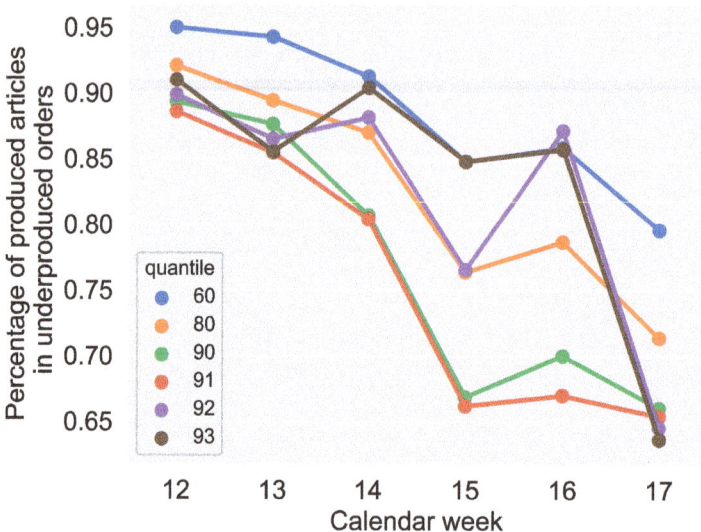

Figure 18. Average percentage of underproduction in orders producing too few items due to scrap.

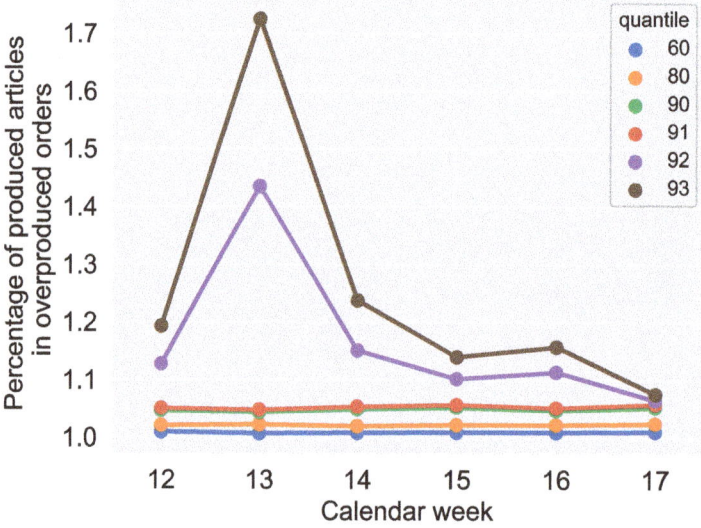

Figure 19. Average percentage of overproduction in orders producing too many items due to quantile method.

Figure 16 shows the ratio of orders that produce at least one less than the weekly demand. So, jobs are identified for that the weekly demand did not fulfil. This figure also validates our method to use scrap quantiles to avoid as many unfulfilled orders as possible. This demonstrates that the probability of unfulfilled orders decreases with increasing values for the different quantile values in the expected rates. The effects on the makespan show that the quantile value of 91% is preferable and can already be found in the optimization results of Figures 8–13 and are also validated by simulation with Figure 17.

Figures 16 and 19, when analyzed together, show that it is not realistic to reduce the probability of unfulfilled orders below 10 % without an extreme overproduction of orders. Furthermore, Figure 19 also confirms what could be expected from Figures 8–13, and Figure 17: the makespan increases, starting with the 92% quantile, because of significantly more overproduced parts in orders with overproduction.

In contrast, the results in Figure 18 do not indicate a clear correlation. For quantiles 60–91%, the rate of produced jobs decreases by increasing the quantile value, but quantiles 92% and 93% do not validate this assumption. Considering only this figure, quantiles 92% and 93% provide more preferable results. Although Figure 18 indicates that another quantile value should be chosen instead of the 91% quantile, the analyses of Figures 16, 17 and 19 confirm that the 91% quantile should be preferred for production planning in the application case. Because the most important indicators in our application case are the unfulfilled orders, in the following, we use the 91% quantile for our analysis.

To summarize the results under almost real conditions and to indicate which method returns the schedules with the best makespan and which schedule is most robust against uncertainties, e.g., in processing times or setup times, Figure 20 shows the makespans for week 12 of different schedules resulting from the seven algorithms analyzed by simulation. The box plots also indicate how the makespan varies in simulation runs of the same schedule. The borders of the boxes describe the first and third quartiles. Upper and lower limits show the minimum and maximum makespan of the simulation runs. Outliers are not included in Figure 20. For each schedule, 40 parallel replications are performed, requiring about 9 min. A good schedule should result in a small value for makespan and a small box, indicating robustness. The most robust solution in this week is provided by random descent (swap), but the average makespan is higher than the one provided by Steepest Descent (swap). Since the schedule resulting from Steepest Descent (swap) shows only small differences between the results of the different simulation runs and has a small average makespan for the production program of week 12, it should be selected for this week.

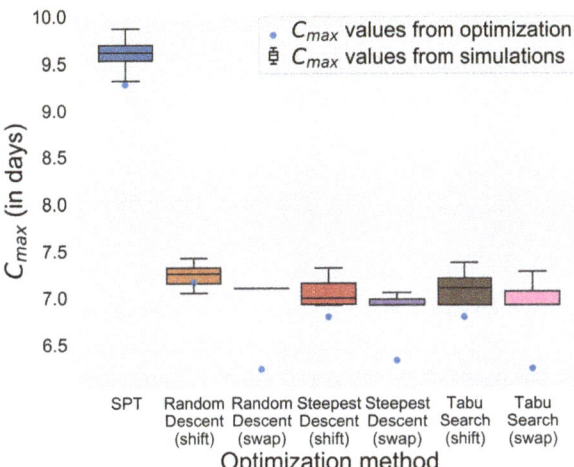

Figure 20. Comparison of simulation results per optimization method for calendar week 12 with quantile 91%.

9. Conclusions

In this paper, we solve a hybrid flow shop scheduling problem under uncertainties derived from a real industrial use case. It is shown that the combination of data analysis to estimate model parameters, heuristic and metaheuristic optimization and detailed stochastic simulation results in robust schedules that can be used in real systems. In addition, we have shown that, depending on the application, quantile analysis for scrap is an adequate method to reduce unfulfilled orders. Above a certain value of the quantile, their effect on preventing incompletely fulfilled demand positions is adversely affected by extreme overproduction and increased makespans. Thus, it is of high importance to analyze the quantiles and makespans depending on the application case.

Our approach can be developed further by using more efficient forecasting techniques to predict model parameters, by developing an upper bound for scrap rates, by additional heuristics and metaheuristics to generate schedules for the optimization model, and by combining the simulation model with additional techniques to optimize schedules. With the mentioned extensions, more efficient schedules are possible with regard to limiting overproduction, and achieving optimum production is possible. However, it is not expected that we will obtain significantly closer results to the simulation with modifications to the optimization methods because the simulation results are already very near to the results of the deterministic optimization.

Author Contributions: Conceptualization, C.S.; methodology, C.S.; software, C.S.; validation, C.S.; formal analysis, C.S.; investigation, C.S.; resources, P.B.; data curation, C.S.; writing—original draft preparation, C.S. and P.B.; writing—review and editing, C.S. and P.B.; visualization, C.S.; supervision, P.B.; project administration, C.S.; funding acquisition, P.B. All authors have read and agreed to the published version of the manuscript.

Funding: This research was funded by Deutsche Forschungsgemeinschaft (DFG, German Research Foundation), grant number 276879186/GRK2193, within the Research Training Group GRK 2193 "Adaption Intelligence of Factories in a Dynamic and Complex Environment".

Acknowledgments: Special thanks goes to the company that generously provided us with the data for the use case and, in particular, to the production planer for their excellent cooperation. We want to express our great gratitude to our (former) student assistants– Kevin Fiedler, Nico Gorecki, Dominik Mäckel, Alina Esfahani and Emily Veuhoff—for their engagement and support with the project. In addition, we wish to thank the other members of the GRK 2193 for their productive collaboration.

Conflicts of Interest: The authors declare no conflicts of interest. The funders had no role in the design of the study; in the collection, analyses, or interpretation of data; in the writing of the manuscript, or in the decision to publish the results.

Abbreviations

The following abbreviations are used in this manuscript:

SPT	Shortest Processing Time
ECT	Earliest Completion Time

References

1. Borshchev, A.; Grigoryev, I. *The Big Book of Simulation Modeling*; AnyLogic: Chicago, IL, USA, 2014.
2. Ruiz, R.; Şerifoğlu, F.S.; Urlings, T. Modeling realistic hybrid flexible flowshop scheduling problems. *Comput. Oper. Res.* **2008**, *35*, 1151–1175. [CrossRef]
3. De Siqueira, E.C.; Souza, M.; de Souza, S.R. A Multi-objective Variable Neighborhood Search algorithm for solving the Hybrid Flow Shop Problem. *Electron. Notes Discret. Math.* **2018**, *66*, 87–94. [CrossRef]
4. Graham, R.L.; Lawler, E.L.; Lenstra, J.K.; Kan, A. Optimization and approximation in deterministic sequencing and scheduling: A survey. In *Annals of Discrete Mathematics, Proceedings of the Advanced Research Institute on Discrete Optimization and Systems Applications of the Systems Science Panel of NATO and of the Discrete Optimization Symposium Co-Sponsored by IBM Canada and SIAM Banff, Aha, Vancouver, BC, Canada, 1–31 August 1977*; Hammer, P.L., Johnson, E.L., Korte, B.H., Eds.; Elsevier: Amsterdam, The Netherlands, 1979; Volume 5, pp. 287–326. [CrossRef]

5. Pinedo, M. *Scheduling: Theory, Algorithms, and Systems*, 5th ed.; Springer: Cham, Switzerland; Heidelberg, Germany; New York, NY, USA; Dordrecht, The Nertherland; London, UK, 2016. [CrossRef]

6. Ruiz, R.; Vázquez-Rodríguez, J.A. The hybrid flow shop scheduling problem. *Eur. J. Oper. Res.* **2010**, *205*, 1–18. [CrossRef]

7. Ribas, I.; Leisten, R.; Framiñan, J.M. Review and classification of hybrid flow shop scheduling problems from a production system and a solutions procedure perspective. *Comput. Oper. Res.* **2010**, *37*, 1439–1454. [CrossRef]

8. Komaki, G.M.; Sheikh, S.; Malakooti, B. Flow shop scheduling problems with assembly operations: A review and new trends. *Int. J. Prod. Res.* **2019**, *57*, 2926–2955. [CrossRef]

9. Jabbarizadeh, F.; Zandieh, M.; Talebi, D. Hybrid flexible flowshops with sequence-dependent setup times and machine availability constraints. *Comput. Ind. Eng.* **2009**, *57*, 949–957. [CrossRef]

10. Kurz, M.E.; Askin, R.G. Comparing scheduling rules for flexible flow lines. *Int. J. Prod. Econ.* **2003**, *85*, 371–388. [CrossRef]

11. Johnson, S.M. Optimal two- and three-stage production schedules with setup times included. *Nav. Res. Logist. Q.* **1954**, *1*, 61–68. [CrossRef]

12. Nawaz, M.; Enscore, E.E.; Ham, I. A heuristic algorithm for the m-machine, n-job flow-shop sequencing problem. *Omega* **1983**, *11*, 91–95. [CrossRef]

13. Low, C.; Hsu, C.J.; Su, C.T. A two-stage hybrid flowshop scheduling problem with a function constraint and unrelated alternative machines. *Comput. Oper. Res.* **2008**, *35*, 845–853. [CrossRef]

14. Naderi, B.; Ruiz, R.; Zandieh, M. Algorithms for a realistic variant of flowshop scheduling. *Comput. Oper. Res.* **2010**, *37*, 236–246. [CrossRef]

15. Burdett, R.L.; Kozan, E. Evolutionary algorithms for flow shop sequencing with non-unique jobs. *Int. Trans. Oper. Res.* **2000**, *7*, 401–418. [CrossRef]

16. Burdett, R.L.; Kozan, E. Evolutionary Algorithms For Resource Constrained Non-Serial Mixed Flow Shops. *Int. J. Comput. Intell. Appl.* **2003**, *3*, 411–435. [CrossRef]

17. Dios, M.; Fernandez-Viagas, V.; Framinan, J.M. Efficient heuristics for the hybrid flow shop scheduling problem with missing operations. *Comput. Ind. Eng.* **2018**, *115*, 88–99. [CrossRef]

18. Logendran, R.; deSzoeke, P.; Barnard, F. Sequence-dependent group scheduling problems in flexible flow shops. *Int. J. Prod. Econ.* **2006**, *102*, 66–86. [CrossRef]

19. Kaczmarczyk, W.; Sawik, T.; Schaller, A.; Tirpak, T.M. Optimal versus heuristic scheduling of surface mount technology lines. *Int. J. Prod. Res.* **2004**, *42*, 2083–2110. [CrossRef]

20. Geiger, M.J. Randomised Variable Neighbourhood Search for Multi Objective Optimisation. In Proceedings of the 4th EU/ME Workshop: Design and Evaluation of Advanced Hybrid Meta-Heuristics, Nottingham, UK, 4–5 November 2008; pp. 34–42.

21. Almeder, C.; Hartl, R.F. A Metaheuristic Optimization Approach for a Real-world Stochastic Flexible Flowshop Problem with Limited Buffer. *Int. J. Prod. Econ.* **2013**, *145*, 88–95. [CrossRef]

22. Burdett, R.L.; Kozan, E. Techniques to effectively buffer schedules in the face of uncertainties. *Comput. Ind. Eng.* **2015**, *87*, 16–29. [CrossRef]

23. Figueira, G.; Almada-Lobo, B. Hybrid simulation–optimization methods: A taxonomy and discussion. *Simul. Model. Pract. Theory* **2014**, *46*, 118–134. [CrossRef]

24. Juan, A.A.; Faulin, J.; Grasman, S.E.; Rabe, M.; Figueira, G. A review of simheuristics: Extending metaheuristics to deal with stochastic combinatorial optimization problems. *Oper. Res. Perspect.* **2015**, *2*, 62–72. [CrossRef]

25. Law, A.M. *Simulation Modeling and Analysis*, 5th ed.; Series in Industrial Engineering and Management; McGraw Hill: New York, NY, USA, 2015.

26. Murray, P.W.; Agard, B.; Barajas, M.A. Forecasting Supply Chain Demand by Clustering Customers. *IFAC-PapersOnLine* **2015**, *48*, 1834–1839. [CrossRef]

27. Lee, H.L.; Padmanabhan, V.; Whang, S. The bullwhip effect in supply chains. *Sloan Manag. Rev.* **1997**, *38*, 93–102. [CrossRef]

28. Kück, M.; Scholz-Reiter, B. A Genetic Algorithm to Optimize Lazy Learning Parameters for the Prediction of Customer Demands. In Proceedings of the 12th International Conference on Machine Learning and Applications (ICMLA), Miami, FL, USA, 4–7 December 2013; Sayed-Mouchaweh, M., Wani, M.A., Eds.; IEEE Computer Society; IEEE: Piscataway, NJ, USA, 2013; pp. 160–165. [CrossRef]

29. Scholz-Reiter, B.; Kück, M.; Lappe, D. Prediction of Customer Demands for Production Planning—Automated Seelction and Configuration of Suitable Prediction Methods. *CIRP Ann.* **2014**, *63*, 417–420. [CrossRef]

30. Schumacher, C.; Buchholz, P.; Fiedler, K.; Gorecki, N. Local Search and Tabu Search Algorithms for Machine Scheduling of a Hybrid Flow Shop Under Uncertainty. In Proceedings of the 2020 Winter Simulation Conference, Orlando, FL, USA, 13–16 December 2020.

31. Van Hentenryck, P.; Bent, R. *Online Stochastic Combinatorial Optimization*; MIT Press: Cambridge, MA, USA, 2006.

32. Juan, A.A.; Panadero, J.; Reyes-Rubiano, L.S.; Faulin, J.; de la Torre, R.; Latorre, J.I. Simulation-Based Optimization in Transportation and Logistics: Comparing Sample Average Approximation with Simheuristics. In Proceedings of the 2019 Winter Simulation Conference, WSC 2019, National Harbor, MD, USA, 8–11 December 2019; pp. 1906–1917. [CrossRef]

33. Arthur, D.; Vassilvitskii, S. *k-means++: The Advantages of Careful Seeding*; Stanford University: Stanford, CA, USA, 2007.

34. Leskovec, J.; Rajaraman, A.; Ullman, J.D. *Mining of Massive Datasets*, 2nd ed.; Cambridge University Press: Cambridge, UK, 2014. [CrossRef]

Publisher's Note: MDPI stays neutral with regard to jurisdictional claims in published maps and institutional affiliations.

Article

A Simheuristic Algorithm for Solving the Stochastic Omnichannel Vehicle Routing Problem with Pick-Up and Delivery

Leandro do C. Martins *, Christopher Bayliss, Pedro J. Copado-Méndez, Javier Panadero and Angel A. Juan

Internet Interdisciplinary Institute (IN3)–Computer Science Department, Universitat Oberta de Catalunya, 08018 Barcelona, Spain; cbayliss@uoc.edu (C.B.); pcopadom@uoc.edu (P.J.C.-M.); jpanaderom@uoc.edu (J.P.); ajuanp@uoc.edu (A.A.J.)

* Correspondence: leandrocm@uoc.edu

Received: 24 August 2020; Accepted: 15 September 2020; Published: 19 September 2020

Abstract: Advances in information and communication technologies have made possible the emergence of new shopping channels. The so-called 'omnichannel' retailing mode allows customers to shop for products online and receive them at home. This paper focuses on the omnichannel delivery concept for the retailing industry, which addresses the replenishment of a set of retail stores and the direct shipment of the products to customers within an integrated vehicle routing formulation. Due to its *NP-Hardness*, a constructive heuristic, which is extended into a biased-randomized heuristic and which is embedded into a multi-start procedure, is introduced for solving the large-sized instances of the problem. Next, the problem is enriched by considering a more realistic scenario in which travel times are modeled as random variables. For dealing with the stochastic version of the problem, a simheuristic algorithm is proposed. A series of computational experiments contribute to illustrate how our simheuristic can provide reliable and low-cost solutions under uncertain conditions.

Keywords: omnichannel retail stores; vehicle routing problem; pick-up and delivery; biased-randomized heuristics; simheuristics

1. Introduction

Today, people are changing their shopping behavior. Recent advances in information and communication technologies have introduced new shopping channels and models, which make possible the expansion of e-commerce and, consequently, the emergence of new challenges in operational research, transportation, and logistics areas. Specifically, regarding modern e-commerce business models, new decision variables and constraints have been incorporated in them, leading to emerging variants of distribution problems in supply chain management.

Unlike brick-and-mortar stores, where salespeople are available to support and help customers to make their purchases, the popularization of mobile devices with access to the Internet has promoted the use of different shopping channels. The online channel is an example that has emerged as a competitive marketing channel to that of traditional retail centers, transforming e-commerce into a global trend and an important tool for every business worldwide [1]. With e-commerce, customers are immersed in an environment of a plethora of information, opinions, and access to a vast combined supply of stock, which together allows them to browse through different stores in an online environment. According to some experts, the online shopping channels were predicted to kill off the physical ones. However, they co-exist and have completely transformed the way customers shop nowadays [2]. The use of a variety of shopping channels is referred to as 'omnichannel retailing,' where, instead of having only the single option of physically visiting a store to buy products, consumers can also buy them via online shopping to be delivered at their homes. Hence, the company also becomes responsible for delivering goods ordered online to consumers. Therefore, this new retailing environment has introduced the need to design integrated distribution systems for both serving online customers and for replenishing the stocks of retailer stores [3].

This paper focuses on the emerging omnichannel vehicle routing problem (OM-VRP) concept, which is an extension of the classical vehicle routing problem (VRP) in which a two-echelon distribution network is considered. The VRP aims to design cargo vehicle routes with minimum transportation costs, and sometimes the problem also considers facility location costs [4]. The generated routes are designed to distribute goods between depots and a set of final customers during a planning period [5]. Since the OM-VRP tackles simultaneously the replenishment of a set of retailer stores and the direct shipment of the products from those retailer stores to customers in an omnichannel retailing environment, the OM-VRP can be seen as an integrated problem that combines both the VRP and the pick-up and delivery problem (PDP). In the OM-VRP, which was first introduced by Abdulkader et al. [1], a single distribution center supplies a group of retailer stores–i.e., the first-echelon. In turn, this set of retail centers serve a set of online customers–the second-echelon–by using a single fleet of vehicles in both delivery levels in order to reduce transportation costs. Apart from reducing operating costs and improving supply chain competitiveness, the optimization of this two-echelon problem holds the potential to improve customer service levels and to enhance the on-time delivery of customer orders [6]. VRPs and PDPs are frequently considered in the literature as deterministic problems, where customers' demands and travel times are constant values. In real-life, however, it is frequent that both demands and travel times are exposed to some degree of uncertainty. In these scenarios, it is more accurate to model these constant variables as random variables. In this paper, we extend the previous OM-VRP formulation by replacing the deterministic travel times by stochastic ones. To the best of our knowledge, it is the first time that a stochastic version of the OM-VRP has been considered.

Since the VRP and the PDP are both *NP-hard* problems [7,8], the OM-VRP is, consequently, *NP-hard* as well. Therefore, we propose a multi-start procedure, which employs a savings-based [9] biased-randomization heuristic technique [10]. The multi-start approach is able to generate a variety of good and feasible solutions in short computing times. Finally, in order to deal with the stochastic OM-VRP, the multi-start approach is combined with Monte Carlo simulation and extended into a simheuristic algorithm [11]. Simulation-optimization methods, and simheuristics in particular, allow us to properly deal with stochastic versions of combinatorial optimization problems [12,13], such as the one proposed in this work, where travel times are modeled as random variables. The simheuristic approach is also employed to measure the 'reliability' level of the proposed distribution plan, i.e., to measure the probability that the plan can be deployed, without any route failure, in a realistic scenario under uncertain travel times. To the best of our knowledge, this is the first time that a stochastic version of the OM-VRP has been considered in the scientific literature.

The remainder of the paper is arranged as follows: Section 2 presents a brief literature review on related topics; Section 3 describes, in more detail, the addressed problem; Section 4 introduces the proposed solving methodologies; Section 5 presents an analysis of the results and a comparison between the proposed heuristic and another solution methodology; finally, Section 6 highlights the main conclusions of this work and proposes some future lines of research.

2. Literature Review

With recent advances in information and communication technologies, different shopping channels have emerged which have attracted the attention of customers. Nowadays, customers use different channels to shop, giving them a multichannel shopping environment [14]. The transition from multichannel to omnichannel retailing has been discussed by Verhoef et al. [15] and Hübner et al. [16]. On the one hand, in multichannel retailing, the online and offline channels are treated as separate businesses. On the other hand, the use of both channels in an omnichannel environment is completely integrated, providing consumers with a seamless experience [17]. Therefore, the customer experience is different although multichannel and omnichannel retailing environments are often considered the same. Beck and Rygl [18] presented a complete categorization and definition of retailer channels: multi, cross, and omnichannel are clearly defined. According to Hübner et al. [3], there are several operations within the omnichannel distribution system which are responsible for its excellence, such as expanding delivery modes, increasing delivery speed, and service levels.

As mentioned, the OM-VRP combines the VRP and a PDP. The classical VRP, originally proposed by Dantzig and Ramser [19], has been extensively studied by practitioners and academics due to its wide applications in several areas. The VRP belongs to a set of *NP-hard* combinatorial optimization problems (COPs) [7]. Therefore, the use of exact algorithms is efficient only for solving small-sized VRP instances. Mostly, these exact approaches are based on the combination of column and cut generation algorithms [20,21]. On the other hand, approximate algorithms, such as metaheuristics, are frequently very efficient for solving large-sized instances of COPs. Several metaheuristics have been proposed to solve the VRP, which include tabu search (TS), genetic algorithms (GA), ant colony optimization (ACO), and some hybrid methodologies [22–25]. Pick-up and delivery problems have also been studied for more than 30 years. These problems incorporate some route order dependencies in which some nodes should be visited before others in order to transfer inventory between them. Similar to the VRP, the PDP is also an *NP-hard* problem [8], and some exact methodologies, based on branch-and-cut and branch-and-cut-and-price algorithms, have been developed to optimally solve small-sized PDP instances [26,27]. Moreover, several heuristics and metaheuristics algorithms have been developed to solve the PDP and some of its variants. We highlight the use of TS [28], GA [29], large neighborhood search heuristics (LNS) [30], adaptive LNS (ALNS) [31,32], particle swarm optimization (PSO) [33], and greedy clustering methods (GCM) [34]. A literature review and classification of PDPs is presented by Berbeglia et al. [35].

To the best of our knowledge, Abdulkader et al. [1] were the first authors to address the omnichannel VRP as a combination of the VRP and the PDP in an omnichannel retailing context. For solving this novel integrated problem, the authors proposed a two-phase heuristic, based on: (i) inserting consumers into retailers routes and on correcting infeasible solutions, and (ii) on joining the routes through the maximum-savings criterion, i.e., the Clarke & Write Savings heuristic (CWS) [36]. Apart from this two-phase heuristic, a multi-ant colony algorithm (MAC) was proposed. A complete set of instances have been generated to test their methodologies, and the MAC outperformed the heuristic's performance. Martins et al. [9] proposed a simple and deterministic heuristic for solving the OM-VRP. Although no best-known solutions were found, the heuristic showed to be promising since feasible solutions were provided in short computational time and no repair operations were needed. Recently, the same problem have been also solved by Bayliss et al. [37] and Martins et al. [38]. In contrast to Bayliss et al. [37], Martins et al. [38] have framed the problem in the humanitarian logistics field, providing an agile optimization solving methodology–which combines parallel computing with biased-randomized heuristics–which was proposed for solving it in real-time. Competitive results were found in milliseconds, enabling the agile optimization technique able to outperform other heuristics from the literature. On the other hand, Bayliss et al. [37] formulated the OM-VRP as a mixed-integer program (MIP) and proposed a two-phase local search with a discrete-event heuristic for solving the problem. In contrast to Abdulkader et al. [1]'s model, their formulation avoids the need to directly assign retailers to vehicles, since the pick-up and delivery constraints are modeled through routing variables. The first phase of the approach employs a discrete-event constructive heuristic, while the second phase aims to refine the most promising solutions obtained in stage one, by applying a sequence of local search neighborhoods. The authors have found new best-known solutions for the vast majority of problem instances, and improved lower bounds for a set of small instances were obtained.

Constructive heuristics are simple deterministic procedures that follow a logical sequence of decisions and which always generate the same solution when starting from the same point. Biased-randomized algorithms incorporate non-symmetric random sampling in order to diversify the behavior of a base constructive heuristic [39]. At each stage of the base constructive heuristic, a list of candidate decisions is considered. The list is sorted in decreasing order of the benefit concerning an objective function, and a candidate is then randomly selected. In this random selection process, the higher-ranked candidates receive a higher probability of being selected. Biased-randomized algorithms have been employed for solving different COPs in transportation [40–42], scheduling [43,44], and facility location problems [39,45].

Simheuristic algorithms combine the use of approximate methods, such as heuristics or metaheuristics, with simulation techniques, in order to cope with stochastic combinatorial optimization problems. They have proven to be an efficient approach to solve stochastic problems [46]. The extension of traditional metaheuristics into simheuristics is gaining popularity, and they have already been applied to solve a wide set of stochastic optimization problems, in different fields such as permutation flow-shop [47], facility location problems [48], inventory routing problems [48–50], telecommunication networks [51] and finances [52].

Other examples of simheuristics include Lam et al. [53], Lopes et al. [54], and Santos et al. [55]. Lam et al. [53] employs a simheuristic approach for evolving agent behavior in the exploration of novel combat tactics. They use a genetic algorithm to find the states, during a flight maneuver, at which an aircraft should transit into the next phase of the maneuver. Lopes et al. [54] tackles a stochastic assembly line problem using a simheuristic approach. Demands for different product types are stochastic and occur in real-time. The optimization task lies in assigning tasks to stations in such a way that task precedence constraints are respected and the expected throughput is maximized. Santos et al. [55] develops a simheuristic based decision support tool for an iron ore crusher circuit. They propose and validate a simulation model of throughput efficiency depending on the amount of equipment active in each phase of the crusher circuit. The simheuristic integrates the simulation model with an iterated local search (ILS) metaheuristic. Their solutions improve throughput and reduce energy consumption compared to the all active equipment solution.

Despite the fact that travel times are stochastic in most real-life transportation activities, in the past only deterministic versions of the OM-VRP have been considered. Hence, our work goes one step further by considering random travel times and proposing a simheuristic algorithm to solve the stochastic version of the OM-VRP.

3. Details on the Stochastic OM-VRP

Usually, retail stores must be supplied from the depot with a large number of products, which are packed and frequently measured in terms of the number of pallets. In turn, and in contrast to retail stores' demand, online customer orders are of negligible size but require processing at a physical retail store before their delivery. Since orders must be processed at retail stores before delivery, products ordered online cannot be shipped directly from the central warehouse to online customers.

In the OM-VRP, a single fleet of vehicles is employed to simultaneously perform three different operations: (i) bulk deliveries to retail stores from a main central depot; (ii) the pick-up of online customer orders from these retail stores; and finally, (iii) the deliver of online customers' orders. Different product types are available at each retail store. Likewise, each retail store has a limited inventory of processed products that can be delivered to online customers. Therefore, the vehicle responsible for a particular online order must first visit a retail store with that product in stock. The available processed inventory and bulk demand for each retail store are known in advance. It is assumed that bulk inventory does not contribute to a retailer's available inventory since bulk deliveries cannot be processed within the drop time of delivery. As a simplifying assumption, each online customer orders a single product. When more than one item is ordered, the consumer is replicated in the same location as a 'virtual' consumer, and each product is delivered separately. According to Abdulkader et al. [1], this strategy of considering single-item orders by consumers guarantees the solution feasibility and also minimizes the distribution cost.

Figure 1 depicts how the processes of visiting retail centers and online customers are performed by the same fleet of vehicles. A route starts from the single and central depot, and the same cargo vehicle visits a set of retail centers and customers. Deliveries to customers cannot be directly performed from the depot. Hence, drivers must meet precedence constraints in order to pick-up customer orders from the retail centers before they can be delivered. Since retailers are supplied by the depot, these nodes are both delivery and pick-up points. On the other hand, customers require only the delivery of items from these retail centers, making them, delivery nodes. Apart from precedence and inventory constraints, the service of each route is limited by a maximum tour length and vehicle capacity limit.

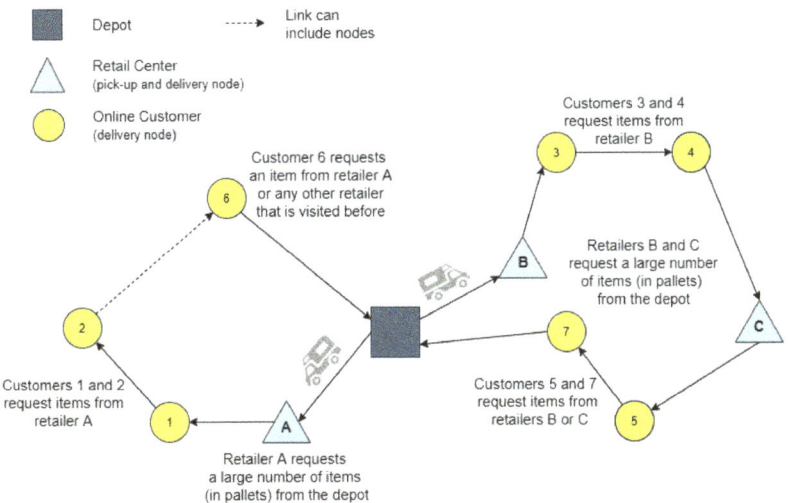

Figure 1. A general schema of the OM-VRP.

We can define the distribution network of the OM-VRP as directed graph $G = (V, A)$. The set of vertices $V = \{0, 1, 2, \ldots, r + c\}$ is composed of a single depot (0), r retail centers, and c online customers. In other words, the problem is represented by a set R of retail stores, which are supplied by the depot 0, and a set C of online customers, which are posteriorly supplied by the retail centers. The set $N = R \cup C$ comprises both sets R and C, in which $R = \{1, 2, \ldots, r\}$ and $C = \{r + 1, r + 2, \ldots, r + c\}$. The same fleet of capacitated vehicles, initially stationed at the central depot at the start time t_0, is employed for serving both the retail centers and consumers. For the complete mathematical formulation of this problem, readers are referred to Abdulkader et al. [1]. In this work, we extend previous work on this topic by considering the case in which edge-traversal times are stochastic. We define the time to traverse edge (i, j) as $T_{ij} = t_{ij} + D_{ij}$ where t_{ij} is the deterministic edge-traversal time (which represents the edge-traversal time under 'ideal' traffic conditions), D_{ij} is a log-normally distributed delay term, and T_{ij} denotes the distribution of edge-traversal times. The objective of this extended problem is to minimize the total travel cost of the vehicle routes such that: (i) every route starts and ends at the depot; (ii) the routes do not violate the maximum tour length; (iii) every node $i \in N$ is visited by only one vehicle and only once; (iv) the total load of the vehicle does not exceed the vehicle capacity; (v) the total consumer demand to be fulfilled by a vehicle for a specific product does not exceed the inventory picked up by the vehicle; (vi) the retail store determined to satisfy the consumer's demand must be visited before the consumer and by the same vehicle; and (vii) the routes must have a reliability level greater than a user-set parameter, R_{min}. The reliability level of a set of routes is defined as the probability that all routes are completed within the maximum time limit of T_{max}.

Two alternative mathematical formulations of the deterministic OM-VRP can be found in Abdulkader et al. [1], Bayliss et al. [37]. The differences in this case are a stochastic objective function and probabilistic constraint regarding route completion reliability. Let x_{fkij} be a binary decision variable indicating whether or not vehicle f in the fleet F traverses edge ij in the kth node visit in its route. The stochastic objective function is given in Equation (1), where D_{ij} is the stochastic delay associated with traversing edge ij.

$$min \; E \left(\sum_{f \in F} \sum_{k \in K} \sum_{i \in V} \sum_{j \in V} x_{fkij} \left(t_{ij} + D_{ij} \right) \right). \tag{1}$$

The probabilistic route completion reliability constraint is given in Equation (2).

$$R_{min} \leq P \left(\sum_{i \in V} \sum_{j \in N} \sum_{k \in K} \left(t_{ij} + \tau + D_{ij} \right) x_{fkij} + \sum_{i \in V} \sum_{k \in K} \left(t_{i0} + D_{i0} \right) x_{fki0} \leq T_{max}, \; \forall f \in F \right). \tag{2}$$

Equation (2) also accounts for the drop times (τ) that are required when performing deliveries and pickups. In this work we employ a simheuristic approach for addressing the stochastic aspects of the OM-VRP. The main novelty of the OM-VRP, in comparison to other VRPs, is the precedence constraints regarding the collection of customer orders from retailers and subsequent delivery to customers. The vehicle capacity constraint regarding the retailer demands that can be satisfied are expressed by Equation (3), where OP_j denotes the number of ordered product units of node j (which is zero for customer nodes) and H denotes the vehicle capacity.

$$\sum_{i \in N} \sum_{j \in V} \sum_{l=1}^{k} x_{flij} OP_j \leq H, \; \forall f \in F, \; \forall k \in K. \tag{3}$$

The customer order precedence constraints are expressed by Equation (4), where OD_{jq} denotes the number of items of type $q \in Q$ ordered by node j (which is zero for retailer nodes) and P_{jq} denotes the number of items picked up of type $q \in Q$ at node j (which is zero for customer nodes).

$$\sum_{i \in V} \sum_{j \in V} \sum_{l=1}^{k} x_{flij} \left(P_{jq} - OD_{jq} \right) \geq 0, \; \forall f \in F, \; \forall k \in K, \; \forall q \in Q. \tag{4}$$

Table 1 provides the details for a small-sized instance, which is composed of one central warehouse, four retail stores, and nine online customers. For this instance, Table 1 provides: the geographic coordinates (X and Y) of each node, the demand required from the depot by each retail center $i \in R$, the demands for each customer j for each product type q (OD_{jq}), and the inventory of each available product P_{iq}, $q \in \{1, 2, 3\}$ at the retail centers. Since the products are negligible in terms of capacity, they do not affect the vehicle load capacity. Accordingly, Figure 2 presents the optimal solution for the provided example. The routes are performed with a total cost of 455.91 distance units, and a fleet of vehicles each with a capacity of 100 weight units is employed for performing the routes. In the first route, customers 8, 5, and 9 are served by retail center 1, while customers 12 and 13 are served by retail 3. The route requires 272.37 distance units, and the vehicle starts with 93 loaded demand units. Note that the retail centers are first visited by the vehicle in order to deliver the required demand from the depot and to pick-up the products ordered by the customers. Similarly, in the second route, customers 11 and 10 are supplied by retail center 4 while customers 6 and 7 are served by retail store 2. The route requires 183.53 distance units, starting with 79 loaded demand units.

Table 1. Problem instance data.

Node	X	Y	OP_i	OD_1	OD_2	OD_3	Inventory		
							P_1	P_2	P_3
0	48	23	0	0	0	0	0	0	0
1	91	20	44	0	0	0	1	0	2
2	25	9	36	0	0	0	1	0	1
3	56	68	49	0	0	0	1	2	0
4	71	1	43	0	0	0	1	2	1
5	26	94	0	0	0	1	0	0	0
6	30	15	0	1	0	0	0	0	0
7	4	51	0	0	0	1	0	0	0
8	35	78	0	1	0	0	0	0	0
9	79	72	0	0	0	1	0	0	0
10	16	33	0	0	1	0	0	0	0
11	61	6	0	1	0	0	0	0	0
12	78	89	0	0	1	0	0	0	0
13	77	61	0	0	1	0	0	0	0

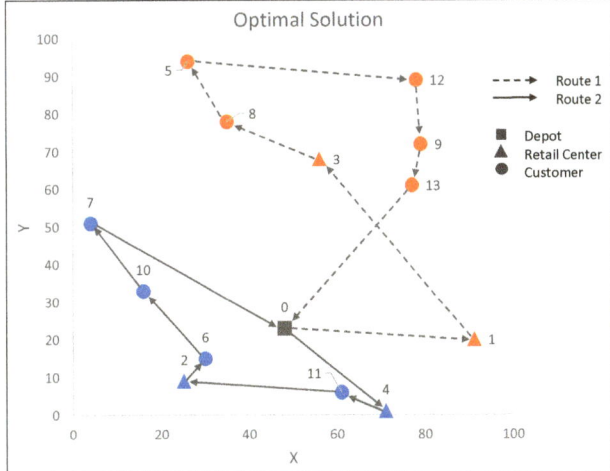

Figure 2. The optimal solution routes for Table 1.

4. Methodology

The multi-start framework belongs to a family of metaheuristics algorithms [56] which includes approaches such as Evolutionary Algorithms [57,58] and Swarm Intelligence Algorithms [59–62], among others. Metaheuristics were introduced in order to provide high-quality solutions using a reasonable amount of computation time and memory. Typically, they require a time-consuming parameter tuning process. Although, there are approaches that provide self-adaptive parameter control [58], our methodology has been devised to work with a reduced number of parameters, providing an excellent trade-off between simplicity, computational time, and solution quality.

In order to solve the stochastic OM-VRP, a simheuristic approach is proposed. Our methodology combines a biased-randomized savings-based heuristic with simulation techniques to deal with the stochastic aspects of the problem. Biased-randomized heuristics can be extended into simheuristics in a natural way. Starting from a savings-based heuristic, which is completely deterministic, this solution method is then extended into a biased-randomized multi-start algorithm. Also, a local search procedure is applied to search for locally optimal solutions. Finally, the multi-start framework is extended into a simheuristic approach in order to deal with stochastic travel times.

4.1. Savings-Based Heuristic

As introduced, the savings-based heuristic (LH) [9] is based on greedy decisions and designed to solve the deterministic OM-VRP. The LH is composed of the following three stages:

1. In the first stage, a dummy solution is created, where each route in this dummy solution serves one node $i \in N$, which can be either a consumer or a retail store. Routes depart from the depot, travel to the node, and then return to the depot.

2. The second stage of LH, named as CWS_1, is presented in the Figure 3, where the dummy routes from stage 1 are merged using a maximum-savings criterion [36]. Each box from Figure 3 is numbered to aid the following explanations.

   Initially, a savings list (SL) is constructed (step 1). This list considers all possible pairs of nodes–i.e., edges–from the problem. For each edge $\{i, j\}$, the corresponding savings value is calculated as $s_{ij} = t_{0i} + t_{j0} - t_{ij}$, where t_{ij} represents the deterministic travel time between nodes i and j. That is, candidate solutions are generated using 'ideal' traffic conditions for the edge-traversal times.

   Initially, all edges from SL are eligible. The list is sorted in descending order of the savings value (step 2), and the edge with the highest saving is selected (step 3). At this stage, the selection of edges is restricted to guarantee the assignment of a retail center to each consumer in the problem (step 5). In other words: a route containing one single customer can only be merged with a route containing a retail center, i.e., the selection is restricted to eligible edges $\{i, j\}$, where node j is a consumer in a dummy route and i is a node in a route with a retailer that can supply consumer j. According to Martins et al. [9], these attempts at only merging routes containing at least one retail center, which can supply a single consumer, are made first in order to avoid infeasible solutions–i.e., solutions in which some customers are not assigned to any retailer. This approach of addressing solution feasibility first is based on the observation that the availability of feasibility restoring merges will only decrease as the algorithm progresses.

   Based on CWS route-merging conditions (step 6), the two corresponding routes, i and j, of an edge $\{i, j\}$ (obtained in steps 4.1 and 4.2) can be merged only if: (i) nodes i and j are exterior in their respective routes (a node is exterior if it is adjacent to the depot); (ii) i and j belong to different routes; (iii) the maximum tour length is not violated; and (iv) the vehicle capacity is not violated.

   The selected edge is deleted from SL (step 9) only if: (a) the corresponding merge is performed (step 7); or (b) at least one of the CWS constraints ((i)–(iv)) are violated (in step 6). Otherwise, the edge becomes temporarily ineligible (step 10), but it is not removed from the list since subsequent merges might restore eligibility. This can occur when a different retail center is merged into a route, increasing the available processed inventory for subsequent consumers. For example, when selecting an edge (i, j), the evolving route of i may have insufficient processed inventory for customer j at this time. However, if in subsequent iterations route i is merged with another route containing retailers, the evolving route of i may then be able to serve customer j.

   When a merge is successfully performed (step 7), the entire SL becomes eligible (step 8), since a new inventory scenario is generated.

   At the end of this stage, all the consumers are supplied by the retail centers, guaranteeing a feasible final solution. Notice that this is achieved without solving separate assignment and routing problems, as done in Abdulkader et al. [1].

3. Finally, the third stage (CWS$_2$) tries to improve the solution generated in the previous step. To do that, the algorithm cycles through the SL list, which includes the remaining saving edges that were discarded in the previous step, with the aim of identifying more beneficial merges. Unlike the procedure used in the CWS$_1$ stage, in this phase all the customers are already assigned to a retail center, so step 5 of Figure 3 is not required. Hence, all edges are eligible. The process attempts all the available merging possibilities which may improve the solution. Each time a new edge is selected from the SL list, it is removed from the list, whether the corresponding merge is performed or not–due to it violating any of the constraints (i)–(iv). In each new iteration, the highest saving edge is selected to restart the merge process. This process is repeated until *SL* is empty. At the end of the procedure, a feasible solution is generated, without the necessity of repair operations.

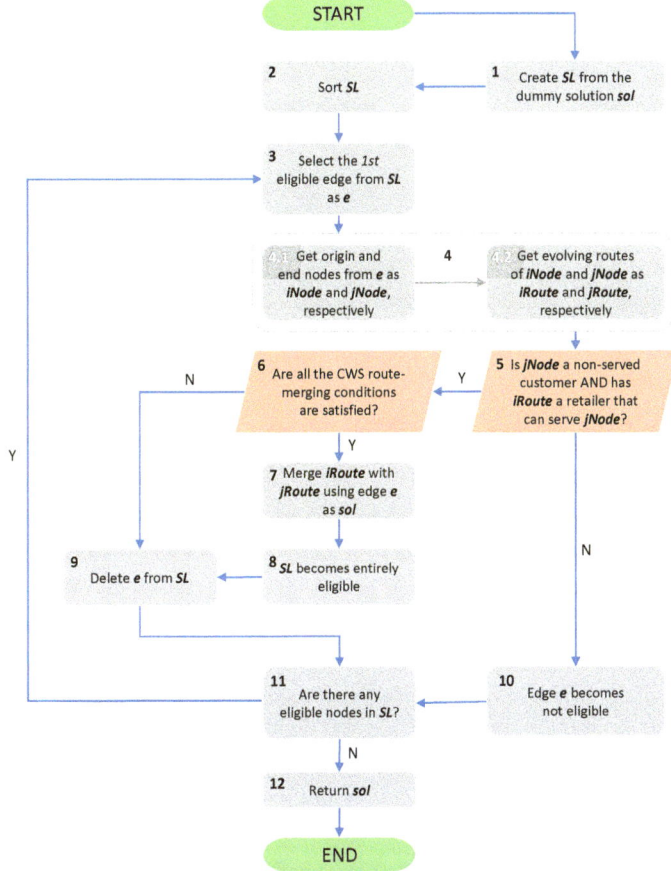

Figure 3. The flowchart of CWS$_1$.

4.2. Introducing a Local Search

Once an initial and feasible solution is constructed, a fast local search is applied to improve its quality. This local search mechanism is based on a *2-opt* movement. Since this problem has some precedence particularities, the *2-opt* movement, which consists of the reversal of sub-sequence of nodes, is restricted to movements that do not violate the precedence order between customers and their suppliers–hence, the feasibility of the solution is preserved.

4.3. Extending to a Biased-Randomized Algorithm

To modify the original greedy and deterministic behavior of our heuristic, the selection of candidates from the *SL* is randomized by introducing a skewed probability distribution into the selection process. For the biased-randomized component, we employ a geometric distribution, which is controlled by a single parameter, $\beta \in (0, 1)$. β values closer to 1 increase the probability that the highest saving merges are selected. On the contrary, as β approaches 0, a near-uniform randomization is obtained. In this way, β controls the level at which the selection probabilities decrease along the sorted *SL*. Hence, unlike deterministic heuristics, which always generate the same solution when starting from the same initial solution, different decisions are taken at each selection iteration, consequently generating different solutions. Algorithm 1 represents the selection process of LH with biased-randomization, which replaces the greedy selection of edges from the SL.

Algorithm 1: brSelection.

Data: savings list *SL*, parameter $\beta \in [0, 1]$
1 $l \leftarrow$ getNumberOfEligibleEdgesFromList (*SL*);
2 Randomly select position $x \in \{1, ..., l\}$ according to distribution Geom (β);
3 $e \leftarrow$ selectTheXthEligibleEdgeFromList (x, *SL*);
4 **return** e;

Considering all of the stages which have been introduced, Algorithm 2 represents the overall structure of our biased-randomized algorithm with local search (BRLH). This algorithm is then embedded into a multi-start procedure in order to obtain a variety of solutions (MS$_{\text{BRLH}}$).

Algorithm 2: BRLH.

Data: set of nodes *V*, geometric distribution parameter β
1 $sol \leftarrow$ createDummySolution (*V*);
2 $sol \leftarrow$ CWS$_1$ (*sol*, β);
3 $sol \leftarrow$ CWS$_2$ (*sol*, β);
4 $sol \leftarrow$ localSearch (*sol*);
5 **return** *sol*

4.4. Extending to a Simheuristic Approach

Deterministic travel times are widely assumed in transportation problems. However, when dealing with real-life problems, which are often fraught with uncertainty, travel times are usually stochastic in nature. As introduced in Section 3, the deterministic travel time employed to traverse edge (i, j), t_{ij}, can be seen as the travel time required under ideal traffic conditions. In the proposed extension, the stochastic time to traverse (i, j) is computed as $T_{ij} = t_{ij} + D_{ij}$, where D_{ij} follows a *logNormal*(μ, σ) probability distribution, and represents a random delay resulting from uncertain conditions. Since the *logNormal* probability distribution can only take positive values, it follows that $T_{ij} > t_{ij}, \forall (i, j)$ in the set of connecting edges.

Algorithm 3 describes our simheuristic approach (Sim$_{\text{BRLH}}$). Initially, a solution is generated by our BRLH in line 1 (Algorithm 2), by employing the greedy approach (i.e., $\beta \approx 1$). A short simulation is then performed on this initial solution (line 2), in order to estimate its average stochastic cost. This initial solution is set as the best-found stochastic solution cost (line 4). While the termination criterion is not met (line 6), different solutions are generated by BRLH (line 7). The deterministic cost of the initial solution is considered for guiding the search. Therefore, a solution is accepted for being submitted to the simulation module (line 10) only if its deterministic cost is smaller than the best-found deterministic solution cost plus $m\%$ of its value (line 9). This solution filtering approach reduces the amount of time spent on testing unpromising solutions in computationally expensive simulations. Moreover, by allowing the acceptance of moderately worse solutions, controlled by the parameter m, a better exploration of the solution space can be achieved [63]. At this stage, q_{short} Monte Carlo simulation runs are used to test the accepted solution. Each simulation run replaces the deterministic travel times of a solution with randomly sampled ones–according to the assumed probability distribution. From this complete simulation process, the average stochastic cost of each solution is computed. Every time a new best stochastic cost is found (line 15), this solution is introduced into a pool of 'elite' solutions E (line 17). This process is repeated while the termination criterion is not met. On this reduced set of solutions, q_{long} Monte Carlo simulation runs are performed (line 23) in order to generate more accurate results for solutions in stochastic environments. During the simulation process we also obtain an estimate of the reliability rate of a solution [64]. This estimate is computed as the rate at which all routes show completion times lower than the maximum allowed travel time. At the end, the set of elite solutions is sorted in descending order of their expected cost (line 25), and the best-found stochastic solution is provided to the manager.

Algorithm 3: Sim_{BRLH}.

Data: set of nodes V, geometric distribution parameter β, acceptance margin m, number of short simulations q_{short}, number of long simulations q_{long}, log normal distribution parameters μ and σ, maximum number of iterations max_{iter}

1 $baseSol \leftarrow \text{BRLH}\,(V, 1.0)$;

2 simulation $(baseSol, q_{short}, \mu, \sigma)$;

3 $bestCost_d \leftarrow baseSol.getDeterministicCost()$;

4 $bestCost_s \leftarrow baseSol.getStochasticCost()$;

5 $n_{iter} \leftarrow 0$;

6 **while** $n_{iter} < max_{iter}$ **do**

7     $sol \leftarrow \text{BRLH}\,(V, \beta)$;

8     $cost_d \leftarrow sol.getDeterministicCost()$;

9   **if** $cost_d < bestCost_d + bestCost_d \times m$ **then**

10   simulation $(sol, q_{short}, \mu, \sigma)$;

11       $cost_s \leftarrow sol.getStochasticCost()$;

12   **if** $cost_d < bestCost_d$ **then**

13          $bestCost_d \leftarrow cost_d$;

14   **end**

15   **if** $cost_s < bestCost_s$ **then**

16          $bestCost_s \leftarrow cost_s$;

17          $E \leftarrow E \cup \{sol\}$;

18   **end**

19   **end**

20    $n_{iter} \leftarrow n_{iter} + 1$;

21 **end**

22 **foreach** $sol \in E$ **do**

23   simulation $(sol, q_{long}, \mu, \sigma)$;

24 **end**

25 $E \leftarrow \text{sort}\,(E)$;

26 $bestStochSol \leftarrow E.get(0)$;

27 **return** $bestStochSol$

---

5. Results and Discussion

To test the proposed methodologies, we have used the 60 problem instances introduced in Abdulkader et al. [1]. These instances differ in the number of retail centers ($r \in \{10, 15, 20, 25\}$), online customers ($c \in \{20, 50, 75, 100, 150\}$), and also in the inventory scenarios of the retail centers (tight, relaxed, and abundant). Therefore, for each inventory scenario, 20 different problem combinations are generated. The maximum tour length of the routes and the vehicle capacity are set to 8 h and 100 weight units, respectively. While the BRLH is guided by a single parameter, β, the simheuristic approach is also controlled by the maximum running time $time_{max}$, the acceptance margin of worst solutions m, and the number, q_{short} and q_{long}, of simulation repeats in short and long simulation runs, respectively. The stochastic travel times for each edge are set by the log-normal distribution parameters, μ and σ.

Table 2 summarizes the setup of the parameters employed during the computational experiments. For calibrating these parameters, we have used the methodology proposed in Calvet et al. [65], which is based on a general and automated statistical learning procedure. Regarding the maximum run time $time_{max}$, the value was set depending on the size of the instance $(c + r) \times 0.342$, which leads to a maximum execution time of 60 s in the case of the largest instance. This stopping criterion is employed in both the multi-start and simheuristic strategies.

The algorithms were coded in Java and all tests were performed on an Intel Core i7-8550U processor with 16 GB of RAM.

Table 2. Parameter setup.

β	m	μ	σ	q_{short}	q_{long}	$time_{max}$
$[0.45, 0.75]$	20%	0	$\{1.55, 1.9, 2.5\}$	100	1000	$(r + c) \times 0.342$

Note that three different values have been considered for the σ parameter, which is used to modify the deterministic travel times. Since the maximum tour length is fixed independently of the size of the instances, small-sized instances are more likely to generate short routes. Therefore, a larger value for σ introduces more variability in the travel times, which increases route failure rates. On the other hand, large-sized instances are often composed of larger routes, then a small value for σ is introduced. In particular we have, $\sigma = 2.5$ for small instances (composed of 25 customers), $\sigma = 1.55$ for large instances (composed of 150 customers), and $\sigma = 1.9$ for the remaining medium-sized ones. This approach ensures that small, medium, and large instances each have similar levels of difficulty with respect to the risk of route failure.

The initial analysis aims to compare the solutions generated by our greedy heuristic (LH) and by our MS$_{BRLH}$–in which β is (uniformly) randomly selected in the interval $[0.45, 0.75]$–with the solutions obtained by the two-phase heuristic (AH) and multi-ant colony metaheuristic (MAC) proposed by Abdulkader et al. [1]. Their methodologies were performed on four 2.1 GHz processors with 16-cores each and a total of 256 GB RAM. That is, we initially focus on comparing each algorithm in terms of deterministic travel cost. Tables 3–5 present the results obtained for tight, relaxed, and abundant inventory scenarios, respectively. For each problem instance (I), we present results for: the cost of the best-found solution obtained by the different methodologies; the average cost of our MS$_{BRLH}$; the CPU time (in seconds) required by each methodology; and their percentage gaps. The best results returned by the solution methodologies are highlighted in bold. Figures 4 and 5 present how both the gap and the cost of the solutions, i.e., the objective function (OF) value, behave according to the employed solution approach and inventory scenario, respectively.

Table 3. Comparison of the results obtained by our methodologies (LH and MS$_{\mathrm{BRLH}}$) with those obtained by Abdulkader et al. [1]'s methods (AH and MAC) in the tight inventory scenario.

I	|*R*|	|*C*|	*1*	*2*	*3*	*4*	*Avg. Cost*	*Time (sec.)*				*Gap*		
			LH	MS$_{\mathrm{BRLH}}$	AH	MAC	*(2)*	*(1)*	*(2)*	*(3)*	*(4)*	*(1)–(2)*	*(3)–(2)*	*(4)–(2)*
b1	10	25	1277.5	1110.9	1631.6	**1002.5**	1119.6	0	7	0	7	−13%	−32%	11%
b2	10	50	1641.1	1378.2	2057.5	**1192.0**	1392.0	0	8	0	47	−16%	−33%	16%
b3	10	75	2663.7	2437.2	3006.2	**1815.4**	2450.7	0	25	0	79	−9%	−19%	34%
b4	10	100	2415.1	1930.3	2830.2	**1529.0**	1980.7	0	15	0	286	−20%	−32%	26%
b5	10	150	2678.2	2395.3	3478.7	**1905.2**	2408.9	0	38	0	576	−11%	−31%	26%
b6	15	25	1540.5	1389.4	1774.4	**1313.7**	1400.6	0	4	0	7	−10%	−22%	6%
b7	15	50	2059.0	1769.3	2461.8	**1522.3**	1803.7	0	0	0	44	−14%	−28%	16%
b8	15	75	3105.3	2620.5	3545.1	**2101.8**	2630.3	0	6	0	131	−16%	−26%	25%
b9	15	100	3121.5	2836.9	3529.0	**2329.5**	2860.5	0	1	0	209	−9%	−20%	22%
b10	15	150	4292.4	3787.2	4916.8	**3012.2**	3797.4	0	45	0	430	−12%	−23%	26%
b11	20	25	2035.2	1817.1	2432.6	**1611.3**	1838.4	0	10	0	11	−11%	−25%	13%
b12	20	50	2335.4	2109.1	2695.3	**1800.9**	2112.8	0	1	0	50	−10%	−22%	17%
b13	20	75	3212.7	2765.1	3936.7	**2406.0**	2796.2	0	12	0	127	−14%	−30%	15%
b14	20	100	3025.2	2842.7	3826.1	**2483.8**	2881.4	0	20	0	327	−6%	−26%	14%
b15	20	150	3934.3	3308.0	4496.1	**2679.2**	3332.1	0	50	0	708	−16%	−26%	23%
b16	25	25	2019.4	1847.2	2254.9	**1669.6**	1858.0	0	8	0	13	−9%	−18%	11%
b17	25	50	2665.9	2434.8	3020.8	**1965.6**	2442.8	0	17	0	46	−9%	−19%	24%
b18	25	75	3207.6	2853.4	3963.5	**2449.8**	2885.8	0	18	0	136	−11%	−28%	16%
b19	25	100	4064.0	3551.0	4933.9	**2788.5**	3588.7	0	42	0	257	−13%	−28%	27%
b20	25	150	3782.7	3512.8	4721.3	**2890.3**	3525.5	0	17	0	712	−7%	−26%	22%
Average								**0**	**17**	**0**	**210**	**−12%**	**−26%**	**19%**

Table 4. Comparison of the results obtained by our methodologies (LH and MS$_{\mathrm{BRLH}}$) with those obtained by Abdulkader et al. [1]'s methods (AH and MAC) in the relaxed inventory scenario.

I	|*R*|	|*C*|	*1*	*2*	*3*	*4*	*Avg. Cost*	*Time (sec.)*				*Gap*		
			LH	MS$_{\mathrm{BRLH}}$	AH	MAC	*(2)*	*(1)*	*(2)*	*(3)*	*(4)*	*(1)–(2)*	*(3)–(2)*	*(4)–(2)*
b21	10	25	1233.0	1030.0	1571.6	**879.2**	1048.9	0	5	0	10	−16%	−34%	17%
b22	10	50	1490.8	1275.7	1920.6	**1083.7**	1293.9	0	4	0	85	−14%	−34%	18%
b23	10	75	2468.0	2021.9	2699.2	**1591.5**	2049.5	0	18	0	167	−18%	−25%	27%
b24	10	100	1885.0	1632.2	2305.1	**1437.7**	1645.3	0	7	0	528	−13%	−29%	14%
b25	10	150	1998.6	1980.4	2700.4	**1520.5**	1981.8	0	39	0	1836	−1%	−27%	30%
b26	15	25	1591.4	1268.0	1665.2	**1180.8**	1308.9	0	4	0	11	−20%	−24%	7%
b27	15	50	1940.7	1652.1	2320.7	**1329.3**	1660.9	0	9	0	73	−15%	−29%	24%
b28	15	75	2436.3	2101.7	3016.5	**1692.4**	2160.4	0	3	0	279	−14%	−30%	24%
b29	15	100	2648.3	2395.4	3302.4	**2016.4**	2412.5	0	25	0	567	−10%	−27%	19%
b30	15	150	3373.2	2819.0	3919.0	**2399.6**	2847.6	0	18	0	1407	−16%	−28%	17%
b31	20	25	1835.5	1679.1	1993.6	**1495.8**	1682.7	0	11	0	16	−9%	−16%	12%
b32	20	50	2320.5	1960.7	2713.0	**1656.9**	1965.7	0	6	0	76	−16%	−28%	18%
b33	20	75	2404.6	2267.2	3393.3	**1799.6**	2269.8	0	28	0	262	−6%	−33%	26%
b34	20	100	2751.9	2469.3	3127.5	**2018.5**	2490.6	0	34	0	740	−10%	−21%	22%
b35	20	150	3157.4	2818.0	3742.2	**2291.0**	2824.5	0	32	0	2141	−11%	−25%	23%
b36	25	25	1844.0	1683.7	2032.1	**1550.0**	1700.9	0	13	0	15	−9%	−17%	9%
b37	25	50	2663.9	2322.3	3130.5	**1939.5**	2357.5	0	22	0	73	−13%	−26%	20%
b38	25	75	2790.7	2559.7	3433.2	**2088.6**	2569.7	0	30	0	283	−8%	−25%	23%
b39	25	100	3352.9	3038.1	3824.5	**2244.1**	3053.6	0	27	0	656	−9%	−21%	35%
b40	25	150	2971.1	2830.6	3447.9	**2229.4**	2837.7	0	37	0	2077	−5%	−18%	27%
Average								**0**	**19**	**0**	**565**	**−12%**	**−26%**	**21%**

Table 5. Comparison of the results obtained by our methodologies (LH and MS$_{BRLH}$) with those obtained by Abdulkader et al. [1]'s methods (AH and MAC) in the abundant inventory scenario.

I	$|R|$	$|C|$	1 LH	2 MS$_{BRLH}$	3 AH	4 MAC	Avg. Cost (2)	Time (sec.) (1)	(2)	(3)	(4)	Gap (1)–(2)	(3)–(2)	(4)–(2)
b41	10	25	805.4	760.5	897.6	**711.3**	760.5	0	1	0	16	−6%	−15%	7%
b42	10	50	1014.2	**870.4**	1287.8	875.2	871.2	0	8	0	143	−14%	−32%	−1%
b43	10	75	1463.5	1259.6	1531.1	**1132.1**	1266.4	0	9	0	358	−14%	−18%	11%
b44	10	100	1379.4	1284.9	1636.5	**1224.1**	1294.1	0	30	0	978	−7%	−21%	5%
b45	10	150	1499.3	1364.3	1551.8	**1273.9**	1385.3	0	43	0	2085	−9%	−12%	7%
b46	15	25	1137.5	1024.3	1264.3	**996.9**	1028.8	0	6	0	22	−10%	−19%	3%
b47	15	50	1247.6	1135.1	1488.1	**1080.3**	1141.0	0	17	0	159	−9%	−24%	5%
b48	15	75	1595.3	1355.2	1815.2	**1252.4**	1361.2	0	17	0	559	−15%	−25%	8%
b49	15	100	2021.3	1777.8	2242.4	**1594.0**	1798.9	0	24	0	1167	−12%	−21%	12%
b50	15	150	2059.6	1869.2	2459.5	**1691.4**	1873.6	0	26	0	4126	−9%	−24%	11%
b51	20	25	1507.2	1414.7	1660.9	**1302.9**	1418.2	0	11	0	33	−6%	−15%	9%
b52	20	50	1464.7	1366.8	1740.7	**1301.0**	1368.4	0	7	0	156	−7%	−21%	5%
b53	20	75	1797.7	1591.5	2096.8	**1421.8**	1599.7	0	18	0	605	−11%	−24%	12%
b54	20	100	2066.2	1881.8	2226.4	**1640.6**	1883.9	0	23	0	1370	−9%	−15%	15%
b55	20	150	2214.0	2025.1	2518.2	**1763.3**	2030.0	0	52	0	5321	−9%	−20%	15%
b56	25	25	1423.2	1368.1	1550.7	**1311.6**	1372.3	0	7	0	36	−4%	−12%	4%
b57	25	50	1670.8	1559.7	1835.4	**1468.1**	1570.2	0	11	0	203	−7%	−15%	6%
b58	25	75	2047.5	1845.3	2276.9	**1654.9**	1847.5	0	7	0	791	−10%	−19%	12%
b59	25	100	1856.4	1797.8	2061.9	**1575.7**	1801.0	0	15	0	1262	−3%	−13%	14%
b60	25	150	1968.1	1837.3	2347.8	**1653.3**	1849.1	0	60	0	4549	−7%	−22%	11%
Average								0	19	0	1197	**−9%**	**−19%**	**9%**

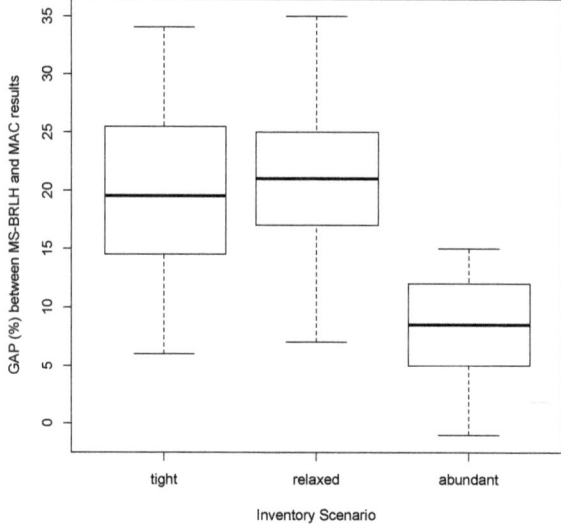

Figure 4. Gap between our best-found solutions (from MS$_{BRLH}$) and the MAC's results, for each inventory scenario.

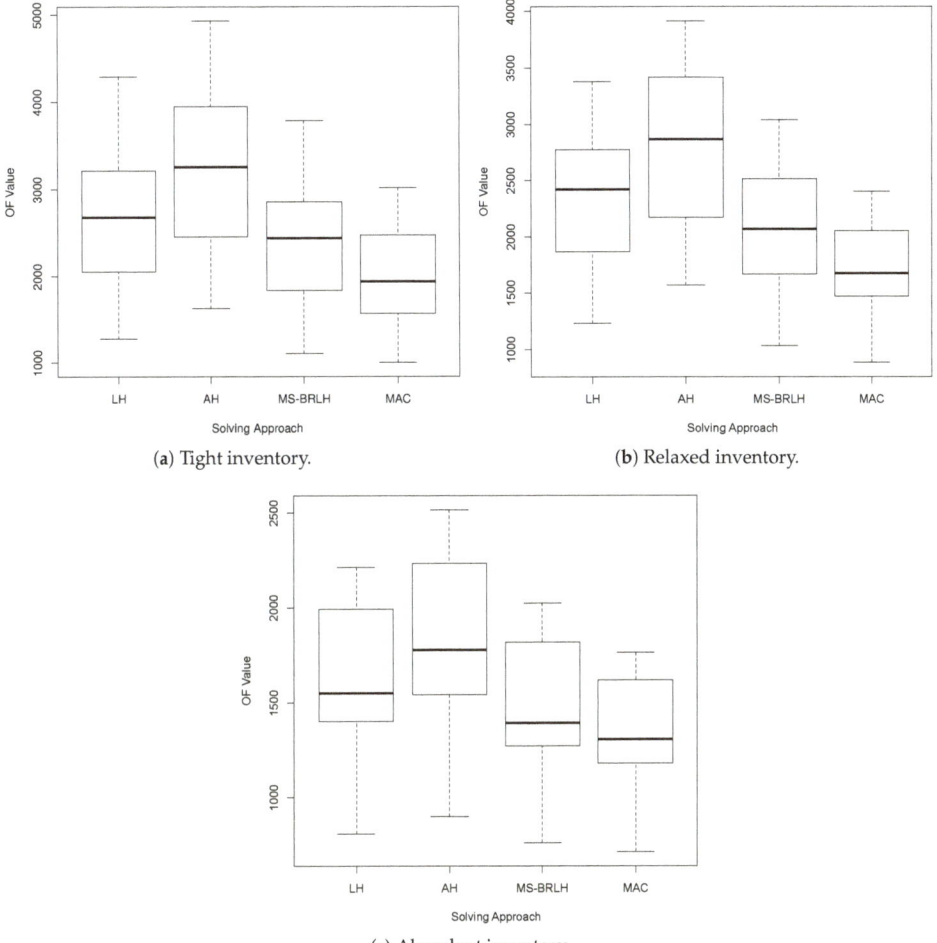

(a) Tight inventory.

(b) Relaxed inventory.

(c) Abundant inventory.

Figure 5. Comparison of the solutions cost (OF value) from each solving approach, for each inventory scenario.

By analyzing Tables 3–5, we can observe that our MS_{BRLH} algorithm is able to improve previous results (from LH) by 9–12%, on average (column *gap (2)–(1)*). When comparing the MS_{BRLH} with the AH heuristic (column *gap (3)–(2)*), our approach is able to reduce solution costs by up to 26% in short computational times (about 18 s on average). On the other hand, when comparing our results with those generated by the MAC approach (column *gap (4)–(2)*), our solutions are between 9% and 21% worse, on average. Particularly, in the abundant inventory scenario, MS_{BRLH}'s results are only 9% worse than MAC. Notice, however, that the processing time required by MAC is substantially larger in all inventory scenarios. By analyzing Figure 4, it is evident that MS_{BRLH} performs better in the abundant inventory scenario, being able to find one better solution and several others with a maximum gap of 8%. Moreover, we can observe a variability of around 10% in the gap between MS_{BRLH} and MAC on average. This variability is reduced to around 8% for the relaxed and abundant scenarios. These results demonstrate the robustness of our solution approach for the deterministic case. When analyzing Figure 5, which presents the overall performance of each solution approach for each inventory scenario, we can observe that our multi-start strategy is more efficient than both LH and AH heuristics, by generating solutions with a lower cost. To complement these box-plots, an ANOVA test was run for each inventory scenario. The *p*-values associated with the tight, relaxed, and abundant inventory scenarios were, respectively, of 0.001, 0.000, and 0.000. Also, the Fisher's LSD test suggests significant differences in all tree scenarios between MAC and AH, between MS-BRLH and AH, as well as between MAC and LH. However, cost differences between MAC and MS-BRLH were not significant in any scenario, despite the fact that MAC employed a noticeably higher amount of computing time than MS-BRLH.

Next, in Figure 6, we present the convergence of three problem instances' solutions, including one from each different inventory scenario (instances *b6*, *b26*, and *b46*), by comparing the MS$_{BRLH}$ with the best-known solutions, in terms of gap. As introduced, these instances require approximately 15 s of processing time, given their magnitude.

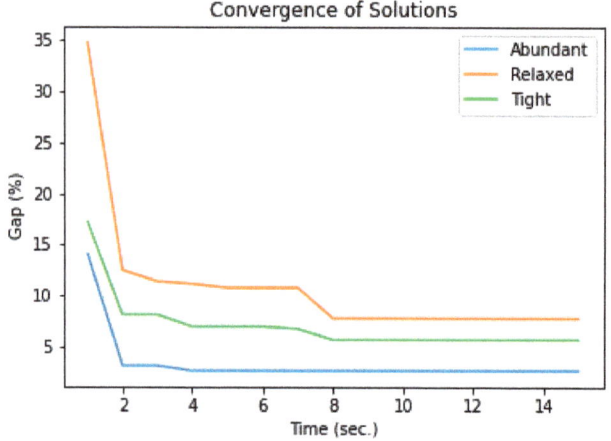

Figure 6. Comparison between MS$_{BRLH}$ and MAC on solving large-sized instances.

As we can see in Figure 6, the instances demonstrate the same convergence behavior as solution time increases. It is noticeable that the convergence rate is abrupt during the first few seconds. However, contrary to the tight and relaxed inventory scenarios, where the solutions continue improving over time, the search demonstrates more stable convergence during the remaining execution time in the abundant scenario. Being more efficient in the more flexible inventory case, our multi-start approach quickly achieves its best solutions.

Next, we want to compare the quality of the solutions generated for the deterministic scenario (MS$_{BRLH}$) against the solutions generated for the stochastic scenario (Sim$_{BRLH}$). Since the only difference between the deterministic and stochastic scenarios is that stochastic delays are added to edge traversal times, we can consider the deterministic cost of the best solutions generated by MS$_{BRLH}$ as a lower bound (LB) of the stochastic travel times of the best Sim$_{BRLH}$ solution. Moreover, since MS$_{BRLH}$ does not account for stochastic travel times, we can consider the stochastic travel time of the best MS$_{BRLH}$ solution as an upper bound (UB) for the stochastic travel time of the best Sim$_{BRLH}$ solutions. Table 6 provides both LBs and UBs values and the best-found stochastic travel times obtained by our Sim$_{BRLH}$. The solutions reported in the Sim$_{BRLH}$ column are the best-found stochastic travel times.

Table 6. Analysis of the results obtained by our Sim_{BRLH} on scenarios of tight, relaxed and abundant inventory.

I	*Tight Inventory*			*I*	*Relaxed Inventory*			*I*	*Abundant Inventory*		
	LB	Sim_{BRLH}	UB		LB	Sim_{BRLH}	UB		LB	Sim_{BRLH}	UB
b1	1110.9	2164.5	2167.0	b21	1030.0	2096.3	2154.6	b41	760.5	1731.0	1858.7
b2	1378.2	2084.7	2084.7	b22	1275.7	1996.6	1996.6	b42	870.4	1574.1	1636.8
b3	2437.2	3465.3	3465.3	b23	2021.9	3043.9	3043.9	b43	1259.6	2239.4	2239.4
b4	1930.3	3184.3	3184.3	b24	1632.2	2891.1	2989.5	b44	1284.9	2553.4	2553.4
b5	2395.3	3790.2	3790.2	b25	1980.4	3363.6	3363.6	b45	1364.3	2753.9	2753.9
b6	1389.4	2628.3	2775.6	b26	1268.0	2487.9	2487.9	b46	1024.3	2269.2	2269.2
b7	1769.3	2544.9	2544.9	b27	1652.1	2446.5	2446.5	b47	1135.1	1919.3	1944.4
b8	2620.5	3715.6	3715.6	b28	2101.7	3178.6	3178.6	b48	1355.2	2420.6	2442.4
b9	2836.9	4209.9	4209.9	b29	2395.4	3725.6	3725.6	b49	1777.8	3138.7	3146.9
b10	3787.2	5258.7	5258.7	b30	2819.0	4269.7	4269.7	b50	1869.2	3308.8	3312.6
b11	1817.1	3261.5	3401.5	b31	1679.1	3099.3	3099.3	b51	1414.7	2814.0	3095.4
b12	2109.1	2978.8	2983.5	b32	1960.7	2819.4	2832.9	b52	1366.8	2233.4	2250.7
b13	2765.1	3917.1	3917.1	b33	2267.2	3412.4	3412.4	b53	1591.5	2732.9	2732.9
b14	2842.7	4312.3	4312.3	b34	2469.3	3891.5	3914.8	b54	1881.8	3289.1	3304.1
b15	3308.0	4813.7	4813.7	b35	2818.0	4311.4	4311.4	b55	2025.1	3510.5	3510.5
b16	1847.2	3460.4	3591.6	b36	1683.7	3267.0	3273.6	b56	1368.1	2944.6	3180.0
b17	2434.8	3377.2	3393.7	b37	2322.3	3266.1	3268.6	b57	1559.7	2497.4	2497.4
b18	2853.4	4082.6	4082.6	b38	2559.7	3782.0	3788.0	b58	1845.3	3065.6	3065.6
b19	3551.0	5039.2	5039.2	b39	3038.1	4548.9	4548.9	b59	1797.8	3287.3	3287.3
b20	3512.8	5088.2	5088.2	b40	2830.6	4384.5	4385.9	b60	1837.3	3380.0	3380.0

As we can see in Table 6, all the Sim_{BRLH} solution costs are between the LB and the UB, as expected. For 24 problem instances, the solution returned by our simheuristic is better than the best deterministic solution when it is tested in the stochastic scenario (the *UB* column). From this, we can assert that our Sim_{BRLH} is able to generate competitive results for the stochastic scenario. The reliability value is calculated by simulation for each solution and represents the probability that all routes are completed within maximum tour duration. For visualizing this trade-off between the deterministic cost of the solutions and their reliability rate, which are conflicting objectives, a Pareto frontier of non-dominated is presented. Accordingly, Figure 7a–c present the non-dominated solutions for three different instances (*b17*, *b37*, and *b57*), each one belonging to a different inventory scenario. A solution is non-dominated if, no other solution has a greater reliability and a lower or equal travel cost, or if no other solution has a lower travel cost and a greater or equal reliability level. The *b17* solution was randomly chosen, while the *b37* and *b57* solutions are for the same problem but set in the two other inventory scenarios. The square orange dot represents the best deterministic solution found by our MS_{BRLH}, while the remaining ones, round and blue, represent different solutions with a higher reliability rate, but with higher operating costs.

As we can see in Figure 7, despite being the solutions with the lowest cost, the best deterministic solutions (square dots) are the least reliable ones for stochastic scenarios. Particularly in Figure 7a, the best deterministic solution is approximately only 21% reliable under stochasticity. By selecting higher-cost solutions, the reliability rate reaches more than 70%. The same behavior is noticed in Figure 7b,c, however, the deterministic *b57* solution is reasonably reliable. Usually, low-cost solutions are made up of a small number of large vehicle routes, in terms of travel distance and time. Therefore, when increasing the travel time variability in those scenarios, the risk of exceeding the time constraint is higher. On the other hand, higher cost solutions are built from a larger number of smaller routes, and smaller routes exhibit a lower risk of violating the maximum tour duration constraint in stochastic scenarios. In this way, decision-makers should consider that low-cost solutions under deterministic scenarios might not necessarily be the best option when stochasticity is taken into account.

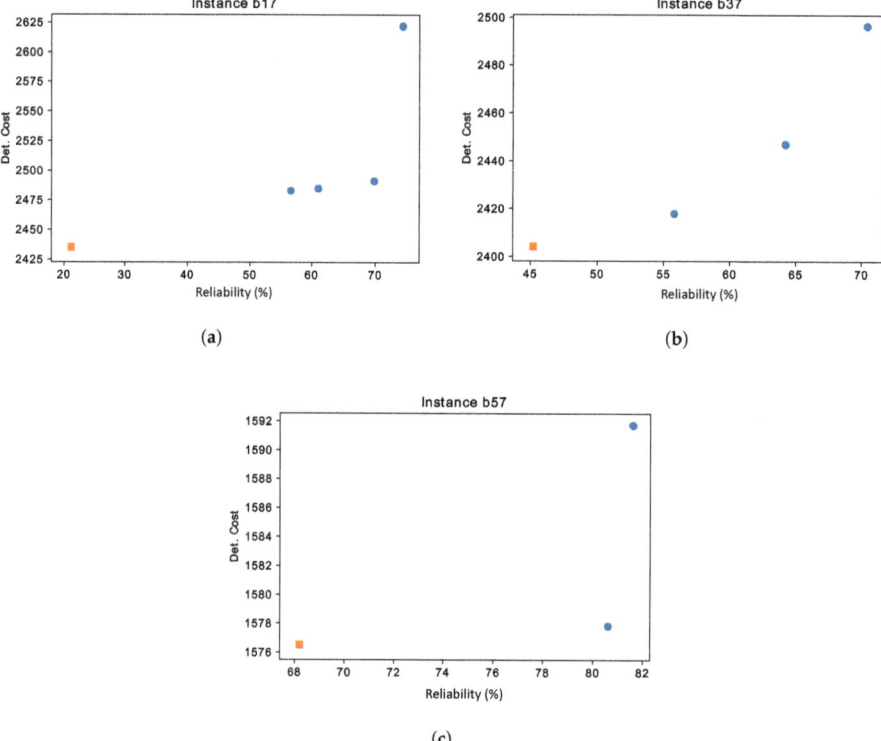

Figure 7. Set of non-dominated solutions of problem instances *b*17 (**a**), *b*37 (**b**) and *b*57 (**c**). (**a**) Non-dominated solutions for problem instance *b*17 (tight inventory). (**b**) Non-dominated solutions for problem instance *b*37 (relaxed inventory). (**c**) Non-dominated solutions for problem instance *b*57 (abundant inventory).

6. Conclusions and Future Work

With the emergence of online retail channels and the popularization of mobile devices, new retailing modes have become popular. Some of these retailing practices allow customers to browse through different online stores and, then, to get the items bought directly delivered to their homes. Hence, new versions of the vehicle routing problem (VRP) considering additional decision variables and constraints have emerged. Omnichannel retailing leads to an integrated problem combining the VRP and the pick-up and delivery problem. In omnichannel distribution systems, a set of retail stores need to be replenished and, at the same time, products have to be sent from these stores to final customers. The resulting omnichannel VRP consists in two stages: (i) a group of retail stores that must be served from a distribution center; and (ii) a set of online consumers who must be served, by the same fleet of cargo vehicles, from these retail stores.

For solving the deterministic OM-VRP, a simple heuristic was initially introduced. This heuristic was then extended into a multi-start biased-randomized algorithm, which is tested against the state-of-the-art methodologies. Our biased-randomized algorithm performs reasonably well in a set of 60 instances of the deterministic OM-VRP, which allows us to extend it into a full simheuristic for solving the stochastic version of the problem. This is a more realistic version of the OM-VRP where travel times are modeled as random variables following a log-normal distribution. Our simheuristic approach is also capable of measuring the reliability of any proposed solution when it is employed in a stochastic scenario. To the best of our knowledge, this is the first time that such a stochastic variant of the problem has been solved in the literature. Regarding the simheuristic results, we conclude that the best deterministic solutions may perform badly when used in a stochastic scenario. Those solutions are often not reliable in terms of completing all routes within a time limit. On the other hand, our simheuristic approach was able to generate reliable and competitive results for these stochastic scenarios. Therefore, our methodology enables decision makers to choose the solution that better fits his or her utility function in terms of cost and reliability level.

Two-echelon distribution systems, as the one considered here, are typically characterized by the use of different fleets of vehicles at each distribution level. Apart from considering a single fleet of vehicles for serving both delivery levels, the products ordered by customers were assumed to not affect the vehicles' capacity. Therefore, future directions of research include the consideration of non-negligible sized online customer orders, heterogeneous vehicle fleets, and the incorporation of positive demands for multiple product types for each customer. Regarding the solution approach, different perturbation stages and local search operators could be tested in order to speed up the convergence process towards near-optimal solutions. This might be particularly relevant when considering large-sized instances.

Author Contributions: Conceptualization, L.d.C.M., C.B. and A.A.J.; methodology, L.d.C.M., C.B., P.J.C.-M., J.P. and A.A.J.; software, L.d.C.M. and P.J.C.-M.; writing, L.d.C.M., C.B., P.J.C.-M., J.P. and A.A.J.; validation, L.d.C.M., P.J.C.-M., J.P. and A.A.J. All authors have read and agreed to the published version of the manuscript.

Funding: This research received no external funding.

Acknowledgments: This work has been partially supported by Rhenus Freight Logistics GmbH & Co. KG and by the Spanish Ministry of Science, Innovation, and Universities (PID2019-111100RB-C21, RED2018-102642-T). We also acknowledge the support of the Erasmus+ Program (2019-I-ES01-KA103-062602).

Conflicts of Interest: The authors declare no conflict of interest.

References

1. Abdulkader, M.M.S.; Gajpal, Y.; ElMekkawy, T.Y. Vehicle routing problem in omni-channel retailing distribution systems. *Int. J. Prod. Econ.* **2018**, *196*, 43–55. [CrossRef]
2. Gallino, S.; Moreno, A. Integration of online and offline channels in retail: The impact of sharing reliable inventory availability information. *Manag. Sci.* **2014**, *60*, 1434–1451. [CrossRef]
3. Hübner, A.; Holzapfel, A.; Kuhn, H. Distribution systems in omni-channel retailing. *Bus. Res.* **2016**, *9*, 255–296. [CrossRef]
4. Quintero-Araujo, C.L.; Gruler, A.; Juan, A.A.; Faulin, J. Using horizontal cooperation concepts in integrated routing and facility-location decisions. *Int. Trans. Oper. Res.* **2019**, *26*, 551–576. [CrossRef]
5. Crainic, T.G.; Laporte, G. *Fleet Management and Logistics*; Springer Science & Business Media: Berlin/Heidelberg, Germany, 2012.
6. Cheng, B.Y.; Leung, J.Y.T.; Li, K. Integrated scheduling of production and distribution to minimize total cost using an improved ant colony optimization method. *Comput. Ind. Eng.* **2015**, *83*, 217–225. [CrossRef]
7. Lenstra, J.K.; Kan, A. Complexity of vehicle routing and scheduling problems. *Networks* **1981**, *11*, 221–227. [CrossRef]
8. Savelsbergh, M.W.; Sol, M. The general pickup and delivery problem. *Transp. Sci.* **1995**, *29*, 17–29. [CrossRef]
9. Martins, L.D.C.; Bayliss, C.; Juan, A.A.; Panadero, J.; Marmol, M. A savings-based heuristic for solving the omnichannel vehicle routing problem with pick-up and delivery. *Transp. Res. Procedia* **2020**, *47*, 83–90. [CrossRef]
10. Quintero-Araujo, C.L.; Caballero-Villalobos, J.P.; Juan, A.A.; Montoya-Torres, J.R. A biased-randomized metaheuristic for the capacitated location routing problem. *Int. Trans. Oper. Res.* **2017**, *24*, 1079–1098. [CrossRef]
11. Juan, A.A.; Kelton, W.D.; Currie, C.S.; Faulin, J. Simheuristics applications: dealing with uncertainty in logistics, transportation, and other supply chain areas. In Proceedings of the 2018 Winter Simulation Conference, Gothenburg, Sweden, 9–12 December 2018; pp. 3048–3059.

12. Gonzalez-Martin, S.; Juan, A.A.; Riera, D.; Elizondo, M.G.; Ramos, J.J. A simheuristic algorithm for solving the arc routing problem with stochastic demands. *J. Simul.* **2018**, *12*, 53–66. [CrossRef]
13. Gruler, A.; Fikar, C.; Juan, A.A.; Hirsch, P.; Contreras-Bolton, C. Supporting multi-depot and stochastic waste collection management in clustered urban areas via simulation–optimization. *J. Simul.* **2017**, *11*, 11–19. [CrossRef]
14. Mosquera, A.; Pascual, C.O.; Ayensa, E.J. Understanding the customer experience in the age of omni-channel shopping. *Icono14* **2017**, *15*, 5. [CrossRef]
15. Verhoef, P.C.; Kannan, P.K.; Inman, J.J. From multi-channel retailing to omni-channel retailing: introduction to the special issue on multi-channel retailing. *J. Retail.* **2015**, *91*, 174–181. [CrossRef]
16. Hübner, A.; Wollenburg, J.; Holzapfel, A. Retail logistics in the transition from multi-channel to omni-channel. *Int. J. Phys. Distrib. Logist. Manag.* **2016**, *46*, 562–583. [CrossRef]
17. Heitz-Spahn, S. Cross-channel free-riding consumer behavior in a multichannel environment: An investigation of shopping motives, sociodemographics and product categories. *J. Retail. Consum. Serv.* **2013**, *20*, 570–578. [CrossRef]
18. Beck, N.; Rygl, D. Categorization of multiple channel retailing in Multi-, Cross-, and Omni-Channel Retailing for retailers and retailing. *J. Retail. Consum. Serv.* **2015**, *27*, 170–178. [CrossRef]
19. Dantzig, G.B.; Ramser, J.H. The truck dispatching problem. *Manag. Sci.* **1959**, *6*, 80–91. [CrossRef]
20. Laporte, G.; Mercure, H.; Nobert, Y. An exact algorithm for the asymmetrical capacitated vehicle routing problem. *Networks* **1986**, *16*, 33–46. [CrossRef]
21. Fukasawa, R.; Longo, H.; Lysgaard, J.; de Aragão, M.P.; Reis, M.; Uchoa, E.; Werneck, R.F. Robust branch-and-cut-and-price for the capacitated vehicle routing problem. *Math. Program.* **2006**, *106*, 491–511.
22. Barbarosoglu, G.; Ozgur, D. A tabu search algorithm for the vehicle routing problem. *Comput. Oper. Res.* **1999**, *26*, 255–270.
23. Nazif, H.; Lee, L.S. Optimised crossover genetic algorithm for capacitated vehicle routing problem. *Appl. Math. Model.* **2012**, *36*, 2110–2117. [CrossRef]
24. Ezzatneshan, A. A algorithm for the Vehicle Problem. *Int. J. Adv. Robot. Syst.* **2010**, *7*, 14. [CrossRef]
25. Lin, S.W.; Lee, Z.J.; Ying, K.C.; Lee, C.Y. Applying hybrid meta-heuristics for capacitated vehicle routing problem. *Expert Syst. Appl.* **2009**, *36*, 1505–1512. [CrossRef]
26. Lu, Q.; Dessouky, M. An exact algorithm for the multiple vehicle pickup and delivery problem. *Transp. Sci.* **2004**, *38*, 503–514. [CrossRef]
27. Ropke, S.; Cordeau, J.F. Branch and cut and price for the pickup and delivery problem with time windows. *Transp. Sci.* **2009**, *43*, 267–286. [CrossRef]
28. Nanry, W.P.; Barnes, J.W. Solving the pickup and delivery problem with time windows using reactive tabu search. *Transp. Res. Part B Methodol.* **2000**, *34*, 107–121. [CrossRef]
29. Pankratz, G. A grouping genetic algorithm for the pickup and delivery problem with time windows. *OR Spectr.* **2005**, *27*, 21–41. [CrossRef]
30. Ropke, S.; Pisinger, D. An adaptive large neighborhood search heuristic for the pickup and delivery problem with time windows. *Transp. Sci.* **2006**, *40*, 455–472. [CrossRef]
31. Li, Y.; Chen, H.; Prins, C. Adaptive large neighborhood search for the pickup and delivery problem with time windows, profits, and reserved requests. *Eur. J. Oper. Res.* **2016**, *252*, 27–38. [CrossRef]
32. Ghilas, V.; Demir, E.; Van Woensel, T. An adaptive large neighborhood search heuristic for the pickup and delivery problem with time windows and scheduled lines. *Comput. Oper. Res.* **2016**, *72*, 12–30. [CrossRef]
33. Ai, T.J.; Kachitvichyanukul, V. A particle swarm optimization for the vehicle routing problem with simultaneous pickup and delivery. *Comput. Oper. Res.* **2009**, *36*, 1693–1702. [CrossRef]
34. Nadizadeh, A.; Kafash, B. Fuzzy capacitated location-routing problem with simultaneous pickup and delivery demands. *Transp. Lett.* **2019**, *11*, 1–19. [CrossRef]
35. Berbeglia, G.; Cordeau, J.F.; Gribkovskaia, I.; Laporte, G. Static pickup and delivery problems: A classification scheme and survey. *Top* **2007**, *15*, 1–31. [CrossRef]
36. Clarke, G.; Wright, J.W. Scheduling of vehicles from a central depot to a number of delivery points. *Oper. Res.* **1964**, *12*, 568–581. [CrossRef]
37. Bayliss, C.; Martins, L.D.C.; Juan, A.A. A Two-phase Local Search with a Discrete-event Heuristic for the Omnichannel Vehicle Routing Problem. *Comput. Ind. Eng.* **2020**, *148*, 106695. [CrossRef]

38. Martins, L.D.C.; Hirsch, P.; Juan, A.A. Agile optimization of a two-echelon vehicle routing problem with pickup and delivery. *Int. Trans. Oper. Res.* **2020**, *28*, 201–221. [CrossRef]
39. Estrada-Moreno, A.; Ferrer, A.; Juan, A.A.; Bagirov, A.; Panadero, J. A biased-randomised algorithm for the capacitated facility location problem with soft constraints. *J. Oper. Res. Soc.* **2019**, *0*, 1–17. [CrossRef]
40. Dominguez, O.; Guimarans, D.; Juan, A.A.; de la Nuez, I. A biased-randomised large neighbourhood search for the two-dimensional vehicle routing problem with backhauls. *Eur. J. Oper. Res.* **2016**, *255*, 442–462. [CrossRef]
41. Belloso, J.; Juan, A.A.; Faulin, J. An iterative biased-randomized heuristic for the fleet size and mix vehicle-routing problem with backhauls. *Int. Trans. Oper. Res.* **2019**, *26*, 289–301. [CrossRef]
42. Dominguez, O.; Juan, A.A.; de La Nuez, I.; Ouelhadj, D. An ILS-biased randomization algorithm for the two-dimensional loading HFVRP with sequential loading and items rotation. *J. Oper. Res. Soc.* **2016**, *67*, 37–53. [CrossRef]
43. Al-Behadili, M.; Ouelhadj, D.; Jones, D. Multi-objective biased randomised iterated greedy for robust permutation flow shop scheduling problem under disturbances. *J. Oper. Res. Soc.* **2019**, 1–13. [CrossRef]
44. Ferone, D.; Hatami, S.; González-Neira, E.M.; Juan, A.A.; Festa, P. A biased-randomized iterated local search for the distributed assembly permutation flow-shop problem. *Int. Trans. Oper. Res.* **2020**, *27*, 1368–1391.
45. Pages-Bernaus, A.; Ramalhinho, H.; Juan, A.A.; Calvet, L. Designing e-commerce supply chains: A stochastic facility–location approach. *Int. Trans. Oper. Res.* **2019**, *26*, 507–528.
46. Rabe, M.; Deininger, M.; Juan, A.A. Speeding up computational times in simheuristics combining genetic algorithms with discrete-Event simulation. *Simul. Model. Pract. Theory* **2020**, *103*, 102089.
47. Hatami, S.; Calvet, L.; Fernández-Viagas, V.; Framiñán, J.M.; Juan, A.A. A simheuristic algorithm to set up starting times in the stochastic parallel flowshop problem. *Simul. Model. Pract. Theory* **2018**, *86*, 55–71.
48. Gruler, A.; Panadero, J.; de Armas, J.; Moreno, J.A.; Juan, A.A. A variable neighborhood search simheuristic for the multiperiod inventory routing problem with stochastic demands. *Int. Trans. Oper. Res.* **2020**, *27*, 314–335.
49. Gruler, A.; Panadero, J.; de Armas, J.; Moreno, J.A.; Juan, A.A. Combining variable neighborhood search with simulation for the inventory routing problem with stochastic demands and stock-outs. *Comput. Ind. Eng.* **2018**, *123*, 278–288.
50. Onggo, B.S.; Panadero, J.; Corlu, C.G.; Juan, A.A. Agri-food supply chains with stochastic demands: A multi-period inventory routing problem with perishable products. *Simul. Model. Pract. Theory* **2019**, *97*, 101970.
51. Cabrera, G.; Juan, A.A.; Lázaro, D.; Marquès, J.M.; Proskurnia, I. A simulation-optimization approach to deploy Internet services in large-scale systems with user-provided resources. *Simulation* **2014**, *90*, 644–659.
52. Panadero, J.; Doering, J.; Kizys, R.; Juan, A.A.; Fito, A. A variable neighborhood search simheuristic for project portfolio selection under uncertainty. *J. Heuristics* **2020**, *26*, 353–375.
53. Lam, C.P.; Masek, M.; Kelly, L.; Papasimeon, M.; Benke, L. A simheuristic approach for evolving agent behaviour in the exploration for novel combat tactics. *Oper. Res. Perspect.* **2019**, *6*, 100123. [CrossRef]
54. Lopes, T.C.; Michels, A.S.; Lüders, R.; Magatão, L. A simheuristic approach for throughput maximization of asynchronous buffered stochastic mixed-model assembly lines. *Comput. Oper. Res.* **2020**, *115*, 104863. [CrossRef]
55. Santos, M.S.; Pinto, T.V.; Júnior, Ê.L.; Cota, L.P.; Souza, M.J.; Euzébio, T.A. Simheuristic-based decision support system for efficiency improvement of an iron ore crusher circuit. *Eng. Appl. Artif. Intell.* **2020**, *94*, 103789. [CrossRef]
56. Glover, F.W.; Kochenberger, G.A. *Handbook of Metaheuristics*; Springer Science & Business Media: Berlin/Heidelberg, Germany, 2006; Volume 57.
57. Dulebenets, M.A.; Moses, R.; Ozguven, E.E.; Vanli, A. Minimizing carbon dioxide emissions due to container handling at marine container terminals via hybrid evolutionary algorithms. *IEEE Access* **2017**, *5*, 8131–8147. [CrossRef]
58. Dulebenets, M.A.; Kavoosi, M.; Abioye, O.; Pasha, J. A self-adaptive evolutionary algorithm for the berth scheduling problem: towards efficient parameter control. *Algorithms* **2018**, *11*, 100. [CrossRef]
59. Anandakumar, H.; Umamaheswari, K. A bio-inspired swarm intelligence technique for social aware cognitive radio handovers. *Comput. Electr. Eng.* **2018**, *71*, 925–937. [CrossRef]

60. Brezočnik, L.; Fister, I.; Podgorelec, V. Swarm intelligence algorithms for feature selection: A review. *Appl. Sci.* **2018**, *8*, 1521. [CrossRef]

61. Slowik, A.; Kwasnicka, H. Nature inspired methods and their industry applications—Swarm intelligence algorithms. *IEEE Trans. Ind. Inform.* **2017**, *14*, 1004–1015. [CrossRef]

62. Zhao, X.; Wang, C.; Su, J.; Wang, J. Research and application based on the swarm intelligence algorithm and artificial intelligence for wind farm decision system. *Renew. Energy* **2019**, *134*, 681–697. [CrossRef]

63. Talbi, E.G. *Metaheuristics: From Design to Implementation*; John Wiley & Sons: Hoboken, NJ, USA, 2009; Volume 74.

64. Faulin, J.; Juan, A.A.; Serrat, C.; Bargueno, V. Predicting availability functions in time-dependent complex systems with SAEDES simulation algorithms. *Reliab. Eng. Syst. Saf.* **2008**, *93*, 1761–1771. [CrossRef]

65. Calvet, L.; Juan, A.A.; Serrat, C.; Ries, J. A statistical learning based approach for parameter fine-tuning of metaheuristics. *SORT-Stat. Oper. Res. Trans.* **2016**, *1*, 201–224.

algorithms

Article

Simheuristics Approaches for Efficient Decision-Making Support in Materials Trading Networks

Markus Rabe *, Majsa Ammouriova, Dominik Schmitt and Felix Dross

IT in Production and Logistics, Faculty of Mechanical Engineering, TU Dortmund, 44227 Dortmund, Germany;
majsa.ammouriova@tu-dortmund.de (M.A.); dominik.schmitt@tu-dortmund.de (D.S.);
felix.dross@tu-dortmund.de (F.D.)
* Correspondence: markus.rabe@tu-dortmund.de

Abstract: The distribution process in business-to-business materials trading is among the most complex and in transparent ones within logistics. The highly volatile environment requires continuous adaptations by the responsible decision-makers, who face a substantial number of potential improvement actions with conflicting goals, such as simultaneously maintaining a high service level and low costs. Simulation-optimisation approaches have been proposed in this context, for example based on evolutionary algorithms. But, on real-world system dimensions, they face impractically long computation times. This paper addresses this challenge in two principal streams. On the one hand, reinforcement learning is investigated to reduce the response time of the system in a concrete decision situation. On the other hand, domain-specific information and defining equivalent solutions are exploited to support a metaheuristic algorithm. For these approaches, we have developed suitable implementations and evaluated them with subsets of real-world data. The results demonstrate that reinforcement learning exploits the idle time between decision situations to learn which decisions might be most promising, thus adding computation time but significantly reducing the response time. Using domain-specific information reduces the number of required simulation runs and guides the search for promising actions. In our experimentation, defining equivalent solutions decreased the number of required simulation runs up to 15%.

Keywords: simulation; optimization; machine learning; logistics; distribution networks

Citation: Rabe, M.; Ammouriova, M.; Schmitt, D.; Dross, F. Simheuristics Approaches for Efficient Decision-Making Support in Materials Trading Networks. *Algorithms* **2021**, *14*, 23. https://doi.org/10.3390/a14010023

Received: 14 December 2020
Accepted: 8 January 2021
Published: 14 January 2021

1. Introduction

Managing distribution networks is a challenging task for decision-makers. The specific challenge in this field is the complex structure of a typical network, which is a multi-echelon system with horizontal and vertical shortcuts in combination with huge numbers of nodes as well as transported parts, each kind of which is defined as a stock keeping unit (SKU). In addition, this kind of logistics operates in a highly volatile environment, requiring continuous adaptations by the responsible managers who need to conduct frequent maintenance and improvement decisions, especially on tactical horizons. In practice, decision-makers face a substantial number of potential improvement actions, spanned by the huge number of objects that can and have to be combined for suitable maintenance of the network [1,2]. Furthermore, conflicting goals, such as simultaneously maintaining a high service level and low costs, characterized by specifically defined key performance indicators (KPIs) [3], add to the complexity of the problem. Short delivery times versus low costs as well as a large number of delivered SKUs by their due date versus a large number of fully completed orders are other examples of conflicting goals in the network.

The first challenge is the specific shape of the problem. Traditional parameter optimisation tasks—easily found in the broad literature—are described by a given (finite) number of parameters, each with a given number of possible values. The size of the solution space, in this case, is defined as the product of the number of all parameters. However, in the network covered in this paper, there is an (in principle) unlimited number of actions to change the network, each of which could be any of a given limited set of actions, applied to any of the object combinations. Therefore, traditional algorithms are not applicable because of the daunting combinatorics. Just as an example, traditionally a parameter entry of the algorithm stands for a specific characteristic of the underlying system. Here, however, it only stands for any kind of action. Therefore, it is also the case that the sequence of the elements is clearly relevant, in contrast to the cases that are usually found in the state-of-the-art literature.

Due to their complexity, real-world networks cannot obtain a closed mathematical formulation of the goal functions [4]. Therefore, an application might resort to a three-stage solution procedure. In the first stage, changes to the system are defined that are expected to keep or even improve the KPIs. In the second stage, a discrete event simulation (DES) model [5] is run to determine basic logistical data, such as throughput times, in-time delivery, or utilisation of resources. In the last stage, these data are used as in the real world to calculate the KPIs, which then serve to judge the quality of the changes that have been set up in the first stage.

This three-stage process can, of course, be conducted manually by human experts, but there have been a number of trials to automate the optimisation of distribution networks. Unfortunately, due to the huge solution space, there is again no closed mathematical formulation to find a minimum or maximum of the desired KPIs, leading to the necessity of applying heuristic algorithms, which do not deliver the optimum, but—hopefully—a "suitably good" solution in finite time [6,7]. Specific heuristics would raise extremely high development and implementation effort for such complex applications. Therefore, reported implementations exploit metaheuristics, often biology-inspired, such as evolutionary algorithms [8]. Metaheuristics are optimisation algorithms that are—at least up to a point—independent of the specific application problem, with the great advantage that new developments can be exploited for a multitude of applications, and, thus, very sophisticated and efficient algorithms are available.

The scientific solution approach applied in this paper is consequently the method of simheuristics [9], which combines DES used as an evaluation function with metaheuristics for the optimisation. The major drawback of this approach is the time to produce promising action proposals. The tremendous time requirements originate from the huge solution space described before in combination with the significant runtimes of the complex simulation models [10], the latter being in the range of minutes to even hours per single run.

There have been very different approaches proposed to face this problem. Optimisation of the metaheuristics performance itself is hardly promising, as the processing of these algorithms covers only a very minor part of the total run time—by far the major part is covered by the DES. An obvious idea is to develop advanced simulation models that can evaluate the distribution system faster. Alternatives address the effort to obtain statistical relevance, for example, find better controls for the number of required replications or adapt such numbers to the degree that a specific solution seems to be promising [11–13]. This article explores two different innovative ways.

Actually, the real performance challenge is not to minimise the effective computation time T_C of the computer resource, but to reduce the time required to present a decision proposal T_D, defined as the time span between the availability of data and the provision of acceptable solution proposals. With metaheuristics, such as an evolutionary algorithm (EA) [7], T_D can only be reduced with respect to T_C when additional resources are applied. For example, using four computer processors instead of one will cut T_D to about 25% of T_C. With ten computers, it will reduce to about 10% (assuming that the distribution overhead is negligible). However, the tactical decisions are performed, for example, once per month with a decision request three days after availability of field data in the data warehouse. Thus, ten computers might idle 27 days waiting for the next decision request. The solution approach is to apply machine learning, where a learning algorithm is operating for 90% of the time, and in the concrete decision situation the acquired knowledge is used to quickly find promising solutions. We consider deep reinforcement learning for this purpose, as it allows us to estimate the impact of specific changes, even if these have never been simulated in the past, by using the "fuzzier" knowledge within the deep learning's neural network [14,15].

The second innovative idea is to get domain-specific information (DSI) back into our metaheuristic algorithm [16]. We analyse three different approaches to use contextual information for the acceleration of the heuristics machine. One approach exploits experience from previous (actual or simulated) applications of actions, following the idea that actions that have shown to be helpful in the past might lead to good results in the future as well. This method also allows us to exploit the idle time between the decision periods to collect experience about the actions' success and, thus, to improve the forecast power of the success indicators. A second approach uses the classification of actions that either change the network's structure or else just its parameters, assuming that structural changes would be more targeted if applied among the first actions of the action plan. The last idea assumes that the actions are not independent, and one action being performed will influence the impact of further actions. In this approach, the correlation among actions is computed for data from the past and projected into future action plans. Again, idle time can be used to calculate and continuously improve the correlation indicators.

Finally, the number of simulation runs could be reduced, and we discuss two ways towards this goal. On the one hand, different action plans are analysed to determine whether they can be predicted to gain identical results without the need to simulate both of them. This would lead to performance improvement without reducing the result quality (or, from a different point of view, to achieve better results within the same time frame). On the other hand, the reduction of the solution space itself by grouping actions into fewer selectable items is considered [17]. It can be assumed that this approach, quite usual in real-world decision making, will lead to a significant reduction of simulation runs. However, the reduction of the research space might exclude some even better solutions, which in fact could be acceptable if the method leads to better solutions within a limited given time frame.

For all these approaches, we have developed suitable implementations and evaluated them with subsets of real-world data. In this paper, we give an overview of the implementation, present exemplary results, and make conclusions about the suitability of the investigated approaches. The paper is organised as follows—Section 2 presents the related work and Section 3 the considered optimisation approaches. Section 4 introduces the general ideas and architecture of the developed logistics assistance system, and it clarifies the relationship to real-world data. Sections 5–7 discuss the above-mentioned approaches one by one, followed by an evaluation of the novel concepts in an evaluation based on real-world data in Section 8. The discussion relates the major findings to the previous state of the art and derives future research paths, followed by a summary of the achievements in Section 9.

2. Related Work

2.1. Simulation of Distribution Systems

Management of logistics distribution systems is a complex task; hence, decision-makers use models to represent and study these systems. A model is a "simplified reproduction of a planned or existing system with its processes in a different conceptual or concrete system" [18] (p. 3). In the models, decision variables are under the control of decision-makers and present the input to the models [19]. Decision-makers change the values of decision variables and use the output of models to study the relationships between the variables and the performance of the modelled system.

Distribution systems have a high degree of interaction between their entities and are characterised as having time-dependent variables [18]; thus, mathematical models [5] reach their limits in modelling distribution systems and, instead, simulation is used to model them.

Simulation studies are conducted in several phases that are, for example, illustrated in the procedure model presented by Rabe et al. [20]. This model shows the phases targeted to guarantee the building of a representative model of the system under study. It highlights the importance of verification and validation of the model as well as the data in the simulation study [21].

A variety of model representation techniques using simulation modelling have been developed, such as DES [22]. The discrete event simulation is characterised as modelling a system by focusing on its discrete states. Fanti et al. [23] claimed that DES is the most preferred simulation approach for logistics systems. Pujawan et al. [24] modelled a cement distribution system using DES to estimate costs and service level. In another study, Fang and Li [25] evaluated various inventory scenarios using DES. Ivanov [26] studied the effect of disruption at one point in a network using DES; he used DES to perform a sensitivity analysis.

2.2. Optimisation of Distribution Systems

In optimisation problems, decision variables are optimised. These variables might have continuous values or countable values [7]. Optimisation problems with countable decision variables are integer programming problems, sometimes called combinatorial optimisation problems [27]. Such problems are based on combinatorics [28], in which a solution is formed from a finite space of elements to optimise an objective function [29]. Optimisation of distribution systems could be formulated as a combinatorial optimisation problem [30], such as the travelling salesman problem, in which the task is to arrange a tour through a number of cities to minimise the total travelled distance.

Greedy algorithms have been used to find the approximately optimal solutions of simple combinatorial optimisation problems [31]. Adding constraints to these problems or increasing their size increases the difficulties to solve them, and the problems might become NP-hard [4]. The travelling salesman problem is an example of an NP-hard problem that is solved by approximate methods (such as metaheuristics) to find promising feasible solutions [31]. "A metaheuristic is a high-level problem-independent algorithmic framework that provides a set of guidelines or strategies to develop heuristic optimisation algorithms" [32] (p. 960).

Researchers used metaheuristics to solve a variety of combinatorial optimisation problems, such as Osaba et al. [33]. Cybulski [34] found that evolutionary algorithms exhibited promising performance in different benchmark combinatorial optimisation problems. Other researchers combined metaheuristics and other methods in a hybrid approach [7], such as the simheuristics approach [35].

2.3. Simheuristics

For the optimisation of complex systems, simulation and optimisation methods are combined in simulation-optimisation methods [36], which depend on the optimisation algorithm that is used *and* the simulation purpose. The VDI-Guideline 3633.12 [37] classifies the relation between simulation and optimisation algorithms into four categories: "Category A" in which simulation follows optimisation, "Category B" with optimisation following the simulation, "Category C" integrating an optimisation algorithm in the simulation, and "Category D" in which simulation is integrated in an optimisation algorithm.

A variety of optimisation algorithms could be combined with simulation, for example, metaheuristics. The integration of simulation in metaheuristics is called simheuristics [35] and is classified as "Category D" by VDI-Guideline 3633.12 [37]. Simheuristics combines the power of metaheuristics and simulation. The metaheuristic algorithm forms solutions that are evaluated by simulation with respect to the objective function in the optimisation problem.

Researchers have used simheuristics to solve a variety of combinatorial optimisation problems. For example, Juan and Rabe [35] proposed an approach that outperformed a traditional method to solve an inventory routing problem. They combined Monte Carlo simulation and the best-known heuristic that solves the problem. Juan et al. [9] proposed a framework to handle a stochastic type of combinatorial optimisation problems with moderate volatility. Jackson et al. [38] combined DES and a genetic algorithm to handle the stochasticity in an inventory management problem. Discrete event simulation and a genetic algorithm were used to design a supply network by Gutenschwager et al. [39]. Pages-Bernaus et al. [40] investigated a facility location problem. They found that a simheuristic approach outperformed other stochastic programming methods to solve the problem.

2.4. Literature Summary and Contributions

Distribution networks are complex networks with a large number of possible actions that might be used to improve them. These networks are difficult to model adequately in a mathematical formulation, and, thus, simulation is often used for their study. In order to optimise such networks with their conflicting goals, metaheuristic algorithms could be used to provide a "good solution". Because these networks are complex, researchers have found it beneficial to combine simulation and metaheuristics in a simheuristic approach to optimise them. This approach forms the basis for a logistics assistance system (LAS) that is described in Section 4. In the LAS, actions are selected to construct action plans in which the order of the actions is significant. However, the LAS has a long decision proposal time, because simulation forms the major part of the optimisation run time.

Researchers have suggested approaches to reduce the number of evaluations in an optimisation algorithm, such as screening solutions [41]. Other researchers proposed random biased selection of the solution's elements to improve the optimisation [42]. None of these strategies addressed the presented action plan problem that is a combinatorial optimisation problem in which actions are selected.

Since decision-makers look for a "good solution" in a reasonable time for the decision proposal even in large and complex networks, our paper proposes innovative approaches to reduce this time. In the first approach, reinforcement learning is proposed to reduce the decision proposal time. Sections 3.2 and 5 describe reinforcement learning and its innovative implementation in the LAS. Another innovative approach defines a network's domain-specific information and utilises it to recommend actions (Section 6). The last proposed approaches reduce the number of simulation runs by defining equivalent solutions and reducing the actions' search space (Section 7).

3. Optimisation Approaches

3.1. Evolutionary Algorithms

Evolutionary algorithms are metaheuristic algorithms developed to solve optimisation problems. In evolutionary algorithms (EAs), solutions are represented as individuals in a population. The individual's definition and encoding depend on the optimisation problem to be solved [43]. The individual might be presented as a string of binary numbers or real numbers. A fitness value assigned to each individual represents the objective function value associated with it. These individuals evolve in each generation and form a new population. The fittest individuals evolve inspired by the theory of evolution defined by Darwin. The selection of the individuals to evolve is facilitated by a biased selection, such as roulette-wheel or tournaments [44,45].

In addition to "individual", "population", and "fitness" terms used in the EA, other terms are used, such as "offsprings", "crossover", and "mutation" [7,43,45]. Offsprings are individuals from the population that are reproduced using crossover and mutation. In a crossover, parts of the individuals' genes are exchanged between two individuals. The crossover form depends on the number of exchange points along the individual's length, for example, one-point crossover, two-point crossover, and uniform crossover. In uniform crossover, multiple crossing points are defined along the individual's length. Mutation modifies one individual to reproduce an offspring. One or more parts of the individual are changed. Both crossover and mutation can be customised based on the optimisation problem.

The evolution of the individuals continues until a termination criterion is met, such as reaching a specified number of generations or stagnation [7,45]. Stagnation is defined when the best-found solution is not changed by the algorithm over a specific number of generations.

Evolutionary algorithms can handle optimisation problems in different domains. For example, an EA was used to minimise the service costs in marine container terminal operations [46]. Pasha et al. [47] compared an EA and other algorithms for solving the vehicle routing problem with a "factory-in-a-box" concept. The EA found the nearest solution to the optimum in small-scale problem instances and better solutions than other algorithms in large-scale problem instances. Evolutionary algorithms can detect promising regions in the search space and be utilised in the learning process while solving optimisation problems [48,49]. In online optimisation, the problems' features change over time and are unknown in advance. A learning-based EA was proposed to handle this problem [49]. Additionally, EAs were used to solve combinatorial optimisation problems, such as the vehicle routing problem and the travelling salesman problem [7,48].

Evolutionary algorithms can handle multi-objective optimisation problems [50]. In these problems, the non-dominated solutions, which outperform other solutions at least in one of the objective functions, are stored, and the algorithm looks for solutions along the Pareto front. Moradi [48] used a multi-objective evolutionary algorithm to minimise the number of vehicles and the total travelled distance in the vehicle routing problem. Researchers have utilised EAs in optimisation problems, including minimisation of energy consumption. For example, Ji et al. [51] solved a multi-objective green express cabinet assignment problem in urban last-mile logistics using probability-guided EA. They minimised total costs and energy consumption. The total makespan and total energy consumption were minimised in the flow shop scheduling problem with sequence-dependent setup times [52]. Petrowski and Ben-Hamida [43] stated that EAs for multi-objective problems provide promising solutions in problems with less than four objective functions. Other approaches proposed combining an EA and DES to solve optimisation problems, such as optimising lead time and total inventory holding costs in job sequencing and buffer size optimisation problems [53].

3.2. Deep Reinforcement Learning

In the field of reinforcement learning, the primary goal is to produce autonomous agents that interact with their environments to learn optimal behaviours, improving over time through trial and error. Although considerable successes in this field have been reported in the past [14,54,55], previous approaches often lacked scalability and were inherently limited to fairly low-dimensional problems [56]. In order to apply reinforcement learning to problems approaching real-world complexity, agents need to be able to derive efficient representations of the environment from high-dimensional inputs, and use these representations to generalize past experiences to new situations [15]. In recent years, improvements in the ability to process large amounts of data have led to considerable progress in this field [57]. A major reason for the development in this regard is the rise of deep learning, a class of representation learning with multi-layer artificial neural networks [58–60]. The neural networks are called deep, because they have numerous hidden layers between the input layer and the output layer and have, thus, an extensive internal structure [61–63]. Combining several layers, a deep neural network can be used to find compact low-dimensional representations in high-dimensional data, for example, in audio, text, and images. Hence, deep neural networks can, hence, be used to progressively build up abstract representations of data, and, thus, enable abstract learning. A particularly successful type of deep neural network is the Convolutional Neural Network (CNN) [15,64]. CNNs leverage the fact that the analyzed data are composed of smaller details—referred to as features—and trigger a decision about the entire data set by analyzing each feature in isolation. By using the mathematical concept of convolution, CNNs are able to learn patterns, for example, to associate object categories to raw image data. Applied in the context of reinforcement learning, a CNN can be used to approximate the internal value function of the agent, and, thus, to map actions to constellations of data in a particular state [65]. In this regard, effective progress has been made in addressing the curse of dimensionality in the field of reinforcement learning [15,56]. Deep reinforcement learning is supposed to be able to scale to decision-making problems that were previously unsolvable, for example, settings with high-dimensional state and action spaces. Recent work in this field has shown outstanding progress, which started with an algorithm that could learn to play a range of Atari 2600 video games at super-human level, directly from screen pixels [65]. A comprehensive survey of efforts in deep reinforcement learning can be found in Reference [66].

4. Solution Architecture

4.1. A Logistics Assistance System

A logistics assistance system has been developed to assist decision-makers in distribution networks using the Python programming language [16]. This LAS utilises basic components related to a transactional system in a distribution network, such as Enterprise Resource Planning. Figure 1 shows the architecture of the LAS. The data are extracted from the transactional system and loaded into a data warehouse. KPIs are calculated, and any deterioration of the value of a KPI beyond the previously assigned limit triggers an alert in a corresponding key performance indicator management system (KPIMS) [67]. These systems recommend potential actions that are designed to improve the value of the KPI. A recommended action by the KPIMS is expected to increase the intrinsic value of the KPI that triggers the alert, but it could reduce the intrinsic value of other KPIs. Since each of the KPIMS recommends actions independently from the others, the LAS aims to consider the impact of the actions on the entire network and improve the network's performance as a whole.

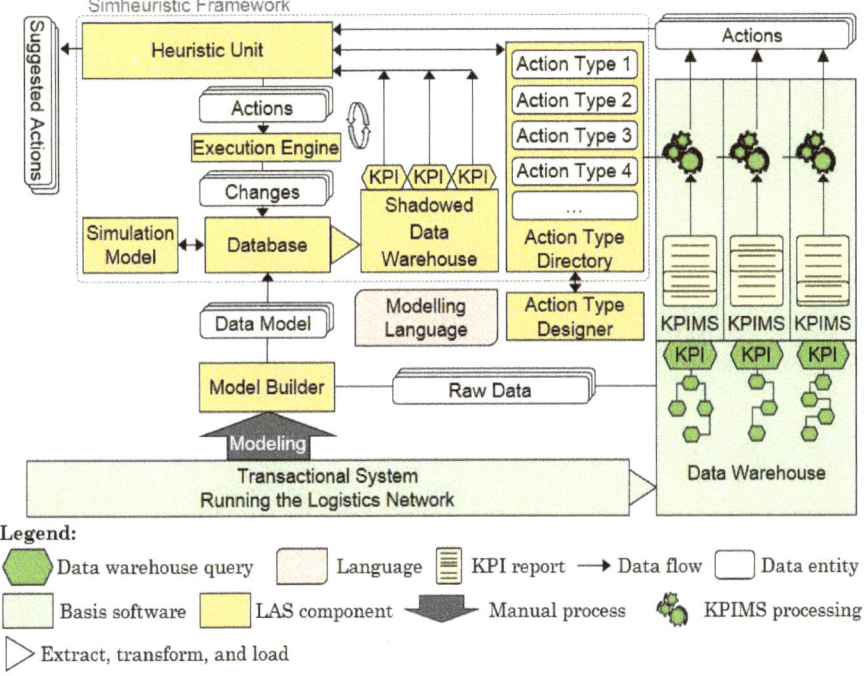

Figure 1. The architecture of the developed Logistics Assistance System (LAS) [68].

In addition, the data are extracted from the transactional system by the model builder into a data model to form the database of a data-driven simulation tool (Figure 1). Rabe and Dross (2015) proposed the use of data-driven simulation tools to apply actions using SQL statements, such as SimChain, which is a generic supply chain simulation model based on the Siemens Plant Simulation tool [69]. The developers of the LAS used SimChain to model a similar distribution network previously [70].

In the LAS, actions are derived from action types [71], which are defined by simulation experts. An action type represents a generic description of an action, for example, centralising an SKU in a site without specifying the SKU and the site. To derive actions from the action types, input parameters are specified, for example, SKU 1 in site A. Action types are defined in the action type designer by decision-makers of the LAS using a domain-specific modelling language. The action types are stored in an action type directory that can be accessed by the KPIMS and the heuristic unit in the simheuristic framework (cf. Figure 1). The actions recommended by the KPIMS and the actions derived from action types form the search space of actions for the heuristic unit.

In the heuristic unit, the simheuristic approach is represented by simulation and a metaheuristic algorithm. The metaheuristic algorithm explores the search space and constructs action plans to be evaluated. The changes applied by actions are executed as SQL statements in the database. These data are then transferred to a "shadowed data warehouse", which mimics the calculation of the operational KPI, but for simulated data. The shadowed data warehouse is introduced in order to avoid any potential mix-up of the simulated (experimental) data with the real operational data sets. The (simulated) KPIs calculated from the shadowed data warehouse form the objective values to be optimised by the metaheuristic. The construction and evaluation continue until a termination condition is met. Then, suggested actions as an action plan are recommended to decision-makers, who are the main users of the LAS.

4.2. Semantic Model for Action Types in Wholesale Logistics Networks

To increase the LAS's flexibility and usability,decision-makers can model and integrate user-generated action types. For this purpose, decision-makers can utilize a specifically developed domain-specific modelling language, which is tailored to the model of action types in wholesale logistics networks. Accessing the developed domain-specific modelling language can be performed via the Action Type Designer, an integrated development interface (IDE), providing all benefits of common IDEs such as code completion or syntax highlighting.

All action types are based on the same semantic model. Therefore, the semantic model of an action type must be capable of representing all required information for all possible action types in a logistics network. Action types can be instantiated by adding type-specific parameters to the semantic model's attributes [72].

The attributes of the semantic model serve different purposes and are, thus, divided into different categories. The first category of attributes has informative purposes, such as the action type's *name* , *description*, *id*, the *owner's id*, and a list of ids for representing the involved modellers.

Action types represent changes to the underlying simulation model. For the specification of these changes, functional attributes are used. The attribute *input* is used to define the affected entities of the logistics network. To specify the effects on those entities, *statements* of the domain-specific modelling language are used.

Meta information of action types is stored in meta-attributes of the semantic model. For example, it may take some time to fully execute a set of actions in the real logistics network. Therefore, the required time for executing actions is stored in the attribute *time till effect*. Additionally, executing an action may entail costs. The costs of an action are stored in the attribute *total costs*.

The semantic model additionally includes domain-specific information [68,73,74], for example, the *frequency* or the *impact* of an action type on the logistics network, which can be stored in corresponding attributes of the model. Changes to the network can be categorised into two different groups, *structural* and *parametrical* changes. A structural change alters the structure of the network, for instance, adding new routes, sites, or SKUs to a site. Actions that affect attributes of the logistics network's entities are categorised as parametrical, for example, increasing the safety stock or changing the frequency of a route. In addition, *correlations* between different action types and their actions' impact on the network can be modelled. For example, when "centralising an assortment", "increasing the safety stock" of any centralised SKU might be a promising candidate for further actions. Thus, a positive relation is defined between "centralise" and "increase the safety stock".

After the parameterisation of an action type, the corresponding derived actions can be stored in the semantic model's attribute *actions*. An overview of the semantic model is given in Table 1.

Table 1. The semantic model for action types in wholesale logistics networks, based on Reference [72].

Attribute	Description	Category
Actions	List with all derived actions, depending on the logistics network's state.	Functional
Correlation	Domain-specific information that specifies possible correlations and their correlation factors with other action types.	Domain-specific
Description	Free description of the action type.	Informative
Frequency	Domain-specific information that specifies the frequency of the implementation of derived actions.	Domain-specific
Id	Id of the action type.	Informative
Impact	Domain-specific information that specifies the impact of derived actions to the underlying logistics network's performance.	Domain-specific
Input	List of input parameters.	Functional
Modelers	List with ids of the involved modelers.	Informative
Name	Name of the action type.	Informative
Owner	Owner of the action type.	Informative
Parametrical	Domain-specific information that specifies, for an action type, whether the corresponding changes are parametrical.	Domain-specific
Statements	List of statements, representing changes to the underlying logistics network.	Functional
Structural	Domain-specific information that specifies whether the corresponding changes of the action type are structural.	Domain-specific
Time till effect	Required time for a corresponding action to take effect.	Meta
Total costs	The costs associated with the implementation of derived actions.	Meta

4.3. Abstracting the Modelling of Action Types from the Underlying Simulation's Data Base

Actions are closely related to the underlying simulation's data model, resulting in multiple issues. Modelling action types requires in-depth knowledge of the database's structure, for example, for specifying the areas of the database that are affected by applying corresponding actions. Another issue arises when the database's structure changes, for example, when the simulation software is updated or a new simulation tool is introduced. To address these problems, the authors propose to decouple the modelling of action types from the underlying simulation data model [75].

When applying an action, a set of corresponding entities of the logistics network needs to be adapted, accordingly. In a data-driven simulation, an entity can be described by entries in a database's table. To identify the correct entities, the table's name and the entities' attributes are defined as part of statements in the modelling process of an action type (Section 4.2). Thus, when applying an action, multiple entries in the database might be changed (Figure 2).

However, the simulation's database and, therefore, the data model, are typically predefined by the simulation tool that is being used. Thus, the data model is not easily adjustable. When decoupling the modelling of action types from the data model of the underlying simulation, an additional data model is required: an enterprise-specific data model. This enterprise-specific data model can be structured in the way that best suits the decision-makers' knowledge and needs.

Using an enterprise-specific data model, action types can be specified against this model and not against the simulation data model. To correctly convert actions into changes to the simulation data model, each attribute of the simulation data model must be distinctly linked to the corresponding attribute of the enterprise-specific data model (Figure 3). Such a mapping can be defined, for example, in the form of a JSON-file. In the process of executing an action, the information for the mapping between the two models is read from the JSON-file, so that changes can be applied to the simulation data model, accordingly [75].

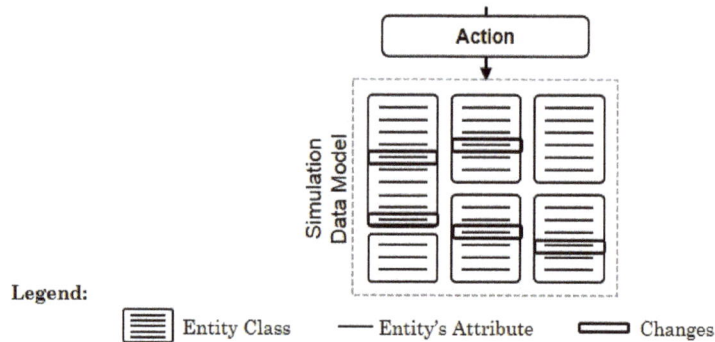

Figure 2. Applying an action directly to the simulation's database.

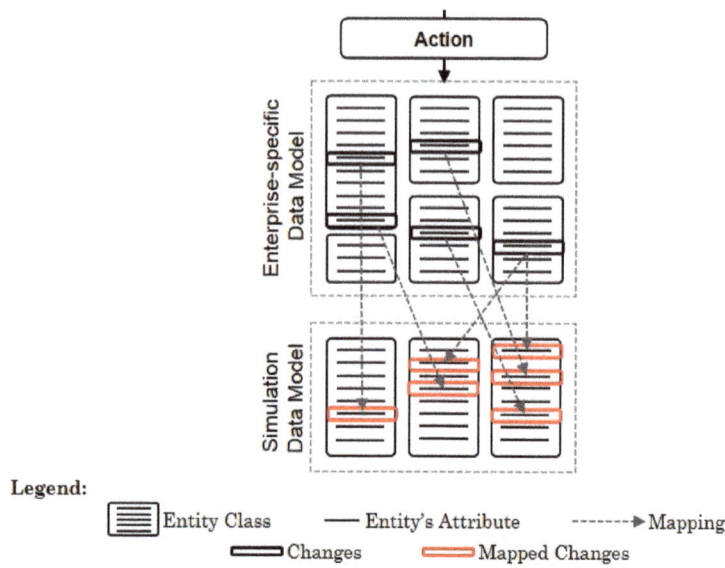

Figure 3. Applying an action to the enterprise-specific data model and mapping the resulting changes to the simulation data model.

By utilizing this approach, action types can be modelled against an enterprise-specific data model, which can be adapted to the modellers' knowledge and needs. This approach allows decision-makers to become modellers and to specify action types against a common data structure and with known names of the entities and their attributes. Another advantage of this approach is that when the simulation data model changes, only the mapping must be adjusted and not all the definitions of the action types. This saves resources, reduces the risk of faults, and improves the acceptance of the method in general.

5. Addressing the Performance Challenge: Deep Reinforcement Learning

As mentioned above, creating an algorithm that is able to master a varied range of challenging tasks by teaching itself in a trial-and-error procedure is one of the major goals of reinforcement learning. Reinforcement learning in general considers tasks in which an agent interacts with an environment through a sequence of observations, actions, and rewards. To use reinforcement learning successfully in situations approaching real-world complexity, however, agents are confronted with a challenge: they have to derive efficient representations of the environment from high-dimensional sensory inputs and use these to generalize past experiences to new situations (cf. Section 3.2). The authors of Reference [15] approached this challenge by creating an algorithm that used a Deep Q-Network (DQN) as the central value function approximation.

Almost all reinforcement learning algorithms are based on estimating value functions. The algorithm used for the DQN agent, Q-learning, is based on the Q-function, a function of state-action pairs that expresses how beneficial it is for the agent to perform a given action in a given state with respect to the expected return [76]. More formally, the Q-function expresses the value of taking an action a in a state s under a policy π with respect to the expected return starting from s, taking the action a, and thereafter following policy π. For small problems, the Q-function can be stored as a table, but for larger problems, this table quickly gets too large to be stored in memory. Moreover, the time and data required to fill the table accurately would be too high. In many tasks to which one would like to apply reinforcement learning, most states encountered will never have been experienced exactly in the same way before. The only way to learn anything at all in these cases is to generalize from previously experienced states to ones that have never been seen before. Hence, for larger problems, the key issue is that some sort of function approximation is included. In this regard, advances in deep neural networks have made it possible to approximate the Q-function, for example, with a CNN.

Mnih et al. [15] tested an agent with a DQN on the Arcade Learning Environment (ALE), which is a software framework designed to simplify the development of agents that play arbitrary Atari 2600 games and, therefore, offers a method to evaluate the development of general, domain-independent reinforcement learning agents [77]. Its source code is publicly available on the Internet [78]. Through the ALE, researchers have access to several dozen games through a single common interface. Eighteen actions can be input to the game via a digital joystick: three positions of the joystick for each axis, plus a single button. The DQN approach of Reference [15] outperformed the best existing reinforcement learning methods on 43 of the 49 games without incorporating any of the additional prior knowledge about the Atari 2006 games used by other approaches. In conclusion, the DQN algorithm trained itself and reached super-human performance just by using the game pixels as the observation and the game score as the reward signal from the environment.

The work by Mnih et al. [15] inspired the authors to test the DQN agent as a reinforcement learning approach to the performance challenge, as discussed earlier in this article (cf. Section 1). For the experiments, the general working principles of the DQN agent have been retained, but the parameters of this agent have been slightly adjusted. The implementation of the DQN has been built with the Python API for TensorFlow, an open-source software library for numerical computations using data flow graphs [79]. After the reinforcement learning agent applies an action to the database, the simulation model is instantiated and the simulation is run as described above. A reward calculation function generates the reward signal from the simulation output data by computing a scalar reward signal, using the changes in costs and performance. The reward signal is then routed back to the DQN for training [80]. In order to express the state *s* of the logistics system configuration as an image, a feature extraction function selects the different features from the tables in the MySQL database and composes them into an image (Figure 4).

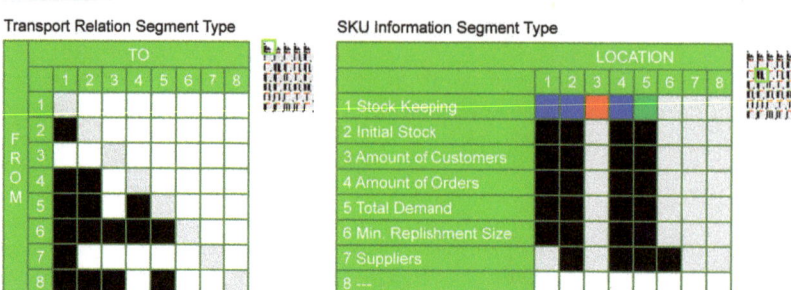

Figure 4. Graphical state representation (small image) and details of two exemplary image segments (large images) [80].

The image has been designed to look similar to an Atari game screen in order to make the problem accessible for the DQN agent. The general idea behind the design of the state representation as an image is to profit from the research regarding further domain-independent agents in the future.

Since the agent needs to learn a mapping from states to actions, the state representation also needs to encode information that enables for concluding from states to actions. For instance, if the agent is intended for learning to make a decision regarding the inventory, useful information to make such a decision, for example, inventory levels and customer demands, needs to be included in the state representation. For actions regarding, for example, machines, other information is needed in the state representation. Thus, the information needed in the state representation heavily depends on the action types available in the system (see Section 4.2). Consequently, the features that have to be selected from the MySQL database for the state *s* are derived from the action types used. In order to address the requirements regarding the scalability of the state representation, the state image is built from different image segments. Each segment corresponds to a segment type, similar to the previously explained relationship between actions and action types. The size of each segment is fixed. The actual segment size is derived from the size of the largest segment type. The overall design was chosen to enable the CNN to more easily identify patterns within the state data.

In order to generate a scalar reward signal for the reinforcement learning agent, a decrease in the total costs after taking an action is translated into a positive reward. An increase in the total costs, on the other hand, is translated into a negative reward. Furthermore, besides the bare costs, the difference in the logistics performance before and after applying the action is also incorporated into the reward. The authors have decided to define a penalty cost that is multiplied with the percentage change in the service level. If the service level decreases, a penalty is generated. If the service level increases, a bonus payment is generated. The service level costs are meant to express the loss of customer orders in the future due to unsatisfied customers, or the increase of customer orders from satisfied customers. The difference in the logistics costs and the service level costs are summed up and interpreted as the total costs caused by an action. Finally, these total costs are scaled down to generate the final reward signal, which is sent back to the agent. The scaling is done to get as close as possible to the architecture used in the original DQN implementation.

6. Addressing the Performance Challenge: Exploiting Domain-Specific Information

The performance of the LAS can be evaluated based on the impact of the recommended action plans on the distribution network and on the number of simulation runs. This section focuses on guiding the metaheuristic algorithm in the heuristic unit to find promising actions to be added to the action plan. The approach investigates the potential actions and explores information to guide the search. This information is called domain-specific information and is added to the action type definitions, such as the type of changes, success, and correlation (Section 4.2) [68,73,74].

6.1. Utilizing the Characteristics of Action Type Classes

The first illustrated DSI concerns the type of changes applied by an action. An action can change a parametrical value of an entity in a distribution network, for example, the stock level of an SKU at a site. Actions of this kind are called parametrical actions. For example, an action that increases the stock level of SKU 1 at site A is a parametrical action.

Other actions might add an entity to the network or delete an entity. These actions cause structural changes in the network, such as centralising SKU 1 at site A. These actions cause structural and parametrical changes. Centralising SKU 1 at site A is realised by several changes, for example, adding SKU 1 to site A if it is not at site A, removing SKU 1 from the other sites, establishing transport relations between site A and the other sites if not currently existing, and specifying the parametrical values of SKU 1 at site A. This action should define the parametrical values for the newly added entities, for example, SKU 1 at site A, and the transport relations between site A and the other sites.

Accordingly, actions are classified as structural or parametrical based on their type of changes. Structural actions cause significant changes in the network. Their changes delete the impact of previously applied parametrical actions if they affect the same entity in the network. For example, action a_1 increases the stock level of SKU 1 at site B, and a_2 centralises SKU 1 at site A. Action a_2 removes SKU 1 at site B from the network when it is applied. If a_2 follows a_1, the change in the stock level caused by a_1 is removed by removing the entity by a_2.

In order to consider the structural and parametrical changes in the selection of actions, the selection probability of an action is biased according to its type of changes and its position in an action plan. Structural actions are preferred at the beginning of an action plan and parametrical actions at its end. Figure 5 shows a proposed probability distribution of actions' types of changes that changes linearly along the length of an action plan, l. In Equations (1) and (2), $prob_i^S$ is the selection probability of structural actions at position i of an action plan. If structural changes are selected, a structural action is selected from the potential structural actions.

$$prob_i^S = prob_1^S - \frac{prob_1^P - prob_1^S}{l-1}(i-1), \ i = 1, 2, ..., l \tag{1}$$

$$prob_i^P = 1 - prob_i^S. \tag{2}$$

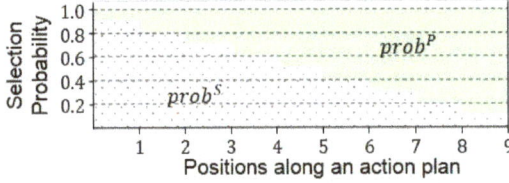

Figure 5. Probability distribution of actions' types of changes along the length of an action plan.

6.2. Building on Success Experience

Another DSI is the success of actions in improving the performance of a distribution network. The term success is defined with respect to an action. The impact of an action on a network is investigated to determine whether it increases or decreases the performance measures. For example, Figure 6 shows actions, a_1 and a_2, that increase the service level and an action, a_4, that reduces the service level. Actions that increase the service level get a higher success value than the actions that decrease the service level. Within the actions that increase the service level, their impact of the actions varies, and accordingly, their success value varies, such as a_1 and a_2 in Figure 6.

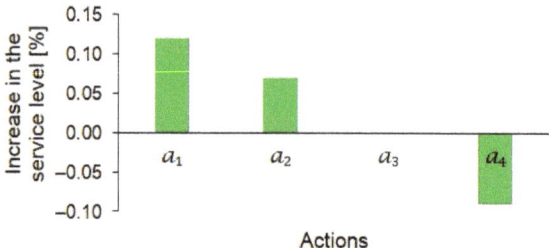

Figure 6. Impact of actions on the service level.

Actions with a high success value tend to increase the performance of the network, and hence, increasing their selection probability might guide the metaheuristic algorithm to construct promising action plans. Actions with a high success value get a higher selection probability than actions with a lower success value. For example, the selection probabilities of the actions in Figure 6 might be assigned as 0.32, 0.28, 0.24, and 0.16 to actions a_1, a_2, a_3, and a_4, respectively.

While the success values of concrete actions can only be measured for the single and parametrized actions themselves, these values cannot be expected to contribute to the performance improvement, directly, because there is a low probability that the specific current action has already been evaluated before and, thus, owns a success attribute. Therefore, success may have to be regarded only indirectly: Measured success values of actions are summarized for the respective action types, and this success attribute of the action types is then used to steer the construction of action plans. With this procedure, action types are preferred if the associated actions have often led to improvements in the past.

6.3. Defining Relations between Actions

The last DSI that we propose is the correlation between two actions and their impact on the performance of the network. In this context, the joint impact of a sequence of two actions on the performance of a network is compared to their expected impact if they are applied individually. In Figure 7, the expected impact of applying actions a_1 and a_2 is an increase of 0.19% in the service level, given by the summation of the impact of the single actions a_1 (0.12%) and a_2 (0.07%). Actually, the sequence a_1 followed by a_2 increases the service level by only 0.15%. Thus, applying these two actions as $[a_1, a_2]$ has a negative influence ("$-$"). The sequence $[a_2, a_1]$ causes an increase in the service level by 0.28%. Thus, it has a positive impact ("+") compared to the expected impact of the single actions. Another example of the positive impact is the sequence $[a_1, a_3]$. If the expected impact of a sequence does not differ from the actual impact, the relation is a weak relation ("$\sim$"), for example, sequence $[a_2, a_3]$ in Figure 7.

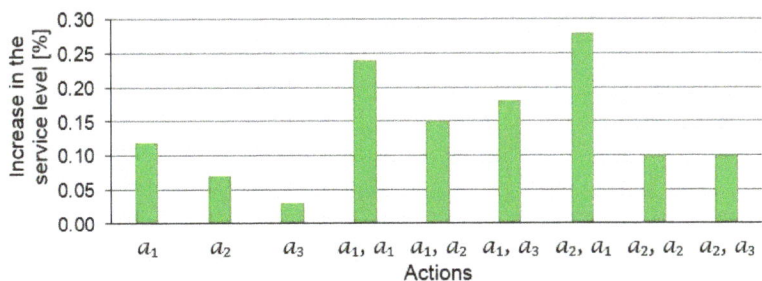

Figure 7. Impact of sequence of actions on the service level.

The correlation between actions could be tabulated in a correlation matrix. Rows represent the first applied action in the sequence, and columns represent the second applied action. The cells show the relation between the impact of a sequence of actions and their expected impact on the network as "+", "~", and "−" for positive, weak, and negative relations, respectively. The relations extracted from Figure 7 are tabulated in Table 2. The rest of the correlation matrix shows relations between other actions in the search space.

Table 2. Correlation matrix example.

	a_1	a_2	a_3	a_4	a_5	a_6	...
a_1	$\sim$	$-$	$+$	$\sim$	$-$	$-$	
a_2	$+$	$-$	$\sim$	$-$	$\sim$	$\sim$	
...							

The cell between a_1 and a_1 is a duplication of an action. An action can be duplicated by applying it twice. If an action increases the stock level of an SKU at a site by 10 units, its duplication increases the stock level by 20 units. Accordingly, the performance of the network is affected and might vary from the expected impact.

Similar to the previous section, applying actions affects the performance of the network, and their impact might be used to guide the selection of actions to construct promising action plans. The selection probability of actions is increased if the actions are in a positive relation with already selected actions. For example, if action a_2 is selected, then the recommended action is a_1 to increase the service level (Table 2). Selecting a_2 does not increase the service level as expected, and selecting a_3 does not influence the expected increase in the value. Thus, the selection probability of a_1 becomes higher than a_3.

7. Addressing the Performance Challenge: Reducing the Number of Evaluations

Another performance measure of the LAS is the number of simulation runs, which we define to be the number of objective function evaluations. In order to reduce the number of evaluations of the objective function, a selective evaluation might be performed, or evaluations might be skipped. In this research, the evaluation of the impact of an action plan is skipped if the action plan has previously been evaluated [81].

Previously evaluated action plans might be identical to newly formed action plans, or they can be equivalent to them. Equivalent action plans have an identical impact on the performance of the distribution network, but are not identical action plans. Figure 8 shows an example of equivalent action plans. These action plans cause the same changes in the network and, hence, result in the same impact on the performance. The performance of an equivalent action plan can directly be used, without again evaluating the performance of the newly formed plan.

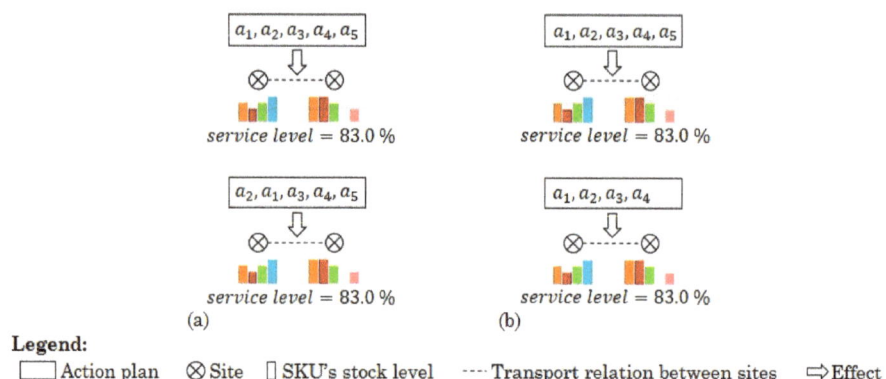

Legend:

▢ Action plan ⊗ Site ▯ SKU's stock level ---- Transport relation between sites ⇨ Effect

Figure 8. Equivalent action plans: (**a**) action plans with interchangeable actions and (**b**) action plans with redundant actions.

In order to identify equivalent action plans we define interchangeable and redundant actions. Interchangeable actions can be reordered in an action plan without affecting the impact of the action plan on the performance of the network (Figure 8a). Actions a_1 and a_2 in Figure 8a have been reordered without affecting the applied changes and the impact of the action plan on the service level; a_1 and a_2 are interchangeable actions. Actions that affect different entities in the network can be reordered without affecting the impact of the action plan. These actions are interchangeable if they do not interfere with an overall parameter of the network, such as the capacity of a site. For example, a_1 increases the stock level of SKU 1 at site A, and a_2 increases the stock level of SKU 2 at site A. Both actions affect different entities in the network, SKU 1 at site A and SKU 2 at site A. Applying the changes by any of the actions does not affect the changes applied by the other action. However, if the total capacity of site A reaches its limit after applying any of these actions, the resulting applied changes differ when the actions are swapped.

Redundant actions can be removed from the action plan without affecting the impact of the action plan on the distribution network (Figure 8b). Action a_5 has been removed from the action plan in Figure 8b. The resulting action plan applies the same changes as the original action plan, without removing a_5, and the service remains unchanged. Action a_5 is a redundant action, because its removal has no effect on the changes applied in the network. These actions can be duplicated structural actions. A structural action adds or removes entities from the network, and its duplication repeats these changes without causing additional changes in the network. A duplicated parametrical action that causes incremental changes is not redundant, because it causes an incremental increase or decrease in the value of the affected parameter.

Defining the equivalent action plans based on interchangeable and redundant actions enables skipping the evaluation of an action plan. An action plan is rated as its equivalent action plan that was evaluated previously.

Another approach reduces the number of actions to reduce the number of evaluations. In this approach, actions are grouped. The grouped actions replace actions and form a smaller search space of actions to be explored. For example, if two actions are grouped, the search space of actions can be reduced from 100 actions to 50 actions. Exploring the search space of 50 actions obviously requires a smaller number of evaluations.

The grouping criteria might be defined by the decision-maker, for example, grouping actions that affect SKUs based on an SKU assortment at a site [17]. For example, a distribution network has two sites, site A and site B. Assortment 1 includes SKU 1 and SKU 2, and assortment 2 includes SKU 3 and SKU 4. Then, action a_1 that increases the stock level of SKU 1 at site A and action a_2 that increases the stock level of SKU 2 at site A are grouped to form a new action a_1^* that increases the stock level of SKUs in assortment 1 at site A. Similarly, action a_3 that increases the stock level of SKU 1 at site B and a_4 that increases the stock level of SKU 2 at site B are grouped to form the new action a_2^* that increases the stock level of SKUs in assortment 2 at site B. The reduction in the number of actions depends on the number of actions assigned to an assortment. As a result, the optimisation algorithm explores a smaller number of actions.

In order to construct an action plan from the grouped actions, the number of selected grouped actions is almost certainly lower than the length of the action plan. Four actions are selected to form an action plan of length four. If two actions are grouped, they form an action plan of length four. Therefore, this reduction in the number of selected actions further reduces the number of potential action plans and the number of evaluations.

8. Evaluation and Results

In order to test the proposed approaches, we used a database from a distribution network of an international material trading company. The database was extracted from their enterprise resource planning system and was verified and validated according to a procedure model presented by Rabe et al. [82]. In this research, we filtered this database down to a subset of five sites and 30 SKUs. This database represents the database in Figure 1. Then, we adapted the *evolutionary algorithm* to utilise the actions' DSI. This information is assigned to the action types, and from there then it is inherited to the derived actions from the action types. The selection probability of actions is changed based on their DSI. For example, considering the actions' type of changes, the actions are classified as structural and parametrical actions. The selection probability of these classes is changed according to Equations (1) and (2). An action is selected randomly from the respective selected class. Thus, the selection probability of actions is biased based on their type of changes.

We compared a completely random selection of actions with a biased selection of actions in the construction of action plans in the EA's initial generation. The number of generations that were required to stagnate and the quality of the corresponding recommended action plans were recorded for the comparison. The quality of the action plans has been evaluated based on the costs and the service level. Fifty individuals form a generation in the EA. The crossover and mutation probabilities were set to 0.8 and 0.3, respectively. The crossover forms, CR, were the one-point crossover, the two-point crossover, and the uniform crossover. In mutation, MU, one randomly selected action was replaced, or multiple actions were selected to be replaced. Each experiment setup was run ten times. Table 3 records the average performance and demonstrates the gap analysis of the difference between random selection and the biased selection of actions.

Table 3. Comparison between random selection of actions and biased selection in an evolutionary algorithm (EA) experiment using the gap analysis (CR = crossover form, MU = mutation form).

CR	MU	Random Selection			Biased Selection			Gap (Biased − Random)		
		c (€)	sl (%)	N_s	c (€)	sl (%)	N_s	c (€)	sl (%)	N_s
1-point	1-action	90,420	84.58	76	90,309	84.74	31	−111	0.2	−45
1-point	multi	91,414	84.65	41	90,045	84.79	41	−1369	0.1	0
2-point	1-action	90,630	84.72	73	90,806	84.81	34	176	0.1	−39
2-point	multi	90,673	84.69	65	91,340	84.83	43	667	0.1	−22
uniform	1-action	90,086	84.75	89	88,039	85.11	37	−2047	0.4	−52
uniform	multi	91,699	84.72	63	92,292	85.03	32	593	0.3	−31

Next, we have tested the approach that exploits the definition of equivalent action plans. In this experiment, the EA selected actions randomly, and the evaluation of an action plan was skipped if an equivalent action plan was previously evaluated. Figure 9 shows the time distribution during an experiment run when the crossover and the mutation probabilities were set to 0.8 and 0.3, respectively. The number of simulation runs decreased by more than 15%.

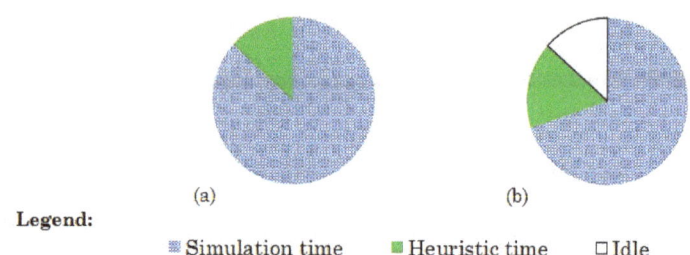

Legend:

⬚ Simulation time   ■ Heuristic time   □ Idle

Figure 9. The time distribution in (**a**) a reference EA experiment and (**b**) an EA experiment utilising the equivalent action plans approach.

For the experimentation with the *DQN agent*, the authors assumed that one training episode for the reinforcement learning agent consists of taking three actions. Hence, once the three actions have been taken, the simulation is reset to its initial state and the agent can start a new training episode. The hyper-parameters of the architecture have been kept mostly the same for all the experiments. However, further architectures for the internal DQN were tested. For each architecture, the reinforcement learning agent was trained with at least 1000 episodes, each consisting of taking three actions, which resulted in at least 3000 evaluative simulation runs for each architecture. In most of the cases, the agent was able to gradually learn to take the best three actions possible for the initial state of the logistics network after about half of the training episodes. By conducting these experiments, the authors could demonstrate that a general reinforcement learning agent was able to generate action plans just from its trained internal value function approximation. Hence, in general, the presented approach can be used to reduce the response time T_D (cp. Section 1). However, as a drawback, the total runtime of each experiment took several days. As expected, the bottleneck in terms of computing performance was not the back-propagation through the CNN, but the simulation time needed for each evaluative simulation run. Although the experiments have been performed on relatively small test models of a logistics network, the results of the experiments with the DQN implementation were promising, since they showed that a general purpose reinforcement learning agent can in fact be trained to optimize a logistics network model solely from a state representation, a reward signal, and the available actions types.

9. Discussion

The approaches explained in Sections 4 and 5 aim to improve the performance of the LAS. This performance is evaluated based on the performance of the simheuristic's components – metaheuristics and simulation. The quality of found solutions is a major performance measure to evaluate the metaheuristics used to solve an optimisation problem [7]. Additionally, the run time of the algorithm is used to evaluate it [83]. In this research, we used the objective values of the found solutions and the number of simulation runs to evaluate the recommended approaches. The number of simulation runs represents the number of objective function evaluations, which is an indicator of the run time of an algorithm to recommend a solution [27].

Researchers proposed approaches to improve the performance of the metaheuristics by focusing on the analysis of the search space. For example, Bode et al. [41] screened solutions before their evaluation. Karimi et al. [84] clustered the problem's search space before exploring it, and Ku and Arthanari [85] replaced the search space with a smaller space. Furthermore, researchers have filtered the solutions to reduce the number of objective function evaluations, such as Cai et al. [86] and Alsheddy et al. [13].

Other approaches have examined the search algorithms. They investigated improvements to the local search, such as Alsheddy et al. [13], who aimed to escape from a local optimum by introducing penalties. Other researchers have investigated machine learning and data mining to learn from the patterns [87,88]. Amaran et al. [89] stated that problem information could be used to construct initial promising solutions as an input to the optimisation algorithm. Forming these solutions by selecting its parts randomly based on problem information is called randomly biased selection [42].

In Section 6, we introduced an approach to guide the search of a metaheuristic algorithm. In this approach, DSI is used to prioritise which actions to select while constructing action plans. The experiments utilising the type of changes to construct action plans showed promising results for identifying initial solutions for the algorithm. We used the Mann-Whitney U test [90] to compare our approach to random selection of actions. The null hypothesis in comparing the random selection and the biased selection is rejected concerning decreasing costs, increasing the service level, and reducing the number of generations to stagnate at p-values of 0.0961, 0.0000, and 0.0000, respectively. These results suggest a significant impact of DSI on the performance of the metaheuristics of the LAS, and our claims of recommending better solutions' quality and decreasing the number of generations to stagnate are accepted.

The domain-specific information can be used to alter the variation operators of the found action plans in the subsequent iterations in a metaheuristic algorithm. In our research, these operators are represented as modified crossover and mutation. Because initial solutions based on the type of changes helped the algorithm to recommend better solutions than the random selection of actions, we expect to get a similar effect in implementing them in crossover and mutation. Combining different DSI is a field for further investigation.

In addition, we propose an approach to reduce the number of simulation runs by defining equivalent solutions. This approach keeps a list of evaluated solutions and increases the EA's computational time a bit; but this is compensated by a reduction in the number of simulation runs (Figure 9). The memory usage might be overcome if the algorithm can have access to a table where this list of evaluated solutions is stored.

In conclusion, simulation runs consume a large portion of the computational time of the algorithm run in a simheuristic approach. Our approach reduced this percentage and enabled the algorithm to recommend solutions in shorter time.

10. Summary and Outlook

In this research, we have developed a logistics assistance system to support decision-making in material trading networks. Decision-makers face a challenging task in selecting actions to improve the performance of the networks. The developed LAS is based on a simheuristics framework that combines simulation and metaheuristics. For the metaheuristics, we have studied reinforcement learning and evolutionary algorithms. Additionally, we have proposed approaches to address performance challenges of the LAS that are represented as the quality of recommended actions and the number of simulation runs. Our approaches are based on utilising domain-specific information, reducing the number of actions, and defining equivalent solutions.

We have developed a suitable implementation and used a subset of real-world data to evaluate our LAS. Our results show that reinforcement learning requires a significant training time. However, after learning, it recommends promising actions upon request. The domain-specific information approach guides the search of an optimisation algorithm to select promising actions, and hence, improves the performance of the LAS. Defining equivalent action plans has reduced the number of simulation runs by up to 15%.

Our approaches are limited to distribution networks. We defined and tested them on a distribution network of an international trading company. In other networks or applications, the specific definition of the domain-specific information as well as of the equivalency of action plans should be studied.

For further research, we investigate other domain-specific information to guide the selection of actions in the LAS. Taking advantage of combining reinforcement learning and the evolutionary algorithm is another approach to be investigated. This combination requires the study of the schema to integrate both approaches. Furthermore, new parameters might become necessary to be defined and initialised.

Author Contributions: Conceptualization and research supervision, M.R.; General methodology of LAS and implementation of decision support system, F.D.; Development of domain-specific description language, D.S.; Development and evaluation of reinforcement learning approach, F.D.; Development and evaluation of domain-specific biasing methods, M.A.; Design of paper M.R. and M.A.; Original draft preparation, M.A.; Editing, M.R. and M.A.; Supervision, M.R. All authors have read and agreed to the published version of the manuscript.

Funding: This research was partially funded by the German University of Jordan, the Graduate School of Logistics in Dortmund (Germany) and by thyssenkrupp Materials International GmbH.

Data Availability Statement: This research has been based on real enterprise data taken from the IT systems of a German company. These data have been handed out under strict NDA and experience specific procedures to ensure their classification, which unfortunately hinders their free release.

Conflicts of Interest: The authors declare no conflict of interest.

Abbreviations

The following abbreviations are used in this manuscript:

SKU	stock keeping unit
KPI	key performance indicator
EA	evolutionary algorithm
DES	discrete event simulation
LAS	logistics assistance system
CNN	Convolutional Neural Network
KPIMS	key performance indicator management system
IDE	integrated development interface
DGN	Deep Q-Network
ALE	Arcade Learning Environment
DSI	domain-specific information
CR	crossover form
MU	mutation form

References

1. Stadtler, H. Supply Chain Management—An Overview. In *Supply Chain Management and Advanced Planning: Concepts, Models, Software, and Case Studies*; Stadtler, H., Kilger, C., Eds.; Springer: Berlin/Heidelberg, Germany, 2008; pp. 9–36.
2. Ravindran, A.R. Managing Supply Chains: An Introduction. In *Multiple Criteria Decision Making in Supply Chain Management*; Ravindran, A.R., Ed.; CRC Press, Taylor and Francis Group: Boca Raton, FL, USA, 2016; pp. 1–14.
3. Sürie, C.; Wagner, M. Supply Chain Analysis. In *Supply Chain Management and Advanced Planning: Concepts, Models, Software, and Case Studies*; Stadtler, H., Kilger, C., Eds.; Springer: Berlin/Heidelberg, Germany, 2008; pp. 37–64.
4. Buriol, L.S. Network Optimization. In *Handbook of Heuristics*; Martí, R., Pardalos, P.M., Resende, M.G.C., Eds.; Springer: Cham, Switzerland, 2018; pp. 1123–1140.
5. Law, A.M. *Simulation Modeling and Analysis*, 5th ed.; McGraw-Hill: New York, NY, USA, 2015.
6. Bianchi, L.; Dorigo, M.; Gambardella, L.M.; Gutjahr, W.J. A Survey on Metaheuristics for Stochastic Combinatorial Optimization. *Nat. Comput.* **2009**, *8*, 239–287. [CrossRef]
7. Talbi, E.G. *Metaheuristics: From Design to Implementation*; John Wiley and Sons: Hoboken, NJ, USA, 2009.
8. Datta, S.; Roy, S.; Davim, J.P. Optimization Techniques: An Overview. In *Optimization in Industry: Present Practices and Future Scopes*; Datta, S., Davim, J.P., Eds.; Management and Industrial Engineering; Springer International Publishing: Cham, Switzerland, 2019; pp. 1–11.
9. Juan, A.A.; Faulin, J.; Grasman, S.E.; Rabe, M.; Figueira, G. A Review of Simheuristics: Extending Metaheuristics to Deal with Stochastic Combinatorial Optimization Problems. *Oper. Res. Perspect.* **2015**, *2*, 62–72. [CrossRef]
10. Banks, J.; Carson, J.S., II; Nelson, B.L.; Nicol, D.M. *Discrete-Event System Simulation*, 5th ed.; Pearson: Upper Saddle River, NJ, USA, 2010.
11. Ding, H.; Benyoucef, L.; Xie, X. Stochastic Multi-objective Production-distribution Network Design Using Simulation-based Optimization. *Int. J. Prod. Res.* **2009**, *47*, 479–505. [CrossRef]
12. Deininger, M. *Modellierungsmethode für die Simulationsbasierte Optimierung Rekonfigurierbarer Produktionssysteme*; Fortschritte in der IT in Produktion und Logistik, Cuvillier: Göttingen, Germany, 2019.

13. Alsheddy, A.; Voudouris, C.; Tsang, E.P.K.; Alhindi, A. Guided Local Search. In *Handbook of Heuristics*; Martí, R., Pardalos, P.M., Resende, M.G.C., Eds.; Springer: Cham, Switzerland, 2018; pp. 261–297.

14. Singh, S.; Litman, D.; Kearns, M.; Walker, M. Optimizing Dialogue Management with Reinforcement Learning: Experiments with the NJFun System. *J. Artif. Intell. Res.* **2002**, *16*, 105–133. [CrossRef]

15. Mnih, V.; Kavukcuoglu, K.; Silver, D.; Rusu, A.A.; Veness, J.; Bellemare, M.G.; Graves, A.; Riedmiller, M.; Fidjeland, A.K.; Ostrovski, G.; et al. Human-level Control through Deep Reinforcement Learning. *Nature* **2015**, *518*, 529–533. [CrossRef]

16. Rabe, M.; Dross, F.; Schmitt, D.; Ammouriova, M.; Ipsen, C. Decision Support for Logistics Networks in Materials Trading Using a Simheuristic Framework and User-generated Action Types. In *Simulation in Production and Logistics 2017*; Wenzel, S., Peter, T., Eds.; Kassel University Press: Kassel, Germany, 2017; pp. 109–118.

17. Rabe, M.; Schmitt, D.; Ammouriova, M. Improving the Performance of a Logistics Assistance System for Materials Trading Networks by Grouping Similar Actions. In Proceedings of the 2018 Winter Simulation Conference, Gothenburg, Sweden, 9–12 December 2018; pp. 2861–2872.

18. VDI-Guideline 3633.1. In *Simulation of Systems in Materials Handling, Logistics, and Production: Fundamentals*; Beuth: Berlin, Germany, 2014.

19. Schmidt, J.W.; Taylor, R.E. *Simulation and Analysis of Industrial Systems*; Irwin Series in Quantitative Analysis for Business; Irwin: Homewood, IL, USA, 1970.

20. Rabe, M.; Spieckermann, S.; Wenzel, S. *Verifikation und Validierung für die Simulation in Produktion und Logistik: Vorgehensmodelle und Techniken*; Springer: Berlin/Heidelberg, Germany, 2008.

21. Gutenschwager, K.; Rabe, M.; Spieckermann, S.; Wenzel, S. *Simulation in Produktion und Logistik: Grundlagen und Anwendungen*; Springer Vieweg: Berlin/Heidelberg, Germany, 2017. [CrossRef]

22. Balci, O.; Fujimoto, R.M.; Goldsman, D.; Nance, R.E.; Zeigler, B.P. The State of Innovation in Modeling and Simulation: The Last 50 Years. In Proceedings of the 2017 Winter Simulation Conference, Las Vegas, NV, USA, 3–6 December 2017; pp. 821–836.

23. Fanti, M.P.; Iacobellis, G.; Ukovich, W.; Boschian, V.; Georgoulas, G.; Stylios, C. A Simulation Based Decision Support System for Logistics Management. *J. Comput. Sci.* **2015**, *10*, 86–96. [CrossRef]

24. Pujawan, N.; Arief, M.M.; Tjahjono, B.; Kritchanchai, D. An Integrated Shipment Planning and Storage Capacity Decision Under Uncertainty: A Simulation Study. *Int. J. Phys. Distr. Log.* **2015**, *45*, 913–937. [CrossRef]

25. Fang, D.J.; Li, C. Simulation-based Hybrid Approach to Robust Multi-echelon Inventory Policies for Complex Distribution Networks. *Int. J. Simul. Model.* **2014**, *13*, 377–387. [CrossRef]

26. Ivanov, D. Simulation-based Ripple Effect Modelling in the Supply Chain. *Int. J. Prod. Res.* **2017**, *55*, 2083–2101. [CrossRef]

27. Spall, J.C. *Introduction to Stochastic Search and Optimization: Estimation, Simulation and Control*; Wiley-Interscience: Hoboken, NJ, USA, 2003.

28. Lawler, E.L. Combinatorics. In *Encyclopedia of Operations Research and Management Science*; Gass, S.I., Fu, M.C., Eds.; Springer: Boston, MA, USA, 2013; pp. 192–194. [CrossRef]

29. Schrijver, A. Polyhedral Combinatorics and Combinatorial Optimization. *J. Ann.-Rech. Oper.* **2004**, *15*, 59–74.

30. Taylor, B.W. *Introduction to Management Science*, 11th ed.; Pearson: Boston, MA, USA, 2013.

31. Korte, B.; Vygen, J. *Combinatorial Optimization: Theory and Algorithms*, 6th ed.; Algorithms and Combinatorics; Springer: Berlin/Heidelberg, Germany, 2018; Volume 21. [CrossRef]

32. Sörensen, K.; Glover, F. Metaheuristics. In *Encyclopedia of Operations Research and Management Science*; Gass, S.I., Fu, M.C., Eds.; Springer: Boston, MA, USA, 2013; Volume 1, pp. 960–970. [CrossRef]

33. Osaba, E.; Carballedo, R.; Diaz, F.; Onieva, E.; de La Iglesia, I.; Perallos, A. Crossover Versus Mutation: A Comparative Analysis of the Evolutionary Strategy of Genetic Algorithms Applied to Combinatorial Optimization Problems. *Sci. World J.* **2014**. [CrossRef]

34. Cybulski, R. Vergleich zwischen Algorithmen zur Optimierung Logistischer Netzwerke. Bachelor's Thesis, TU Dortmund University, Dortmund, Germany, 2018.

35. Juan, A.A.; Rabe, M. Combining Simulation with Heuristics to Solve Stochastic Routing and Scheduling Problems. In *Simulation in Production andLogistics—Entscheidungsunterstützung von der Planung bis zur Steuerung*; Dangelmaier, W., Laroque, C., Klaas, A., Eds.; HNI-Verlagsschriftenreihe: Paderborn, Germany, 2013; pp. 641–649.

36. Figueira, G.; Almada-Lobo, B. Hybrid Simulation—Optimization Methods: A Taxonomy and Discussion. *Simul. Model. Pract. Theory* **2014**, *46*, 118–134. [CrossRef]

37. VDI-Guideline 3633.12. *Simulation of Systems in Materials Handling, Logistics, and Production: Simulation and Optimisation*; Beuth: Berlin, Germany, 2016.

38. Jackson, I.; Tolujevs, J.; Reggelin, T. The Combination of Discrete-event Simulation and Genetic Algorithm for Solving the Stochastic Multi-product Inventory Optimization Problem. *Transp. Telecommun. J.* **2018**, *19*, 233–243. [CrossRef]

39. Gutenschwager, K.; Wilhelm, B.; Völker, S. Speeding up Simulation-based Optimization of Supply Networks by Means of a Multi-population Genetic Algorithm and Reuse of Partial Solutions. In *Proceedings of the 2018 Winter Simulation Conference*; Rabe, M., Juan, A.A., Mustafee, N., Skoogh, A., Jain, S., Johansson, B., Eds.; IEEE: Piscataway, PA, USA, 2018; pp. 3036–3047. [CrossRef]

40. Pagès-Bernaus, A.; Ramalhinho, H.; Juan, A.A.; Calvet, L. Designing e-Commerce Supply Chains: A Stochastic Facility—Location Approach. *Int. Trans. Oper. Res.* **2019**, *26*, 507–528. [CrossRef]

41. Bode, F.; Reed, P.; Reuschen, S.; Nowak, W. Search Space Representation and Reduction Methods to Enhance Multiobjective Water Supply Monitoring Design. *Water Resour. Res.* **2019**, *55*, 2257–2278. [CrossRef]

42. Grasas, A.; Juan, A.A.; Faulin, J.; de Armas, J.; Ramalhinho, H. Biased Randomization of Heuristics Using Skewed Probability Distributions: A Survey and some Applications. *Comput. Ind. Eng.* **2017**, *110*, 216–228. [CrossRef]

43. Pétrowski, A.; Ben-Hamida, S. *Evolutionary Algorithms*; Metaheuristics Set; Wiley-Iste: London, UK, 2017; Volume 9.

44. Ahn, C.W. *Advances in Evolutionary Algorithms: Theory, Design and Practice*; Studies in Computational Intelligence; Springer: Berlin/Heidelberg, Germany, 2006; Volume 18. [CrossRef]

45. Chong, E.K.P.; Żak, S.H. *An Introduction to Optimization*, 4th ed.; Wiley: Hoboken, NJ, USA, 2013.

46. Dulebenets, M.A. An Adaptive Island Evolutionary Algorithm for the Berth Scheduling Problem. *Memetic Comput.* **2020**, *12*, 51–72. [CrossRef]

47. Pasha, J.; Dulebenets, M.A.; Kavoosi, M.; Abioye, O.; Wang, H.; Guo, W. An Optimization Model and Solution Algorithms for the Vehicle Routing Problem With a "Factory-in-a-Box". *IEEE Access* **2020**, *8*, 134743–134763. [CrossRef]

48. Moradi, B. The New Optimization Algorithm for the Vehicle Routing Problem with Time Windows using Multi-objective Discrete Learnable Evolution Model. *Soft Comput.* **2020**, *24*, 6741–6769. [CrossRef]

49. Zhao, H.; Zhang, C. An Online-learning-based Evolutionary Many-objective Algorithm. *Inf. Sci.* **2020**, *509*, 1–21. [CrossRef]

50. Coello Coello, C.A. Multi-objective Optimization. In *Handbook of Heuristics*; Martí, R., Pardalos, P.M., Resende, M.G.C., Eds.; Springer: Cham, Switzerland, 2018; pp. 177–204.

51. Ji, S.F.; Luo, R.j.; Peng, X.S. A Probability Guided Evolutionary Algorithm for Multi-objective Green Express Cabinet Assignment in Urban Last-mile Logistics. *Int. J. Prod. Res.* **2019**, *57*, 3382–3404. [CrossRef]

52. Jiang, E.d.; Wang, L. An Improved Multi-objective Evolutionary Algorithm based on Decomposition for Energy-efficient Permutation Flow Shop Scheduling Problem with Sequence-dependent Setup Time. *Int. J. Prod. Res.* **2019**, *57*, 1756–1771. [CrossRef]

53. Kang, P.S.; Bhatti, R.S. Continuous Process Improvement Implementation Framework using Multi-objective Genetic Algorithms and Discrete Event Simulation. *Bus. Process. Manag. J.* **2019**, *25*, 1020–1039. [CrossRef]

54. Kohl, N.; Stone, P. Policy Gradient Reinforcement Learning for Fast Quadrupedal Locomotion. In Proceedings of the IEEE International Conference on Robotics and Automation, 2004. ICRA '04. 2004, New Orleans, LA, USA, 26 April–1 May 2004; pp. 2619–2624.

55. Ng, A.Y.; Coates, A.; Diel, M.; Ganapathi, V.; Schulte, J.; Tse, B.; Berger, E.; Liang, E. Autonomous Inverted Helicopter Flight via Reinforcement Learning. In *Experimental Robotics IX*; Siciliano, B., Khatib, O., Groen, F., Ang, M.H., Eds.; Springer: Berlin/Heidelberg, Germany, 2006; Volume 21, pp. 363–372.

56. Arulkumaran, K.; Deisenroth, M.P.; Brundage, M.; Bharath, A.A. Deep Reinforcement Learning: A Brief Survey. *IEEE Signal Process. Mag.* **2017**, *34*, 26–38. [CrossRef]

57. Scholkopf, B. Artificial Intelligence: Learning to See and Act. *Nature* **2015**, *518*, 486–487. [CrossRef] [PubMed]

58. Hinton, G.E.; Salakhutdinov, R.R. Reducing the Dimensionality of Data with Neural Networks. *Science* **2006**, *313*, 504–507. [CrossRef]

59. Bengio, Y. Learning Deep Architectures for AI. *Found. Trends Mach. Learn.* **2009**, *2*, 1–127. [CrossRef]

60. Krizhevsky, A.; Sutskever, I.; Hinton, G.E. ImageNet Classification with Deep Convolutional Neural Networks. In Proceedings of the Advances in Neural Information Processing Systems 25 (NIPS 2012), Lake Tahoe, NV, USA, 3–6 December 2012.

61. McClelland, J.L.; Rumelhart, D.E. *Parallel Distributed Processing: Explorations in the Microstructure of Cognition*, 1st ed.; A Bradford Book; MIT Press: Cambridge, MA, USA, 1986.

62. LeCun, Y.; Bengio, Y.; Hinton, G. Deep Learning. *Nature* **2015**, *521*, 436–444. [CrossRef]

63. Goodfellow, I.; Bengio, Y.; Courville, A. *Deep Learning*; MIT Press: Cambridge, MA, USA, 2016.

64. Lecun, Y.; Bottou, L.; Bengio, Y.; Haffner, P. Gradient-based Learning Applied to Document Recognition. *Proc. IEEE* **1998**, *86*, 2278–2324. [CrossRef]

65. Mnih, V.; Kavukcuoglu, K.; Silver, D.; Graves, A.; Antonoglou, I.; Wierstra, D.; Riedmiller, M. Playing Atari with Deep Reinforcement Learning. 2013. Available online: arxiv.org/abs/1312.5602 (accessed on 14 December 2020).

66. Li, Y. Deep Reinforcement Learning: An Overview. 2017. Available online: arxiv.org/abs/1701.07274 (accessed on 14 December 2020).

67. Dross, F.; Rabe, M. A SimHeuristic Framework as a Decision Support System for Large Logistics Networks with Complex KPIs. In Proceedings of the 22nd Symposium Simulationstechnik, Berlin, Germany, 3–5 September 2014; pp. 247–254.

68. Rabe, M.; Ammouriova, M.; Schmitt, D. Utilizing Domain-specific Information for the Optimization of Logistics Networks. In Proceedings of the 2018 Winter Simulation Conference, Gothenburg, Sweden, 9–12 December 2018; pp. 2873–2884.

69. SimPlan AG. SimChain. 2018. Available online: www.simchain.net (accessed on 14 December 2020).

70. Rabe, M.; Gutenschwager, K.; Fechteler, T.; Sari, M.U. A Data Model for Carbon Footprint Simulation in Consumer Goods Supply Chain. In Proceedings of the 2013 Winter Simulation Conference, Washington, DC, USA, 8–11 December 2013; pp. 2677–2688.

71. Rabe, M.; Schmitt, D.; Dross, F. Method to Model Actions for Discrete-event Simulation of Logistics Networks. In Proceedings of the 2017 Winter Simulation Conference, Las Vegas, NV, USA, 3–6 December 2017; pp. 3370–3381.

72. Rabe, M.; Schmitt, D. Domain-specific Language for Modeling and Simulating Actions in Logistics Networks. In Proceedings of the 2019 Winter Simulation Conference, National Harbor, MD, USA, 8–11 December 2019; pp. 1579–1590.

73. Rabe, M.; Schmitt, D.; Ammouriova, M. Utilizing Domain-specific Information in Decision Support for Logistics Networks. In *Dynamics in Logistics: Proceedings of the 6th International Conference LDIC 2018, Bremen, Germany*; Freitag, M., Kotzab, H., Pannek, J., Eds.; Lecture Notes in Logistics; Springer International Publishing: Cham, Switzerland, 2018; pp. 413–417.

74. Rabe, M.; Ammouriova, M. Constructing Action Plans Based on Correlation between Sequential Actions and their Performance in Logistics Distribution Networks. In Proceedings of the 13th International Conference of Research in Logistics and Supply Chain Management, Le Havre, France, 7–9 October 2020.

75. Rabe, M.; Schmitt, D.; Klueter, A.; Hunker, J. Decoupling the Modeling of Actions in Logistics Networks from the Underlying Simulation Data Model. In *Advances in Production, Logistics and Traffic: Proceedings of the 4th Interdisciplinary Conference on Production Logistics and Traffic (ICPLT)*; Clausen, U., Langkau, S., Kreuz, F., Eds.; Springer: Cham, Switzerland, 2019; pp. 32–44.

76. Watkins, C. Learning from Delayed Rewards. Ph.D. Thesis, Kings College, Cambridge, UK, 1989.

77. Bellemare, M.G.; Naddaf, Y.; Veness, J.; Bowling, M. The Arcade Learning Environment: An Evaluation Platform for General Agents. *J. Artif. Intell. Res.* **2013**, *47*, 253–279. [CrossRef]

78. ALE. The Arcade Learning Environment. 2020. Available online: https://github.com/mgbellemare/Arcade-Learning-Environment (accessed on 14 December 2020).

79. TensorFlow. 2020. Available online: https://www.tensorflow.org/ (accessed on 14 December 2020).

80. Rabe, M.; Dross, F.; Wuttke, A. Combining a Discrete-event Simulation Model of a Logistics Network with Deep Reinforcement Learning. In Proceedings of the 12th Metaheuristics International Conference (MIC), Barcelona, Spain, 4–7 July 2017; pp. 438–447.

81. Rabe, M.; Ammouriova, M.; Schmitt, D.; Chicaiza-Vaca. An Approach for Reducing the Search Space for Simheuristics Applications in Logistics Network in Trading. In *Simulation in Production and Logistics*; Putz, M., Schlegel, A., Eds.; Verlag Wissenschaftliche Skripten: Auerbach, Germany, 2019; pp. 335–344.

82. Rabe, M.; Dross, F.; Vennemann, A. A Procedure Model for the Credible Measurability of Data Warehouse Metrics on Discrete-event Simulation Models of Logistics Systems. In *Simulation in Production and Logistics 2015*; Rabe, M., Clausen, U., Eds.; Fraunhofer Verlag: Stuttgart, Germany, 2015; pp. 168–176.

83. Silberholz, J.; Golden, B.; Gupta, S.; Wang, X. Computational Comparison of Metaheuristics. In *Handbook of Metaheuristics*; Gendreau, M., Potvin, J.Y., Eds.; International Series in Operation Research and Management Science; Springer International Publishing: Cham, Switzerland, 2019; pp. 581–604.

84. Karimi, M.B.; Isazadeh, A.; Rahmani, A.M. QoS-aware Service Composition in Cloud Computing Using Data Mining Techniques and Genetic Algorithm. *J. Supercomput.* **2017**, *73*, 1387–1415. [CrossRef]

85. Ku, D.; Arthanari, T.S. On the Abstraction Method for the Container Relocation Problem. *Comput. Oper. Res.* **2016**, *68*, 110–122. [CrossRef]

86. Cai, K.Q.; Zhang, J.; Xiao, M.M.; Tang, K.; Du, W.B. Simultaneous Optimization of Airspace Congestion and Flight Delay in Air Traffic Network Flow Management. *IEEE Trans. Intell. Transp. Syst.* **2017**, *18*, 3072–3082. [CrossRef]

87. Blenk, A.; Kalmbach, P.; Kellerer, W.; Schmid, S. O'zapft is: Tap Your Network Algorithm's Big Data! In *Proceedings of the Workshop on Big Data Analytics and Machine Learning for Data Communication Networks (Big-DAM'17)*; Association for Computing Machinery: New York, NY, USA, 2017; pp. 19–24. [CrossRef]

88. Umetani, S. Exploiting Variable Associations to Configure Efficient Local Search Algorithms in Large-scale Binary Integer Programs. *Eur. J. Oper. Res.* **2017**, *263*, 72–81. [CrossRef]

89. Amaran, S.; Sahinidis, N.V.; Sharda, B.; Bury, S.J. Simulation Optimization: A Review of Algorithms and Applications. *Ann. Oper. Res.* **2016**, *240*, 351–380. [CrossRef]

90. Sheskin, D. *Handbook of Parametric and Nonparametric Statistical Procedures*, 5th ed.; CRC Press: Boca Raton, FL, USA, 2011.

MDPI

St. Alban-Anlage 66

4052 Basel

Switzerland

Tel. +41 61 683 77 34

Fax +41 61 302 89 18

www.mdpi.com

Algorithms Editorial Office

E-mail: algorithms@mdpi.com

www.mdpi.com/journal/algorithms